A History of Clocks and Watches

Horology (from the Latin, Horologium) is the science of measuring time. Clocks, watches, clockwork, sundials, clepsydras, timers, time recorders, marine chronometers and atomic clocks are all examples of instruments used to measure time. In current usage, horology refers mainly to the study of mechanical time-keeping devices, whilst chronometry more broadly included electronic devices that have largely supplanted mechanical clocks for accuracy and precision in time-keeping. Horology itself has an incredibly long history and there are many museums and several specialised libraries devoted to the subject. Perhaps the most famous is the *Royal Greenwich Observatory*, also the source of the Prime Meridian (longitude 0° 0' 0"), and the home of the first marine timekeepers accurate enough to determine longitude.

The word 'clock' is derived from the Celtic words *clagan* and *clocca* meaning 'bell'. A silent instrument missing such a mechanism has traditionally been known as a timepiece, although today the words have become interchangeable. The clock is one of the oldest human interventions, meeting the need to consistently measure intervals of time shorter than the natural units: the day, the lunar month and the year. The current sexagesimal system of time measurement dates to approximately 2000 BC in Sumer. The Ancient Egyptians divided the day into two twelve-hour periods and used large obelisks to track the movement of the sun. They also developed water clocks, which had also been employed frequently by the Ancient Greeks, who called them 'clepsydrae'. The Shang Dynasty is also believed to have used the outflow water clock around the same time.

The first mechanical clocks, employing the verge escapement mechanism (the mechanism that controls the rate of a clock by advancing the gear train at regular intervals or 'ticks') with a foliot or balance wheel timekeeper (a weighted wheel that rotates back and forth, being returned toward its centre position by a spiral), were invented in Europe at around the start of the fourteenth century. They became the standard timekeeping device until the pendulum clock was invented in 1656. This remained the most accurate timekeeper until the 1930s, when quartz oscillators (where the mechanical **resonance** of a vibrating crystal is used to create an electrical signal with a very precise **frequency**) were invented, followed by atomic clocks after World War Two. Although initially limited to laboratories, the development of microelectronics in the 1960s made **quartz clocks** both compact and cheap

THE
WATCH ADJUSTER'S MANUAL

A Practical Guide for the Watch and Chronometer Adjuster in Making, Springing, Timing and Adjusting for Isochronism, Positions and Temperatures

BY

CHARLES EDGAR FRITTS
("EXCELSIOR")

Author of Practical Hints on Watch Repairing; Practical Treatise on the Balance Spring; Electricity and Magnetism for Watchmakers; How to Take In, Warrant and Deliver Work; etc., etc.

Formerly Member of the British Horological Institute, London, England

FIFTY-SIX ORIGINAL ILLUSTRATIONS

THIRD EDITION
Revised and Corrected by the Author

Copyright © 2013 Read Books Ltd.
This book is copyright and may not be
reproduced or copied in any way without
the express permission of the publisher in writing

British Library Cataloguing-in-Publication Data
A catalogue record for this book is available from the
British Library

to produce, and by the 1980s they became the world's dominant timekeeping technology in both clocks and **wristwatches**.

The concept of the wristwatch goes back to the production of the very earliest watches in the sixteenth century. Elizabeth I of England received a wristwatch from Robert Dudley in 1571, described as an arm watch. From the beginning, they were almost exclusively worn by women, while men used pocket-watches up until the early twentieth century. This was not just a matter of fashion or prejudice; watches of the time were notoriously prone to fouling from exposure to the elements, and could only reliably be kept safe from harm if carried securely in the pocket. Wristwatches were first worn by military men towards the end of the nineteenth century, when the importance of synchronizing manoeuvres during war without potentially revealing the plan to the enemy through signalling was increasingly recognized. It was clear that using pocket watches while in the heat of battle or while mounted on a horse was impractical, so officers began to strap the watches to their wrist.

The company H. Williamson Ltd., based in Coventry, England, was one of the first to capitalize on this opportunity. During the company's 1916 AGM it was noted that '...the public is buying the practical things of life. Nobody can truthfully contend that the watch is a luxury. It is said that one soldier in every four wears a wristlet watch, and the other three mean to get one as soon as they can.' By the end of the War, almost all enlisted men wore a wristwatch, and after they were demobilized, the fashion soon caught on - the British *Horological Journal* wrote in 1917 that '...the wristlet watch was little used by the sterner sex before the war, but now is seen on the wrist of nearly every man in uniform and of many men in civilian attire.' Within a decade, sales of wristwatches had outstripped those of pocket watches.

Now that clocks and watches had become 'common objects' there was a massively increased demand on clockmakers for maintenance and repair. Julien Le Roy, a clockmaker of Versailles, invented a face that could be opened to view the inside clockwork – a development which many subsequent artisans copied. He also invented special repeating mechanisms to improve the precision of clocks and supervised over 3,500 watches. The more complicated the device however, the more often it needed repairing. Today, since almost all clocks are now factory-made, most modern clockmakers *only* repair clocks. They are frequently employed by jewellers, antique shops or places devoted strictly to repairing clocks and watches.

The clockmakers of the present must be able to read blueprints and instructions for numerous types of clocks and time pieces that vary from antique clocks to modern time pieces in order to fix and make clocks or watches. The trade requires fine motor coordination as clockmakers must frequently work on devices with small gears and fine machinery, as well as an appreciation for the original art form. As is evident from this very short history of clocks and watches, over the centuries the items themselves have changed – almost out of recognition, but the importance of time-keeping has not. It is an area which provides a constant source of fascination and scientific discovery, still very much evolving today. We hope the reader enjoys this book.

PREFACE TO THIRD EDITION.

In issuing this Third Edition of The Watch Adjuster's Manual, it is opportune to state for the information and assurance of the reader, that since the work was first published only two slight errors were brought to the notice of the author, and these were of such a trivial nature that they scarcely called for correction. This fact shows the extreme care and thoroughness with which the work was originally prepared, and is also proof of its accuracy and reliability of statement. It is also opportune here to make general acknowledgment of the letters received by the author from all parts of the world, giving assurance that the work was in truth what it was intended to be, the practical workman's standard authority.

Unlike most technical treatises, the progress of time has added greatly to the value of this work. Railroad watch inspection, which has now become almost universal, has made the very finest workmanship imperative, and such workmanship implies a thorough knowledge of the methods described in this book. And in this connection it may be added that the workman who is qualified for railroad watch inspection has the best recommendation for the patronage of the community.

THE PUBLISHERS.

CONTENTS.

PART FIRST.
PREPARATORY.

	PAGES
CHAPTER I.—Suggestions to Workmen,	1 to 7
CHAPTER II.—Preliminary Examination of the Movement,	8 to 14
CHAPTER III.—Magnetism and Magnetized Watches,	14 to 18
CHAPTER IV.—The Demagnetization of Watches, Watch Parts, etc,	19 to 27

PART SECOND.
MAKING BALANCE SPRINGS.

CHAPTER V.—Treatment of Steel for Making Hair Springs,	28 to 35
CHAPTER VI.—Making Cylindrical or Helical Springs,	35 to 41
CHAPTER VII.—Making Flat Spiral and Breguet Springs,	41 to 46
CHAPTER VIII.—The Modern American Method of Making Hair Springs,	46 to 49

PART THIRD.
WATCH BALANCES.

CHAPTER IX.—Balance Making,	50 to 56
CHAPTER X.—Selecting and Testing Watch Balances,	57 to 64
CHAPTER XI.—Correcting and Finishing Balances,	64 to 69

PART FOURTH.
SPRINGING AND TIMING.

	PAGES
CHAPTER XII.—Conveniences for Timing,	70 to 78
CHAPTER XIII.—Means for Registering and Comparing Times,	78 to 80
CHAPTER XIV.—Calculating the Proper Number of Vibrations,	81 to 84
CHAPTER XV.—Counting the Vibrations,	84 to 90
CHAPTER XVI.—Testing and Timing Hair Springs,	90 to 96
CHAPTER XVII.—Hair Spring Fitting Tools,	96 to 108
CHAPTER XVIII.—Fitting Hair Springs,	109 to 124
CHAPTER XIX.—On Poising,	124 to 131
CHAPTER XX.—Quick Ways of Bringing a Spring to Time,	131 to 134
CHAPTER XXI.—Regulating Watches,	134 to 145
CHAPTER XXII.—Regulating Fine Watches,	146 to 157
CHAPTER XXIII.—Rating,	158 to 167

PART FIFTH.
SPECIAL AND "NATURAL" COMPENSATIONS.

CHAPTER XXIV.—The Four Principal Escapements,	168 to 170
CHAPTER XXV.—Cylinder Escapement Watches,	171 to 179
CHAPTER XXVI.—Duplex Watches,	180 to 188
CHAPTER XXVII.—Lever Watches,	188 to 200
CHAPTER XXVIII.—Box and Pocket Chronometers,	200 to 212

PART SIXTH.
THE ADJUSTMENT FOR ISOCHRONISM.

CHAPTER XXIX.—Isochronism,	213 to 221
CHAPTER XXX.—Why Springs are Isochronous,	221 to 231
CHAPTER XXXI.—Methods of Securing Isochronism,	232 to 243
CHAPTER XXXII.—Isochronizing by Terminal Curves,	243 to 252

CONTENTS. xi

PAGES
CHAPTER XXXIII.—Isochronizing the Cylindrical Spring, . 252 to 258
CHAPTER XXXIV.—Isochronizing the Flat Spiral Spring, . 258 to 263
CHAPTER XXXV.—Isochronizing the Breguet Spring, . . 263 to 271
CHAPTER XXXVI.—The Isochronal Adjustment, . . . 271 to 287

PART SEVENTH.
THE ADJUSTMENT FOR POSITIONS.

CHAPTER XXXVII.—Position Faults, ... 288 to 298
CHAPTER XXXVIII.—Adjusting for Positions, . . . 298 to 313

PART EIGHTH.
THE ADJUSTMENT FOR HEAT AND COLD.

CHAPTER XXXIX.—Compensation, ... 314 to 320
CHAPTER XL.—Apparatus for Adjusting the Compensation, . 320 to 327
CHAPTER XLI.—Adjusting the Compensation, . . . 327 to 342

TO THE READER.

A note of the following corrections should be made on the margins of the pages referred to:

TIME SIGNALS.—The methods of sending out noon time signals from the U. S. Naval Observatory, at Washington, D. C., as described on page 71, has been slightly changed. The signals now begin at 11.55′ A.M. instead of 11.56′.45″ A.M., as before, and continue for five whole minutes, giving sixteen opportunities for comparing time. During this period a signal is sent out for each second, except the following, which are omitted: the 29th second of each minute, the last 5 seconds of the first 4 minutes, and finally, the last 10 seconds of the last minute are omitted, followed by a signal at exactly 12 o'clock noon, standard time.

The method of utilizing the signals is the same as before described.

OVER-BANKING IN LEVER WATCHES.—It should be stated at the end of paragraph 469, page 196, that over-banking in lever watches is a fault of the safety action (469), and is due to the lever being too short, or some other fault, which lets the safety pin (or guard point) get past the roller in the wrong direction, or before the proper time, or before the safety pin gets in the crescent. It is most frequently caused by setting the hands backward.

Whenever the instructions say that the safety pin or guard point is "too short," and the like, that of course means that the lever is too short, and that the safety pin or the guard point should be set forward, or towards the balance staff, and *vice versa*. See (469), lines 5 to 8, and especially line 14 to end of section. Also, see (465), lines 6 to 8; and (472), items No. 11, 14 and 15. The necessary instructions will all be found there somewhere, in their proper places. These corrections should always be made before beginning to work on the adjustments.

THE WATCH ADJUSTER'S MANUAL.

PART FIRST.

PREPARATORY.

CHAPTER I.

Suggestions to Workmen.

(1.) This book will be pre-eminently practical. Not that we would disparage theory—far from it. A knowledge of the theoretical principles of any art is the proper preparation for the most successful practice in it. But the majority of watchmakers would give more for an account of the actual practice among good workmen than for all the theoretical treatises ever published. This is not as it should be, but it is considered the part of wisdom to take things as they are. Hence the work has been made practical and exhaustive, going to the bottom of the subject, and useful to the most advanced workmen, as well as those with less experience. At the same time, enough of the theory of the different procedures is introduced, to enable the reader to understand the reason why he should do as described, as well as how to do it.

(2.) *Need of such a book.*—The truth is that a very large share of our watchmakers are but imperfectly educated, either in theory or practice. The foreign system of long apprenticeships is not in vogue here, and even if it were, the most of our employers are not really competent to instruct apprentices. Many of them are not workmen at all—only dealers in the goods of our line. Such as are good workmen are becoming more and more averse to taking apprentices because their time is too valuable to allow of giving thorough instruction, as they could better afford to do under the old apprentice-laws, which on the whole were certainly better for both masters and men. The result is that half-fledged workmen abound—most of them conscious of their shortcomings and anxious to learn, but they are compelled to educate themselves, and to make their living while doing so.

Again, many workmen have fully learned their trade, according to the old style, but everything has changed greatly since then, even within the last ten years, and they find that they are getting out of date. There are new kinds of work to be done, new tools and machinery to be used, new materials, new ways of working, and above all, greater excellence in every respect is required than would have sufficed in the old verge and lepine days. This change is constantly going on, even now, and the good workman of to-day will soon be left among the old fogies unless he keeps himself informed of all the current improvements.

(3.) *The way to become a good workman.*—Let no one feel discouraged because he has never had proper instruction in the trade. If he really desires to be a good workman, and has true grit in him, there can scarcely be any training more severe and improving than patient study and practice, growing out of his own resources, and being held responsible for the performance of his work, either by an employer or by a customer of his own. If he will persist in doing *the best he can*, and improve every opportunity to learn, he will gradually regain the ground he should have made during his apprenticeship, and may in time become the equal of any, and the superior of those with greater opportunities but less determination to excel. A large share of our very best workmen are thus largely self-taught— thorough, independent, versatile and progressive, but the lack of a long and rigid apprenticeship has cost many of them a fearful loss of their time in the best years of their lives—a loss which it is the object of this book to lessen for its readers.

Habits are all-powerful with a workman, and I feel the importance of not leading any one into faulty or inferior ways of working. I shall try to tell all that is worth the telling, and worthy of being included in a first-class method of procedure— in fact, to give the latest and most advanced state of practical horology, so far as concerns the subjects treated herein. This involves the examination and comparison (either experimentally or judging from general experience) of perhaps scores of different tools, methods, etc., each claimed to be the best, in order to sift out and arrange a complete, uniform and practically reliable system in each branch of work.

(4.) *Contents of the book.*—While I shall not give all the new but visionary ideas floating about, I shall also exclude many old and generally accepted ones which I consider wrong in principle or superseded by better methods. I shall not only treat of things not generally known, but also of things very commonly done, but seldom done well, at least by learners, and which they need to know about, as they are at the root of all good work; of some things that are highly important, and also of "little things." But those little things are often just what constitute the difference between the good workman and the botch, which the former has learned by long and bitter experience, the fruit of years of labor, study and trials.

Much of what I shall say will, of course, be the standard practice among good workmen, and therefore not new to them. But I must take the risk of telling what is familiar to such, for the sake of that much larger class who have not had the opportunities of the former for learning. Another large share, however, will be the results of my own experience, investigations and observation, new and valuable even to experts and first-class workmen. I shall not claim perfection, either in judgment or experience, but simply lay the information before them and leave them free to accept or reject it as they think best.

What we need in our trade is more life, study, interest; more discussions and even quarrels, if necessary, to wake us up; more rivalry in letting such light as we have shine for the benefit of all. And if I should use rather sharp language in regard to some persons and things in the course of these pages, as I propose to do, my sole object in stirring them up will not be any personal feeling or prejudice, but a desire to tell the exact facts, according to my knowledge and belief.

(5.) *Must put the directions in practice.*—But let them mark this:—They can never really know a thing till they have actually done it, and discovered by experience the peculiarities, dangers and difficulties of each operation. It matters not how carefully they read and understand, they must practice also. Instructions alone will not make one a workman, any more than a book of prescriptions makes a man a doctor. Therefore they should take the first opportunity, or make one, to put my directions in practice. They will then learn many minor points which space compels me to omit, will understand better what I do say, and they will remember it. Otherwise, as soon as they lose sight of the book they will know scarcely more about it than they did before. So when a small tool or fixture is described let them go to work and make one. Each one will take but little time, which they will never miss, but they will soon have a goodly collection of them, at the mere cost of material, which they could not buy for any money, for the good reason that most of them are not on sale; and, having made them, they will know how to use them. The directions being in print, they can refer back to my very words and details a hundred times if necessary, and study and practice on them *ad libitum*, till they are perfectly familiar with every point. The unusually copious Index will be a great assistance in quickly finding whatever is wanted.

(6.) *Annotating the book.*—The workman who makes a specialty of some particular class of work can somewhat simplify matters by carefully going over the book and marking in the margin of each page the parts which apply to his specialty. This will both familiarize him with the rules, and also aid him to instantly find any part to which he wishes to refer for further suggestions. Another way to annotate the book would be to mark every rule and section which is applicable only to some particular kind of watch. " M. Chr." could be used to indicate marine chronometer: " P. Chr." for pocket chronometer; " D. L.," for detached lever; etc. " H. Sp." could mean helical spring;" " F. Sp.," for plain flat spiral; " Br. Sp.," for Breguet, and so on. Parts not so marked would be understood to have a general application to all kinds of watches or springs. The mere effort to analyze the meaning, and determine to what cases the rule applied, would make him more thoroughly acquainted with the subject than reading the book a dozen times over.

(7.) *Cross-references.*—Another useful habit is to mark in the margin the number of any other section which bears on that point. This will greatly assist him in reading up on any particular point, and collecting all the information relating to it. The sections are numbered, in order to facilitate this, and to avoid repetitions, so that any directions once given may afterwards be referred to for full details, and easily found. A great many such cross-references are already given in the text, but the intellectual peculiarities of each reader, and his way of reasoning, may make others beneficial to him.

(8.) *Make the book a bench companion.*—The book gives the results of the investigations, studies and experience of horologists and practical men up to this time, and no better methods or rules are known to the trade. All available sources of information have been consulted, in order to make it complete, reliable and inclusive of the best theories and practices followed or known.

The reader may reasonably depend upon it that, so long as the present styles of watches are used, the directions in this book cannot be superseded nor materially bettered, nor can experience add very much that is new in the future, for they are the results of innumerable experiments, trials and inventions by the best watch and chronometer makers and adjusters everywhere. Moreover, it is the only special guide published, for practical watch and chronometer springers and adjusters. He should therefore make it his *bench companion*, keeping it always within reach, ready for constant reference, until he knows its contents perfectly. This habit of instantly looking up a point and settling it, makes the difference between a man who is constantly learning and improving, and one who is rapidly forgetting what he does know.

(9.) *Honest, thorough work indispensable.*—Before closing, I wish to give a few words of advice which will have a very wide application, although addressed especially to young or inexperienced workmen. They should clearly understand that there is no royal road to success in our trade. No amount of experience or knowledge, no costly instructions, or "trade secrets"— *nothing whatever* will suffice except good, honest, thorough work. Whatever other advantages they may have, that is the one indispensable thing. A watch is a machine; when it is all right, throughout, it will perform properly, and not before. Experience *with* thoroughness will make a fast workman, but never without. He should never knowingly slight any part, however small, for even after he has done his best, there will always be enough to apologize for. And, as my old master used to say, "you can't do it *too well*, if you try." This is what all old workmen will tell him, and he should settle down at once and forever upon that basis, and dismiss all ideas that there are any "secret ways," or ways that are not secret, known to any one, which will enable him to dispense with that requisite. Therefore it will be well for him to make up his mind never, under any circumstances, to shirk his work. He should do this for the sake of his reputation as a workman, of his self-respect as an honest man, and of avoiding the habit of shirking, which will surely grow upon him if indulged, till he will become actually incapacitated for doing a thorough job, by indifference and indisposition to exert himself.

(10.) *Don't do too much.*—On the other hand, don't do too

much. This is a great fault with the inexperienced. They file, and bend, and hammer, and cut off, and make the most radical changes, on the slightest grounds or none at all. Now, a workman has no business to change any part of a watch unless he knows the precise purpose of that part, and of its peculiar construction; knows that it ought to be changed, and why; knows what object it is desirable to accomplish by changing it; knows that the proposed change will accomplish that object, and how to make that change in a workmanlike manner. If he does not know the difficulty and its cause, and the proper remedy, he has no right to butcher a watch on the "cut and try" principle. When he cannot improve it he should at least not injure it, but rely more on head-work and less on guess-work. That, after all, is the real secret of excellence. Of two men, alike in every other respect, the best thinker is invariably the best workman.

(11.) *The right way and the wrong way.*—It will be noticed that the custom in some cases is to make the watch imperfect or wrong, *i.e.*, different from what would be strictly proper or right, in order to correct some error in the timing or to secure some special action. As examples I will mention the setting of the hair spring excentrically, putting the balance out of poise, opening the regulator pins widely, etc. If you should change such an arrangement in "putting the watch in order," you would ruin the adjustment, and make the watch worse off, instead of better. On the other hand, such imperfection may *not* be intentional, and *then* it probably ought to be corrected. It is necessary, therefore, to use good judgment in making repairs, so as to do whatever is really necessary and proper *in that particular case*, and no more.

(12.) *The right way.*—Perhaps the only way to determine that point is to inquire, when the watch is left, what kind of time it has kept, and by whom it has previously been kept in order. If it has been in skilful hands and has performed well, it may safely be left as it is, unless the directions are to "put it in perfect order," in which case you should do your best to carry out the instructions. Even then, you will often be compelled to choose between long and expensive changes and some quicker makeshift which, while theoretically wrong, is practically about as good as you would get it by the other way. In such cases, the decision will be largely determined by the value of the watch—and the temper of its owner. If it is an ordinary one, you would hardly be justified in making a bill of repairs almost equal to the value of the watch; but if it is a fine and valuable article and the owner is willing to pay for having it put in perfect order, do that. It may seem rather out of place to advise the doing of imperfect work, but if that kind is what we are expected to do, and it will satisfy the customer, it may be considered excusable.

(13.) *Be careful what you do.*—Especially when you get hold of a fine watch, be very careful what you do. Even when you see something which, according to the rules, is wrong, it may have been intentionally left so, or put so, as before stated. It may be a part of a laborious co-ordination of the various actions in order to secure a good rate. If you change any part of it, you at once destroy the whole arrangement. The watch may not keep very close time and you may think that a certain alteration will improve it. You try it, and find the rate worse than before. You try this, that, and the other way, and finally you find that the way it was at first gives the best results—not so close as it ought to be, but the best that that watch is capable of doing without a radical overhauling and reconstruction. Almost every one has had some such experience. Hence the advice to be careful what you do when handling a fine watch, or even an ordinary one which has been performing reasonably well. In addition to the suggestion in section (12), a good rule in all such cases is to notice how everything is, before taking it apart—making memoranda of every point, to prevent mistakes or forgetfulness—so that when putting it together again you can get everything precisely as it was before.

(14.) *Apparent contradictions.*—Should there be any seeming inconsistencies in different parts of the book, it will be due to the effort to give a complete and candid statement of all the different opinions and methods. The reader will perceive that some contradictions of the kind are unavoidable, after comparing the various opposing opinions on the subject of isochronism (536 to 541), and reflecting that opinions on other subjects are nearly as contradictory. I have endeavored to reconcile the old and the new as well as I could, and to be strictly fair and impartial in the statement of every case, but the reader can have no difficulty in knowing what my opinion is, if he wants it—and at the same time he is in a position to use his own judgment in the matter and to follow his own opinion if he thinks it better. The book is not a set of rigid rules which must be obeyed, but it gives him full information of the opinions and methods of the best men in the trade, so that he is *educated* and posted up to date, and can intelligently make such use of his knowledge as he likes.

CHAPTER II.

Preliminary Examination of the Movement.

(15.) *Prerequisites.* It is not sufficient for the workman to perform his special work properly. There are numerous extraneous points about the movement which, if not correct, will either prevent his job from giving satisfaction, or will so influence its performance as to give the appearance of faults which do not exist, and will perhaps render it difficult or impossible for him to secure a good adjustment or rate. I will therefore specify some of the points which should be looked after, and they will serve to suggest others which he may find incorrect. It is elsewhere stated how the hair spring should be pinned in the collet and stud, and various other matters relating to the spring, and I will proceed to mention other points seldom attended to as carefully as they should be.

(16.) *The Regulator.*—As a general rule, the regulator-pins should be as close together as possible and yet leave the spring free between them. But if they are found otherwise, they should not be closed without good reason, for they may have been so opened for a purpose, by some one who fully understood the effects of so doing. But wide pins may justly be regarded with suspicion. The effect of having the pins very open is not only to render the spring less susceptible to control by the regulator, but also to cause sudden and violent checks to its motion, making uniform progression of force (35²) difficult, if not impossible. Moreover, the spring vibrates upon the pin against which it rests, as a pivot or fulcrum, and the part beyond the regulator vibrates in a direction contrary to that of the normally acting portion, rendering it uncertain or difficult to regulate. The regulator is intended to act as the real stud, at the end of the acting part, and the pins should properly be as close together as they can be without binding on the spring when moved. The regulator should stand pretty well back towards the "slow" when the watch is regulated. The pins should both be tight in their places, so that they cannot yield any when the spring presses against them. If one of them has a foot, to close the bottom of the opening between them, the spring should be entirely free from it, nor should any dirt be allowed to accumulate there and touch the spring.

See that the outer coil stands perfectly free between the regulator pins as they are moved through the whole of their sweep from "slow" to "fast," not moving nearer to or against either pin at any point in the sweep. When you have occasion to take a watch apart for cleaning or any other purpose, which does not involve a change in the rate, it should be put together in such a way that the regulator should be at the same place, and the hair spring should occupy the same position between the regulator pins, as before it was taken down. To insure this, a careful examination should have been made, with the balance at rest, free from the motive force of the mainspring, and the position of both the regulator and hair spring noted down—for in a fine watch both of them have probably been carefully adjusted, and changing either of them or opening or closing the regulator pins might seriously damage the adjustment. Even in cheap watches, following this rule will frequently save several days in bringing them to time.

But if a watch does not perform satisfactorily on trial, or if the workman is sure from inspection that it will not do so, the defective conditions must of course be changed and corrected.

(17.) *The end-stones*, if not held in settings, should be fastened there by cement. A loose end-stone is an abomination. When it is uppermost, it rests on the end of the pivot, and often can be seen wobbling about with every vibration of the balance. When the movement is inverted, the pivot rests upon the cap jewel and presses it down, but its position is very uncertain. It may possibly be level, but is much more likely to be otherwise, and may even tip up sideways so as to give little or no support to the pivot. Always fasten the end-stone in its cap or setting, either by a bezel or with cement.

(18.) *To cement the end-stone level*, a good way is to put some shellac in the cavity, soften it by heat, place the end-stone in position, and while the cement is soft invert the cap upon the paper over the board, press the cap firmly down, and hold till cool. Pressing the cap down forces the jewel into the soft wax up to its proper place where it has the support of the metal, and insures that its surface will be level with the cap. If not so, it must be heated again till it becomes so. Generally, a cap or foot jewel should be just even with the surface of its setting or cap, not lower, nor sticking out any above it. But cases occasionally occur requiring a variation from this rule. Before altering or cementing a cap jewel, feel of it with a sharp-pointed piece to see if it is tight in its place. Also notice if it is pushed as far towards the hole jewel as it can be. The cap jewel should not quite touch the hole jewel unless the latter has been cupped on the back side (726). If necessary, fit in a larger jewel, so as to bring its flat surface, when cemented, as it was before, if that was correct.

(19.) *How cemented.*—A cap or foot jewel must invariably be fixed parallel with the under surface of the cap, or the upper surface of the slip, so as to present a perfectly horizontal support for the end of the pivot. Otherwise it will slide down the inclined surface of the jewel and be wedged in against one side of the jewel-hole. This point must be carefully attended to. In the case of the foot jewel, which is out of sight, a little wax left outside of the jewel does no harm, and considerably strengthens the jewel. But for cap jewels, where no wax must appear to the eye, after prying the cap off the paper, and scraping the superfluous shellac from the under surface, see that the jewel is flat and true, lay it down on the bench, the jewel underneath, and carefully scrape the wax from the outside of the socket, without loosening the jewel. It will do no harm to leave a very little around the edge, as by again melting carefully, (and pressing down on the bench as before,) it will take a smooth, shining surface, and not be noticed. There are many workmen who denounce "sticking jewels in" with shellac as botchwork. So far as hole jewels are concerned I agree with them, but with cap and foot jewels it is often a necessity, and it is certainly far better than to plug the holes around the jewels with paper, slivers of wood, etc., as we see every day. Doubtless our carping friends would sooner leave them loose than "stick them in" with wax. But then, *some* people are so *very* nice!

(20.) *The hands and their operating mechanism.*—If the minute-hand, cannon pinion, or center post is suspected to touch the glass, place the thumb nail on the glass and run it along just over the hand, and by getting the light right, and looking through the edge of the glass, you can see the exact distance between its under surface and the hand. Or, put a small slip of paper over the post or hand, shut the glass on, hold the movement edgewise and tap on the glass. If free, the paper will drop off. Or, turn the hands and listen for any grating or squeak. Also look for any mark on the glass over the cannon pinion. If there be the slightest evidence of touching, a higher glass should be substituted. If that cannot be done, confine the end play of the center pinion or post, or, if that is correct, the top must be taken off a little. Be sure to turn the minute-hand once around, examining it frequently to see that it nowhere touches either glass or dial, and does not "cant up" on one side and down on the other. If it does, the center pinion wants uprighting. Also try if the hour-hand is perfectly free *at every point* during this revolution of the minute-hand. If not, it must be made so, for any binding will affect the time if it does not stop the watch. A black mark in the hole in the dial shows that either the hour wheel or the socket of the hand rubs there. If the hour-hand trembles or bobs or jumps as it is turned, it shows something wrong about the fitting of the dial wheels. If the seconds-hand points higher on one side than on the other, bring the hour-hand over it at its highest position to see if there is any possibility of their interfering. Also try if the point of the minute-hand can touch it anywhere.

(21.) *Putting together.*—In putting together a movement, the dial should first be fastened firmly to the plate so that it cannot move about or become loose, then the seconds-hand should be put on and trained as closely as possible to the dial without touching at any point of its revolution. The hour-hand is next put on firmly, turned to point exactly to the I, and the minute-hand put on pointing to the dot of the XII. This position will cause the hour-hand to point correctly to all the other figures, if the dial is correctly marked. In fitting it upon the hour wheel, the hour-hand when at its lowest end-shake must clear the seconds-hand at its highest, and the minute-hand, in turn, must clear the hour-hand at *its* highest, and, finally, the glass must clear the minute-hand at *its* highest point. *Try this*, by pushing the upper hand down to its lowest possible end-shake, and, while so, lift the lower hand to its highest end-shake, one being just over the other.

(22.) *Freedom of the hands.*—Hence the play of the different hands should be no greater than will give perfect freedom of motion. If the hour-hand has too much play, a spring foil washer should be placed on the hour wheel to prevent end-shake, but it must still remain perfectly free to revolve. The washer is not designed to exert any pressure upon the wheel when in its correct position, but only to prevent it getting out of its proper place and having unnecessary play. These washers are sold by all material dealers, and are so cheap that there is no excuse for the use of unyielding paper plugs between the hour wheel and dial. Further details concerning the dial and the seconds-hand will be found in Chapter XXIII. (See *Dial*, in Index.)

(23.) *Trying the hands.*—Finally, bring the minute- over the hour-hand at the most dangerous place, hold the movement dial downwards, and with the key turn the minute-hand back and forth past the other while in that position, watching closely when they pass each other. Too much care cannot be given to the perfect fitting of the hands and the mechanism propelling them, for any trouble here may prevent the most perfect movement from doing even decent service, and it is useless to undertake the regulation until it is corrected. If the glass is thin and it is suspected that it may be sprung down upon the center post and interfere with running, put a little rouge and oil on the tip of the post, shut down the glass and press it cautiously with the fingers, after pushing the post to its highest end-shake. If any contact occurs, the rouge will be found on the glass. Or the oily rouge can be left on the post while the watch is worn in the pocket for a few days, and the glass then examined. When satisfied that there is no contact, absorb the oil off the post with tissue paper.

(24.) *Cannon pinion and center square.*—If the cannon pinion or center post is loose, it may be tightened by twisting the arbor or post around between the jaws of a pair of dull cutting pliers. The sharp edges raise a couple of ridges or rings around the arbor, making it practically so much larger. If too large, twist the arbor in the flat pliers, which will flatten the ridges a little, till they just fit the cannon or center pinion snugly enough to surely carry the hands, but no tighter than that. By holding the arbor or post *straight* across the jaws of the cutting pliers and using reasonable care, there is not the least danger of either cutting or breaking the post off, or even bending it in the slightest degree. If this operation will not enlarge it enough, it is better to fit a new one than to tighten it with bristles or to flatten it with a hammer as many workmen do, for the former lasts but a little while, and both are sure to make the post and hand one-sided and probably cause "canting," besides lengthening it and disarranging the dial wheel mechanism. When the post is soft and but little enlarging is needed, it is often done by rolling it between two sharp files with a heavy pressure, thus producing a multitude of fine burrs on its surface. In a cheap watch, the cannon pinion is sometimes filed in at one side, nearly to the bore, then a punch causes the thin metal to project into the bore enough to secure a tight fit. Just as I am finishing, a method is mentioned to me which, if practical, would be useful for tightening a cannon-pinion arbor or center square. I have not tried it. Make a solution by dissolving 1 part of cyanide of silver and 10 parts of cyanide of platinum in 100 parts of water. Immerse the worn part of the center post (or other worn piece) in this solution and leave it there till the deposit upon it is sufficient to make it tight in place. If too tight, the surplus metal can of course be filed off. Clean it well before putting in the bath, and wash thoroughly in water and alcohol after taking it out.

(25.) A cannon pinion on a center post must be proof against any possible accidental turning. But if on a center-pinion arbor, it must only be tight enough to certainly carry the hands. If it has a tendency to work up and become loose by setting the hands, making a ridge near the top end of the arbor will generally cure this. But if the arbor is very much tapering, the part of it which forms the bearing in the cannon should be made more nearly cylindrical, or smaller at the base, then properly tightened. If the cannon pinion is tight enough in some places, but on turning it a little further around becomes loose, this fault should be corrected by taking the "humps" off the arbor, then ridging it at some place where it is round. In stem-winders, see that the stud holding the intermediate steel wheel is tight in place, also the stud of the minute wheel, and that both wheels operate properly, and cannot pass by, nor tip up and stick. Oil both studs, also the cannon pinion *slightly*, to prevent rust. See that the stem-setting mechanism cannot touch the dial wheels except when in action.

(26.) *Fuzee, chain, going barrel, etc.*—In fuzee watches, see that the end of the fuzee arbor cannot touch the case or dial, that the dust cup on the winding square does not rub where it goes through the dust cap; that the chain or its hooks do not rub—especially, if the mainspring has broken and bulged the barrel; examine when the bulged side is outermost, and the chain is on its highest part; if the teeth of the great wheel in a fuzee watch, or of a going barrel, are near the joints of the case, or where the ends of the case springs come when pressed in, be sure that they cannot touch.

(27.) *The balance, cock, etc., in full-plate movement.*—The screws in the balance should be tight, so that they cannot work out of themselves. See that the balance is free from the head of the barrel where it projects through the upper plate, and from the projecting point of the brace which supports the outer end of the mainspring. Both the brace and the barrel or its head may at times project upwards much higher than usual. Get the barrel up to its highest end shake, and see if the balance has ample clearance. See that an excess of oil does not exude to the top of the barrel, and hairs or dirt stick in it and clog the balance. See that the balance does not hit end of center-pinion pivot, steady pins, etc.

(28.) *Three-quarter plate movement.*—See that the balance

screws are free from the chain on the barrel, (especially after a broken mainspring,) or on the fuzee; from the teeth of the going barrel, and great wheel; from the center or fourth wheel pinion leaves; from the adjacent parts of the dust cap, or of the case, joints, springs, etc. If the balance has a banking pin, test its freedom by slowly moving the pin past the dangerous points. Do the same with the wings on the balance of a duplex. See if the wings are tight. See that the balance is free from the regulator where it passes over or under it.

(29.) *Sundry faults.*—See that the dust cap cannot be pressed down so as to touch the balance, (or its screws), nor press against the sides of the balance cock and displace it. See that the inner case cannot touch the regulator center, or some screw or prominent point on the top of the balance cock, springing the latter down and interfering with the freedom of the balance. If doubtful, or if the case is thin and liable to be pressed in sufficiently to touch, put a little rouge and oil on the highest or most probable points, and cautiously squeeze the case in, (listening at the same time, to see if it interferes with the vibration,) or wear it so for a few days. Look out for bent pivots on the balance staff, if the steady pins are tight and the balance cock comes off hard. See that the guard pin on the lever (in a full plate watch), cannot touch the regulator center. Turn the regulator in all positions, (with the balance out,) with the guard pin on each side, (*i.e.*, with the lever banked on each side,) to see that the guard pin cannot touch, and interfere with the locking, in English lever watches.

The foregoing are of course not all the points which require looking after in a watch, but merely those which might affect the timing or rate, and perplex the workman if he did not know where the trouble was.

CHAPTER III.

Magnetism and Magnetized Watches.

(30.) *Effects of magnetism.*—Besides the mechanical condition of the watch itself, we have to guard against an external disturbing influence which often produces vagaries in the regulation so incomprehensible as to cause the workman to give up in despair of overcoming them. This influence is magnetism or electricity, and is more commonly felt than is supposed by the majority of workmen. It has already been said that the balance should not be magnetized. Chronometer makers fully appreciate the importance of this point, and try to guard against it by causing their balances to vibrate a turn and a quarter. By this means a balance is secured from the injurious effect, so far as it can be done. A magnetized balance has a constant tendency to turn to some particular position, like the needle of a compass, or to point to any other magnetized part near it, but with the above arc of vibration this tendency is partially neutralized, by the retarding and accelerating influences counterbalancing each other during the course of the vibration, so that less effect is produced upon the rate. If the magnetism is at all strong, however, the difference will not save the rate from being ruined. Another advantage of vibrating 1¼ turns is that the effect of a want of poise is less than if the arcs are either greater or smaller. It is scarcely necessary to say that the advantages thus secured are not confined to marine chronometers, but may be obtained in the same way for all watches, by giving that vibration, when their balances are wholly or partly of steel, iron or nickel. Balances of palladium, gold or brass are not affected by magnetism, but steel screws used in their rims, or elsewhere in their construction, may have a disturbing influence. In going-barrel watches, whose balances have varying arcs from the varying motive forces, if we make the average between the largest and smallest vibrations to be 1¼ turns, we practically secure the advantages named as well as can be done in such cases.

(31.) But the above precautions will not prevent evil effects from the application of a magnet near to a watch, and the effect is the same whether the case be open or shut. Powerful electro-magnetic batteries or machines will magnetize a watch at a distance of several feet, and persons who work around batteries, etc., should lay their watches aside during working hours. Even if the balance is of gold or brass, the magnet may attract the lever so strongly as seriously to disturb the rate. If the balance, balance spring, and lever with its pallets, are made of non-magnetic metal, it is of little or no consequence whether the rest of the watch is magnetized or not. But a magnetized lever or balance spring is very injurious, and a magnetized balance fatal to good time-keeping. Never allow any magnet or magnetized piece, loadstone, electric machine, galvanic battery, conducting wires, etc., near a fine watch, or carried in the pocket with it. Thousands of watches have been ruined by fooling around them with magnets, etc., either knowingly or ignorantly, and when the watches are not injured by such a practice, their running is disturbed. It is often thought that a solid or uncut steel balance cannot be affected by magnetism, because it is a circle. But the arms have ends, and may be magnetized or attracted the same as plain bars, notwithstanding that they are attached to a rim. The rim itself can be magnetized with two poles, or perhaps with several. A watchmaker should take no chance in such matters, but avoid even the possibility of his adjustments being interfered with by this or any other influences known to be injurious. If the owner insists on exposing his watch to injury, it is his privilege to do so,—and to pay for it.

(32.) *Effect of dynamos, electric motors, etc.*—At the present day magnetism is encountered almost everywhere. The electric motor is used on street railways, for elevators in buildings, for running machinery of all kinds and in all places, even for working electric fans in offices, restaurants, residences, etc. Powerful dynamos may be within a few feet of us in the building or under the sidewalks. Telegraph instruments, district messenger calls, telephones, and a multitude of other apparatus to be found in almost every house, contain magnets, which magnetize everything near them that is composed of iron or steel. A balance while vibrating is less affected than when still, and a hard balance or piece is less easily magnetized than a softer one, but the magnetism is more permanent and more difficult to remove. Every time a watch is worn on an electric car, it is almost certain to be magnetized.

(33.) *Different kinds of magnets.*—Tempered steel, when magnetized, remains so, and is called a permanent magnet. Soft iron is a magnet while acted upon by another magnet or by an electric current, but loses its magnetism when the magnetizing influence is removed, and is therefore a temporary magnet. A coil of wire in which a current is flowing is a magnet, and one end of it is a North pole and the other a South pole, the same as a bar of steel or iron. When an iron or steel rod is placed in the coil, it becomes magnetized by it. Not only the coil, but the wire itself when straightened out, is magnetic while the current flows through it. A straight rod of magnetized iron or steel is called a bar magnet; when made in U shape, so that the poles or ends are near together, it is called a horseshoe magnet. A coil of wire with an iron core in it is an electro-magnet.

(34.) *Action of magnetism.*—A magnet of any kind acts by means of what are called magnetic *lines of force*, which spread out through the space near it. In the case of a powerful magnet, these lines of force can be detected at least a hundred feet distant, and could probably be detected many times that distance if we had sufficiently sensitive means for testing. The lines of force are closed circles. They come out of the North end or pole of the magnet, curve around through the neighboring space, and into the South end, completing the circle in the magnet itself. In the magnet there may be millions of these lines, but outside they diverge in every direction and fill the entire space around, being most numerous near the poles, and less so as the distance increases. The magnetism is said to be powerful or weak, according to the number of lines of force passing through the object being tested.

Magnetic attraction is due to the attraction of these lines for other lines of opposite direction. They tend to unite and contract or shorten themselves up. Magnetic repulsion is due to the repulsion between lines of force having the same direction—whether the lines belong to the same magnet or to different ones.

(35.) *All substances permeable by magnetism.*—Magnetism passes freely though all substances, whether animate or inanimate. It will pass through a brick or stone wall, a wooden partition, a human body, living or dead, precisely as if they were not there. Nothing can stop it. Air, water, glass, paper, cloth, metals, and everything else are permeable by magnetism. A magnet will therefore act on a balance in the case as well as if outside. The only difference is that when it acts upon a complete watch, its strength is distributed among all the steel or iron parts it contains, while the whole strength could be directed upon the balance by taking that by itself. Hence you must take the watch apart if your magnet is weak; but if it is strong enough you can magnetize or demagnetize the whole watch at once with it.

(36.) *Magnetic metals.*—Although all substances are permeable by magnetism, only the magnetic metals can be magnetized. They are iron, both wrought and cast, and steel in all forms; nickel is slightly magnetic, chromium and manganese much less so. But for all ordinary purposes, we may call iron and steel the magnetic metals. While the magnetic lines of force are passing through them, they are magnets. Magnets attract the magnetic metals and the latter attract magnets, the attraction being mutual. But two magnets attract each other more strongly than one magnet and an unmagnetized piece. A magnetized balance attracts every other magnet and piece of magnetic metal in the neighborhood, whether in the watch or out of it, and is attracted by them. Hence it is useless to demagnetize a balance, and leave other parts magnetized such as pinions, case springs, etc. The attraction between them is diminished, but it is still acting upon the balance and they will gradually remagnetize it. The only proper course is to demagnetize every piece of steel or iron in the movement and case, and to keep magnetized articles away from it. A magnetized pocket-knife, steel chain, button hook, suspender buckles, spectacles, buttons, truss or other springs, and similar articles on the person, will affect the motion of the balance. In the same way, magnetized iron beams or parts in the building, magnetized tools on the bench, and the like, will affect the running while in the shop.

(37.) *Testing for magnetism.*—Take a piece of perfectly soft iron (not steel) binding wire, about one-half inch long, and say No. 20 to 24, tie a fine silk fibre around the middle of it, and fix the other end of the fibre in a slit in a stick of pegwood. This "tester" will swing freely, and will point in any direction indifferently, so long as it is not influenced by a magnet. But if there is a magnet in the vicinity acting upon it, the tester will *point* towards the magnet. Turn it away, and if it swings back and points in the same direction as before, move it in the direction it points, and you will find where the magnet is. If it ceases to point, when you move it so, you are going the wrong way, and should move in the opposite direction; when you get it close to the magnet, it will be drawn bodily towards it, and, if allowed to touch, will stick to it. To test a watch, hold it around the rim of the case, or open the case and hold it over the suspected piece. Remember that magnetism acts through the case, glass, etc., as well as through air. If there is no magnetism present, it will not be attracted nor "point;" if there is, it will point, and will be attracted to the magnetized piece. You can thus test a balance or a watch without taking it apart. It is well to make two of these, so that you can discover if either of them has become slightly magnetized, as in that case they will attract each other and stick together. They should then be heated red-hot to remove the magnetism, and again suspended, without bending, hardening or working at them in any way. When in proper order, they will not attract each other at all.

CHAPTER IV.

THE DEMAGNETIZATION OF WATCHES AND WATCH PARTS.

(38.) *Demagnetization.*—A piece which has been magnetized by a powerful magnet, requires correspondingly strong magnetism to demagnetize it, but the latter need not be quite so strong as the former. But if they are not equally distant from the piece, there may be a very great difference in their strengths, for the effects are, roughly speaking, inversely as the cubes of the distances. That is, if the magnet which magnetized the piece was 10 feet from it, while the magnet which is used for demagnetizing is 1 foot from it, and both are of the same strength, their influences upon it will be in the ratio of 1 to 1,000. Consequently a magnet close to it could remove the magnetism produced by another magnet 1,000 times as strong —provided the latter was 10 times as far away. It is from this reason that ordinary magnets can undo the effects of powerful dynamos, etc. But if a watch is held close to the dynamo or magnet, or in contact with its poles, as is sometimes foolishly done, a demagnetizer of nearly equal strength will be required to thoroughly remove the magnetism.

(39.) *The principles of demagnetization.*—Demagnetization is accomplished by causing the lines of force to pass through the magnetized piece in the wrong direction. Supposing the piece to be a balance whose center bar has North polarity at one end and South polarity at the other, its lines of force come out of the North end and re-enter at the South end, as before explained. If we take another magnet and present its North end to the North pole of the balance, its lines of force will force their way through the center bar in the unnatural direction, or will prevent the home lines of force from emerging from the center bar, if we may so express it. What really occurs is unknown, but the result is that the molecules of the steel become differently rearranged, and the center bar is no longer magnetized. This is supposing that the opposing influences are nearly equal. But if the magnet is not strong enough, all of the magnetism will not be removed; or if it is too strong, or is continued too long, it will not only remove the magnetism, but will remagnetize the center bar in the opposite direction, *i.e.*, will cause in it lines of force in the same direction as its own. In actual practice with a bar magnet, many trials and corrections are generally required to entirely free the piece from magnetism.

(40.) *Testing the polarity.*—In order to tell what the condition of the piece is, or what effect has been produced, we need a polarity indicator. To make one, we take about an inch of a small sewing-needle, break off the eye and the fine point, and magnetize it powerfully by rubbing one pole of a bar magnet over it several times from end to end. Call the point the North pole; then we rub the South pole of the magnet from the eye to the point of the needle—always in the same direction, and holding the magnet far away while returning it to the eye. Next, we rub the North pole of the magnet from the middle to the eye several times, and finish by repeating the first rubbings, from the middle to the point. The polarity of a piece thus treated is opposite to that of the magnet at the last point of contact. Thus, if the South pole touches the needle last, at its point, the point will be a North pole. Suspend this in a bottle by a fine silk fibre attached to the middle of the cork. When it is not affected by the proximity of magnetic metal, this will point to the North like a compass needle. A delicately balanced pocket compass needle can be used, but is not so good for our purposes, unless we want to know *how much* it is deflected from a true Northern direction; in that case, a compass having a card divided off in degrees would be necessary.

(41.) *Distinguishing magnetized from non-magnetized pieces.*— This needle is attracted by every piece of magnetic metal, whether magnetized or not. If the piece is not magnetized, either end of it will attract either end of the needle; but if it is magnetized, its end will attract one pole of the needle and repel the other, according to the law of magnets, that *unlike poles attract each other but like poles repel.* That is, if the fork end of the lever, for instance, attracts the North pole of the needle, the fork is of South polarity; if it repels the North end of the needle, it also is of North polarity, and the distance that it repels (or attracts) it, shows whether the magnetism is strong or weak. If we tested a piece, then treated it to remove the magnetism, and it again repelled (or attracted) the needle, but not so much as before, we have weakened the magnetism. But if it repelled the needle, and, after treatment, it attracted, we have *reversed* the magnetism. In testing a balance, we first try all parts of the rim, center bar, staff, etc., with the tester (37). If that shows the existence of magnetism, and we want to know its location and polarity, we approach the different parts to the point of the needle, and observe whether they attract or repel it, and how much, thus learning the exact condition of the piece. If the magnetism is strong, we shall need a powerful magnet to remove it.

(42.) *Clark's method of demagnetizing.*—This method is used when the workman has only a small bar magnet to operate with. Each piece is treated separately. Supposing it to be a lever or similar piece, we will call the magnetized ends or poles N. and S. Lay the bar magnet on a paper box or wooden block to raise it an inch above the bench, with the N. pole towards you. Take the piece in brass or wooden pliers, (anything except steel or iron,) bring its N. end up as close to the N. pole of the magnet as possible without touching, then present the S. end to the magnet about $\frac{1}{16}$ inch from it, then the N. end $\frac{1}{8}$ inch away, and so present the ends alternately, and each time a little further away, till it is several inches from the pole of the magnet, when the magnetism will probably be out. This can be told by the tester and the needle. Do not test it with the needle unless the tester (37) shows that it is still magnetized, for the needle will remagnetize it. The distances can be told by holding a divided rule up to it. The balance and hair spring could also be treated in this way, but the balance generally has to be treated on different sides, and the hair spring should be removed from the staff and enclosed between two pieces of card or thick paper having a hole punched for the collet to come through and the edges folded over the spring. Hold the cards tightly together while presenting the spring. Case springs can be demagnetized by heating red-hot and re-tempering them, or as above.

(43.) *The Waldo method.*—Straight and similar pieces are treated with a bar magnet as described below. You can make your own bar magnets from pieces of bar steel, charged in the way described in section (40). They need frequent recharging, as they rapidly lose their magnetism. A strong horse-shoe magnet can be used for charging, by using the proper pole each time. For treating a balance, the bar magnet should be about 3 inches long and $\frac{1}{4}$ inch square. Find where the magnetism is strongest, and its polarity, by hanging it on a brass wire and bringing the pole of the magnet near the end of the arm. If it is attracted towards the magnet, try the other pole and it will be repelled. Take the balance in the hand and touch the pole momentarily to that part of the rim, then test with the tester to see if the magnetism is removed. Continue this till that point is free from magnetism. Then treat the other end of the arm in the same way; also, all around the rim, till the magnetism is all out. As it becomes weaker, use a weaker magnet, to avoid overdoing it and reversing the magnetism. Always use the *like* pole to *repel* or drive the magnetism out (39). It may require half an hour to demagnetize a balance by this method.

(44.) *The Mayer method.*—Prof. Mayer demagnetizes the whole watch at once, by oscillating it before the pole of a strong bar magnet. His method is somewhat modified in the following description, to make it simpler and shorter. Put a slip of paper under the balance, to keep all the parts still during treatment. The watch (in the case) is tested as a whole, by laying it on the bench near the needle, to find the strongest magnetic points and their polarity. Suppose that the side at III (on the dial) has the strongest South polarity, and at XI is the strongest North polarity. You arrange the magnet M at the edge of the bench, as shown in Fig. 1, (or on a book or

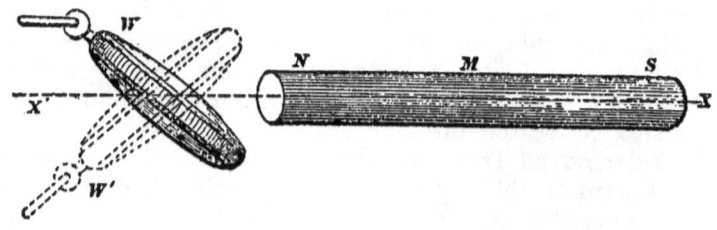

FIG. 1.

wooden block will do,) and hold the watch near it, with the strongest North point (at the figure XI) before the North pole of the magnet, *i.e.*, so that they *repel*. The line X, X', should pass through the center of the watch and also through the axis of the magnet. Taking it in both hands, oscillate the watch, holding it alternately in the positions W and W^1. After doing this several times, reverse the magnet, bring the strongest South point (figure III) opposite the South pole of the magnet and oscillate it as before. Then again find the strongest magnetic points in the watch, and treat them in the same way, repeating this until there is no perceptible magnetism anywhere. As the magnetism gets weaker, hold the watch further from the magnet and oscillate it fewer times, to avoid reversing the magnetism. This should be done at a distance from any iron or steel objects, otherwise they would attract the magnetism and interfere with the operation.

(45.) *The Maxim method* consists in subjecting the watch to rapid alternations of magnetism while slowly withdrawing it from the magnet, and thereby constantly weakening the magnetism till it ceases to be appreciable. This is done by a special machine which is patented, and is rather costly—the price being at one time as high as $250. I will explain the method as elucidating the principles of demagnetization. A bar magnet, carried on a vertical axis, revolves around that axis in a horizontal plane. The watch is carried on another vertical axis and is held in a frame so that it revolves in a vertical plane, while the frame itself revolves in a horizontal plane. The watch is thus turned both horizontally and vertically at the same time before the magnet, which is turning horizontally, and is slowly drawn from it by a horizontal screw.

(46.) *Demagnetizing with horse-shoe magnet.*—It is hardly worth while to fit up special apparatus unless it will demagnetize the whole watch at once. A powerful, permanent magnet should therefore be used, or two to four of them may be arranged together in a magnetic battery. Clamp the magnet in a wood block which can be held in the lathe, so that there will be wood in the bend of the magnets and also between the magnets and the lathe chuck. The central line of the spindle runs through the center of the bend and midway between the legs of the magnet, which revolve around the central line of the spindle. If more than one magnet are used, they are clamped together, with all the North poles on one side and the South poles on the other. While the magnets are revolving, hold the watch flatwise before them as closely as is safe, and very slowly draw it back, say 1 inch in the first 15 seconds, the next inch in 10 seconds, and at that rate till it is a foot away. Then test it, and if any magnetism remains, hold the other side to the magnets and treat as before. If that does not cure it, take out the case spring or other piece that is so strongly magnetized, and treat it separately.

(47.) *Demagnetizing with alternating current.*—If you are on an electric light or power line which uses the alternating current, you can get the company's electrician to wind up a solenoid, or coil without a core, so that an alternating current of high intensity can be sent through it. Hold the watch in this for a few seconds, then slowly draw it away as before described, while the current is still flowing, till it is two or three feet away, when the current may be be cut off. If you are where you can conveniently reach an alternating current dynamo, or powerful motor, it will be still cheaper to hold the watch near to one of the poles and gradually draw it away. But be careful not to touch any part and get the current through you, or you may be demagnetized yourself—and perhaps devitalized.

(48.) *Demagnetizing with an electro-magnet.*—If you are on a continuous or direct current line, you can use the current to energize an electro-magnet, fastened to the lathe spindle, whose arms are parallel with the axis of your lathe, and operate it as before directed for horse-shoe magnets (46). In this way you can make your magnet as powerful as you like, by using a strong current or large coil on the magnet, and can demagnetize a watch thoroughly in a few minutes. It would require too much space to describe the construction so that one not familiar with electricity could make such an apparatus, but any electrician can make you one at small cost. The only difficulty is in making the two contacts for conducting the current to the electro-magnet while revolving. The current *is not reversed in the electro-magnet*, and only plain contacts are required. If not convenient to employ an electrician, you can fit up a different apparatus which will answer all purposes. It consists of a simple *current reverser*, made to screw into the lathe spindle as a chuck, and neither the magnet nor the watch revolves. The magnetism is reversed in the magnet, and the watch slowly drawn away, as described for the horse-shoe magnet (46,), and the effect is the same.

(49.) *Description of the demagnetizing apparatus.*—Fig. 2 is a top view of the reverser, also showing the electrical connections

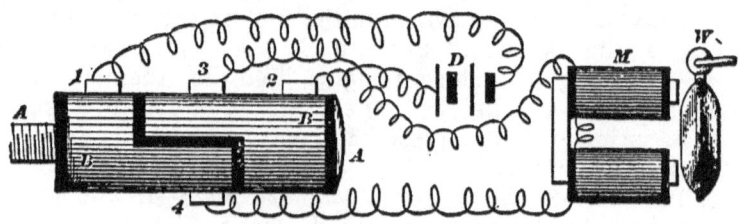

FIG. 2.

between the battery or dynamo and the coils of the magnet. The reverser is a boxwood or hard rubber rod, A, A, covered with a brass tube B, B, cut into two parts as shown. The shape of the cut is the same on both front and back sides, and is filled flush with sealing-wax, to insulate the parts of the tubing from each other. D represents the battery or other source of current, and wires conducting the current to brushes 1 and 2. Fig. 3 is a side view of the chuck and brushes, which are brass springs bearing on the tubing, and faced with thin platinum or silver where they rub on it. Fig. 4 is an end view of the same, showing the brushes on a wooden or rubber block *C*. In Fig. 2, brushes 3 and 4 connect to the electro-magnet *M*, and *W* is the watch to be treated. In the position shown, the current flows through wires and brushes 1, 4, magnet, 3, 2, and back

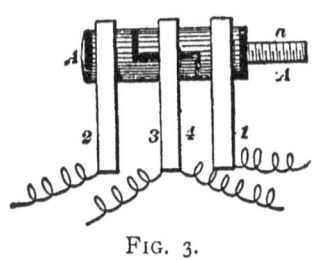

FIG. 3.

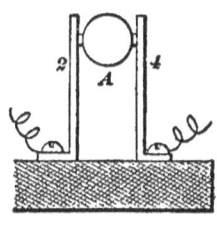

FIG. 4.

to the battery. When the reverser has revolved half a turn, the course will be 1, 3, magnet, 4, 2, thus reversing the direction of the current through the magnet twice in each revolution, and thereby reversing its magnetism. To stop the current, slip a piece of paper between the reverser and one of the brushes, then disconnect the wires wherever most convenient. Or you can use a switch to turn the current on and off. If a battery is used, arrange at least five to ten cells in series. Keep all the contacts clean and free from oil or grease. *Always disconnect the current before the reverser stops revolving.*

(50.) *Demagnetizing apparatus* of different kinds are sold ready made, and will save the trouble of fitting up apparatus, if they are efficacious. To test a machine, magnetize an old balance or a hard case spring on the pole of a dynamo or strong motor, and see if the machine will demagnetize that perfectly. If it is claimed to be able to demagnetize the entire watch at once, test it in that way. The directions already given will explain the principles of the process, and be useful even if you buy a complete apparatus, because you will understand the philosophy of its management and operation, and can work with greater certainty and rapidity.

(51.) *Care of magnets.*—Permanent magnets should always be arranged in a closed magnetic circuit while not in actual use, (*i.e.*, their poles connected by soft iron,) as that preserves their strength, or prevents them from growing weak so fast as they otherwise would do. Horse-shoe magnets are always provided with soft iron "keepers" for connecting the poles, and so closing the circuit with magnetic metal. The keepers must of course be removed while using the magnet. Bar magnets can be preserved in the same way, as shown in Fig. 5, where $b\ b$ are two bar magnets and $k\ k$ are soft iron pieces or keepers, to connect their ends. The poles of the magnets are as shown by N and S on each. When not in use, permanent magnets should be kept in a sheet iron, covered box, which has been heated red-hot and very slowly cooled to soften it. The object of this is to prevent the magnetism from spreading beyond the box and magnetizing everything around. If the tester shows strong magnetism outside of the box, it is not thick enough, and a box should be made of heavier iron. All electro-magnets and magnetic apparatus near the watch bench or watch rack, which *must* remain there, should have a similar shield around them. But they should be removed elsewhere, if possible, and no magnet of any kind, or magnetized piece, allowed there. The action of keepers and shield is due to the fact that soft iron offers many thousand times less resistance to the passage of magnetism than air and most other substances, and the lines of force will pass through the iron rather than the air. By arranging iron so that it will conduct the magnetism *past* any object, it acts as a shield for it. The box and the keepers act by conducting the magnetism from one pole to the other, without the necessity of going through air. This *choice of paths* is the reason that iron or steel "attracts" any magnetism in its vicinity.

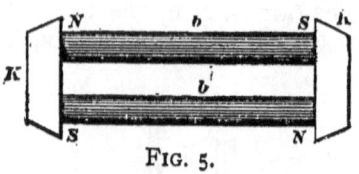

FIG. 5.

(52.) *Care of tools, etc.*—Demagnetize perfectly all tools and *materials* used around watches. The operation of demagnetizing must *not* be done on the watch bench, but in the back shop, and as soon as the article is freed from magnetism remove it *instantly* to the front shop, or it will again be contaminated. Take no tools from the bench to the back shop except for demagnetization, and allow no tools from the back shop on the watch bench. Any watch that is magnetized should be kept away from others.

(53.) *Necessity of understanding this subject.*—Inasmuch as magnetism is well known to affect the rate of watches, and regularity is impossible when they are under its influence, every springer and adjuster should understand how to free them from magnetism, at least, while timing and adjusting, or else he cannot depend upon the rates observed during his trials nor secure a correct adjustment. While the frequency of exposure to magnetizing influences is constantly and rapidly increasing, the methods of protection are not. In fact, it is by no means certain as yet whether we know of either a compensation balance or a balance spring, not liable to be magnetized, which can fill the place of steel and be depended upon to *permanently* retain its good qualities. Palladium balances and springs are giving good results, and it is to be hoped that longer and more extensive use may demonstrate that their good qualities are permanent.

But steel will, for a long time to come, at any rate—continue to be used in ninety-nine hundredths of the watches made, and the watchmaker must necessarily learn how to protect it, or to rescue it, from this insidious enemy. No workman who does not know this can do good work, nor avoid actually injuring the watches which pass through his hands. And what is worse, he cannot even restore those which come to him daily for demagnetization.

PART SECOND.

MAKING BALANCE SPRINGS.

CHAPTER V.

Treatment of Steel for Making Hair Springs.

(54.) *Materials employed for hair springs.*—The material generally used is the very best quality of cast steel, specially prepared and drawn into wire. It has the objection of liability to rust, and to be affected by magnetism, but thus far no substitute has been found which is positively known to have all of its valuable qualities and be free from these defects. Alloys of gold and palladium have been used, and further information regarding them will be given in sections (98) and (100). I will first give the method of making springs of steel, the material almost exclusively used.

(55.) *Imparting elasticity to steel.*—Steel may be made elastic either by hardening and tempering, or by compression, and springs are made in both ways. Springs for marine chronometers are now almost always hardened and tempered, as are those for the finer classes of pocket watches—while cheap springs are wire-drawn and rolled to all degrees of hardness, then wound into shape, and blued by heat, which causes them to "set" in the proper form. The former are more expensive, but are in every way preferable when properly made. Their temper is more uniform, both in the body of the spring and throughout its length; their qualities, whatever they may be, are more permanent, and they are more certainly made of any desired temper. Where the elasticity is given by drawing through wire plates and by rolling, there is the danger of minute cracks being produced in the edges at the final rollings, when the wire is already hard, which, although imperceptible to the sight, will disturb the action of the spring. But if the spring is to be hardened by fire, it can be annealed and kept in safe workable condition till the moment of hardening.

(56.) *Drawing the spring wire.*—In drawing (or rolling) the wire it is important, 1st: To draw always from the same direction, and, if it is rolled upon a spool after each drawing, it must be unwound and re-rolled before drawing again, so as to commence with the same end each time; 2d: To draw at a regular rate of speed—not fast at one time, then slow, etc., for such irregularity of speed will produce irregularity of texture in the wire; 3d: To have as few stops as possible, for there will be a difference of texture at that point of the wire that is in and behind the plate at the time of the stoppage, no matter how short the stop may be. The best way is to draw the whole length of the wire through at a regular speed without stopping at all; 4th: Wind the wire upon *large* spools or bobbins, if at all, and do not cramp or bend it any more than is unavoidable, until it is made up into springs; 5th: Instead of oil use beeswax as a lubricant; that will adhere to the wire under any pressure, while oil will not; 6th: Before heating the wire, either to harden or "set" it, clean it thoroughly by rubbing it lengthways with a rag dipped in pure (or 98 *per cent.*) alcohol, and then do not handle it with the bare fingers, but with clean tools, or by interposing clean paper or cloth between the skin and the steel.

(57.) *Selecting the spring wire.*—First cut off a piece and see if it will harden properly at a cherry-red heat. If not, it is unsuitable for springs, because it is too "mild," *i.e.*, it contains too little carbon for good spring steel, and is more like iron. If, when quenched in cold water, it becomes glass-hard and brittle, it will answer. Then examine the spool, to see if the wire is rusty, twisted, marred or scratched, or full of bends or kinks. If so, reject it. It should be clean, with a bright, polished surface, of a uniform size and shape, and carefully coiled on the spool to avoid short bends.

(58.) *Annealing the steel.*—If you have occasion to anneal and soften the steel, (for drawing, or any other purpose,) wind it on an iron spool or bobbin, as closely and solidly as possible, (without getting any short bends in it,) heat it in a cyanide bath (63) which just begins to be visibly red in a darkened room, till the steel is well heated through, then quickly quench in water. Dry in alcohol, then heat again to a dull red heat in daylight, and lay it in hot ashes, covering it deeply in the hot mass and leave till perfectly cold—an entire day, if necessary. The quenching process, if the heat is just short of the temperature at which the steel will harden, makes it very soft. For ordinary quenching the heat should not go above incipient red heat, (600° or 700°, Cent.,) but some kinds of steel may require to be quenched two or more times, while others will be soft after one quenching, even without the slow cooling process mentioned. If the latter is used, the temperature may be a cherry red, (800° or 900°, Cent.,) the article being packed in dry iron filings or dry powdered wood charcoal, in a crucible or a cast-iron vessel, closely luted up, and the entire pot buried in the ashes. For the quenching process, no such packing is needed.

(59.) *Cleaning blackened steel.*—When steel has been heated in the fire and has acquired a black coating, this oxide can be best removed by pickling or leaving it in dilute sulphuric acid (1 part of acid to 6 or 10 parts of water) till the scale is entirely removed; wash thoroughly in water to remove the last traces of the acid, and carefully wipe dry if the steel is in large pieces. In the case of wire, soak in alcohol to absorb the water and dry it off.

(60.) *Cleaning tarnished or colored steel.*—When the steel has not been so roughly heated as to receive a black coating as described, but is merely colored or has a gray surface, it can be cleaned by immersing in dilute muriatic acid (acid one part, to two parts of water,) till the surface becomes white and clean. Next wash thoroughly in water, then in a weak solution of cyanide of potassium (saturated solution one part, water 4 parts,) and finally in alcohol, as before.

(61.) *To prevent cracking in hardening.*—After being annealed and cleaned as before described, the steel is ready to be worked, with the assurance that it will be perfectly soft, of uniform texture and free from hard spots, fit for drawing or the finest turning. After being worked into shape, and ready for hardening, it is well to again heat it to a blue and let it cool slowly, as that is thought to prevent the tendency to crack or warp in hardening. It will of course be understood that the foregoing treatment of steel is not only for springs, but also for the steel used in making balances, and tools, and for all similar purposes.

(62.) *Hardening steel.*—The method of hardening small articles of steel has entirely changed since the first edition of this book was published. At that time, the steel was covered in some way to protect it from the air; then heated in a coke or charcoal fire, and quenched in water or other bath with the covering still protecting it. Then came the era of the lead bath. The article was heated in a pot of melted lead, in which it could be safely left as long as necessary for heating it through, as the lead protected it from the air; and, if the temperature of the bath was correct, the article could not be overheated, no matter how long it was left in the bath, because it could not be heated higher than the bath. The lead bath was a great improvement, and is still a very important aid in ordinary work.

(63.) *The new method of heating.*—Within a few years, another important change has occurred, especially applicable for the treatment of hair springs and other small articles. The steel is now heated in a bath of melted cyanide of potassium, which protects the steel from the air while heating, in the same way as the lead bath, but it has the additional advantage that, when the article is removed from the bath for quenching, a thin film of cyanide adheres to its surface and protects it from the air, without interfering with the hardening, as it instantly dissolves off in the water. The oxidation and scaling of the surface is avoided, and the tendency to warp and crack in hardening is also prevented (102). The cyanide is melted in a wrought-iron pot, and its temperature is shown by its color. Every part of the article can be heated equally; the thick metal block is brought up to a red heat without overheating the thin spring coiled upon it.

(64.) *The temperatures used in hardening.*—In order to be as precise as possible about the temperature of the bath, it is well to work in a slightly darkened room, or at least not too light, so that the colors can be accurately noted, and do not allow the bath to go above the proper heat, which is invariably shown by the color, and can be known by consulting the table below. It should not be above middle cherry red for cast steel, or clear cherry red for shear steel.

Colors at Red Heat and Upward.

The following table, compiled by Pouillet, gives the temperatures corresponding to the different colors of a body raised to a red heat:—

1. Incipient red heat corresponds to	525° Cent.	980° Fahr.
2. Dull red " "	700° C.	1290° F.
3. Incipient cherry red heat corresponds to	800° C.	1470° F.
4. Cherry red " "	900° C.	1650° F.
5. Clear cherry red " "	1000° C.	1830° F.
6. Deep orange " "	1100° C.	2010° F.
7. Clear orange " "	1200° C.	2190° F.
8. White " "	1300° C.	2370° F.
9. Bright white " "	1400° C.	2550° F.
10. Dazzling white " "	1500° to 1600° C.	2730° to 2910° F.

Frodsham gives the following:—

11. Red heat, visible by daylight	1077° Fahr.
12. Iron red hot in the twilight	884° F.

(65.) *The hardening and quenching bath.*—Notwithstanding all that has been said about special hardening baths, etc., practical men generally are pretty well agreed that a plain water bath can answer all purposes as well as any. It should not be ice cold, but at about 60° F. If the steel has been properly annealed and not injured in working, heated uniformly in every part but not overheated nor scaled, and so immersed in the water as to cool every part as uniformly as possible, the result will be entirely satisfactory. After quenching, remove the article from the bath, place it at once in alcohol to absorb the water, and dry in boxwood sawdust, as usual. If the surface is slightly dull, rubbing it with a little rouge will restore the polish.

Many good workmen claim great virtues for kerosene as the quenching liquid. They heat steel springs or other parts strongly, rub over with common soap while hot, to protect the surface, then heat to a cherry red and quench in a bath of ordinary petroleum. The steel will not twist, and remains perfectly white, ready for immediate annealing, which may be done in oil or with tallow as usual.

(66.) *Tempering steel.*—The usual way is to put the article in an iron spoon, or any metal capsule or vessel, containing melted tallow or oil, and heat it till the oil smokes in a certain way, or takes fire and burns off. The following table will indicate the temperatures and tempers corresponding to different grades of smoke and burning, with tallow or linseed oil:

TEMPERING STEEL IN TALLOW, OIL OR ALLOYS.

No.	Color.	Adapted for	Temperature.	Alloy fusing at same temperature.	Appearance with tallow.
1.	Pale straw...	Lancets and tools for cutting iron.	420° F.	7 lead, 4 tin.	Vaporizes.
2.	Straw........	Watchmakers' tools.	450° F.	8 lead, 4 tin.	Smokes.
3.	Straw yellow.	Penknives and razors.	480° F.	8½ lead, 4 tin.	More smoke.
4.	Nut brown...	Small pinions and arbors.	500° F.	14 lead, 4 tin.	Dense smoke.
5.	Purple.......	Large pinions and arbors.	530° F.	19 lead, 4 tin.	Black smoke.
6.	Bright blue..	Swords and watch springs.	580° F.	48 lead, 4 tin.	Flashes when a flame is applied.
7.	Deep blue...	Watch hair-springs.	590° F.	50 lead, 2 tin.	Continues to burn.
8	Blackish blue.	Chronometer hair-springs.	640° F.	All lead.	All burns away.
9.	Boiling linseed oil indicates a temperature of 640° F.				
10.	Boiling olive oil............................600° F.				

Steel can be tempered by heating in an alloy which is kept just above the point of fusion. The above table gives the melting points of a number of alloys. As soon as the article is heated thoroughly, it may be removed from the bath, and allowed to cool slowly.

(67.) *Other metallic baths for tempering steel.*—The following metallic baths may be used instead of those already mentioned:

Various Melting Points.

1. An alloy of 1 part lead and 1 part tin (by weight) melts at	196° C.	385° F.
2. Metallic tin..................................	"	230° C.	446° F.
3. An alloy of 2 parts lead and 1 part tin........	"	240° C.	465° F.
4. Metallic bismuth.............................	"	270° C.	520° F.
5. An alloy of 5 parts lead and 1 part tin........	"	290° C.	550° F.
6. Metallic cadmium............................	"	310° C.	590° F.
7. Metallic lead.................................	"	320° C.	608° F.
8. Metallic zinc.................................	"	420° C.	790° F.

and volatilizes if raised to a red heat.

(68.) *Method of tempering in metallic baths.*—The difficulty with metallic baths for tempering, is that they are liable to be heated far above the fusing points, without giving any indication of that fact, and the article may have its temper entirely removed. A good way is to dip the (cold) article in the bath and at once take it out again. It will of course be covered with a coating of the metal which has cooled upon it. Then immerse again in the bath till this solid metal has entirely melted off and the article comes out perfectly clean and free from the alloy. Then allow it to cool. Some kinds of steel require to be tempered two or more times to soften them sufficiently. Such steels are troublesome and uncertain, and had better be tempered with the aid of a thermometer (72).

(69.) *Tempering steel by heating in the air.*—Another way very commonly followed is to heat the article in the air till it takes on the color which corresponds to the temper desired. This is a tolerably accurate method, but the article is apt to be left brittle. The color for each temper is given below.

Colors Below a Red Heat.

The following table, by Stoddart, shows the tints which correspond approximately to the various temperatures of a body moderately heated, and the uses for which each temper is adapted:—

1. Very pale straw yellow.....	220° C.	430° F.	Tools for metal.
2. A shade darker yellow......	235° C.	450° F.	
3. Darker straw yellow........	245° C.	470° F.	Tools for wood and screw taps, etc.
4. Still darker straw yellow....	255° C.	490° F.	

5. Brown yellow .... 260° C. 500° F. ⎫
6. Yellow, tinged slightly with   ⎪ Hatchets, chipping
   purple .... 270° C. 520° F.   ⎬ chisels, and other per-
7. Light purple .... 275° C. 530° F. ⎭ cussive tools, saws, etc.
8. Dark purple.............. 290° C. 550° F. ⎫
9. Dark blue................ 300° C. 570° F. ⎬ Springs.
10. Paler blue................ 310° C. 590° F. ⎫
11. Still paler blue .... 320° C. 610° F. ⎬ Too soft for the above
12. Still paler blue, with a tinge   ⎪ purposes.
    of green............... 335° C. 630° F.   ⎭

(70.) The following table is given by C. Frodsham:

No.	Temperature.	Colors.	Adapted for
1.	430° F.	Faint yellow............	Lancets.
2.	450° F.	Pale straw	A little softer.
3.	470° F.	Full yellow.............	Razors and surgeons' instruments.
4.	490° F.	Brown yellow	Small pinions and arbors.
5.	510° F.	Do., with purple spots....	Cold chisels and shears for cutting iron.
6.	530° F.	Purple	Large pinions and arbors.
7.	550° F.	Bright blue.............	Swords and watch springs.
8.	560° F.	Full blue...	Chronometer and watch balance springs.
9.	600° F. to 660° F.	Dark blue, verging on pale black, technically termed white.	Chronometer balance springs.

(71.) "Steel may be tempered in a metallic bath, in linseed or salad [olive] oil, heated to the proper degree. The colors are very imperfect indications of the requisite temperature. Perfection of temper depends not only upon the temperature, but upon the time occupied in the operation."

10. Linseed oil boils at ....640° F.
11. Shellac began to soften at...180° F.
12.   "   was soft and plastic, but showed no signs of fusion at . ...212° F.
13.   "   boiled up at above ....300° F.
14. Water boils at..212° F.
15. Alcohol "   ....174° F.

(72.) *Tempering with a thermometer.*—All of the foregoing ways, although they can be safely followed after sufficient experience, are ordinarily somewhat uncertain and clumsy. The best way is to temper in a bath of melted paraffin, sweet oil, cyanide, or a metallic alloy, (according to circumstances,) heated to the proper degree, and kept there by using a chemical thermometer or pyrometer. Such a thermometer graduated up to 650° or 700° Fahrenheit will cover all temperatures that can possibly be required for any tempering operation, and will only cost a couple of dollars. Then you will know just what heat you are using, without any guesswork about it, and will be able to obtain definite and uniform results. One kind has a double glass stem, with a paper scale of figures within the outer tube. Others have a single stem, with the figures cut on it. The former is clearer, but the latter is more durable. By making an ink-mark at the proper place before you begin, you can see when the desired temperature is reached without any trouble. As soon as that occurs, remove the heat, or remove the oil or other bath from the heat, and let it cool down to about boiling water (212°) before taking out the object, and it will be perfectly tempered. The cyanide bath can also be used for tempering steel, at any of the temperatures between its melting-point and the upper range of the thermometer; it acts to dissolve all oxide off steel or iron, but acts more powerfully upon some of the other metals and alloys, and so injures the surface of the latter.

CHAPTER VI.

Making Cylindrical or Helical Springs.

(73.) *Different forms of springs.*—There are two principal forms for hair springs: the flat spiral, either plain or with the Breguet curve, and the cylindrical or helical. The latter is adapted for chronometers, and the former for most pocket watches. There are many other forms, not often employed, as the spherical, which is largest in the middle and tapering down toward each end, making it globular in form. These are very troublesome to make and set true, and have no practical advantage over the helical form with proper terminal curves. Another method is to make half of the wire in the helical form and the rest is coiled up in the flat form at the end of the helix. This is called the *duo-in-uno* spring. Then there is the reversed helix, being, in effect, a helix broken in two in the middle, and the two ends pinned into a stud in such a way that the upper half of the spring coils up while the lower half is uncoiling, and *vice versa.* It can, of course, be made in one piece. This is difficult and unreliable. The same object is accomplished with flat springs, by using two of them, so attached that one coils up while the other uncoils, as above stated. But no form of spring has yet been tested which produces any better effects than can be obtained from the helix or the spiral, by proper manipulation.

(74.) *Advantages of the different forms.*—There are good workmen who claim that a flat spring cannot be made isochronal—which, in view of innumerable instances to the contrary, is as ridiculous as the claim that the spring-detent or chronometer escapement is, *per se,* superior for keeping time to a detached lever escapement equally well made—a point which I shall touch upon hereafter. Theoretically, the helix, with its coils of equal diameters, is superior to the spiral; but practically, the average of the effects of the numerous coils of different diameters is equal to that of a spring with equal coils of an intermediate diameter. And a spiral spring with its outer end returned by a properly formed terminal curve is fully equal to a helical spring, for pocket watches; but for marine chronometers it is better to make the spring in the helical form, on account of the large size of the wire required for their heavy balances. As both forms are good, I will describe the mode of making each.

(75.) *Making helical springs.*—For the helical spring a cylindrical brass or German silver block is made, and shallow grooves cut in its exterior surface, by a small screw-cutting lathe or otherwise, having the exact shape the spring is desired to take. The wire is then coiled tightly in these grooves, and each end is fastened by screws or pins. Instead of a grooved block, a smooth one can be used, and a narrow extra wire coiled up with the spring wire, to keep the coils at a uniform distance apart—the extra wire being between the coils. It is not really necessary to have the extra wire, as the spring wire can be coiled by itself, and if evenly done the coils will open out enough in the bluing to avoid coming in contact with each other while vibrating. The spring is of course drawn tight and even on the block, before tempering. The object of using German silver blocks is two-fold: If of steel, they would be liable to warp more or less by hardening, and communicate an irregular form to the spring, which is, of all things, to be avoided; and a steel block will scale to some extent by the hardening process, and lose the perfect accuracy of its grooves —whereas a good brass or German silver block can with care be used many times. The block on which the cylindrical springs are hardened should be hollow, so that it will cool quickly. Its thickness should be no greater than will give sufficient rigidity and strength. The thickness is generally from one-eighth to one-sixth of the total diameter of the block, or about $\frac{1}{16}$ to $\frac{1}{8}$ inch thick.

(76.) *Setting helical springs.*—If the spring is given spring temper by drawing and rolling, and is to be simply blued and "set," hold the block with the spring upon it in the flame of the alcohol lamp, turning it constantly, and heating slowly and evenly, till it acquires the proper color, then let it cool. One bluing is sufficient for a rolled string, but coloring a hardened and tempered spring is a very different matter.

(77.) *Hardening helical springs.*—If the spring is to be hardened by fire, it is sometimes wrapped in thin sheet copper or platina foil, while wound on the block, fastened with binding wire or folded over the ends, having been previously well daubed over with common soap, softened by warmth, not moisture, and mixed with wood-charcoal dust, which largely protects it from scaling and coloring by the heat, by keeping it from the air. When so wrapped up it must be hardened in water. But most workmen simply slip the block and its spring into a brass, copper, or iron tube, or even a common clay pipe bowl, and fill it around and over the block with fine wood-charcoal dust, well shaken down to fill all the interstices, and entirely exclude the air while the wire is being heated. A small piece of steel wire must be so placed that it can be occasionally taken out to judge of the heat, as charcoal packing is a very poor conductor of heat, and very deceptive to the inexperienced. Very fine silver filings have been proposed, being a good conductor, but I do not know that this has been tried. Animal charcoal is also used, but it makes the spring very hard and difficult to form the terminal curves.

(78.) The whole must be carefully heated in a charcoal fire: to a cherry red, but no higher, and, as soon as it reaches that, the block with its spring is emptied into oil or water—the preference being for oil, unless the block is wrapped up as stated above, when it should be quenched in soft water. The proper temperature for the quenching bath is about 60° Fahr., as that is found to give sufficient hardness without danger of causing the steel to crack. But if the wrapping is at all thick, a greater degree of cold will be safe, and in fact necessary—but that is to be avoided.

(79.) *Improved method of hardening helical springs.*—The process described is the one usually followed. But the modern method would be to coil the wire on a German silver or copper cylinder and secure the ends by screws as described, heat in a cyanide bath (63) and quench in water, then temper in cyanide, (72), after loosening one of the screws, and drawing the spring tightly upon the block; clean in acid, (60,), and finally color it. The usual way of tempering is as follows.

(80.) *Tempering helical springs.*—If the spring has been hardened in oil, it is now drawn down to a straw color—if in water, to a purple—then removed from the block and polished inside and out, edges and all, with a stick and fine oil-stone dust or "sharpe," again fastened tightly on the block as before, and the color brought down to a rich dark blue. This, however, is a matter which depends somewhat on the quality of the wire used, and can only be fixed by testing your sample. Some steel will be as hard and elastic at a dark blue as another sample will be at a straw color. The aim should be to stop just short of brittleness, so that a piece of the tempered wire may, *with care*, be bent cold to a right angle around your screw-driver, or a round broach, but would snap off if it was bent carelessly or over the square edge of your pliers. If the spring is to be used white, it should be brought to the proper temper before polishing. Others temper the spring by heating in an oil or tallow bath, as described in section (66). When dried after hardening, they draw the spring tight on the block (79), and temper in oil to a blue, then clean and polish as above, ready for coloring or " bluing." In forming the terminal curves the hardened spring must always be bent by heated tools, a subject I shall treat on hereafter under the head of isochronism.

(81.) *In coloring a spring*, it is not always necessary or even advisable to go by the color of the spring itself, as any piece of steel on the block or plates will do just as well. But there are certain precautions to be observed which are not necessary with larger articles of steel, because here even the slightest variation of the temper affects the action of the spring. Supposing the color should be a dark blue, if the mass (spring and block, or plates,) has been heated rapidly, the coloring must be stopped sooner, or at a lighter shade, say a purple or a reddish-brown; or else it will go too far before it stops; while if it has been heated very slowly, it may be carried to the exact shade desired.

(82.) *The color-piece.*—The screw or piece by whose color we are guided should be hardened, as hard steel colors with less heat than a soft piece would do, and consequently there is less danger of reducing the temper too low. Some makers color or heat their springs once only; others clean the bluing off the color-piece and blue again; some even heat their springs five or six times. My own opinion is that if the spring has been properly made, hardened, tempered and polished, one bluing should be sufficient. But if it has scaled in hardening, or minute imperfections, roughness or cracks are feared, it will be safer to heat twice, but never more than three times. If the spring, after that, breaks under the test named in (80), it may be considered imperfect, unless it was packed in animal charcoal, when it will break even after the sixth bluing if bent cold. Such a spring, if smooth and perfect, may be blued three times, and will be sufficiently soft. It is understood, of course, that the color-piece requires a greater heat to bring it to a blue the second time than when it was hard, so that in reality it will be reduced to a lower temper or made a little softer at each bluing, although the color is exactly the same each time. This is also the case with the spring; but this need not be whitened after each heating, nor even loosened (if on a block) till done. But if the color-piece was soft at the start, the temper will not be reduced any lower by bringing it to the same color several times.

(83.) Another point is to avoid what are known as false colors. The color-piece, or some part of it near the middle of the whole mass, if practicable, is first ground off with the oil stone, or even Scotch gray. This bright spot must then be slightly dimmed again, by rubbing the finger over it once or twice before coloring, for the degree of temper cannot be closely judged from the color of a very bright piece, as will be found by trial. In coloring flat springs, as hereafter directed, the color-piece may be screwed in the center of the plates, holding them together, or in the center of the spring-cover of the bluing-pan, and the heating should be very slowly and evenly done, the center of the hair-spring resting just in the center of the pan, and the cover also being central.

(84.) Before leaving the subject of coloring springs, I may add that it furnishes us a ready means of discovering whether they are equally hardened or not. For instance, if the wrapping (77) touches the spring in some places and does not in others, the former will be harder when quenched. So if the wrapping is lapped on one side and thicker than on the other, the spring will not be so hard in the former places as in the latter. This we may test after cleaning the block, but before loosening the spring, by arranging the block to revolve freely between the centers of the "turns," then suspending a trough or half cylinder of sheet copper under it, reaching up on each side, protecting it from the blaze, but leaving the upper half exposed to view. Now apply the heat to this copper trough, which in turn will communicate it to the block, and the latter will be heated more evenly than could be done by applying the blaze directly to it. The block must be constantly turned by a piece of peg wood, and the lathe centers loosened up when it expands. When the spring reaches a purple in its darkest part, take away the lamp and trough, still turning the block till it has cooled somewhat, when an examination will reveal any inequality of temper. Any soft places will be indicated by a lighter color, in spots or streaks, according to its cause. Even the course of a carelessly applied binding wire may be traced. Should any such appearance be found, it must not be passed over as a slight matter, for it is proof positive that the spring is incapable of fine performance, and it must either be rehardened, or, if it has been scaled in the first hardening, it must be rejected entirely and a new one made.

(85.) *Diameter of springs.*—The proper diameter for a hair spring is a matter of calculation in new chronometers and watches, but helical springs are generally one-half the diameter of the balance. But a certain length in proportion to its thickness is indispensable to its free action, and if it is found that there is not room for that length of a helical spring, the coils being of the above-named diameter, then a spring with larger coils must be made, to secure the necessary length of wire. But the repairer should generally be guided by the old spring, if it yet remains, remembering that the new spring, when finished, will have expanded a little larger than the grooves in the block, or its first size before being hardened. If your wire is not of the same stiffness as that of the old spring, more or less coils than the old one had must be used, to get the same strength of spring. But generally the old spring should be copied in all respects, unless there is good reason to believe that it was never satisfactory.

(86.) *The number of coils* for a helical spring is given in section (397), but it is well to make one or two extra coils, to allow for testing the temper at the ends, etc., after which the superfluous length can be broken off. A rather long spring is better than a short one, especially if it is somewhat soft, as the angle of flexion, and the consequent danger of setting by use, are less. A spring should be thin and hard, rather than thicker and lower tempered, both being of the same strength. For the former will maintain the motion of the balance longer (without additional impulse from the hand or the movement), and consequently a watch with such a spring will be less affected by difference in the motive power, or friction, poor oil, jarrings, etc. The less the number of coils the harder the temper should be, and, conversely, the softer the spring the longer it must be. Hardened springs are less liable to be affected by magnetism than soft ones, and are to a great extent, but not entirely, free from the deterioration or loss of force to which all springs are more or less subject by constant action, even when the flexion does not approach the limits of their elasticity. The well-known phenomenon of hardened springs slightly accelerating on their rates, for a few months after being fitted, is an example of this change of condition in the reverse direction. In this case the springs lose a portion of their excessive initial hardness, and gain in pliability and elasticity. After attaining their greatest degree of elasticity they remain nearly constant, while the deterioration of soft springs is comparatively rapid.

(87.) *Making the terminal curves* will be described under the head of Isochronism, as it is properly a part of that adjustment. The foregoing directions will give a clear idea of the process of making helical springs, and will secure a better understanding of subsequent operations. Furthermore, the workman who proposes to fit a helical spring in a chronometer will generally find it necessary to make one to suit. Hence instructions upon that operation must include the making of the spring, as already described. The making of palladium springs will be described in sections (100, 101), and of gold springs in sections (98, 99).

CHAPTER VII.

Making Flat Spiral and Breguet Springs.

(88.) *The usual method.*—In the next chapter I have given the modern improved process followed by the American spring makers, and will now describe the method usually pursued. Flat spiral springs can be bought ready-made, of almost every strength and quality, so that a suitable one can generally be readily selected from a fair stock of them, and thus save time and labor. But cases occasionally occur when nothing suitable can be got, and a knowledge of the operation of making one precisely as wanted will be very useful. The selecting and preliminary treatment of the spring wire are given in Chapter V.

(89.) *The spring winding tool* consists of a sort of box like a mainspring barrel, with flat bottom, and sides turned out vertical to the bottom; the cavity is of the diameter required for holding the required number of coils of spring. A cover fits over the box, with a portion fitting into the cavity, and is held in place by two screws or otherwise. The side walls of the box have openings through which the wire is wound into the box.

These openings are not radial, but nearly tangential, to facilitate the entrance of the wire. Both the box and the cover have a central hole into which fits the winder.

(90.) *The winder.*—This is slightly like a steel barrel arbor, having an outside shoulder which prevents it from entering too far. The part which passes through the box has as many slits sawed down into it as there are springs to be wound, whether two, three or four, and also has a central hole, tapped for a screw. The slits are sawed down to the level of the bottom of the cavity, and the circumference between the slits is "snailed," to correspond to the thickness of wire used, so that each wire will have a true spiral form from its slit onto the wire from the next slit before it.

(91.) *The winding.*—If four springs are to be wound into the box together, the space between the coils will of course be equal to the thickness of three springs. The space between the cover and bottom of the box is equal to the width of the spring wire. The wire being cut into lengths suitable for springs, the ends are put through the openings in the box, and fitted into the slits of the winder, and the central screw secures them in place. The wires are then carefully wound into the box, as closely together as possible and without twisting, till the box is full. The screw is then removed from the winder and the inner ends of the springs freed so that the winder can be taken out. Mr. Logan then takes out the cover and substitutes what he calls a "cap," without any hole in it. That is better than the usual plan, which is to screw the cover down tight, to press the springs perfectly flat, and then stop the holes with a mixture of soft soap and wood-charcoal dust, to exclude the air while hardening. In making cheap springs, they are merely heated till a piece of steel laid on the box becomes blue, to cause them to "set" and remain in that form.

(92.) *Hardening and tempering flat spiral springs.*—To harden them, they are heated to a cherry red, usually in a charcoal fire or a lead bath, (but the cyanide bath is preferable,) and quenched in cold water. The box is then boiled in oil to temper the springs—the usual rule being to temper to a blue. They are then taken out of the box, separated and cleaned in dilute hydrochloric or sulphuric acid—the former being preferred, as the latter is apt to leave dark marks on the surface. For details on any of the above points, see Chapter IV.

The box and cover may be made of German silver, brass or copper.

(93.) *Polishing the springs.*—If the springs are made of good steel, polished and clean when wound in the box, hardened in the cyanide bath, tempered either with cyanide or in oil and then cleaned with hydrochloric acid as described above, it should not need any polishing. But when it does, use a stick with a conical end to hold the spring upon, and scour it with a stiff brush, as a tooth-brush. The stick is held in the left hand, its point in the center of the spring, which is stretched down over it into a shape similar to that of a hoop skirt, and kept in that position by the thumb resting upon it while the outsides of the coils are being polished. The insides of the coils are polished by sharpening a piece of peg wood and forcing the spring into the same shape, while resting it on a flat piece of cork, rubbing it by moving the stick in both an oscillating and lateral direction, very carefully, to avoid bending the coils. The edges are polished by rubbing the spring around on a piece of smooth paper, by means of a cork pressed gently upon it. In all cases the polishing powder should be plentifully supplied. Springs should not be polished any more than necessary to obtain a clean smooth surface, lest some parts should be reduced more than others and cause irregular action.

(94.) *Coloring the spring.*—After being well cleaned, it is laid in the bluing-pan and heated till it acquires the proper color, and is then thrown off to cool. If the spring does not make good contact with the pan in all its coils, while coloring, a heavy plate is laid over it, or held down by a spring, or even a screw. Of course, the under surface of the plate and the surface of the pan must be perfectly flat.

(95.) *Making Breguet springs.*—The Breguet spring is ordinarily made first as a flat spiral, and tested in that form to find the proper length for timing the watch. The time, or what is the same thing, the number of vibrations, given by a spring depends on *its length* between the stud and collet, and not on its form. Consequently, when the length suitable for the watch has been found, the curve can afterwards be formed in such a way as to make the long and short arcs equal in time. This could not safely be done before testing, because the adaptability of the spring and the proper place for the elbow could not be known till after this trial. The making of the elbow and shaping of the curve will be described under the head of Isochronism.

(96.) *Hardening the terminal curve in form.*—For more than thirty years some workmen have made the elbow on the Breguet spring, and then hardened it with both the main and supplemental coils already at their proper levels, but the terminal curve was not fully formed till the final fitting of the spring in the watch. This could of course be done when the required size and number of coils and the proper place for the elbow were already known, as might be the case in factories where large numbers of movements were made alike, after a model known to be correct. Mr. Logan, at the Waltham watch factory, made two important improvements in the art. He entirely dispensed with the elbow, by causing the supplemental coil to *rise gradually* to its proper height, and he hardened and tempered the whole spring in its final form, including the spiral body, the incline and the terminal curve, thus avoiding any distortion or straining of the metal at the elbow, and securing a curve hardened in form.

(97.) The means for accomplishing this are very simple. The spring box is made to contain the proper number of coils of the spiral, as usual. The spiral openings are tangential, and from the opening is cut a groove, in a manner similar to that on a fuzee, on the outside of the spring box, curving upward and then inward, precisely as the spring is desired to be. The spring wires being wound into the box till it is full, the ends outside are fitted tightly in the grooves and secured in position, after which the hardening and tempering are performed as for the ordinary spiral form. It is obvious that any desired curve can be cut in the spring box, and the most difficult and perfect forms can be reproduced with certainty.

(98.) *Making gold springs.*—At one time gold springs seemed likely to be extensively used, but long experience has shown that they are not so reliable as steel. The alloy is more difficult to work properly than that metal. The gold is alloyed with copper or silver, (generally, 18 K,) and its hardness is greater in proportion to the amount of the alloy. It is also made harder by drawing and rolling, but is very brittle. Instead of hardening and tempering by heat, as for steel, they are made elastic by annealing, in boiling oil, or by coiling on a block or plate, and heating to a blue but no higher. Cylindrical springs coiled on a block as above, are put in a metal tube, with a steel cover or a steel screw in the cover to indicate the temperature. The tube is heated till the steel becomes blue, then removed from the flame and allowed to cool slowly. Flat springs on a steel plate are annealed in a similar way.

(99.) *Objections to springs of gold.*—Its expansibility in heat being greater than that of steel, it requires heavier adjusting screws in the balance, thus introducing a train of evils which more than offset any advantages over steel in respect to being free from liability to rust or to be affected by magnetism. If carefully prepared and worked it retains its elasticity for a long time. But being heavier than steel, a gold spring is more liable to tremble and sag. The loss of elastic force when heated is greater than that of steel, and as that is really the greatest failing in steel springs, it is still more objectionable in those of gold. At present the use of gold springs is practically limited to the unlocking springs of the detents in chronometers.

(100.) *Making palladium springs.*—Springs are now made from different alloys of palladium. They do not become tarnished by exposure to air, sulphurous acid or sea-water. Their elasticity is imparted by wire-drawing and rolling, and can be made equal to that of steel tempered to a blue. They do not become distorted in form by heating, and on cooling recover their original elasticity. Their loss of elastic force when heated is less than that of steel, but the precise amount has not been determined. Their expansion by heat is also somewhat less than that of steel. Their limit of elasticity is less than that of hardened and tempered steel springs, and they are more easily pulled or drawn out of shape. They must be bent with great care, lest they be bent too much and injure the texture of the metal at that point; they are easily marred by blows or pressure. Not having their molecular condition changed, as occurs when steel is fire-hardened, but being in a condition similar to steel tempered by drawing and rolling, they must be classed with soft springs and handled accordingly. But it has been found that palladium springs accelerate on their rates (381) less than those of hardened steel, and the middle temperature error (614) is also less. They are heavier than steel, and therefore sag more. In making them into the Breguet form, greater space must be allowed between the body and the terminal curve to avoid possible contacts. The curves are easily formed with the tweezers.

(101.) Palladium is a silvery white metal, non-magnetic, heavier than silver or lead, with a hardness equal to that of wrought iron. When heated sufficiently in air it oxidizes on the surface and becomes blue. The compositions of the alloys used for balance springs are not known. Springs of the different alloys can be obtained already made, in either the spiral or cylindrical form, or the spring wire, ready for coiling, can be purchased in London, where it is drawn. Whether palladium springs will prove to retain their elasticity and other properties as long, or nearly as long, as those of steel is yet uncertain. But strong claims are made for them, and they certainly have a promising outlook. They are now being used quite largely, and by makers of the finest grades of timepieces, so their merits and demerits must soon become positively known. Thus far, they are the only rivals of steel.

CHAPTER VIII.

THE MODERN AMERICAN METHOD OF MAKING HAIR SPRINGS.

(102.) Mr. A. J. Logan has kindly written a description of the method of making the world-renowned American watch hair springs, hardened and tempered. As the Logans have probably made more watch hair springs than all the other makers in the world put together, all of them high-class springs, a statement of the method employed must be regarded by the trade as of unusual interest and value. It is as follows:—

(103.) "Below you will find answers to your queries regarding the making and tempering of hair springs.

1st. The spring should be coiled in a copper box, which should be turned out perfectly true, the right diameter for the springs. Four springs are wound up together in the box, by a special tool made for the purpose. This done, the tool is taken out, and a cap that is also turned true is put on to fit into the box, then forced down very tightly to keep the springs flat. Two boxes are then put together with the caps facing out, and wound together very tightly with binding-wire. They are now ready for hardening.

2d. To harden, heat cyanide of potassium in a wrought-iron pot, (No. 1,) to a cherry red heat, put in the boxes, heat till they come to a red heat, cool in cold water.

3d. To temper, heat another pot (No. 2) to a low red heat; dip the boxes in the cyanide and take out quickly; then put them back in and leave them in till all the cyanide is melted off; then cool them in water and you obtain the right temper.

4th. The springs are then taken out of the boxes and picked apart, great care being taken not to put them out of true.

5th. Clean the springs with chemically pure muriatic acid one part and water two parts, swill them well with water, then put them in cyanide water to kill all traces of acid, then into alcohol, and dry with sawdust.

6th. Draw down to a straw color, on a steel plate over a gas stove; then remove the color, using the same process as described in No. 5.

7th. Then they are put over a gas stove and drawn to a blue, on a steel plate.

8th. The number of coils, in flat spiral springs, mostly used for 18-size American movements is 15. Some factories use 14 coils for 18-size movements. In small springs, 13 or 14 coils are used. All flat springs are pinned in even coils, to get the best effect.

9th. The numbers of coils used in the Breguet spring is 13¾, for all sizes. The ¾ is for the over-coil, which is curved to the center and makes it equal to 14 coils.

10th. By hardening and tempering with cyanide, the over-coil needs no covering, and when cleaned with the acid it is all right for bluing.

11th. I do not cut blocks to order for making Breguet springs with the over-coil hardened and tempered in shape. The patent is now owned by the American Waltham Watch Co., and I only make them for that company. The other companies form the over-coil with tweezers, like the samples I sent you. I have made tweezers for nearly all of them. With a little practice, the over-coil can be made very accurately and quickly.

. . . .

The information here enclosed has cost me thousands of dollars and years of experience. Hoping it will be an addition to your book, Yours respectfully,
A. J. LOGAN,
Waltham, Mass."

(104.) The American Waltham Watch Company gives the following details:

"DEAR SIR:—In reply to your letter to Mr. Fitch, relating to replies to certain questions concerning the manufacture of Breguet hair springs. . . . For your further information we will say that we make substantially the same number of concentric coils (14–15) in all sizes of springs. (Q. 1)

We make by far the larger number with gradual curve to over-coil, but for the high grade movements we use the Phillips curve. (Q. 2)

The proportions of thickness to width of our springs are 1 to 4, and 1 to 3½. (Q. 4)

Our over-coils make about ¾ of one turn. (Q. 5)

We harden and temper in same form. (Q. 6 and 7).
Yours truly,
AMN. WALTHAM WATCH CO.,
E. A. MARSH, Asst. Supt."

(105.) *Number of coils in Breguet hair springs.*—It will be seen from the foregoing that the American watch companies do not follow the usual rule to give the Breguet spring about 50 per cent more coils than the flat spiral, but use the same number of coils (14–15) for both forms. As they use the same size of spring wire for both forms, it would not do to make the Breguet spring longer than the other form, as the middle coils would then sag and tremble too much. Some may claim that a short spring cannot come so near being theoretically isochronous as the long one would be, but it is on that account more practically isochronous, (660,) and is therefore able to be more widely adjusted and correct greater errors, and so give better satisfaction than the long one. This fact was doubtless ascertained by many practical trials, but it is strictly in conformity to the theory suggested for the flat spiral spring in sections (556, 558). Inasmuch as the over-coil enables the spring to expand equally on all sides of the center and avoid side pressure, if it can also be made perfectly isochronous there would seem to be no good reason why that number of coils should not be sufficient. It is well known that the American watches can be isochronized as closely as any others, and closer than the majority of other adjusted watches. As results are always the best guides, it follows that that number is sufficient for all purposes. On examination of various movements, it appears that they sometimes vary from that number. The following instances may be cited, giving the makers, sizes, numbers of the movements and length of springs from the collet to the stud:

Waltham, 6^s S, No. 6,011,117, $11\frac{1}{8}$ coils.
" 6^s K, " 5,746,501, 12 coils.
Elgin, 6^s, No. 4,777,330, $17\frac{1}{8}$ coils.
" 16^s, 114, No. 5,502,264, $14\frac{7}{8}$ coils.

Here is a range from $11\frac{1}{8}$ to $17\frac{1}{8}$ coils, from which we see that the exigencies of the isochronal adjustment are the final arbiters as to the number of coils required, and that it is impossible to specify any particular length of springs which will *always* be isochronous.

(106.) *Further improvements suggested.*—As is stated in Part Sixth (560) the effect of short springs is to give greater difference of rate between the long and short arcs than long springs, and thus enable them to correct greater errors caused by change of positions, frictions, etc. In the American springs, from the method of their manufacture, the distance between the coils is the same from the center to the outside, the effect of which is to reduce the difference between the long and short arcs to a minimum. It is known that if the distance between the coils increases from the center to the outside of the spring, the difference between the long and short arcs is made greater, (574,) and it can of course correct greater position errors than an equidistant spring could. For watches which are not to be adjusted, an equidistant spring would be preferable, but the other kind would be better in watches which are to be closely adjusted, and would obviate the necessity of making such changes in the lengths of the springs, as before mentioned, (105,) and they could also be adjusted more closely.

(107.) *How to make them.*—By the ordinary method of making hardened and tempered springs, the coils are necessarily equidistant. When springs are not hardened and tempered, but wire-drawn and rolled, and then set in shape by bluing, the coils open out and become much further apart at the outside than at the centre. But the demand is for hardened springs. I would therefore suggest the following method of making such springs as I have recommended: First, draw and roll the wire, wind the springs and set them by bluing, as described. By this process two springs would be made at once, and might be in one piece, connecting through the winder at the center. Second, take these springs, having the shape we desire but being still "soft," clamp them between two perfectly flat copper or German silver plates, and harden and temper them in that shape in the usual way (92, 103). Two pairs of plates with two springs between each pair could be clamped together or held by binding wire, and hardened and tempered together, and the springs then cut apart at the center. One of the plates could have a slight boss at the center (to hold the springs central) fitting into a hole in the other. The cost of manufacture in the factories would not be sensibly greater than for the equidistant springs, but any one who will compare the springs will find the former far superior to the others for isochronal purposes, either for the Breguet or the flat spiral form. This method of making such springs can be followed even by the ordinary watch repairer, who wishes to fit in one of the best possible form and kind.

4

PART THIRD.

WATCH BALANCES.

CHAPTER IX.

Balance Making.

(108.) *Making a plain balance.*—The best material for a plain balance is gold. Although its expansion in heat is somewhat greater than that of steel, it is not liable to rust or be affected by magnetism like steel. The making of the balance presents no special difficulties to the workman, except the cutting out to form the arms. The plate, whether of steel or of gold, (having been well hammered and made hard and elastic, if of gold,) is made smooth and flat on its under side and cemented to another plate of brass or zinc, then centered in the lathe, and the whole surface of the gold is turned off, (the cutter being sharp and taking off very thin cuts,) and made smooth and flat, ready for crossing out the arms.

(109.) *Crossing out.*—Put it on the dividing plate, and mark the positions of the arms and their width. They must of course be at exactly equal distances apart. Also mark the inner edge of the rim—the outer edge can be turned out in the lathe. The best way to cut out the arms is to rest the (double) plate against a block of wood and drill a series of holes along the sides of the arms, rim and boss, of such size that their peripheries will come barely short of touching the marks, to allow for finishing. Drill the holes through the gold, but not through the brass, or zinc, to avoid producing any burr outside, as that would prevent your holding the plate flat while drilling. If the back plate is of zinc, you will know when the drill is out of the gold, by the shavings being all white. When the holes are all drilled, remove the balance from the zinc plate, and separate the metal. The finishing is easy, being careful to avoid bending the arms. If they become stretched and too long, carefully hammer the rim to bring them level. Then shape and polish the rim, etc. For a screw balance, see section (110).

(110.) *Making a compensation balance.*—The compensation balance of ordinary construction consists of a steel center-bar carrying a circular compound rim, which is cut into two or four sections, each having one free end and the other end attached to the center-bar. This rim is composed of two metals, which are unequally affected by heat and cold, usually steel and brass. The first balances of this kind were made by fastening the steel and brass strips together by rivets at frequent intervals, and afterwards they were soft-soldered together. Next they were united by hard-solder, but at present they are generally united by melting the brass upon the steel.

(111.) *Making a balance.*—In making this balance, a piece of the best cast steel is selected, a hole of proper size drilled through the center, it is then mounted on an arbor and turned perfectly flat on both sides and on the edges, which should be parallel to the sides of the center-hole and at right angles to the flat sides. We then have a round piece or disc of steel, of the thickness of the rim of the proposed balance, and of the exact diameter to be given to the steel part of the rim. The brass is then either melted on the outside, or a piece of brass is stamped, or turned out, of the right size, and soldered on. Or a ring of drawn brass (to get a fibrous texture) is fitted to the steel. Some prefer one method, some the other. But there is probably but little difference between the products of each, when equally well made.

(112.) *Uniting the metals by fusion.*—When the brass is to be melted on, the hole in the center of the circular steel disc is first filled up with plumbago, pipe clay, or even fine chalk pressed in wet and allowed to dry. Some turn out a plug of slate pencil to fit the hole perfectly, and many other means are employed to prevent the melted brass from entering the hole during the process. It is indispensable that this hole remain unaltered, as upon it depends the truth of all the parts and the equal action of the segments when finished. The outer edge of the disc must be perfectly clean, to secure a perfect union and adhesion of the metals throughout the whole rim, and thereby insure equal and uniform action in all its parts. Some makers even gild the steel to prevent any danger of oxidation of the metal. The surface is then coated with powdered borax and water in the usual way, before being touched with the fingers, which is allowed to dry, the steel disc is then placed in a crucible, or in a heated mold of fire-clay or soapstone. In the former case, enough of the best brass is put into the crucible to surround and cover the steel disc when melted, covered with powdered borax, and the whole is exposed to the fire in a suitable stove or furnace, till the brass melts and flows freely, then the whole is shaken or stirred with an iron rod to cause impurities to rise, and immediately removed and allowed to cool while the steel disc is forced to the bottom and held there with the rod till the brass begins to solidify. After the brass is well melted and the steel forced to the bottom, it is advisable to cool the crucible or mold rapidly, to prevent liquation, or the tendency of the different parts of the alloy to separate and produce a difference in the composition or texture of the metal in different portions of the mass, and also the tendency to crystallization in the interior during slow cooling. This is readily accomplished by setting the crucible on a cold stone slab or body of metal, which will rapidly conduct the heat away. In the latter case the brass is melted separately. As soon as it becomes thoroughly liquid and the characteristic greenish flame appears, it should be poured into the red-hot mold and the disc held down as before. The side of the disc which was cemented to the chuck should be down. The heat must not be too great, or blisters may arise and make the brass porous. Cool rapidly, as above directed. Old English watch movements are found to furnish brass which is generally very satisfactory. The melting should be done by a charcoal or coke fire. The fumes from coal are very objectionable, especially from soft or bituminous coal, and ordinary wood is not much better, unless thoroughly seasoned and dry. When the brass is to be soldered on, a thin film of silver solder is interposed between the steel plate and brass ring when the latter is driven on, plenty of borax applied, and the whole is carefully exposed to heat till the solder flows satisfactorily.

(113.) *Shaping the balance.*—When cold, the center-hole is cleaned out, the superfluous brass filed off the sides, and also on the edges till it is about three times the thickness it is to be when done, and afterwards turned down nearly to its final diameter; then the rim is carefully hammered to harden the brass without denting it or breaking the grain. This hammering should bring the rim to about the diameter it is to remain, so that as little as possible of the metal will have to be turned off, as that would remove more or less of the hardened surface and impair its value. The edges and outside of the rim are turned perfectly flat and true, and the inside of the steel plate is turned out in such a way as to leave the metal at the bottom of the cavity, of the thickness the center-bar is desired to be, and the steel part of the rim about one-half the thickness which the brass portion outside will have when the balance is finished, and the cavity smoothed with emery powder.

(114.) *Finishing and drilling the rim.*—It is then drilled and tapped for the screws, the number of which varies from twenty to thirty. American watches generally have thirteen holes on each half of the rim. Some makers locate the holes at a progressively decreasing distance apart as they approach the free ends of the segments,—others make them an equal distance apart throughout. This is not material, but it is absolutely indispensable that each opposite pair of screws be exactly in a diametrical line passing through the precise center of the balance. Instead of screws, chronometer makers often use sliding weights, which may be moved along the rims and fastened at any desired point by a set-screw. But the use of screws for compensating is the rule for pocket watches.

(115.) The bottom is next pierced and filed out, leaving the center-bar of exactly the same size and shape on each side of the center, and the rim of the same thickness from edge to edge, without filing or scratching the portion of it which was cut out in the lathe. The balance should now be carefully poised on an arbor, to see that the work has been equally and uniformly done, and then annealed by boiling in olive oil (66) to remove internal strains produced by the working of the metal and bring the whole to a uniform molecular condition. This should be done before cutting.

(116.) *Cutting the rim.*—The balance is then set up in the lathe again, and the rim polished. It is now cut, generally near the center-bar, so as to form two long sections or segments, but sometimes midway between the ends of the center-bar, thus forming four shorter segments. The drilling and cutting are best done by the help of a dividing engine, to insure exactness, and so that the two segments should be of precisely the same length, and shape of cut. It is necessary that all the opposite parts of the balance be of exactly the same thickness, shape and weight, as otherwise, even if the balance was in poise at the mean or middle temperature, it would not be so when the segments had changed their position under the influence of heat or cold, for their unequal motions would carry the compensating screws to different distances from the center, and render the rate utterly unreliable in different positions, or in carrying. It must also be staked or riveted concentrically upon the balance staff, as any fault here would vitiate all previous painstaking.

(117.) *Where to cut the rim.*—Where the rim shall be cut is determined largely by the construction of the balance itself. Every maker tries to have a definite system, which he rigidly adheres to, and by this means he produces balances comparatively uniform, or at least having a certain character. The balances of some makers are more sensitive than those of others. The former do not need so long segments to produce the same effect. And each maker will by careful observation and experience find the length of segment which is suitable to his balances. Very long segments are apt to be irregular in extreme temperatures, while short ones may not have action enough to effect a compensation. If the rim is sufficiently sensitive, it may with advantage be cut into four equal segments. But, in any case, when there are but two compensating segments, the cut should be far enough from the center-bar to afford a good hold upon the balance while handling it, without the fingers pressing on the free ends of the segments. The balance is cemented on a metal plate while cutting, to support and hold the rim. The plate is previously cut, with openings somewhat wider than the cuts will be in the rim. It is not cut radially, but obliquely, so that the end of the short segment laps a little over the adjacent end of the long one, protecting it from injury by rough handling.

(118.) *Making a spring-steel balance.*—By the ordinary method thus far described, the steel part of the rim is left soft. It has often been observed that the balance would be much more stable and uniform in its action, if the steel lamina could be left in the condition of a permanently elastic steel spring, as after being hardened and tempered. But thus far no acceptable way of reaching that result seems to have been found, and I therefore describe my way of producing a permanent spring-steel balance. It is made as before described, by the melting process, until the cavity is turned out,—except that the brass is left about three times the thickness it is to be when done. The arms or center-bar are cut out and the rim finished inside, as in section (113), but the rim is not drilled nor cut, although it is turned to its final width, *i.e.*, from the top to the bottom.

(119.) *Stays for hardening and tempering.*—Turn up a disc of cast iron exactly fitting the inside of the rim, resting on the center-bar and reaching up exactly level with the steel edge of the rim. This is easily done, even in making a single balance. But in factories, where the sizes of all the parts are uniform, it would involve scarcely any expense, as the stays can be used continuously. On each side of the balance lay a cap, with its under edge perfectly flat. One is in contact with the under surface of the rim and center-bar, the other with the rim and the disc, which in turn supports the inside of the rim and the top of the center-bar. The whole is screwed fast in a malleable iron clamp, and is ready to be heated in the cyanide bath, (62, 73,) quenched in water, and tempered either in cyanide, (72, 103,) or boiling oil, (66,) thus giving the steel rim the same temper as a hair spring.

(120.) Figs. 6 and 7 show the balance B, the disc A, the caps C, C, and clamp D. The disc can be made nearly as wide as the rim, and have a slot cut in one side to take in the center-bar, but it is not really necessary. For safety, a narrow strip of writing-paper can be laid on the center-bar, the disc over that, and the clamp screwed down hard to crush the paper and

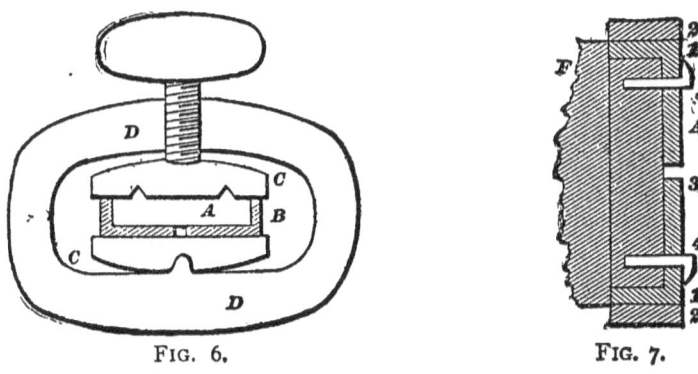

FIG. 6.   FIG. 7.

make perfect contact. Short conical points (screwed in) may project from the surface of the disc and sit into cavities in the caps, to hold the parts in proper position, after the manner of short, stubby steady pins. Or the caps can be turned out so as to sit down a little over the edge of the balance, as shown, for the same purpose. The caps may also have a central cavity for the screw of the clamp, to give central pressure. The clamp is wide, to expose all parts of the rim to equal heating and cooling. Or the caps can be held together in any other convenient way.

(121.) *Finishing the balance.*—Make a lathe chuck, F, to fit inside the rim snugly, with a shoulder sitting over the steel part, 1, of the rim, but leaving the brass, 2, exposed. Pins, 4, rest against the edges of the center-bar, 3, to turn it by, or it is held and fastened on, in any convenient way. The brass may be compressed and hardened by bearing on it with a milling-tool with fine notches, and then turning off the notches, and repeating this till the brass is reduced nearly to its final thickness, then harden and compress with a smooth roller; or it can be turned down nearly to size, and then brought to size with the flat roller, or by cautiously hammering it evenly all round the rim. It is finally centered accurately in a lathe, the rough edges turned off, and the outside turned perfectly true and to size. Then poise, anneal in oil as described for ordinary balances, except that I prefer to leave these balances as hard as is safe, (say, not draw the steel below a straw color,) because hard steel is much less liable to be magnetized than that which is carried to a lower temper. Then cut the rim, as before.

(122.) *Rounding a balance.*—When the rim is cut apart, the segments fly "out of round," and require to be trued up. This is always done by hand, by very gradual and gentle curves, and is a somewhat tedious operation. In trueing a balance, whether new or one that has been bent, use no pliers or other tools to bend it into shape, but spring it very carefully with the fingers. If a rather sharp bend is wanted at any particular point, place the thumb or finger-nails at that point as a support, and spring the segment on each side, against the nail. The novice must use the utmost care, or he will bend it too much, or in some screw-hole, and will be very likely to crack it, when it will be ruined, beyond the power of the cleverest workman to remedy. At first he had better practice only on abandoned balances, till he has acquired a little skill and experience.

This finishes the work of the balance maker. Further instructions for trueing and poising are given in the next chapter.

(123.) *Making non-magnetic balances.*—There are several varieties of non-magnetic balances now in use. For a plain balance, gold, brass, aluminum, bronze, or any metal except iron, steel, or nickel can be employed. For compensating balances, the most promising construction yet tried is that with the Paillard alloys of palladium. In some, the inner lamina is of the palladium alloy and the outer one of brass; in others, the outer lamina is made from a palladium alloy having a rate of expansion for heat different from that of the inner one. Other makers also use palladium alloys. (Alloys of platinum and other metals have also been tried.) The compositions of the various alloys used, and the methods of making and working them, are not made known, but the palladium balances can be bought ready-made, by those who wish to use them.

CHAPTER X.

Selecting and Testing Watch Balances.

(124.) *The balance is the governor.*—The balance is the governor or regulator of the time-keeping mechanism. Upon it depends the possibility of the watch keeping time. If its size and weight are not correctly proportioned to the motive force and the movement generally, no adjustment or combination of the balance spring and other parts can make the watch a good timepiece. The spring is always secondary to the balance, and by many makers the construction of the entire movement is required to conform to the weight and proportions of the standard balance. In other cases, the particular construction adopted for the balance is determined by careful tests of the performances of different balances with a standard type of movement.

(125.) *Effects of improper size and weight.*—If a balance is too heavy, there is more variation in the different positions; especially if the pivots have been made larger on account of its weight; if much too heavy, it will be impossible to time it in positions. A heavy balance, with slow vibrations, is more affected by all resistances and frictions which oppose its motion, jarring, shaking, etc. When the motive force is too great relatively to the balance, the watch will gain in the horizontal and lose in the vertical positions. If the balance is too light it will be too sensitive to variations in the motive force, although, if it is both light and large, there will be little friction on the pivots, and little variation between the horizontal and hanging positions. If heavy and also too small, there is excessive friction at the pivots and variation in positions, but it is less affected by external disturbing influences.

(126.) *Calculating the proper size for balance.*—In calculations of the size of the balance, the diameter is not necessarily the external diameter as measured. Supposing all the weight of the balance to be concentrated in a sphere or ball at each end of a center-bar without any weight, the distance from the center of the balance to the center of the sphere would be the *radius of gyration*, and the distance between the centers of the two spheres would be the *geometrical diameter*, or diameter of gyration of the balance. In a plain balance or one with few and light screws, the center of weight would come about at the center of the rim, or a little inside of that. In compensation balances, with numerous and heavy screws, the radius of gyration is generally taken as the distance from the center of the axis to the outer edge of the rim.

(127.) *The moment of inertia* of a balance is its resistance to a change of velocity, or, commonly speaking, its controlling power,—and is calculated by the formula:

$$A = W \times r^2, \qquad (1)$$

where A is the moment of inertia; W, the weight of the balance; and r is the radius of gyration. This means that the controlling power of the balance increases in proportion to its weight, and also in proportion to the square of its radius of gyration, *i.e.*, of its semi-diameter measured as stated in section (126) above.

(128.) *The period of vibration*, of a balance with a spring attached, is usually calculated by the following formula:

$$T = \pi \sqrt{\frac{A \times L}{M}}, \qquad (2)$$

where T is the period of a single vibration in seconds; A is the moment of inertia of the balance; L is the acting length of the hair spring; M, the moment of elasticity of the spring; and π is equal to 3.14159.

(129.) *Example.*—The actual calculation of the period of vibration by this formula is rather difficult and tedious, but for purposes of mere *comparison* of different balances, the operation can be greatly simplified and shortened. If we wish to compare any two balances, one of which may be correct and the other different from it, we distinguish the symbols referring to them by the figures 1 and 2, written after them and below the line; thus, T_1 would mean the period of the first or standard balance, whose proportions and performance we know, and T_2 would indicate that of the second or trial balance, which we are studying or testing; W_1 and W_2 would be their respective weights, A_1 and A_2 their moments of inertia, and r_1 and r_2 their radii of gyration. In comparing two balances, we have this proportion:

$$T_1 : T_2 :: \pi \sqrt{\frac{A_1 \times L}{M}} : \pi \sqrt{\frac{A_2 \times L}{M}}. \qquad (3)$$

(130.) *Simplifying the formula.*—In this proportion, the symbols L and M refer to the spring, and as they and the symbol π are *not changed* in our consideration or comparison of different balances, and as they are found in *both* the third and fourth numbers of the proportion, we can omit them from the proportion without affecting its truth. Doing so, our proportion becomes:

$$T_1 : T_2 :: \sqrt{A_1} : \sqrt{A_2}, \qquad (4)$$

which means that the periods of vibration of the two balances will be in proportion to the square roots of their moments of inertia. As A equals $W \times r_2$, (127,) we substitute that for A in the proportion, and it then becomes:—

$$T_1 : T_2 :: \sqrt{W_1 \times r_1^2} : \sqrt{W_2 \times r_2^2}. \qquad (5)$$

We have now eliminated everything which does not relate to the balance.

(131.) *Calculating the number of vibrations.*—But it is much easier for most workmen to think of the number of vibrations in a given time, say, one minute, than of the period or duration of a vibration. For instance, in an 18,000 train, the period of the vibration, T, would be $\frac{1}{5}$ second, while the number of vibrations per minute, V, would be 300. It is also plain that as the period T becomes greater, the number V becomes smaller, and in order to make a proportion expressing their ratios, we must reverse the order in which they are written, thus:

$$T_1 : T_2 :: V_2 : V_1; \text{ or } T_2 : T_1 :: V_1 : V_2. \qquad (6)$$

Both expressions are true; and if we take the latter, and substitute the equivalents of T for that symbol in formula (5), we have the proportion:

$$V_1 : V_2 :: \sqrt{W_2 \times r_2^2} : \sqrt{W_1 \times r_1^2}. \qquad (7)$$

In order to get rid of the square roots, we will square all four members of the proportion, which will not affect its truth, and it then becomes:

$$V_1^2 : V_2^2 :: W_2 \times r_2^2 : W_1 \times r_1^2. \qquad (8)$$

(132.) *Calculating the vibrations for balances of different weights.* —If we wish to compare two balances *attached to the same hair spring,* and having *the same* radii of gyration but differing in weight, we can omit the symbol r in the above formula, because it would be *the same* in both the third and the fourth members; and the proportion would then be:

$$V_1^2 : V_2^2 :: W_2 : W_1 \qquad (9)$$

which means that the squares of the numbers of vibrations of the two balances will be inversely proportional to their weights, expressed either in grammes or grains—which is not at all difficult to work out.

(133.) *Calculating the vibrations for balances of different sizes.*—On the other hand, if the balances have the same weight, but different geometrical diameter (126,) *i.e.*, have different radii of gyration, we can drop the symbol W from the third and fourth members of formula (8), and we would then get the proportion:

$$V_1^2 : V_2^2 :: r_2^2 : r_1^2. \qquad (10)$$

It will be observed that all four members of this formula are squared. To save some trouble in calculating, we will take the square roots of all four members, which will not affect the truth of the proportion, and we have:

$$V_1 : V_2 :: r_2 : r_1, \qquad (11)$$

which means that the vibrations of the two balances will be in inverse proportion to their radii of gyration, *i.e.*, the number of vibrations will become less in proportion as the size of the balance becomes greater.

(134.) *Observations.*—Formulas (9) and (11) are good working proportions, by which any one can easily make all necessary calculations. I have taken considerable trouble to explain fully how we have arrived at them, step by step, and their meanings, so that even those who have no mathematical training can understand them and how to use them.

(135.) *Calculating the number of minutes per hour.*—In these calculations, instead of the number of vibrations per minute, we can take the number of minutes passed over by the watch hands in an hour, or 60 minutes. Thus, if one watch or balance went correctly, while the other lost 5 minutes in an hour, the proportion would be 60 : 55. If the second watch or balance gained 5 minutes in an hour, the numerical value of $V_1 : V_2$ would of course be in the ratio of 60 to 65.

(136.) *Method of using the formulas.*—In making calculations by these formulas put the *figures* representing the different letters in place of the letters, so far as known. Calculation will then give you the value of the letter whose value you seek. Instead of the radius (semi-diameter) of gyration, it will be the same thing to take the diameter of gyration, or the geometrical diameter, measured as in section (126). Multiply the first and fourth numbers together, and the second and third together;

the two products will be equal. Then get the unknown symbol on one side of the equation, and all the figures on the other side, and they will give the value of the symbol or letter.

(137.) *Example.*—Suppose a balance weighing six pennyweights runs 10 minutes slow in an hour, what must be the weight of a similar balance to run correctly? Substituting the above values for V and W in formula 9, and squaring the numbers or values of V, we have:

$$2500 : 3600 :: W_2 : 6,$$

i.e., the square of the number of minutes (50) given per hour by the first balance, is to the square of the correct number (60) per hour, as the weight of the second balance (unknown) is to the weight of the first balance (6), which, after multiplying, gives us the equation

$$3600 \times W_2 = 15,000, \text{ or } W_2 = 4.166,$$

or $4\frac{1}{6}$ pennyweights. By using the number of grains the first balance weighs, you will get the weight of the second balance in grains.

(138.) Suppose a balance of a certain weight having a diameter (of gyration) of .648 inch, gives 380 vibrations per minute, what must be the geometrical diameter of a similar balance, of the same weight, to give 300 vibrations per minute? According to formula (11),

$$380 : 300 :: r_2 : .648,$$

which on multiplying gives $300 \times r_2 = 246.240$, or $r_2 = .821$ inch—a trifle over $\frac{82}{100}$ inch in diameter.

These examples will show how to ascertain the value of any member of the proportion, when the values of the other three members are known. Care must be taken to observe the proper *order* of the symbols, as shown by the figure under each one in the formulas.

(139.) *Empirical rules for size of balance.*—The foregoing calculations arrive at the proper size and weight for the balance by a process of *comparison* with some other balance which has been tested, so that both its performance and its weight and dimensions are known. That is the ultimate recourse of the manufacturer. He tries to learn the best proportions from all previous experience—both of his own and of others. Having found the proportions which give the best performance, he adopts that balance as his standard of comparison. But in ordinary practice, much shorter methods are followed. One rule is that the diameter of the balance should be the same as that of the cover of the mainspring barrel. Others say, for a ¾ plate watch, it should equal the inside diameter of the barrel. Another rule is, that it should be half the diameter of the upper or potance plate of the watch. Others say that it should be from 2 to 2½ times the diameter of the escape wheel, or be 5 times the width of the mainspring. But these methods evidently can only secure a more or less close approximation to correctness, leaving the further corrections to be made either by calculation, as already described, or by the tests of performance given in sections (141, 142).

(140.) *Following good models.*—But it should be remembered that the best performance is obtained only when there is a certain proportion between the size and weight of the balance and the number of vibrations it makes. That is to say, a balance which would perform well at 18,000 vibrations per hour might be very unreliable at 16,200 or 20,000 vibrations, even if the motive force and the hair spring were modified correspondingly. There is no better guide, therefore, than a similar movement which is known to perform well. And copying it is not mere slavish imitation, but a wise profiting by experience.

(141.) *Testing the balance for weight and size.*—After the balance is in the watch, it can be tested as follows:—Block the train with a bristle, so that the balance is perfectly free from the motive force or other influence, and stands in its central position or at the point of rest. Now mark on the plate, with a speck of rouge or whiting in oil, the position of the banking pin, or of the cut in the rim, or of some prominent screw or other mark, by which you can easily and surely note the extent of the balance vibrations. Then start the watch, and when the balance has acquired its normal or regular arc, mark the point attained by the banking pin, etc. This mark indicates the full arc of vibration. Now gently stop the balance and bring the pin to its central position, then let it start to running, and count the number of vibrations it requires for reaching its full arc. Watch the banking pin with the eye-glass, and repeat the test if necessary.

(142.) *Indications of this test.*—If the balance is too light, it will acquire its full arc almost immediately; if too heavy, it may require 15 or 18 vibrations to do so. These indications refer to the proper or improper *weight* of the balance. To test the *size*, after the balance has acquired its full arc, gently increase the strength of the motive force, (by pressing against the arm of the center wheel, or in some similar way,) and if the balance is very sensitive to the change, it is generally too small; if the vibrations are hardly any affected by the pressure, it is too large. This test (of size) evidently applies mainly to the lever and chronometer, since the frictional escapements are self-compensating for changes in the motive force. By making such tests for both size and weight on all perfect watches that pass through his hands, he will have a standard of behavior for each kind of watch, which will enable him to quickly detect any which vary from the correct proportions.

In box chronometers, there is not the same objection to heavy balances as there is in watches, because the former are always kept in one position. A heavier balance with slow vibrations can therefore be used, and its greater momentum secures a steadier rate than a lighter balance would give.

(143.) *Selecting compensation balances.*—The foregoing remarks apply to any kind of balance, having reference merely to the size and weight. In selecting a compensating balance, it must also be of such construction as to respond to variations in the temperature promptly, *i.e.*, at least as quickly as the hair spring, (259,) and to act *sufficiently* to compensate for those variations. A thin rim is more sensitive to changes of temperature than a thicker one, but it must be thick enough to hold its shape while vibrating and not allow the screws to fly outwards by centrifugal force. As to the sufficiency of the compensation, that can only be told by actual trial in different temperatures.

(144.) *Expansion balances.*—All balances having a rim composed of two metals, made and cut as before described, are technically called expansion balances. They may be well made and capable of compensating if adjusted, in which case they can properly be termed compensation or chronometer balances —the former being the correct title. Or they may be merely imitations of compensation balances, incapable of compensating. This generally can be told only by trial—unless there is some glaring mechanical imperfection which shows that they cannot compensate.

(145.) *Distinguishing "adjusted" balances.*—No one can tell by mere inspection when a balance is adjusted, for there is absolutely no difference in appearance between one adjusted and one not adjusted. One may be as near perfect as the highest skill and many efforts can get it, while the other may be "wild," but no one can distinguish them by their looks—only by trial in the watch. So of the balances sold by material dealers,—they may be from an excellent maker, made with every care, and all apparently equally good in every respect. Yet a trial will show that no two will act just alike. While some will be good, others may be worthless for accurate performance. The only way to ascertain is to test their running in heat and cold. It may be said, however, that the thinner and higher the rim the stronger the compensating action will be. These remarks of course refer only to balances completed and cut as already described.

(146.) *Imitation expansion balances.*—Very many watches are provided with balances having rims of steel and brass, with screws inserted, the same as before stated, except that the rims are not cut, or are cut only partly through, which amounts to the same thing. These may be in fact expansion or compensation balances, but the *laminæ* or compensating segments cannot compensate, because they are not allowed to act. Any balance the rim of which is not cut entirely through, is certainly not "adjusted," although it may be called a compensation balance. It is no better than the common balances of one metal, with screws in their rims, which are only imitations of chronometer balances. Such balances, however, are better than plain ones, in that they may be timed by these screws, either turning them in or out, or putting in lighter or heavier screws, to suit the strength of the hair spring. They are also safer from injury while being handled by bungling workmen, and add something to the appearance of the movement, which is all that many people judge by. They are good enough for customers who do not comprehend the value of a real compensation balance, and are unwilling to pay the additional price,—and consequently they cannot expect anything better than an imitation balance.

CHAPTER XI.

Correcting and Finishing Balances.

(147.) *General correction of balances.*—There are various manipulations and corrections needed by balances, which are not connected with the adjustment for temperatures, and all such faults will be treated in this chapter, whether they relate to the balance before it is fitted in the watch, or before or after the compensation adjustment.

(148.) *Eccentric balance.*—The defect which is easiest to detect, even before the balance is fitted in the watch, is eccentricity, in which case the hole is not exactly central with the rim at the ends of the center-bar. The hole could of course be changed and made central, if that was all. But the existence of such a fault shows that the maker has not observed the most important principles of balance making, and in all probability the entire balance is made with equal disregard of proper methods, and the safest plan is to reject it. To test a loose balance, mount it on a perfectly true arbor, and try it in the calipers, or even in the turns, with sufficient pressure on the points of the arbor to hold it in any position it may be placed in. Then set the slip-piece of the calipers (or the lathe rest) to barely escape touching the outer edge of the rim with its sharp corner. With a strong magnifying glass, see if the rim is concentric with the hole while the balance is turned around. If so, the outside of the rim, at each end of the center-bar, will be equally distant from the center, or will touch the slip-piece or the rest, alike. If not, perfect action cannot be expected, for it is evident that the two segments have different centers of motion from which to act in either direction under change of temperature. Then test the inner edge of the rim in the same way.

(149.) *Testing a balance on the staff.*—If it is already on the staff, test it as before described, and if found to be eccentric at the ends of the center bar, drive it off the staff and test again. If the error is in the balance reject it; but if the balance is concentric in itself, and the fault is in the staff, the quickest and best remedy is, probably, to turn the staff down a little smaller, so that the balance will go on somewhat loosely, then, by riveting it a little harder on one side than the other, throw the balance a little further out on that side, and make the rim concentric. If the balance hole was already too large for the staff, and that was the cause of the eccentricity, re-staking properly will bring it concentric with the pivots. Or if the arbor of the staff was not concentric with the pivots, it should be made so in the lathe, and the balance then riveted concentrically upon it. Never attempt to bend the arms of the center-bar, except to straighten or level them after some botch has bent them out of shape; such a balance is of little value for accurate performance.

(150.) *Trueing up the balance.*—If the balance is concentric at the ends of the center-bar, but not at other places on the rim, it must be trued up at mean temperature. Avoid touching the balance with the fingers or otherwise warming it, while testing it, but turn it slowly with a stick of pegwood, and note where the rim begins to go in or out from the true circle indicated by the sharp corner of the slip-piece or rest. Have ready a little whiting and oil, mixed, and mark the rim with a speck of this, on the outside where it begins to go out, on the inside where it begins to go inward. So go around the whole rim, marking every such place, and you will have a clear idea of the condition of the balance. In trueing, take one segment at a time, begin at the center-bar and work from there to the end of the segment, testing it after every alteration before making another, till it is true to the end. Then true the other segment in the same way. All this should be done at the middle temperature for which the balance is to be adjusted. If the extremes are to be 30° and 120°, the mean will be 75°, at which temperature the balance should be caused to be round or concentric. If the extremes are 55° and 95°, the mean will be 65°. The temperature of the adjustment-room should be kept nearly at that degree, and if the heat of the sun, stove, lamp, fingers or breath, should warm the balance above that, it should be cooled in a dish of alcohol before testing the roundness in the calipers, as the balance will not be round when it is either warmer or colder than that temperature. Should there be jewels on the staff which are fastened in with shellac, the alcohol would loosen them, and benzine or ether should be used instead.

(151.) *Tempering or setting the balance.*—After rounding the balance, it is then heated on a metal plate to about 212° Fahr., and, when cooled to the above temperature, if not round, it is rounded again as before. This heating and rounding are repeated if necessary. The object is to temper the balance, and free it from the tension or strain which the bending process produces in the metals. Otherwise, it would be very likely to change its form gradually, while running, and derange the rate. If the balance is new, and has been hammered too much in making, or not heated enough afterwards, the rim will probably curve inwards and "set" in that shape, causing a gain in time. Or, if not hammered enough, or heated too much, it will spring outward and lose time. In warm weather, merely handling the balance with the bare fingers is liable to cause the segments to "set" differently. They should therefore be handled as little as possible. See that the rim is true in "the flat," as well as in "the round," which should always be tried with the balance in the vertical position, or edge upwards, so that the segments may assume their natural position as regards flatness.

(152.) *Poising the balance.*—Then poise it accurately, (292,) with the screws turned clear in, but not tight. If they were screwed in tightly, the pressure of their heads against the rim would affect its curvature while the brass part of it was expanded under the influence of heat, and might even cause a change of shape in the rim, which, from the method of its production, is comparatively soft. The above directions apply only to new balances. We often find balances in use having their screws all considerably turned out to make the rate slower. In that case we must let them remain so, if the rate is correct and the opposite screws are at equal distances from the center, as turning them in might necessitate the fitting of a new hair spring. But if we have orders to make everything *perfect*, and as it should be, we ought to turn the screws home, as directed above, then fit a hair spring which will give correct time,—provided the balance is of the right size and weight for the movement. If not, it should be entirely discarded, and a new one put in. Also now test the balance for magnetism, (30, 34, 37,) if it has not been done before.

(153.) *Irregular action.*—Whenever a balance shows any irregularity in time, it should be tested as to its *poise in extreme temperatures*, say 35° and 120° Fahrenheit. And it is well to test the balances of all fine movements before beginning the compensation—also all new balances. Sometimes the brass and steel are not firmly united, and will separate more or less under change of temperature. This defect may not be so great as to be discoverable by prying the metals apart, and yet cause the two segments to operate very irregularly and differently. Sometimes the rim is very slightly "out of round," or not truly circular, when the segments will spring in or out differently, from their different shape or curvature. Sometimes one segment has been bent accidentally and trued up again, or for some other reason one segment has been bent back and forth more than the other, and as this bending impairs the elasticity and changes the condition of the metals, its action will be different from that of the other segment. It is of the highest importance to handle a compensation balance with the utmost care, to avoid the slightest springing or straining of the segments. Flaws or defects in the metal or workmanship of the balance will also cause a difference of action in the segments. If one side has been bruised or dented in the hammering process, that side will show the effects ever after. Care should also be taken not to expose a balance to a heat much exceeding 130° to 140° in waxing it on the lathe, or for any other purpose, and not for any length of time to that temperature, as it is liable to cause the segments to "set" more or less differently from their former shape.

(154.) *Poising in extremes* may be done by placing the balance on a hot or cold metal plate, to bring it to the desired temperature, and then laying it on the straight-edge poising tool. If it changes its position, and comes to rest each time with a certain side up, the segment found down in cold, or up in heat, has acted more strongly than the other, and both should be closely examined. If its position has remained unchanged it may be inferred that the error is very small, if any exists. But if one side is repeatedly found down, either in heat or cold, the fault must be traced out and corrected before going further.

(155.) *Faults in compensation or expansion balances.*—Among the faults which concern the expansion balance, the following may be mentioned:

1. Centrifugal force may throw the two segments out unequally while vibrating, and throw it out of poise.

2. Ditto; this may be different in the long and short arcs, and produce effects wrongly attributed to lack of isochronism in the spring.

3. The balance segments may be too thin, or the screws too heavy for it, and whenever the vibrations become unusually large by jarring, etc., the screws may hit something near them and ruin the regularity of the timing. A good way to detect the above faults is to arrange a circular arc of metal close to the exterior of the balance, but giving all the clearance that it should have. Then if it hit this arc when set going, its motion would be visibly affected, and perhaps audibly. Or a little whiting and oil could be put on the nearest point, and if the screws come out too far they will receive a white mark.

4. The pivots may not be round, or the balance not riveted concentrically on the staff, (or pivot bent,) causing it to be out of poise, and affecting the rate in heat and cold, also the time in different positions, and the isochronism.

5. The two segments may not expand and contract alike in heat and cold, carrying the screws to unequal distances from the center, producing errors in the poise, compensation and isochronism.

6. The segments (or one of them) may have been bent out of the true circular form.

7. A segment may have been bent, and restored to shape, causing a weakening of the rim at that point, with irregular action.

8. Other similar faults might be mentioned. All of them will produce different effects when the watch is held in different positions—according to whether the heavier side is then at the top, bottom, or one side of the balance center.

(156.) *Faults of uncut or plain balances.*—I will only mention the following: 1. When a bi-metallic rim it not cut through, the expansion of the brass of the outside, in heat, causes the rim between the arms or ends of the center-bar to bulge outward into an oval form; in cold, the rim is forced inward; the different parts may also act or yield unequally, and the balance be put out of poise, or spring the arms as well as the rim out of shape. All such balances should have two cuts entirely through the brass, between the arms, *i.e.*, in a three-armed balance, there would be six cuts. But it is much better to use balances of one metal, carrying screws to give the desired weight.

2. Test for magnetism. See Chapter III.

PART FOURTH.

SPRINGING AND TIMING.

CHAPTER XII.

Conveniences for Timing. The Regulator or Standard Clock.

(157.) *The regulator* may be of any variety, provided its rate is constant. The mercurial and the gridiron pendulums are both good, and even wood pendulum rods have done excellent service. All depends on the maker. A good maker can make either kind of clock do first-class service. Of course, each recommends his kind as the best, but the only safe way to buy is to have a guarantee stating *what it will do.* Get as good a one as you can afford, but always insist that its rate shall be regular, and shall be known. If its rate is not known, it has never been regulated, and you will have to take your chances with it.

(158.) *For timing purposes* a regulator beating seconds is the most convenient; but one beating half-seconds is nearly as good, provided it is accurate. But a clock which beats anything except seconds or half-seconds is worthless for timing. It should be compared with some correct time at least as often as every week or ten days, no matter how good its quality or how closely it has been rated. Something may happen at any time to cause an error in running, and perhaps a large error. If you are not watching the clock, you would not know it, but it would be disarranging all your watches to suit the clock. Besides the trouble you would make in extra work, there would be the loss of reputation and the dissatisfaction of customers,—and if your rival across the street should notice it, you would never hear the last of it. *Watch your clock.*

(159.) *Getting correct time.*—Your best way is to get it by telegraph. In most parts of the country, the time is telegraphed from some observatory, or from the headquarters of the telegraph company, at a certain hour, for watchmakers and others on the line. You can ascertain this by inquiring at your telegraph office. If not, the railroad company may send correct time over the road for its own offices and employees—and very likely they would like to have your assistance in taking it off the wire and setting their clocks and watches. In writing down the time, one dash after the figures means minutes, two dashes mean seconds.

The signals are sent over the wire in the following manner. At 11–56′–45″ A.M., *i.e.*, 3′–15″ before noon, all commercial business over the line is stopped, and the time-transmitting apparatus at Washington is switched into the line circuit. The transmitting clock has just been compared with the standard clock of the Naval Observatory and set exactly with it. On the seconds-hand pinion arbor of the transmitting clock is a special wheel of 60 teeth, each tooth of which sends a signal over the line indicating the seconds—each signal being heard at the telegraph offices as a click of the telegraph instruments. The 29th tooth of this wheel is omitted, also, the 55th to 59th, both inclusive. Consequently, no signals are sent for the seconds bearing those numbers, but the telegraph instrument gives a click for all the other seconds, during each minute, until noon.

When the first click is heard, therefore, you know that the correct time is 11–56′–45″ A.M., *i.e.*, 56 minutes and 45 seconds past 11 o'clock. The clicks then continue each second till the 55th, which is omitted; the instrument is then still during the remainder of the minute. At exactly 11–57′–0″ the clicks begin again, continuing each second till the 29th, which is omitted. At 11–57′–30″ they begin again, continuing till the 55th second —and so on, as above described. You thus get signals indicating the minute and half-minute, after a warning silence each time, 7 times, or 4 minutes in succession. This gives you the opportunity to compare your watch 7 times, or to set it and compare again, if you wish. Although it does not affect the result in any way, I would observe that the signals are sent a little differently from the others, in the *last* minute, as the clicks stop at the 50th second, instead of the 55th as in the other minutes. This is to give time for switching in the apparatus for dropping the time-balls, which is done by the signal sent at exactly 12 o'clock, noon. The foregoing is the United States government system for sending out Naval Observatory time, and it is also followed by most of the other Observatories throughout the country. The government sends such signals daily, but in some localities they are only sent on a certain day or days of the week. The signals sent by the government give mean time for the 75th meridian, or meridian of Washington, D. C. In other parts of the country different meridians may be meant. If so, you will find which it is by inquiry at the telegraph office.

(160.) *Taking time off the wire, by a watch.*—Take with you a watch whose seconds dial is evenly divided off, and preferably with a large circle and a long hand. It should have been *accurately set by the regulator* before starting. Seat yourself where you can hear the ticking of the telegraph instrument clearly, and also have a good light on the dial. Arrange a card, slip of paper, or even a finger-nail, on the glass so that you can keep the edge of it close to the point of the hand, *i.e.*, if the hand is after the 60, you draw the card *back* so as to keep the hand just visible until the "time tick," then hold the card still and count the number of seconds to the 60. If the hand is before the 60, you follow it up with the edge of the card till the time tick, then hold it still and count up the seconds as before. Then observe how many minutes (if any) the minute-hand is ahead or behind 12 o'clock—or the hour of sending the time. Make a memorandum of the variation, to avoid any possibility of error or forgetting. Thus, if the time on your watch was 12h, 0′, 13″, you were 13 seconds fast; but if the time was 11h, 59′, 13″, you were 47 seconds slow. In the same way, compare your watch with the other signals, *before* noon. For the method of getting time to fractions of seconds, see sections (206 to 208). By this method you count the beats or jumps of the seconds hand.

(161.) *Another way*, by chronograph, is by means of an independent center-seconds watch. A chronograph, or a split-seconds watch, which is a double chronograph, is preferable, as it admits of observing the fractions of seconds. Two observations are taken, one at the time tick, the other when your watch reaches the hour of signaling. If your watch is slow, you press the push once, at the time tick, to start the chronograph hand from the 60. You press it again when the seconds-hand of your watch reaches its 60 at exactly 12 o'clock, to stop the chronograph hand. The number of seconds it stands after the 60 shows how many seconds you are slow. If your watch is fast, you start the hand at exactly 12 o'clock by the watch, and stop it at the time tick. When you use a split-seconds, you start it shortly before the first push, and stop one hand at 12 o'clock on your watch, and the other at the time tick as before, and compare the two hands. Supposing the watch to have been set by the regulator when starting, you can see when you get back whether it is still exactly with it, which gives you a check upon the correctness of your observation, that you would not have if your watch had not been set beforehand—for you now know that your chronograph is all right, and can safely make the proper change in your regulator. See (159).

(162.) *Getting correct time by observations* of the stars, or of the sun, may be done when telegraphic time is not available. It would take too much space to explain the use of the transits, quadrants, sextants, dipleidoscopes or other instruments employed, the different kinds of time, and the necessary calculations and corrections to be made, and the reader is referred to special treatises on that subject. The most popular and practical work in this line is that of Latimer Clark, which can be obtained from the publishers of scientific books, or of any of the trade journals.

(163.) *Changing the regulator.*—If the error is small, make a note of it on the record, (for you should keep a rate sheet for the clock, as well as for watches,) and wait. If the error is the same, or about the same, the next time—or, at least, is in the same direction, you can safely make the proper correction. But when you have got it as close as you can, it is better not to change it for any slight error, but note the rate and let it go. Possibly something will affect it a hair the other way next time, and remove the error last noted. Even if it does not, it is better to have a slight error, and *know what it is*, than to be always changing the clock and not know whether it is going fast or slow. If you know the error you can keep a card with the amount marked on it for every day, and consult that when making the final adjustments of your watches, or comparing customers' fine watches.

(164.) *Setting the regulator.*—Never set the seconds-hand back, nor do anything to the other hands, or to the wheels, which would cause the escape wheel to turn backwards, as it would smear the oil from the backs of the escape-wheel teeth over the pallets, and probably change the rate of the clock. If the regulator is too fast, stop the pendulum, and start it again at the proper time, or you can put a weight on the pendulum to make it lose rapidly till the error is corrected, then remove the weight. If the clock is slow, the hands can be moved forward; they should not turn too hard, or there is risk of changing or injuring the escapement.

When the clock is but a few seconds, or a fraction of a second slow, (or fast,) it can be set to time by the pendulum. The method followed at the United States Naval Observatory, and many others, is to cause it to vibrate a little more rapidly or slowly, as required. If it is only a small fraction of a second out of the way, merely touching it gently with the finger will be sufficient, either retarding its forward motion, or accelerating it. In the latter case, care must be taken not to make it swing too far. If the clock is much too slow, take hold of each side and vibrate the pendulum more rapidly than usual, till the loss is corrected—moving it far enough to escape and "tick," but no further, else the oil may be displaced and the rate changed.

(165.) *The dial.*—The construction and perfection of the movement and the pendulum are points settled when you purchased the clock. But there are other points, which concern the timing, and are still under your control, and we will note a few which should be looked after. The dial must of course be evenly divided off—especially the circle of the seconds-hand. It must be so fastened to the movement that the arbors or pivots carrying the hands will stand exactly in the center of the dial holes, and *the holes must be exactly in the centre of the circles.* Test these points, for they are important in a fine clock—and these directions refer to fine clocks. If the seconds-hand pivot, for instance, is above the center of its

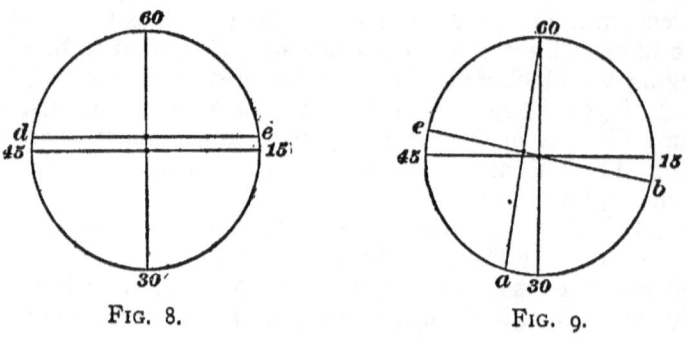

Fig. 8.   Fig. 9.

circle, shown in Fig. 8, at *de*, the hand will be too slow at 15 seconds and too fast at the 45 mark. In the same way, if the pivot stands to the left of the center, as in Fig. 9, so that the point of the hand is moved one second to the right of *the vertical* to make it point to the 60 at the end of the minute, (shown by the line from *a* to 60,) it would point to 30 two seconds too soon, *i.e.*, it would gain 2 seconds in a half minute, and lose 2 seconds in the next half minute, and keep on see-sawing that way all the time—a rather poor reliance for timing.

(166.) *The hands.*—See that the hands, and especially the seconds-hand, do not run too close to the dial, although the point of the last should be as close as is safe; that they do not touch nor run too close in the dial holes; that the minute-hand comes exactly on a minute mark when the seconds-hand is at 60; that when the hour, minute and seconds-hand come over each other, at the XII or elsewhere, they cannot touch each other by any variation of their end-shakes; that neither of them can bind or get tight anywhere, but have sufficient freedom in every position; that the minute-hand, center arbor or seconds-hand cannot touch the glass over the dial. Test this at their highest point of end-shake, and all around the circle. Any bent or unequal teeth in the escape wheel can be detected by the seconds-hand, if it stands in the centre of its circle and that is evenly divided.

(167.) *The pendulum.*—See that the weight cannot come near the pendulum in any position, nor the pendulum too close to the glass in front, or anything behind or near it. Try this very carefully, if the pendulum is ever seen to "wobble" in the least degree while vibrating. Wobbling would indicate either that the escapement is not in good condition, (generally a sliding contact on the pendulum, from front to back,) or the suspension spring has been twisted or bent, and been kinked, or is still so. If you *cannot* correct the cause, be sure that the wobbling pendulum cannot possibly touch anything; if it does, no reliance can be placed on its rate. If the wall or support is subjected to any jarring, it will cause more or less wobbling.

(168.) *Winding.*—Before beginning to wind, press the key gently *backward*, to see that the maintaining click and spring are in action, as the clock might get from 10 to 30 seconds behind while winding, if the maintaining work did not operate, (164), and even stop running. If correct, the spring will be felt to yield a little under the pressure spoken of, and while you are winding the seconds-hand will continue moving *forward*. But if the seconds-hand stops or ticks backwards when you begin to wind, it must be seen to at once.

(169.) *Position.*—The regulator must be protected from the trembling, shaking and jars, especially those recurring at regular intervals, as their period might coincide with that of the pendulum vibrations, and greatly affect their extent and consequently the rate. It should have as solid and firm support as can be obtained in the store. It should also be protected from change of temperature as much as possible—particularly from sudden changes, which may affect the rate before the compensation acts. Artificially heated rooms are generally much warmer near the ceiling than near the floor, especially with low ceilings, and the upper part of the rod and the suspension spring are more affected than the bob, making the compensation irregular. The coolest place in the store would seem to be best in this case—where there would be the least accumulation of warm air near the ceiling—or else a position where the bob would be exposed to radiation from warm surfaces in proportion to the warmth of the room at the top.

Other Means for Keeping Standard Time.

(170.) *Box Chronometers* are very frequently used by watchmakers for keeping standard time where they have not a first-rate regulator. These can be rated by the makers as closely as desired, and are better than ordinary regulators, being more uniform and less affected by external disturbing influences. In almost every city there are chronometer makers or adjusters who will either sell or hire out instruments to watchmakers for timekeeping purposes.

(171.) *Secondary Clock.*—It is frequently inconvenient to stand before the regulator when comparing time, and especially so for the springer and adjuster, or even for winding and regulating custom watches. In order to compare closely, it is necessary not only to be directly in front, but the eye should be nearly on a level with the clock dial to prevent mistakes when the minute-hand gets near the III or the IX, or the seconds-hand near 15 or 45. It is altogether better, therefore, to have a clock specially for timing purposes, arranged where it will be convenient for ordinary work. A good half-seconds regulator is preferable, with perfectly spaced dial circles, and hung low on the wall, so that the workman can take his observations while sitting at the bench or at the watch rack. This can be regulated and set daily, or as often as necessary, to get the time and even the vibrations synchronous with the regulator or standard. It ought to remain synchronous at least one day, or half a day. As before stated, it is imperative that the standard shall always be placed in the most favorable position for securing accuracy in its rate, and where it can have a firm support and be undisturbed. The regulator is for time, and the secondary is for timing, *i.e.*, for everyday regular use, the same as the bench tools, and it should be located suitably for such use. In large shops, two or more secondaries could be used, or electrical secondary clocks employed.

(172.) *Mirror arrangements or time reflectors.*—Another great convenience, either with or without the secondary clock, is an arrangement of mirrors to bring an image of the clock dial directly on the bench, in front of the workman. It is often the case that when he is closely observing or manipulating a watch on the work bench, the clock is at one side or behind him, so that he cannot see both at the same time, to compare them. This is obviated by using mirrors. As one mirror always *reverses* the image, and the clock hand would seem to be moving the wrong way, and to be ahead of the 60 when it was really behind, and *vice versa*, it is better to use two, and get a correct image, as that makes it unnecessary to acquire any new habit or to remember about the image being reversed, and so prevents mistakes.

(173.) *Proper position.*—Supposing the clock to be on your right, the first mirror should be at your left, as nearly in front of, and level with, the clock dial as possible, in order to get a correct and undistorted image of the dial, the same as with the eye (171), but it can be inclined at any angle necessary for reflecting the image where it is required. The second mirror should be in front of you, at such level and position as will be most convenient for looking in it while working. Having found the best place for it by trial, make it a rule to always use it in that precise place, and then incline the first mirror so that it reflects the clock dial perfectly in the second, and incline the latter to reflect the image squarely to the eye. Both mirrors should be large enough to give a good view of the dial, and should be provided with brackets or standards to hold them securely in their proper positions.

(174.) If the first mirror is to be used by two workmen, or by one at two places, its support should be provided with shoulders, notches or pins, so that it can be swung directly into either position and fastened there without any adjustment whatever. The second can be arranged similarly to hang up, or be supported on a sort of easel, and the places for its legs should be plainly marked on the bench, so that it can be at once placed in position. When not in use, the easel and mirror, rigidly fastened together, can be hung up out of the way. When mirrors are used, the clock can be hung higher on the wall than would be convenient for use without them. If the secondary clock has a pendulum marker (175), a single mirror will do to reflect the image to the eye.

(175.) *Vibration marker.*—A good way to mark the exact instant when the pendulum vibration begins or ends, is to arrange a thin diaphragm or screen, say of tissue paper, in front of the pendulum bob, so as to obscure it somewhat except at the very end of each vibration, when its edge comes into full view. The bob is plainly visible all the time, but at the *end* of each vibration it suddenly becomes brighter, and thus marks the exact instant. If a half-seconds pendulum is used, the bob may be so exposed only at *one end* of the vibrations, and thus be equivalent to a seconds-pendulum for timing purposes,—for each brightening would correspond to the end of the vibration in a seconds pendulum. If the bob is not polished or bright enough for clearness, paint it over with varnish or size and bright bronze powder, either yellow or white, at the point of the bob which is to be visible. Even a bit of white paper can be glued on. The proper point is that which has the widest oscillation. The screen may be either inside or outside of the clock case. This method of observing the vibrations is even more convenient than by looking at a seconds-pendulum, and safer than listening to the tick, as that may be faint or drowned out by other noises.

CHAPTER XIII.

Means for Registering and Comparing Times.

(176.) *Apparatus for recording observations.*—In the astronomical observatories, an electric recording chronograph is used, by which the exact instant at which any occurrence (as the passage of a star before the wires in the eye-piece) takes place can be determined within a hundredth part of a second, or even less. This consists of a large cylinder which revolves upon its axis in exactly one minute, its speed being kept perfectly uniform by a governor. A sheet of paper is wrapped around the cylinder, and two or more pens rest upon it, being arranged to be slowly moved by a screw from one end of the cylinder to the other, thus causing each pen to make a spiral line upon the paper. (When the paper is removed from the cylinder, the lines are straight.) The pen can be drawn sideways by a magnet, which can be actuated either by a clock or by an observer touching a key and sending a current through the magnet. Whenever this is done, either by the clock or the observer, the pen is drawn sideways, producing a notch in the line. One line and pen are governed by the clock, another by the observer, and so on. Half a dozen pens may be drawing parallel lines on a paper at the same time, like the lines on a sheet of music. The one controlled by the clock makes a notch at the end of each second; those controlled by the observers make their notches at the instants when a star crossed the line or some other event occurred, and was recorded by making the notch. The time of that event is found by comparing its notch with the time-notch made by the clock. If it is just even with the fifth seconds notch of the minute, it occurred at that second; if it is one-half (or one-twentieth) the distance between that seconds-notch and the next one, it occurred $\frac{1}{2}$ or $\frac{1}{20}$ second later—and so on. These lines are a permanent record, and the notches can be compared and measured at any time, and with any desired closeness. The clock does not close the circuit for making these notches by contacts on its pendulum, but by means of a special wheel on its seconds-hand arbor. The wheel has 60 pointed teeth, one for each second. Each tooth presses a lever sideways to complete the electric circuit, send a current, and make a notch. The foregoing gives a general idea of how the times are recorded and compared.

I had intended to fully describe the apparatus, and then suggest some less expensive modifications of it, suitable for use in comparing watches with the regulator, to ascertain precisely what difference there was between them. As the matter would only be useful to a very limited number of watchmakers, however, I have concluded to omit it. But if any apparatus of the kind, adapted for more general use, should hereafter be devised, it will be described in this chapter, in some future edition.

(177.) *Pocket chronographs.*—Meanwhile, the watchmaker can avail himself of apparatus already in the market, and make his observations and comparisons within $\frac{1}{4}$ or $\frac{1}{5}$ second, which is close enough for most purposes. By using a split-seconds watch, one hand can be stopped when the regulator reaches its 60, and the other when the seconds-hand of the watch being tested reaches its 60 and its minute hand shows the same minute as the regulator. (161.)

(178.) For observation of differences exceeding one minute, a minute chronograph can be used, if desired, but it is hardly necessary, for it is easy to note down the minutes by comparing the minute-hands of the watch being tried and the regulator, after finding the number of seconds they differ.

(179.) *Plain chronograph.*—With a plain chronograph, it is only necessary to start it when the regulator reaches its 60, and stop it when the trial watch reaches its 60, then ascertain the number of seconds between the chronograph 60 and the point of stoppage. If the trial watch is faster than the regulator, the starting must of course be done when its seconds-hand reaches its 60, and the stopping when the regulator reaches its 60. The difference or error should always be counted on the dial of the chronograph, as that of the trial watch may not be evenly divided off.

(180.) *Personal error of the observer.*—It will be found that the hand of the chronograph will not indicate the exact instant of the occurrence, but will be a little behind, due to the observer not pushing the stud quite quickly enough, so that by the time the hand gets started it may be a quarter or half second behind. For instance, when the regulator hand strikes its 60, the intelligence of that fact is transmitted from the eye to the brain, there comprehended, an order sent to the finger to push the stud, the finger muscles contract and do as ordered, and even after the stud is entirely in, a little time is required for the chronograph wheels and hand to get in motion. The same error occurs with the professionals in the observatories, no matter how experienced they are. Some will be quicker than others, but each one will have his own peculiar loss, whatever it may be. This is called the "personal error," and the error of each observer being measured and known, proper allowance is made when recording the observations taken by him.

(181.) *How to be correct.*—In our cases, that error is of no consequence, because if we are $\frac{1}{2}$ second slow at the beginning we are also $\frac{1}{2}$ second slow at the end, and *the difference* between the two points is the same as if we had been exactly on the mark both times. Do not try to be quick, and exactly with the clock, for if you do you will not be *alike* but be quicker at some times than at others, and your observations will be uncertain and unreliable. Keep cool, be natural, take your regular gait, and the error will probably be *the same* every time, which is the most important point. Test yourself by the regulator, till you get your error alike every time. In setting watches to time, the same delay occurs. You should therefore start the watch a little too soon, and then touch the balance an instant to delay it a fraction of a second and so get the watch just right.

CHAPTER XIV.

Calculating the Proper Number of Vibrations.

(182.) *To find the number of vibrations per hour* which a watch should give. As the wheel which carries the minute hand (generally the centre wheel) revolves once an hour, we take that as our starting point in all calculations. Count the number of teeth in the centre, third, fourth, and escape wheels, multiply these numbers together, and double the product, because there are two vibrations to each tooth of the escape wheel. Count the number of leaves in the third, fourth, and escape-wheel pinions, and multiply these numbers together. Then divide the product of the teeth by the product of the leaves, and the quotient obtained will be the number of vibrations per hour. Thus, if the centre wheel has 75 teeth, the third wheel 64 teeth and its pinion has 10 leaves, the fourth wheel has 60 teeth and its pinion 8 leaves, and the escape wheel has 15 teeth and its pinion 6 leaves, it can be written out as follows:—

$$\frac{75 \times 64 \times 60 \times 15 \times 2}{10 \times 8 \times 6} = 18,000 \text{ beats per hour.}$$

By cancellation, as above, much multiplying can be saved, and the operation made easy, short and quick.

(183.) *To find the number of vibrations per minute*, the surest way is to calculate the number of vibrations per hour, as above, then divide that number by 60 (minutes in an hour), as: 18,000÷60=300 vibrations per minute. The whole can be done at one operation, by adding 60 as a divisor to the formula in section (182), thus:

$$\frac{75 \times 64 \times 60 \times 15 \times 2}{10 \times 8 \times 6 \times 60} = 300.$$

(184.) *Another way.*—Many workmen start with the fourth wheel, which revolves once per minute, count the teeth of the fourth and escape wheels, multiply those numbers together and the product by 2, then divide that by the number of leaves in the escape-wheel pinion, thus:

$$\frac{60 \times 15 \times 2}{6} = 300 \text{ vibrations per minute.}$$

In doing so, they assume that the fourth wheel revolves once in 60 seconds. But that is not always the case, even when there is a seconds-hand, and therefore this method is not entirely reliable, but the preceding one is.

(185.) *To find the number of revolutions of the fourth wheel per hour.*—The first point to determine is whether the fourth wheel revolves 60 times per hour, *i.e.*, once in 60 seconds. Count the number of teeth in the centre and third wheels, and multiply the numbers together; then count the leaves in the third and fourth wheels, and multiply; lastly, divide the product of the teeth by that of the leaves, and the quotient will be the number of revolutions per hour, thus:—

$$\frac{75 \times 64}{10 \times 8} = 60.$$

(186.) *To find the number of seconds per revolution of the fourth wheel.*—When the wheels are accessible, count the teeth in the center and third wheels, and the leaves in the third and fourth pinions. We might then ascertain the number of revolutions the fourth wheel makes in an hour as in the preceding section, *i.e.*, in 3,600 seconds, and find the number of seconds to one revolution by dividing 3,600 by the number of revolutions per hour. But we can make one operation of it by inverting the numbers shown in section (185), and adding 3,600 as a multiplier, *i.e.*, multiply the number of leaves in the third and fourth pinions together, and multiply that by 3,600, then divide by the product of the teeth of the center and third wheels, thus:—

$$\frac{10 \times 8 \times 3600}{75 \times 64} = 60 \text{ seconds per revolution.}$$

When the center and third wheels cannot be counted, this method cannot be used; but if the fourth and escape wheels can be reached to count them and the number of vibrations per second is known, the following way can be followed.

(187.) *To find the number of seconds to one revolution of the fourth wheel.*—Count the teeth in the fourth and escape wheels, multiply these numbers together, and multiply the product by 2, then divide by the number of leaves in the escape-wheel pinion multiplied by the number of beats per second. Thus, if there were 5 beats per second, and the train was the same as before, we could put it in this form:—

$$\frac{60 \times 15 \times 2}{6 \times 5} = 60 \text{ seconds per revolution.}$$

(188.) *Another way*, by the seconds-hand, is to start the watch exactly with the regulator, when the seconds-hands of both cross the 60, run the watch till its seconds-hand again reaches its 60, and observe the number of seconds on the regulator dial at that instant. If the regulator shows 1 minute and 12 seconds (or 72 seconds) during one revolution of the watch hand, we have this proportion: number of seconds indicated on the regulator dial is to the number on the watch dial as the number of seconds for one revolution of the regulator hand is to the number per revolution of the watch hand, which we write thus:—

$72 : 60 :: 60 : x$, the unknown quantity.

Multiplying the two extremes together, and the means together, we find that x is equal to 50, and the seconds-hand (and fourth wheel) therefore revolved in 50 seconds. It is necessary to wait till the watch hand gets to its 60, rather than to observe the number of seconds it shows at the end of one minute by the regulator, because the circle on the watch dial may not be evenly spaced off.

(189.) *Another way*, when there is no seconds-hand, but the fourth wheel can be seen, is to make a slight mark on one tooth, and observe the number of seconds (by the regulator dial) during one revolution, *i.e.*, from the instant that the mark passes some fixed point of the movement, close to it and easily seen, till it again passes the same point. Then arrange the proportion as in the preceding section. This gives the required result without any counting of teeth and leaves, which might necessitate taking the movement apart. The mark should be brought exactly at the point convenient for close observation, stop the balance and hold it there till the regulator hand touches its 60, then start it.

(190.) *To find the number of vibrations to one revolution of the fourth wheel*, when not convenient to count the teeth and leaves, but the fourth and escape wheels are visible. Make a minute mark (unless there already is some mark or stain plain enough to answer the purpose) or put a speck of rouge or whiting on the rim of the fourth wheel; stop the watch and put a similar speck on an escape wheel tooth exactly over the other mark. When the two marks exactly coincide start the watch, and count the number of times the escape wheel revolves till the mark on the fourth wheel gets exactly to its starting point. Let us suppose that the escape wheel has 13 teeth, and that it revolved 10 times and 2½ teeth over, *i.e.*, instead of the marked tooth standing exactly over the mark on the fourth wheel, it had passed 2 teeth and half a space beyond that mark. Then we have $13 \times 10 = 130 + 2\frac{1}{2} = 132\frac{1}{2}$ teeth, which we multiply by 2 (as there are 2 vibrations for each tooth), and thus get 265 as the number of vibrations which that movement gives for one revolution of the fourth wheel.

(191.) *To find the number of vibrations per second.*—This can be done by modifying either of the preceding operations. After finding the number of vibrations per hour (which is 3,600 seconds), divide that number by 3,600, thus: $18,000 \div 3,600 = 5$. Or divide the number of vibrations in a minute (which is 60 seconds) by 60, thus: $300 \div 60 = 5$. Or it can be counted with the aid of the regulator (198), or of another watch (214), or a timing balance (218).

(192.) *Another way* is to make it a part of the original calculation of the number of beats per hour or minute. In the case stated in section (182), we write it out as follows:—

$$\frac{75 \times 64 \times 60 \times 15 \times 2}{10 \times 8 \times 6 \times 60 \times 60} = 5.$$

In the case stated in section (187), for finding the number of seconds to one revolution of the fourth wheel, we omit the division by 5 there given, and simply get the number of *vibrations* per revolution, by calculating the train as there described, and add the division by 60 to get the vibrations per second, thus:—

$$\frac{60 \times 15 \times 2}{6 \times 60} = 5 \text{ vibrations per second.}$$

If it is known that the fourth wheel makes one revolution in 60 seconds, this result will be correct.

CHAPTER XV.

COUNTING THE VIBRATIONS.

(193.) *Counting the vibrations of the balance* during a known period of time, as one minute, or one second, is the quickest and easiest way to ascertain whether a watch is running correctly, or if a spring is suitable and will give the number of vibrations which calculation has shown that the train should give. (See Chapter XIV.) The workman should therefore familiarize himself with the different ways of counting, and find which is best adapted for each particular purpose *for his use*, as the temperaments and mental constitutions of different workmen will often render a certain method difficult for one workman to follow, when another workman will find it the easiest and best for him to work by.

(194.) *Vibration registers.*—As it is difficult for some to count up to 300 or 400 vibrations without error, many workmen use some sort of recording apparatus for registering the number counted, so that they can count more easily, and do not depend on memory for the final result. There are several kinds, but they all have a key or push-piece, which is pressed at the proper times, and advances a wheel inside by one tooth for each pressure, carrying forward a hand over the dial and indicating the number of pressures. The workman counts the vibrations up as far as he can do so easily, and without any risk of mistake, then makes a pressure, and begins to count a new series. Some can easily count up to 50 with perfect safety, while others are liable to get the number wrong if they go above 10 or 20. As there is no necessity for going so high that the mind is absorbed in mere counting, it is generally preferable to stop at 10. Anybody can do that almost automatically, and can at the same time give their thoughts to watching the behavior of the balance and other parts.

(195.) *Using the register.*—Having his finger on the push-piece, and the hand pointing to 0, he counts the vibrations up to 10, pressing the push as he says "Ten," then counts another 10 and gives another pressure, and so on, to the end of the minute (or half-minute), noticing how many he had counted (after the last pressure) when the minute ended. If it was 8, and the dial showed 29 pressures of the finger-piece, that would give $29 \times 10 = 290 + 8 = 298$ vibrations. If the spring ought to give 300 vibrations in a minute, this would show that it loses 2 beats (or $\frac{2}{3}$ second) per minute.

(196.) *Registering the vibrations with pencil.*—With a little practice he can register the vibrations with only a pencil and slip of paper, so placed that he can make a plain mark without looking at it. Then at the end of each series of 10 vibrations he makes one mark, the same as described for pressing the push-piece, and the final result is figured out in the same way. The only difficulty is to avoid marking twice in the same place, and getting a false result. To avoid this, he should not only move his hand a little forward each time, but make the marks inclined alternately forward and backward. Even if he should happen to mark twice at the same place, one mark would not be over the other, but across it, forming a letter X, and preventing any miscount. At the end of the minute, write down the surplus beats (those counted after making the last mark), then count the marks and write the number before the odd beats. Thus, if there were 2 extra beats and 31 marks, write down 2, and then 31 before it, making 312 beats altogether.

(197.) *To begin counting.*—You would naturally say "One" when the minute begins, then "Two" at the next beat, and so on. But in reality, when you say "One," there has not been any vibration yet, and so you will get one too many. One vibration in a minute makes four or five minutes per day. To prevent this error, first say "Naught, one," then go on counting. Thus: "Naught, one, two, three, four," etc. The "naught" means you are only beginning to count; the second word, "one," shows one vibration made and counted. This correction is only needed at the *beginning* of the minute; after that, you say: "Eight, nine, ten, one, two, three," etc., as usual. When counting by eye, arrange the watch so that an arm of the balance will be clearly seen at the end of each vibration. If the vibrations are not just one turn, the arm will be in a different place at each end of the vibration. Hold it so that you can see it plainly in both places, and begin counting with the one you see at the beginning of the minute.

(198.) *To commence the minute.*—After getting everything arranged so you can see it conveniently as above stated, get ready to observe the regulator hand in the mirror, (172, 173,) at the beginning of the minute. A good way to know when the regulator seconds-hand is just at the 60 without looking is to look at it five seconds beforehand, after getting the seconds intervals in the mind so that you can count the seconds (or swings of the pendulum) without seeing them, then mentally count the seconds to the end of the minute, while you are getting the motions of the balance well in your eye, and at the 60 begin to count the vibrations. Thus, looking at the clock (in the mirror), when its seconds-hand reaches 55 seconds you say, "Five," looking at your watch, and at each second's interval you say—either aloud or mentally—"Four—Three—Two—One—Naught," and begin to count as directed in section (197). The "Naught" indicates both the instant that the regulator hand strikes its 60, and the beginning of the counting of the vibrations. To distinguish the clock seconds from the number of the vibrations, the former begins with a capital letter; thus "Five—Four—Three—Two—One—Naught, one, two, three, etc. A little practice will make this easy, and the habit will be found a very valuable acquisition. The workman will even get so accustomed to carrying the regular periods in his mind that he can close his eyes for a short time, and continue the counting so accurately that his words will still coincide with the vibrations when he opens his eyes. Counting aloud will be found a great aid, and conducive to accuracy, although not absolutely necessary. Continue to count aloud while you lift your eye to the regulator hand, and notice the exact instant that it reaches the 60 at the end of the minute.

(199.) *Counting alternate vibrations by eye.*—As many workmen find it difficult to count *every vibration*, an easier way is to count only every other vibration. For every vibration to the right there is one to the left. By counting only those to the right, (or to the left, if that will be easier for you), and doubling the number counted, you have the total number as before. It is well to become accustomed to counting both ways, so that you can begin the count with the vibration which occurs at the instant of beginning. If that happened to be a vibration to the left, count the left vibrations throughout the minute, and *vice versa*, making a pencil mark (or pressing the stud of the register) at each 10, as already described. If you had counted 7 extra (after the last mark was made) at the end of the minute, that would mean 14 vibrations, and 16 marks would mean $160 \times 2 = 320$ vibrations, making 334 in all. If you were counting the left vibrations, but the last vibration of the balance was towards the right, that would require the addition of 1 to the number of pairs counted. In the above case, you counted $160 + 7 = 167$ pairs, equal to 334, to which add 1, making 335.

(200.) *Counting the vibrations by ear.*—When the watch is cased, it can be held to the ear, and the vibrations counted while the eye is on the seconds-hand of the clock, either directly or in the mirror (173). It being a little difficult to pronounce the numbers fast enough to count every vibration, it will be found easier to pronounce every other number, omitting the others. Instead of saying: "naught, one, two, three, four, five," etc., pronounce only the even numbers, thus: "naught, two, four, six, eight, ten, two, four," etc., omitting the "naught" after the start, *i.e.*, saying it at the instant that the regulator hand crosses the 60, but not afterwards—and making a pencil mark at each "ten," as before, which can be done without looking at the paper. As the clock hand reaches the 60 at the end of the minute, notice whether it does so on the beat you are counting or the one whose number is not spoken; if on the latter, add 1 to the number counted. For instance, if there were 28 marks, and you counted four after the last mark, besides the odd vibration, that would make 285. Of course, this method can be used by eye, instead of that in section (199) if preferred.

(201.) *Counting alternate vibrations by ear.*—Some may prefer to count only the alternate vibrations, but calling *off all the numbers*, as described in section (198), for the sake of uniformity of method, if for no other reason. In that case, when the regulator hand crossed the 60, they would say: "naught, one, two, three," etc., to "ten, one, two, three," etc. If there were 285 vibrations, as in the last section, there would be 14 marks, two over, (*i.e.*, two pairs,) and the odd vibration, which would be figured up thus: $14 \times 2 = 280 + (2 \times 2) = 284 + 1 = 285$.

(202.) In this method of counting (by ear) there are two points which require some practice, (1), to ignore the alternate beats in counting, and count only every other beat, and (2), at the end of the minute, to notice whether the minute terminated on the beat you counted or on the alternate beat which came after it. A little practice and care will enable you to do both, without risk of mistake.

(203.) *Aids in counting vibrations by ear.*—When the watch is not cased, its beat may not be loud enough to count by ear as above described. But there are various ways of reinforcing the sound and conveying it to the ear, which the watchmaker can adopt if desirable. A resonant box can be made of thin sonorous wood, or of thin and elastic metal (even thin tin might do) of convenient size, say 6 inches long, 3 wide, and 1½ inches high, closed except one end, which is left open. If the movement is laid on this, the sound will be very much louder, especially at the open end of the box. Putting it into any enclosed space with vibratory walls will greatly increase the sound. Even putting the movement in a pasteboard collar box without cover will often be sufficient. Another class of aids is a funnel-shaped piece, to be arranged over or close to the movement, to gather the sound, which is then conveyed through a rubber tube of any convenient length to a sort of hollow nipple, which fits snugly into the orifice of the ear. By having the funnel supported by a standard, and the nipple in the ear, both hands are left free for holding or working at the movement. Such apparatus can be obtained ready made from the telephone and phonograph people.

(204.) *Counting for half a minute*, instead of one minute, will often be sufficient to show whether your spring is suitable, at least for the preliminary trials, and it will lessen the number of vibrations to be counted. When the spring being tested is merely stuck to the balance staff by wax or putty powder, it will hardly bear more than a half or three-quarter turn vibration without becoming loosened, or displaced from the centre, and of course will not continue to vibrate very long. With a good regulator, the half minute can be observed almost as closely as the whole. Another watch would of course answer in place of a regulator, provided it was closely regulated, with a large and plain seconds-dial accurately divided off, so that the 30 would be exactly 30 seconds from the 60.

(205.) *Counting till reversal or coincidence of vibrations.*—If you experience any difficulty in counting the beats and taking the time from the clock as described, you can simply count the balance vibrations till your balance reverses its motion, or reverses twice and again coincides with a timing balance, as described in sections (218) to (222). After starting the two balances together, count the vibrations till your balance gets ahead or behind enough to move in a direction *opposite* to the other, although its vibrations end at the same time as that. It has then gained or lost one beat in the number of vibrations counted. If that number was 300, your watch will vary one minute in 300, or nearly 5 minutes per day. If that number of beats was counted from the start till the balances again vibrate in the *same direction* and end at the same time, that would be gaining or losing 2 beats in 300, or twice as much as before stated.

(206.) *Counting the number of vibrations in one second.*—First get the vibration or swing of the regulator pendulum well in the mind, so that you can nod your head in unison with it, *i.e.*, nod it exactly at the end of each swing (or second), and can continue this nodding correctly while you look at the balance and count the number of its vibrations between two nods. To test whether your nods are correct, continue the nodding after you have finished counting, and again look at the pendulum to see if the nods are still in unison with its swings. If there were 4 or 5 vibrations between 2 nods, each beat would of course correspond to $\frac{1}{4}$ or $\frac{1}{5}$ second. If it does not seem to be even, count for 2 seconds; 9 beats in 2 seconds would be $4\frac{1}{2}$ beats per second. Instead of counting the vibrations you can count the movements of the seconds-hand and find how much each movement means in time. This is often useful in timing a watch closely.

(207.) *Another way.*—Some workmen reverse this process, and nod the head in unison with the balance vibrations (or movements of the seconds-hand), then look at the pendulum, to see whether the terminations of its swing all coincide with the downward motions of the head. If they do, there is an even number of beats per second. If not, continue the trial for several seconds, and if the swings to the right terminate with the downward nods, the number of beats is odd. This will help to determine the right number. A vibration-marker (175) is of great assistance, as it indicates the exact end of each swing.

(208.) *Another way* is to count the number of vibrations of the trial balance (or the beats of the watch or movements of the seconds-hand), during 10 seconds by the regulator, and divide the total number by 10. This is the most reliable, and as easy as any, especially by nodding the head in unison with the pendulum (206).

(209.) *Timing bells.*—Instead of counting the vibrations by a seconds-dial, as described, it can be done with the aid of a small clock arranged to strike a bell at the end of each minute. Several different arrangements of the kind are in the market, varying in the details of construction and arrangement. Most of them give warning strokes a few seconds before the minute stroke, to prepare the workman. A similar arrangement could of course be attached to the secondary clock (171), and be operated by electricity, *i.e.*, the clock would close the circuit, sending a current through wires to an electric bell, which could be placed wherever desired for use. Timing bells are very convenient in counting vibrations, but to be trustworthy they must give the stroke of the bell exactly at the right instant *every time*, and not be liable to strike a little sooner or later at some times than at others. A difference of one-quarter of a second between the initial and end strokes would be equivalent to 6 minutes per day in the running of a watch regulated by it.

CHAPTER XVI.

Testing Hair Springs.

(210.) *Testing by length of cone, or weighing the spring.*—The most common procedure is to hold the outer coil of the spring in the tweezers, with the balance hooked onto the center, and see how far the weight of the balance will stretch the spring. The general rule is that the height of the cone (formed by drawing the center of the spring downward) should be about equal to half the diameter of the balance. The outer coil must of course be held horizontally in the tweezers during the test. But this test is not of much aid, because a spring might be really of the same strength as the old one, and yet be drawn out much further or less by the balance, by reason of being proportionally wider or narrower than that. The stiffness of a spring varies in proportion to its width but as the cube of its thickness. But this test may answer for a first rough trial of a spring, to get some idea of its suitability.

(211.) *Testing with a hair-spring gauge.*—For measuring the strength of hair springs there are several kinds of spring-gauges, and they are very useful in a watch factory, where a great many springs are required of practically the same size as to width, thickness, number and openness of coils, all fitted on collets of equal size, and pinned to the stud at the same place on the same coil. In such a case, measurement by a gauge will give the exact strength of each spring. The balances are also measured and weighed, to find their diameter of gyration and moment of inertia. Rules and tables are prepared from the results of trials and measurements of springs and balances in hundreds of movements, almost exactly alike, showing the best proportion between the spring and the balance. It is then easy by measurement of a spring to know whether it will be suitable for a certain balance, or to select a balance for which it will be adapted, so closely that when put together and timed they will not be more than a quarter or half minute out per day.

(212.) But such gauges are of much less practical use to the ordinary watchmaker, who handles all kinds, sizes, and grades of movements, perhaps no two exactly alike, and has to select from among springs of equally promiscuous sizes, widths, and thicknesses, and to hold each one differently at each end. For his purposes, attaching the spring to the balance it belongs with, and holding the coils in my spring-fitting tool (238), or even in the tweezers, while vibrating the balance, will be fully as convenient, and will give closer and more practically useful results than the hair-spring gauge. In fact, the vibrating test will finally have to be used any way. Some springs require a large, open center, others one that is small and close; but the gauge makes no allowance for that. Those who wish to use them will find further information in Chapter XVIII., on fitting hair springs. Directions for using the tools are always furnished with them. For fitting springs in the usual grades of American watches the gauges are very convenient.

(213.) *Test by vibrating.*—Temporarily attach the spring to the axis of the balance for which it is intended, rest the lower pivot on some hard surface, hold the spring by its outer coil in such a way as to sustain the balance in a nearly horizontal position while resting slightly on the lower pivot, and count the vibrations it makes during a certain time, or during one or more swings of the pendulum; or compare them with another balance making the proper number. The latter is unquestionably the best of all the methods in use, not only for the first short tests, but also for the final long trials, and for regulating the watch quickly.

(214.) *Comparing balances with a watch.*—If you have a movement which makes the same number of vibrations that your spring ought to make, you can arrange its balance and the one you are vibrating close together, start them in unison, and see whether your balance gets ahead or lags behind. If you see a difference immediately, the spring will be so much too strong or too weak as to be totally unsuitable. If you only detect a difference by the end of a half-minute or a minute, it may be likely to answer, and if otherwise suitable you will be justified in pinning it in the collet and making a careful and decisive trial. Even after it is found correct, and finally pinned in the watch and running, the comparison of balances furnishes the easiest, surest, quickest, and best way of quickly bringing the watch to time. A difference of half a vibration can be detected with certainty, which in an 18,000 movement would be $\frac{1}{10}$ second—a difference which could not possibly be detected by any other method available to the ordinary workman. If that error occurred in six minutes, it would only amount to 24 seconds in an entire day. For this use, the movement should be kept in a close, moisture- and dust-proof movement-box, and be closely regulated. It is not necessary to look at the hands, but take the time of beginning and ending the trial from the clock dial. Always keep a pencil and paper handy on the bench, for making memoranda. When you make a trial more than one minute in length, mark down the number of the minute when it began.

(215.) *To start the balances synchronously.*—Grasping the hair spring securely in the tweezers at the proper point, rest the lower balance pivot on the glass of the movement box at a point where that is horizontal, so that it will not slide down the inclined surface and interfere with the vibrations. It should also be where you can see both balances at the same time. Rest the hand holding the tweezers upon some support of convenient height, so that you can hold it stationary without fatigue, and start the balance being tried in such a way that its vibrations are in the same direction as those of the timing balance and also begin and end at the same time with that.

(216.) *When in the movement.*—Probably the easiest way to observe the vibrations of a balance, especially of a small and narrow one, is by noticing its terminations, *i.e.*, where it stands still for an instant while reversing its direction. When regulating a spring which is attached to a balance driven by the movement, so that its vibrations are of uniform extent, you should select an arm of the timing balance which is clearly visible at the end of the vibration, and arrange your trial balance as near it as convenient, with an arm ending its vibration just opposite to the other one, so that you can easily see both, then arrest the trial balance, draw it around to the above-mentioned stopping point, and liberate it so that it will begin its vibration in the same direction, *i.e.*, just as it would if the two rims were in contact—and at the same time, *i.e.*, they both reach the stopping point at the same instant. Then notice the time this trial begins.

(217.) *When not in the movement*, this method would not be suitable if the test continued for more than a few seconds, because the trial balance would rapidly lessen its vibration, and the arm would no longer stop where it could be compared with the other one. When making the first tests of a spring in the tweezers, it is better to arrange the two balances so that when both are at rest, *i.e.*, at the middle of their vibrations, their arms will be *in line* and their ends close together. Let the timing balance acquire its usual motion, then draw the arm of the trial balance around as far as is safe, and liberate it just at the end of the vibration of the timing balance, so that the arms of both balances will pass the line of centers together. With a little practice, this can be done very closely. In this case, you watch their motions at the line of centers (the line between the centers of the two balances) till your trial balance gets ahead or behind. If one balance is still while the other is at the middle of its vibration, the difference is half a vibration; when the arms pass together at the line of centers, but are going in opposite directions, the trial balance has gained or lost one vibration. If you are able to start them off exactly together, it is safe to calculate by the half vibration, or even less—as soon as you can see that your balance is getting ahead or behind. If you cannot do that, it is better to wait till their motions become opposite. For the preliminary tests of springs, the balances can be more easily started together by using a timing balance specially intended for that purpose (218), instead of a watch movement.

(218.) *Timing balance.*—For short tests of springs, the most convenient method is by what is called a timing balance, consisting of a balance on its staff and provided with a hair spring which causes it to make the number of vibrations required for trials. The balance pivots preferably run in jewels as usual, although brass holes will answer if kept clean and well oiled. But jeweled holes can generally be obtained from some condemned watch, and the balance mounted on a small brass plate (say, two by four inches,) leaving vacant space enough at one end to rest the trial balance on the plate alongside of the other one. A balance with three arms and a plain rim is most useful.

Arrange the spring on the staff so that one arm of the balance (the one which will be contiguous to the trial balance) will stand in the central line of the plate. In the same line make a series of shallow, flat-bottomed holes, large enough for the largest pivot to be free in, and, say $\frac{1}{64}$ inch deep. This is for convenience of arranging trial balances at different distances from the timing balance, for comparing their arms while vibrating.

To prevent the timing balance changing its rate of vibration, no regulator should be used with it, but the balance should be brought to time by the hair spring only. Regulate it by a good watch; give it as large a motion as it can have without disturbing the regular action of the spring, so that it will vibrate as long as possible. Start it exactly with the watch balance (215), and see if they exactly coincide in direction and time till the timing balance nearly comes to rest. It is well to have two or three timing balances, giving the most usual numbers of vibrations, with the number engraved on each plate, as:—"18,000—300—5," "14,400—240—4," "16,200—270—4$\frac{1}{2}$," etc.

(219.) *To start synchronously, with timing balance.*—The best way is to arrange the two balances close together but not touching, with an arm of each balance in the line of centers (217) when at rest, then draw both balances around to the same distance, hold them till the proper time to start, and liberate both at the same instant, thus not only starting them exactly together, but with vibrations of equal extents. For holding and starting two balances at once, mount two stiff bristles in a pegwood handle, with their ends sufficiently separated for each one to engage with the arm of its own balance. Move each balance around and catch its arm behind one of the bristles. By lifting the bristles, the same motion liberates both balances. If the trial balance has only two arms, you can rest one bristle against the rim of the timing balance and the other behind the arm of the trial balance, and give them an equal start.

(220.) *Peculiarity of timing balance.*—In testing springs with the timing balance, it should be remembered that it has no regulator, and therefore the point of the trial spring which is held in the tweezers when vibrating correctly is not the point where it should be pinned in the stud in the watch, but it corresponds to the point which falls in the regulator when in the watch. To find the position for pinning in the stud, make allowance for the distance between the regulator pins and the stud. When the spring is held in my hair-spring fitting tool, (233, 238,) which has got a pair of regulator pins and a false stud, the point in the spring which is held in the latter will of course be the place to pin it in the stud of the watch.

(221.) *Testing by opposition.*—Having attached the spring to the balance (269), (270), either temporarily or permanently, start the two balances together, just as the regulator hand reaches the 60, notice whether the trial balance gains or loses, and when it terminates its vibration just as the timing balance is moving at full speed, notice the time on the regulator. The spring has then gained or lost a half vibration (217) in the number of seconds which had elapsed since the test began. With an 18,000 beat timing balance, one vibration is $\frac{1}{5}$ second, and half a beat is $\frac{1}{10}$ second. If the spring lost $\frac{1}{10}$ second in 10 seconds, it would lose 1 second in every 100 seconds, or nearly a quarter of an hour per day. In this way you can soon tell whether a spring is likely to answer. This method is not very close, and is only suitable for the first and coarsest trials.

(222.) *Testing by reversal, and by coincidence.*—A better way is to continue the trial till the two balances end their vibrations at the same instant but vibrate in opposite directions, when your trial spring has gained or lost one beat on the other, in the number of seconds which had elapsed. This is called testing by reversal. A still better way is to keep on till they reverse again, so that the vibrations begin together and are in the same direction, *i.e.*, they coincide as they did at the start, and the trial balance has then gained or lost 2 beats in the number of seconds occupied by the trial. Some can observe more easily and closely by one method than by the others, and each man should choose the one which is best for him, remembering that the longer the trial continues the closer the result will be. For, instance, if he makes an error of a half-second in taking the time from the regulator, and the trial was for 2 beats, the error would be only $\frac{1}{4}$ second per beat; if for 10 beats, only $\frac{1}{20}$ second, etc. The methods of testing given in this Chapter are somewhat easier than those by counting the vibrations, as described in Chapter XV., but some may prefer the latter.

(223.) *Quick test by comparing vibrations.*—In the first rough trials, it is not necessary to continue any longer than till you see that your balance is gaining or losing on the timing balance. If it does so within 20 or 30 vibrations, it will vary so much that it would not be suitable. After you find one which seems to vibrate with the timing balance for a considerable time, it will then be better to make a more formal test, as previously described.

CHAPTER XVII.

Hair-Spring Fitting Tools.

(224.) *Excelsior's hair-spring fitting tool.*—Although twenty years have elapsed since this tool was first described, I have never seen or read of anything equaling it in convenience and completeness. Yet, strange to say, no one has ever thought fit to manufacture it for the trade, although anybody is free to do so. There would certainly be a large sale for it, as every watchmaker who has occasion to do adjusting or testing needs something of the kind, and even for ordinary fitting of hair springs it would save much time and trouble. Its value having been fully demonstrated, I will again describe it, and also some modifications described in other horological works.

(225.) *The original tool* was intended not only for fitting hair springs but also for upright drilling, setting and re-setting jewels, countersinking, chamfering, and many other uses. But I will here only describe it for the first purpose named. By using it, we may test a spring in every way without injuring it in the least, and in a very short time; so that, if it should not prove suitable for the watch on trial, it will still remain as perfect for the finest isochronal adjustment in another watch as when made—a point of considerable importance when working with fine and costly springs.

(226). *Description.*—It is substantially an upright holder, carrying arbors for different uses, and so constructed that the upright portion can be moved in any direction to bring the arbor over any hole in the watch, and there fastened. It consists of a clamp, to be fastened to the movement in any convenient place, carrying a round upright rod, movable up, down and on its own center, and having a head through which moves a horizontal slide carrying the vertical arbors. The general idea of it is shown in Fig. 10, (233).

(227.) The clamp is made from a thick piece of metal, (steel, cast iron or hard brass,) flat on its under surface, nearly rectangular in shape, $1\frac{1}{2}$ inches long, by 1 inch wide, half an inch thick in the center and one-eighth inch at the edges, with one edge hollowed out to form two projections or claws, one at each corner, and about $1\frac{1}{4}$ inches apart. Under each of these claws there is a jaw, made something like the jaws on a universal lathe chuck, capable of being fastened parallel with the surface of the clamp, and at any desired distance from it—so as to be screwed to the potance plate alone, or, if necessary, they can take in the whole thickness of the watch movement. The claws are slipped in between the bridges, or upon the plates, wherever a good bearing can be got, and the jaws screwed up to hold the clamp firmly in place—its flat under surface being, of course, in the same plane with the plate of the watch. The jaws can be faced with thin leather or rubber, if thought best, to give them a good hold without much pressure. In that case, they could be clamped directly on the dial without danger. My own tool is made double, having two claws $1\frac{1}{4}$ inches apart as above, and on the opposite side of the clamp, two other claws or projections only $\frac{3}{4}$ inch apart, so that one side or the other will fit readily upon all sizes of movements. The jaws are also reversible, being turned at their center to point towards either pair of claws which are in use.

(228.) Through the center of this piece or clamp is drilled a vertical hole to take an upright steel rod $\frac{3}{16}$ inch in diameter, and about $1\frac{1}{2}$ inches long, having a head at its top, and fastened at any desired height by a screw, like the centers in a bow lathe. In the head is a rectangular slot through which slides, horizontally, a steel strip $1\frac{1}{2}$ inches long, $\frac{1}{4}$ inch wide, and $\frac{1}{16}$ thick, (a piece of an old pair of tweezers will do,) edge up, and fastened wherever desired by a screw. The strip also has an enlargement or head at its inner end, with a vertical hole to take in the different arbors to be used. These arbors may be the centers of your bow-lathe, or depthing tool, or any others you have already on hand, if you do not wish to make them specially for this tool. But I advise to use tolerably large ones, at least $\frac{1}{8}$ inch in diameter, so that the head will take in arbors for setting jewels, etc., if used for that purpose. But the arbor we use for hair-spring fitting should be reduced to a diameter of about $\frac{1}{16}$ inch for three-quarters of an inch from each end, so as to penetrate into the smallest places, and also to enable us to bring our false regulator pins near to the center when wanted. One end should be brought to a fine central point, the other tapered down a little, and the end truly and centrally countersunk. Or two sets of arbors can be made, one fine, the other larger, each having its own horizontal slide and head.

(229.) The use of this tool is obvious. Having first fastened the clamp *a* firmly to some part of the movement, the upright rod *b* is inserted with its head at any desired height, and the horizontal slide *d* placed so that the point of its arbor *f* will rest in the balance jewel-hole, when the slides are screwed fast. We then reverse the arbor, *f*, and bring the other end, which has the female center, down upon the upper pivot of the balance (or any other piece you are fitting,) and hold it upright the same as would be done by the bridge itself. The angle of this female center should be rather acute, *i.e.*, it should be deeper than it is wide at its mouth, so that it can be raised sufficiently to give the pivot freedom and yet not allow it any play sideways. The surface should be well polished and hard, kept clean and free from rust, and it will form a very tolerable substitute for the balance bridge.

(230.) This arbor has two hubs, *g* and *m*, which slide freely upon it, and are each fastened by a thumb-nut. In each of them is fixed a steel wire, *i* and *o*, $\frac{1}{16}$ inch in diameter, pointing horizontally outward from the center of its hub. Each of these wires has a smaller hub, *k* and *n*, which slides to and from the arbor, and is fastened by a screw. One of them, *n*, has two points, to represent the regulator; the other, *k*, has a clamp to grasp the hair spring instead of the tweezers, and therefore represents a stud. This clamp, *k*, can be either self-acting and spring-tight, or be opened and closed by a screw. The points, *j*, are made thin, so as not to touch the adjacent coils of the spring, and both they and the regulator pins point vertically downwards. The two hubs *k* and *n*, carrying the clamp and the pins, are adjustable independently of each other, as to distance from the arbor, height, and distance from each other, to correspond with the relative positions of the stud and regulator in the watch. The wires which carry the two small hubs are filed flat on one side, making them half-round so that the set-screws can be loosened enough to allow the hubs to slide along, while they cannot turn over. If the spring on trial requires to be altered, we simply open the clamp to release it, and raise the arbor, when the balance can be taken out, and, after altering, can be as readily replaced and refastened, everything being in the same position as before.

(231.) In my own tool I also had holes in different places, in any one of which a small plug, q, with a milled head will fit—the plug being sawed through the center so that the two halves spring outward and hold the plug in any position in which it is placed. This plug carries a stiff bristle, and I place it in any hole suitable to the watch, so that by turning the milled head with the fingers I can lower the end of the bristle upon the balance rim, or raise it, in an instant, for the purpose of holding the balance still or liberating it.

(232.) There may seem to be a good deal of this tool, but it is all perfectly simple and easy to construct, and any man fit to touch a watch ought to make one all complete in a day, at the utmost. If he has much work to do it will save him days and weeks of time, to say nothing of the satisfaction in its use, and the superiority of the work. Perfection is not required in any part for hair-spring fitting—the only point at all essential is that the arbor shall stand vertically or nearly so. There is nothing obligatory about any of the sizes or details given. The rectangular slot can be easily made by riveting together flat pieces, and leaving a space for the horizontal slide. But, whatever time may be required to make it, it is a tool for which every workman will find frequent and profitable use.

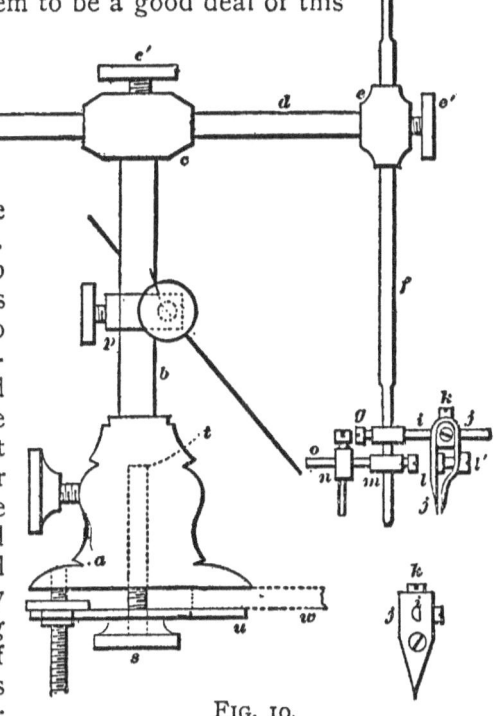

FIG. 10.

(233.) *Simpler forms of hair-spring fitting tool.*—Figure 10 is a sketch of a lighter and cheaper form, adapted only for hair-spring fitting. The clamp, a, was made from a round piece of harness mounting, and the heads, c and e, from a piece of brass lightning-rod point,—showing how refuse scraps may be worked up into valuable tools and save cost. In this holder, the horizontal slide is a half-round rod, and the vertical arbor, f, is in line with the upright rod b, both being vertical to the watch plate. But in the tool as previously described, the slide, d, was flat, to maintain the vertical position of the arbor, f.

In this tool, a is a round clamp, with a thumbscrew, in the center on the back side, while the front edge is filed out to make the two claws; b is the vertical rod, with its head c, and set-screw, c'. This rod slides down in the space between the two jaws, u, which are made from a broad flat piece of steel. The nut, r, runs on a screw fixed in the clamp, a, and the center of the nut passes through the jaws, to give more substance for the screw to hold in. The tightening screws, s, are near enough to the center of the clamp to be bedded in the metal up to t, before coming out. The dotted lines, w, represent a plate to which the holder is supposed to be fastened; d, is the horizontal rod, with its head, e, and set-screw, e'; f is the vertical arbor or runner, point upward. The holes are drilled entirely through the heads, c and e, at right angles, one side of the center taking in the rods, which should be screwed in very tight and fast,—the other side taking in the set-screws; g is the hair-spring hub with set screw and smaller hub, k, sliding on the half-round wire, i, (which is filed flat on one side,) and is fastened thereon by the set-screw seen in front; j is a steel strip bent around the hub, k, to which it is fastened by the screw, k, and terminating in fine points, j, at the lower ends, which grasp the hair spring; l is a brass or steel piece riveted in the back half, to give substance for holding the screw, l', which draws the points together upon the spring. The small figure below is a transverse view of the same. M is the regulator slide, with hub, n, sliding on the half-round wire, o, which is flat on the top; p is a brass strip which slides along the upright rod, b, and turns in any direction, with plug, q, carrying a bristle. The set-screw of this strip is long enough to fasten it upon the rod, b, d, or f,—wherever it will be best to have it. All the parts are drawn in the best position for showing their construction, not for use.

(234.) *Mode of using the tool.*—Our Upright Holder being fastened to the movement so that the point of the arbor rests in the lower balance jewel hole, we select a spring for trial and stick it to the staff, then put the balance into its place in the watch. Reversing the arbor, or runner f, we bring the end with the female center down upon the upper pivot, holding it in position, but leaving it free to vibrate. The hubs *g* and *m* having been previously slipped on the arbor and fastened by their set-screws, we place the hair-spring clamp, *j*, at the proper distance from the center to grasp the spring at the point which, before, we held in the tweezers, and fasten the whole properly. We then place the false regulator pins, *n*, about as the real ones stand in the watch, or should stand, and fasten them also. Then we loosen the screw, *e'*, and turn the whole—the runner *f*, the spring in the clamp, and the regulator pins, *n*,—all together, and bring the balance in beat, or near enough for the watch to go freely, and fasten *f* again.

(235.) *Testing the spring.*—Lastly we turn the balance a little, so that it will start off promptly on being liberated, and lower our bristle upon the rim to hold it so till we are ready to begin, then count the vibrations and proceed as directed in Chapter XVIII., except that we now shift the spring in the clamp *j* instead of in the tweezers. If the number of vibrations is about right, we pin the spring to the collet, (273, 274,) and try again, shifting the spring if necessary till the correct number is obtained, then pin it in the stud at the point grasped by the clamp, put the watch together, and a very little regulation will finish the job. In this way you will never have to change a spring once pinned in the watch, for it is obvious that it will perform almost exactly the same there as in our Holder, provided the regulator and stud occupied the same relative positions in each. In timing springs before breaking off the superfluous outer coils, the claws grasping the proper coil should be raised sufficiently for them to clear the other coils vibrating below. And, of course, the first trials should be made with a small vibration to avoid danger of loosening the spring in the putty powder.

(236.) *Peculiar cases.*—Cases are occasionally found where the tool cannot be used exactly as described, and when it will be required to attach the holder clamp to the balance-bridge, place the upper pivot in its hole, and vibrate the balance by hand, counting, etc., as before. But these instances are exceedingly rare, for in most English lever and other undersprung watches the spring can just as well be stuck to the *upper* pivot for trial, while the balance is placed in the watch for running as usual. And even after the spring is pinned in the collet, that can be stuck on the upper side of the balance with putty powder, concentric with the pivot, and tested as before described, the balance receiving its motion from the movement, the same as if the watch was finished and going.

(237.) *Advantages of this tool.*—As an error of one second in a minute will amount to 24 minutes in a day, it is important to be as exact as possible in our trials. In the usual method of fitting springs, where the balance is caused to vibrate only by the strength of the spring, counteracted by the staggering of the balance as it is supported by the stiffness of the spring itself as held in the tweezers, there is no possibility of any accuracy till the spring is actually pinned and tried in the watch. But with this tool, we may observe correctly from the start. The

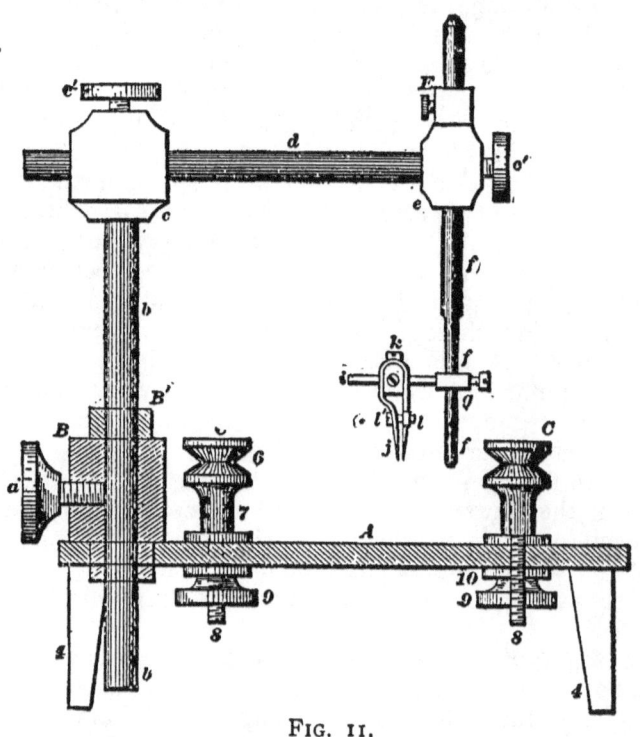

FIG. 11.

Breguet spring can be fitted in half the usual time with this tool, and done better, with no risk of injuring it by numerous trial pinnings in the collet and stud, which is almost unavoidable while following the usual methods. It will also be noted that by raising the point of the runner f out of the way, the balance bridge can be screwed in its place and the watch can run so, while the spring is still held in the false stud and the false regulator. This admits of exact position-timing in this tool.

(238.) *Excelsior's improved hair-spring fitting tool.*—The tool as previously described has a base piece, *A*, arranged to be clamped on the movement or bridge which holds the vibrating balance. In many cases it would be preferable to have the tool stand on its own base, with conveniences for clamping a plate or movement firmly in position during the trial, similarly to an uprighting or upright drilling tool. Fig. 11 shows a base, *A*, of that kind, with a leg, *4*, at each corner for standing on the bench with the clamp screws, *8*, free. Fig. 12 is a plan view, showing the base cut out at the center, *1*, with slots *2, 2, 2*, for the three posts or clamps, *C*, to slide to or from the center, for holding the movement in any desired position, like the clamps on the head of the universal lathe.

(239.) *Movement-holding clamps.*—But the clamps may be very simple affairs. Fig. 14 shows one enlarged, being merely a brass rod turned out as shown at *6* and *7*, with the screw *8*

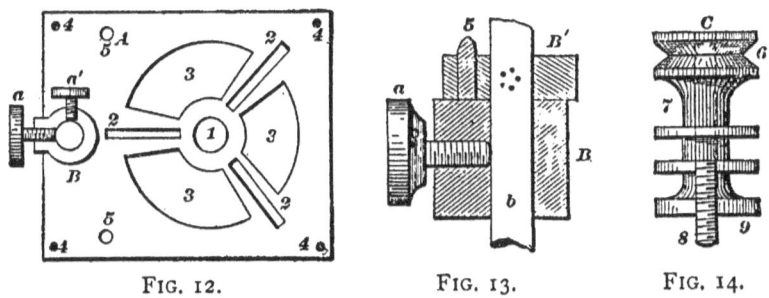

FIG. 12. FIG. 13. FIG. 14.

firmly secured in its center. The part *8* slides in the slot *2* of Fig. 12, and the clamp is secured by the nut *9*, underneath the base plate *A*. The groove *6* may receive and hold either plate of the movement; the hollow *7* is to give room for the pillar plate, when the upper plate is held in groove *6*. A washer, *10*, should be used between nut *9* and the plate. The openings *3, 3, 3*, in the plate are to admit of seeing the watch dial, and noting the positions of the hands, without taking out the movement.

(240.) *The vertical runners or arbors.*—The upright rod *b* should be of cast steel, of spring temper or case hardened, so that the screw *a* may hold it rigidly without marring its surface, and should of course be large enough to hold the head *c* and slide *d* with perfect rigidity. Instead of setting the runner *f* in position by a male center or point on the other end of it, and then reversing *f* to bring the female center down, a special pointed centering runner can be used. The rod *b* runs in a bushing *B*, secured in the bed-plate *A*.

(241.) *Sleeves for obviating repeated adjustments of parts.*—B', Figs. 11 and 13, is a loose sleeve which can be firmly secured on the rod b by thumbscrew a'. It has a hole fitting closely but freely over the pointed pin, 5, like a steady-pin, secured in the bushing B. When the rod b has to be lifted or taken out for any purpose, this arrangement insures that the runner f will be raised vertically upward and cannot twist sideways—and also that everything can be placed exactly in position without any readjustment. In first getting the runner f in position in the pivot hole, with sleeve B' loose and resting on B, tighten thumb-screw a, then a', thereby doubly securing the runner f against side motion. Also add a similar sleeve E, on runner f, resting on the head e, to be secured after f is properly adjusted on the balance pivot. This will admit of lifting f, and replacing it without readjustment, thus saving much time. The letters indicating the parts are the same as in Fig. 10, and the description thereof.

(242.) It will be observed that not only can a spring be held and tested for length, number of vibrations, etc., in fitting a new spring, but the movement can be wound and run for any desired length of time, for regulating, testing the isochronism, etc. To see the hands, or set them, the tool may be inverted, or it can be held right side up over a mirror in which the hands can be seen. When it is to be inverted, or held in different positions for timing, the runner f should have a shallow cylindrical hole with flat bottom drilled vertically into its end, instead of the usual tapering hole, so as to avoid pinching the pivot when held inverted or edgewise, and enable it to run freely. Two or three runners or centers with holes of different sizes will suffice for all sizes of pivots.

(243.) *To time a watch* when held in this tool, arrange the bristle holder, q, Fig. 10, so that turning the plug will bring the bristle down on the balance and hold it, or lift the bristle and liberate the balance. When the watch seconds-hand reaches 60, stop the balance with the bristle, drawing it further around, if necessary, so that it will start off with a good motion when liberated; then set the other hands. As the regulator hand crosses its 60, lift the bristle, and the watch starts off. If it is to be stopped at a certain instant, that is done by lowering the bristle. If the hands are merely to be compared, they are examined by the mirror, or, if the runner has flat-bottomed holes as described, the tool with the watch in it can be inverted, for comparing times.

(244.) *Cheaper fitting tools* can be made by altering over an old uprighting or upright drilling tool, in place of the base *A*—provided there is sufficient thickness of metal in the standard to sustain the screw holding the rod *b*. Rings can be used to raise the movement above the table, and plain clamps to hold it, if desired, as is done with the upright drill, but a better way is to have three clamps or jaws similar to those on the face plate of the universal or American lathe, and movable in slots like them. But the round sliding posts just described will do very well.

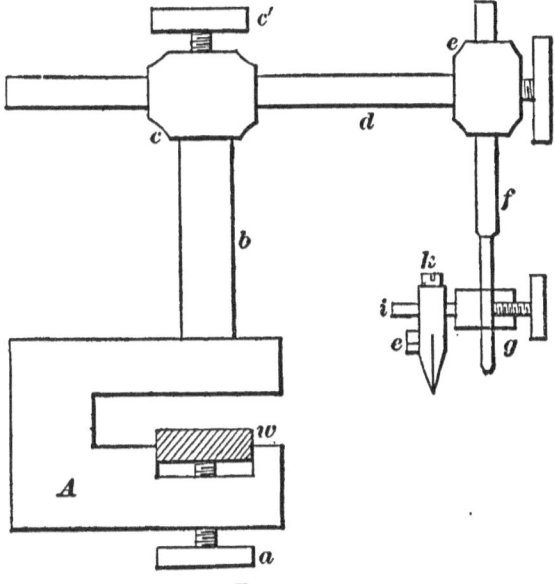

FIG. 15.

(245.) *Spring holder and clamp.*—Fig. 15 is a rigid brass clamp, *A*, to be fastened directly to the watch plate or bridge, by thumb nut *a*, having a loose washer on its point to avoid marring the plate by the screw. The rod *b* is rigidly secured to the clamp, vertical to the inner side of the clamp, and the head *c* is also fast on the rod, and carries the slide *d*, secured by thumbscrew *c'*. At the end of *d* is the head *e*, carrying runner *f*, with spring clamp *g*, as already described. The parts *d*, *e* and *f* may be made as described for Fig. 11, and

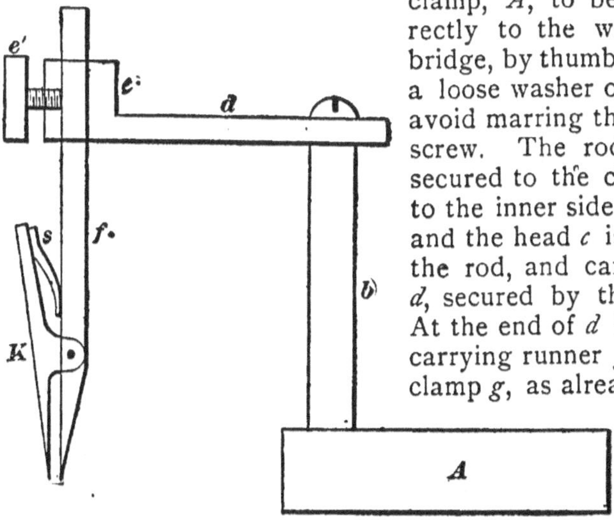

FIG. 16.

so be interchangeable in the different tools. The rod *b* may be two inches long, and the other parts in proportion. The slide *d* is half round, with the flat side vertical. The draughtsman has shown this tool twice the proper size.

(246.) *Standing spring holder, or automatic tweezers.*—Fig. 16 is simply a heavy base, *A*, with rigid upright *b* and arm *d*, at the end of which is the head *e*, carrying the sliding upright runner *f*, secured by thumbscrew as before. In this case, however, the lower end of the runner *f* is provided with a movable jaw *k*, turning on a pivot, both the jaw and the end of the runner being properly formed to grasp a hair spring like a pair of tweezers. The points are held together by the spring *S*. The upright *b* is of such length as to bring the under side of *e* about three inches above the bench, on which this tool stands, in any convenient position for holding the spring properly. The runner *f* is made of the same size as those in Figs. 11 and 15, so that they can be used in this tool if desired. The tool is placed alongside of the watch, or wherever required, and the heavy base keeps it upright. If preferred, the arm *d* can be turned on the upright *b*, but it is seldom necessary.

(247.) *Vibrating tools.*—Special tools are also made, consisting of a hard polished enamel plate, an upright standard with an arm adjustable for height, a balance with a hair spring pinned in the arm as in a stud, arranged to make 18,000 vibrations per hour, (300 per minute,) as a standard of comparison. The trial balance is vibrated alongside of it as before described, being held by the tweezers in the ordinary way. An important improvement would be made by mounting the timing balance in jewel holes, or at least giving the upper pivot of the balance some support while vibrating.

(248.) *Hair-spring gauges.*—The one most familiar to working watchmakers is Bottum's, which needs no description. Much more elaborate kinds are made, but they are principally for watch manufacturers. The ordinary gauge for the use of watch repairers is for ascertaining the relative strengths of all the springs in stock, so that a spring of any required strength can be readily found. Each spring is carefully measured by the gauge, then wrapped in a separate paper, marked on the outside with the kind of spring, and the gauge-number showing its strength. In fitting springs, after one spring has been tested by vibrating, (Chapter XVI.) and not found satisfactory, its gauge-number, and the number of vibrations it gives are used for calculating the gauge-number which will give the required number of vibrations with that balance, according to the rule given in section (266). It is of course obvious that the springs must all be measured *in the same gauge*, as any other gauge-numbers would be useless. The Logan gauge, a well-known and widely used specimen of the tool, adapted for ordinary watch-

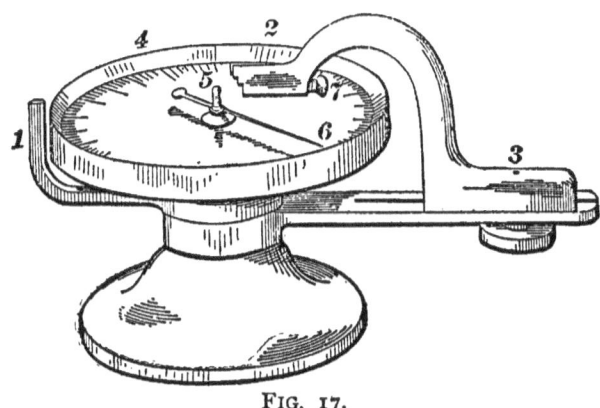

FIG. 17.

makers, is shown in the cut. Directions for use of course accompany all gauges, and need not be explained here.

(249). *Spring-shaping tweezers and pliers.*—The tweezers are used for ordinary watch springs, and the pliers for the heavy springs of marine chronometers, which require more force to work them into shape. At the points, brass blocks are attached to the inner surfaces, one being made hollow, and the other rounding to fit into it. By heating the blocks, and then squeezing the spring between them, it is formed into a curve. Blocks formed to different curvatures are made, for making curves with more or less gradual changes of form. These are intended for making the terminal curves on Breguet and cylindri-

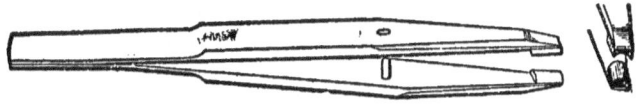

FIG. 18.

cal springs. Fig. 18 shows a pair of curve tweezers from Mr. Logan. Pliers are constructed in the same way, with wooden handles to prevent the heat from burning the fingers.

(250.) *Breguet spring benders* are made in different ways. The simplest and cheapest are heavy tweezers having a small pin near the point, and a pair of them further back, with space enough between the single one and the pair to receive the breadth of the spring wire. The pins fit in corresponding holes through the other point of the tweezers, so that when the tweezers are closed they pinch directly on the flat sides of the coil, while the pins prevent it from moving edgewise. The points of the tweezers are $\frac{1}{8}$ inch broad, and it would be advisable to have them curved inside to conform at least partially to the curvature of the spring coil. Fig. 19 shows elbow bend-

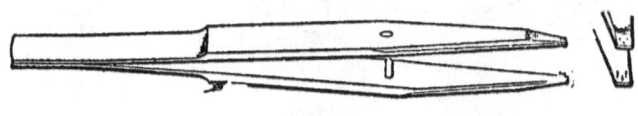

FIG. 19.

ing tweezers, as made by Mr. Logan. Two of these tweezers can be used to grasp the coil at the point where the elbow is to be made, and when the end of the spring has been bent up properly, shift them further along and bend it down, to get the supplemental coil level and parallel with the body of the spring. Or the edge of the spring can be rested on some convenient support, and one of the curve-shaping tweezers (249) be used to hold the coil vertical while being bent. Directions for forming elbows and terminal curves will be found in the chapters on the Adjustment for Isochronism.

(251.) *Poising tools.*—Different kinds are made, which it is unnecessary to describe. If desired, the workman could even file up two runners or centers to knife-edges, fitting into his depthing tool, in default of anything more convenient. Directions for using are given in sections (300, 301,) of Chapter XIX.

(252.) *Various other tools* are on sale, such as diameter gauges, tools for measuring the length of the cone formed in the "weighing" process, (210,) and some others, but as they are of but little assistance to the ordinary working watchmaker, they need not be described.

(253.) Adjusting ovens and ice boxes will be described in the chapters on the Compensation, Part Eighth; a motive-force controller, in section (673); a little tool for holding the Breguet spring while working at it, in section (650); a movement-holder for holding the movement in any desired position while timing it, in section (699); a collet turner, in section (289); apparatus for hardening and tempering compensation balances has already been described in section (120).

CHAPTER XVIII.

Fitting Hair Springs.

(254.) The one chief criterion by which every spring must be judged is this: Is it suitable for the balance it belongs with? If it is, the springer has but little more to do. If the balance itself is not suitable for the movement, or if the movement is not in proper condition, no possible manipulation of the spring can make the watch a fine timekeeper; but if they are suitable, very ordinary skill will enable the springer to secure good time. He should therefore see to those conditions as a necessary part of his work, which he can readily do, as those points have been very fully treated in Chapter II of Part First, in Chapter X, Part Third, and in Part Fifth.

(255.) *Fitting the flat spiral spring.*—I will give the method followed by good workmen in fitting the ordinary plain spiral spring. Fitting the Breguet and helical springs is fully treated in the chapters on Isochronism. It is not to be expected, of course, that pains will be taken to make the hair spring perfectly isochronal, when the workman gets only $1, (which is the price in many places,) for fitting and regulating it. Nevertheless he should have some regard for his own reputation, inasmuch as it will be but little more trouble to approximate very closely to correctness, if he knows how, than to fit the spring in such a manner as to render its good performance impossible. He will therefore understand that the directions to be given in these articles are essential to success, although I omit any discussion or explanation of the reasons therefor till we reach that part of the subject relating to isochronism.

(256.) *Proper condition of tools.*—All tools used in working around hair springs must be kept perfectly clean and dry, not allowed to become magnetized, nor touched with soldering-fluid or other corrosive substances, nor should any such things be allowed on the watch bench at all. Their place is upon the clock and jobbing bench. A pair of fine tweezers must be kept solely for this use. The points should be very slim and thin, flat and rough on the inside, hard tempered, the jaws broad and firmly connected so that they cannot yield sideways and let the points pass each other, and made to come easily together without giving any more spring or stiffness at the points than is just necessary to hold the spring, or a pin. *Too much strength* is the cause of pins snapping away and other "accidents" that bother the beginner, who imagines that the tweezers should not only carry the pin to its place, but hold it firmly enough to force it in. They must not be heated and softened, nor used as a pin punch, for picking teeth, cleaning finger nails, prying off watch dials, or corks out of oil bottles, or picking the sawdust out of keys, nor for anything whatever except working upon hair springs. But if the points do accidentally get injured, it will be a saving of time to put them in perfect condition again before you undertake to work with them. The same remark applies equally to all other tools. There is no surer sign of a good workman than that his tools are always in perfect working order.

(257.) *Ruined springs.*—If a spring has been very much distorted, it probably cannot be made perfectly true in the coils, although it may be true in the flat, and if it belongs in a fine watch, another spring should be fitted. Even if a distorted spring should be worked on with the tweezers till it was restored to exactly its former shape, it would not act the same as before. Every place where it has been bent and restored will be of a different stiffness from the original, and every such place exerts a disturbing influence, rendering a uniform action of the spring impossible. An inexperienced workman will often render a spring worthless for fine time-keeping simply by numerous changes and corrections of shape. A spring should not be bent or altered any more than is absolutely necessary, and any changes of shape should be made by littles, rather than by bending too much and then having to bend part-way back again. The injury caused by bending is greater in soft than in hardened springs. Hence Breguet springs should always be hardened, because they necessarily have to be bent more or less in perfecting the terminal curves.

(258.) *Selecting a spring.*—In selecting a spring for trial, the repairer should be governed largely by the size, number of coils and cross-section (*i.e.*, shape of the wire) of the old spring, unless you have reason to believe that it was not correct. The size is indicated by the position of the stud and regulator pins. The number of coils, if not known from the old spring, can be ascertained, for each kind of watch, by consulting Chapters in Part Fifth.

(259.) The spring should have the same general form and sensitiveness to changes of temperature as the balance to which it is attached, *i.e.*, a wide and thin spring should go with a balance whose rim is comparatively thin and wide, and *vice versa*. A spiral spring should be perfectly flat, evenly coiled, and preferably with the coils becoming more distant from each other as they proceed from the center, being about twice as far apart at the outside as at the center (see Section (574;) and Chapter VIII;) the wire should be of an equal temper, breadth and thickness, throughout its whole length, well polished and free from rust.

(260.) *Enlarging a spring.*—The diameter should generally be one-half that of the balance. If a spring cannot be found of just the right size, one of smaller diameter but having a suitable number of coils may be enlarged by the following process, which is also useful for spreading the coils apart when they are so close as to be liable to interfere with each other. Put the spring on a flat plate of either steel or brass, and over it another thin plate of bright steel, or, if of brass, with a hardened steel screw in the center to act as a color-piece (81, 82.) Heat the whole very slowly and evenly till the top plate or the color-piece becomes blue, then let it cool, and it will be found equally expanded, unless the top plate has been too heavy to allow of free motion. If not sufficient it can be treated in the same way again—as the temper will not be reduced any lower, provided that the heat is not at any time greater than will blue the *hardened* bright plate or color-piece.

(261.) *Flattening a spring.*—If a spring has been warped or bent out of flat, it may be flattened in a similar way, by fastening it *tightly* between two steel plates so as to *prevent* expansion and blue the upper plate, which will cause the spring to "set" perfectly flat. But in all these cases great care must be taken not to exceed the bluing heat or, if the spring is of any other color, not to carry the color of the hardened color-piece beyond the shade of the spring. When the spring has never been hardened and tempered, but merely rolled hard, it will open out too far and become too large when so treated. To prevent this, it should be wound up and the coils made closer and smaller, before heating. That can be done by the aid of the winding tool used in making hair springs (89 to 91), or by similar means.

(262.) *Bulged springs.*—If the center of the spring has been merely sprung up, the best way is to take the collet off the balance and slip it on your pin punch till it fits snugly, then take hold of the outer coil, or of the coil where the "bulge" commences, with a stiff pair of tweezers so that it can be firmly held horizontally, then push the center with the pin punch, in a direction exactly vertical to that in which you hold the outer coil, and the spring can generally be sprung back so truly as to be about as perfect as ever, and with very little trouble.

(263.) *Hardening rolled or soft springs, already made.*—When a watch is found to have a soft spring, *i.e.*, one which is not fire-hardened and tempered but only drawn and rolled, it can easily be hardened and tempered in its present form, by removing it from the stud and collet, taking out any accidental bends and getting it into correct shape, placing it centrally between two perfectly flat plates of copper, which are then screwed tightly together in the clamp shown in Fig. 6, section (120), heating it in the cyanide bath, (63), quenching in water, and tempering in an oil bath, or heating to a blue over a flame. If necessary, clean it in hydrochloric acid (60), again screw tightly in the clamp as before, being careful to get the screw central with the spring, lay a piece of steel on the upper plate, and heat *very slowly* till the steel comes to a blue. A spring so treated will have all the advantages of a hardened and tempered spring, and will time almost exactly the same as before— within a few seconds. The operation will expand the spring a little, and if that would be objectionable, it should previously be wound up in the spring box (90) to make it a little smaller. If the spring is of "mild" steel, it will require a higher heat to harden it (the last cherry red, (64, 78), or it may be so mild that it cannot be fire-hardened at all.

(264.) *The number of vibrations.*—In selecting a spring, it is necessary to know the number of vibrations it should make per minute or half-minute. This can be ascertained by counting the vibrations of that watch, or of one like it, for one minute. Directions for counting vibrations are given in Chapter XV, and for finding the number which that particular watch was intended to make, by counting the teeth and leaves of the train, in Chapter XIV. The general principle is as follows:—

As the center wheel revolves once per hour, we multiply the numbers of teeth in all the wheels from the center to the escape wheels, inclusive of both, into each other, and divide that result by the product of the numbers of the leaves in the pinions of all those wheels (except that of the center wheel), then double the quotient, as there are two vibrations to each tooth of the escape wheel. This gives the number of vibrations the watch makes in an hour, and dividing that by 60 gives the vibrations in one minute. Whenever there is a doubt, or the watch is of an unusual make, it is well to count up and calculate as above. If you have a movement which makes precisely the desired number of vibrations, you need only try your spring alongside of that, as described in (219,) and any divergence between them will be seen at once, without counting.

(265.) *Selecting by hair-spring gauge.*—Many workmen select springs by measuring their strength in some spring-gauge. This gives no indication of the number of vibrations it will make, but is merely a certain gauge number, which is of little or no value unless it can be compared with the strength of the old spring measured in *the same kind of gauge*, or with a spring which has already been tested by vibrating it with that particular balance, found not to give the proper number of vibrations, and then measured in the gauge. For instance, suppose that the spring, when stuck to the balance and vibrated, gave 250 vibrations in a minute, when we required 300. Instead of sticking other springs to the balance and testing them in the same way till we find one to suit, as is usually done, we can test the strength of our first spring in a hair-spring gauge—Bottum's or Logan's is too well known to need description—and examine the rest of our stock of springs by the gauge, without attaching them to the balance, and find what we want by calculation, by the following rule:—

(266.) *Rule for using hair-spring gauge.*—*The forces of two different springs, attached to the same balance, will be in the same proportion to each other as the squares of the numbers of vibrations which each makes.* Expressing this in the same way as was done in sections (133) to (137,) and taking F to represent the force (or gauge number) of the spring, we would have the following formula: $F_1 : F_2 :: V_1^2 : V_2^2$. Supposing that the spring tried gave 250 vibrations, when we want 300, and in the gauge the strength is, say, 20. Then our problem may be stated thus: If a spring which gives 250 vibrations per minute gauges 20, what must a spring gauge that will give 300 vibrations? According to our rule, the square of 250 will be in the same proportion to the square of 300, (the desired number of vibrations,) as 20, the force of our present spring, is to the force of spring which will give 300 vibrations—which is what we want to find out. We will therefore represent that unknown force by the letter x during this calculation, and having squared 250 and 300 (*i.e.*, multiplied each into itself,) we write the proportion down as follows: $62,500 : 90,000 :: 20 : x$. Now multiply the two end terms of the proportion together, and the two middle terms together, and the two products will be equal, according to the law of proportions. Multiplying, we get $62,500 \times x = 1,800,000$, and by dividing we find that one x is equal to about 29, which is the gauge of a spring that will make 300 vibrations per minute; or, to express our process more methodically, $x = \frac{90000 \times 20}{62500} = 29$, nearly. Having found among our stock of springs one that gauges 29, we have but little more to do. Of course, any other figures obtained by the workman in any particular case may be substituted for those given above.

(267.) *Allowance must be made* for the fact that some springs will be used with a wide, open center, others small; some will be held in the stud by the outer coil, others three or four coils from the outside—to suit the watch—and of course they must be held at the same place while measuring their strength or vibrating them.

(268.) *The usual method of selecting a spring* is to lay the balance bridge on the bench bottom upward, and with the regulator pretty well back toward the "slow," where it should be, then taking a spring which you judge likely to give the proper number of vibrations, (264), you place it on the bridge so that its center will come exactly at the pivot hole in the bridge, and one of the coils lying naturally and freely between the regulator pins. This coil can be marked, at a point about one-eighth of an inch back of the regulator pins, (*i.e.*, nearer the stud,) with a speck of rouge or whiting mixed with watch oil. That is the point which must be held in the tweezers while vibrating the balance or measuring the strength of the spring in the gauge. It is also the point to be held in the false stud, when using any of the fitting tools described in Chapter XVII. But to avoid repetitions, I will describe the process as performed with the tweezers, since the same method is followed with the other tools.

(269.) *Vibrating the balance.*—Having now put a little putty powder on the balance-staff, just below the shoulder of the upper pivot, (or the lower one, if more convenient, or on the shoulder where the collet goes), you stick the inner end of the spring to this putty, making a temporary but firm connection between the spring and the staff. Adjust the spring so that it will stand centrally and truly on the staff, then grasp it with the tweezers about one-eighth of an inch back of the point that lay in the regulator-pins, and, while the lower pivot rests on some hard, polished surface, you hold the balance upright by means of the spring, and cause it to vibrate. Care must be taken not to get so large a motion as to loosen the spring in the putty. By holding the coil in the tweezers pretty high, the spring can vibrate without coming in contact with the coils outside of the one held in the tweezers. The hand is rested on some convenient support. Instead of using putty as above, if the center of the spring is very small, and will have to be broken out, any way, the central coil may be bent so as to hug the staff tightly and dispense with the putty. But this should not be done when that coil will have to be bent back into shape again and used.

(270.) *Putty powder for holding springs* is a great improvement over the common way by using wax, as it can be readily dissolved off by placing in alcohol, and leave the balance perfectly clean. But nothing will thoroughly clean wax off except scraping; it will not dissolve off. Doubtless, if the truth was known, thousands of stoppages and timing faults would be rightly laid to traces of wax left on the pivots and other parts, making them sticky, etc.

(271.) *Counting the vibrations.*—Full instructions for starting the balance at the instant the seconds-hand of the regulator crosses its 60 are given in the preceding Chapters of Part Fourth, and the reader will do well to carefully consider all of the methods of counting vibrations described—testing them if necessary for a full understanding of their meanings and merits, and then select those which will be best suited to his temperament and facilities. He should not think that some of them must be superfluous because so many are described, for *every one* of them is useful and valuable, either generally or for special purposes, and he will be the loser if he disregards them. The same may be said with respect to the other details of this book.

(272.) Everything being in readiness, you set the balance in motion, and count the vibrations it makes in exactly one minute. It will be much easier if they are counted only in one direction, as from left to right; then double the number. As already stated in sections (221, 222), if you have a movement or a timing balance (218) making the proper number of vibrations, you can try your spring beside that, causing the two balances to vibrate together at first, and notice whether your spring lags behind or goes ahead. In either case, count the vibrations from the start till they come together again. If your spring loses a beat or gains one in fifteen seconds or less, it is certainly not suitable. It should not lose or gain *more* than a couple of beats in a minute. Or you can rest the balance-pivot on the glass cover of a movement-box, directly over the balance going underneath, and readily compare the two. These trials give you definite information about the performance of the spring and its suitability for the watch, while the gauge will only *compare it* with some other spring.

(273.) *Pinning to the collet.*—If the spring does not give very nearly the desired number of vibrations, or cannot be made to do so by shifting it in the tweezers a quarter or half coil, it is removed and another tried, and so on till one is found which meets the above requirements, when, in the case of a plain spiral spring, it may be pinned to the collet for a final trial. Aside from the convenience of using putty as described, for preliminary trials, there is a grave objection to pinning the spring to the collet at first. Collets differ much in size, and if a spring was cut out at the center to fit properly on a large collet, it would be greatly injured for any watch with a smaller one, if it did not happen to fit the one first tried. But with the temporary putty fastening no injury is done to the spring if it proves unsuitable. If it will be necessary, when pinning it to the collet, to cut out considerable of the inner end, additional length must be allowed at the outer coil to compensate for this shortening at the center—otherwise the watch will of course gain time. Springs are generally made small enough to fit the smallest collets, and often require considerable cutting to go on a large one. And if this additional length outside when allowed for would make the spring too large to lie freely in the regulator-pins, it must be rejected. This can be ascertained before cutting it, by again trying it on the inverted balance bridge. Before pinning the spring to the collet, see section (290) if the collet is not in poise. Also test the poise of the balance.

(274.) *The central coil.*—The manner of pinning it to the collet is important. There should not be a large vacant space at the center of the spring, but the inner coil should be only far enough from the collet to avoid any danger of touching it, even in the longest vibrations—but it must not be too close. We often find springs with the inner coil actually hugging the collet—a certain proof that the watch has been in the hands of a botch. Either end of the pin sticking out so that the coil can hit it, is another evidence of botchwork. The inner end of the spring should be put into the hole in the collet entirely up to the elbow, where the straight joins on the curved portion. From the elbow the curve should diverge from the collet in such a manner that it will meet the regular spiral form in about one-eighth of a coil from the elbow. This is better than running the spiral itself up to the collet, except when the coils are very wide apart, in which case the spiral should reach and be pinned directly to the collet. If the spring diverges too boldly from the collet, its action will not be good. On the other hand, if it diverges too slowly, it will lie so near the collet as to be likely to touch it when closely coiled up, or a minute speck of dirt wedged in between them would produce the same effect. No portion of the spring, however small, should rest on the collet, or on any dirt upon the collet, or on any pin, nor should any coil touch another, even at the extreme end of the longest vibrations the spring will make in use. The repairer should examine every doubtful hair spring that passes through his hands, turning the balance that distance with the finger in each direction, and holding it still while looking over the spring. Although a little out of its order here, I would also say that the spring must not touch anything above, below or around it, except the collet, stud and regulator, and them only at one point. All workmen know that this should be so, but they cannot know whether it *is* so, unless they move the balance to each extreme and hold it while they look as above. It is very common for *two* coils to hit the regulator or the stud.

(275.) *Central coil too open.*—If, however, there is more space at the center than is supposed above, the curve should take more length to reach the regular spiral portion of the spring, but in no case more than 90° or one-fourth of a coil. If that is not enough to reach the spiral, with a moderate divergence, the space is too large. The object we have in view is to bring the entire length of the spring, from the regulator to the collet, into action as uniformly as possible. Any considerable variation from the spiral form at the center causes irregularity of action, *i.e.*, an action different from that of the rest of the spring, and the greater this variation the greater the resulting irregularity. In springs which diverge very boldly, or which have a large open space at the center, this sweep or curve becomes a veritable "terminal curve," modifying the action of the whole spring, always difficult to change or adjust, on account of its position, and frequently defying every effort to neutralize its injurious effects upon the isochronism. It is even necessary sometimes to make the collet larger, or to change the spring.

(276.) *Pin the spring level.*—In pinning the spring many workmen fasten the end "any way it happens," then *bend* the central coil up or down to make the spring stand truly, not knowing that as soon as it is flexed it will be thrown out of its true plane by reason of this central twist. The spring should always be leveled before the pin is tightened, so that when fast it will be true without any twisting. The pin should barely reach through the hole, not sticking out at either end, and particularly not at its large end next to the elbow. It should be made either of hard brass or steel, stiff and tapering but little. After filing it up, flatten one side so that it will go in nearly as far with the spring in the hole as out, and while both are in the hole mark where it projects from the collet on each side, cut it off at the end, file a notch around it at the other mark, then force it to its place and break it off while in the hole. The small end should not be pointed, but flat, so that it can readily be pushed back for altering, if necessary. For this purpose you want a special pin-punch, made from a short needle, perfectly flat on the end, and firmly fixed in a substantial handle.

(277.) *Getting the spring level and concentric.*—While pushing the pin in or out of the collet, you should hold the latter flatwise (the pin-hole being outside of the end of the jaws), in a pair of pliers lined with soft iron or copper—by which you can hold it firmly without any need of marring it. The jaws also serve as guides in getting the spring flat. To try it, slip the collet on an arbor, and revolve it in the turns or calipers, either with a bow or with the fingers, noticing both the flat and also that the coils *rise evenly* from the center to the outside. But if, as your eye runs along the coil while it is turning, there seems to be any waving or "bobbing," the spring is not concentric with the collet, and must be made so by altering the central coil. Being true both in the flat and in the coil, you now put the collet on the balance-staff, and again try if the spring is flat and true, by whirling the balance in the turns, or even between the thumb and forefinger. The collet must be adjusted on the staff at such a hight that the spring, when pinned in the stud, will be perfectly level. If the collet end of the spring is higher or lower than the hole in the stud, the center will be bulged up or down, and satisfactory action will be impossible. It is important, for this reason, that the balance-staff itself should have no more end-shake than necessary.

(278.) *Pinning to the stud.*—Before pinning the spring in the stud, you now verify its proper length more closely, by again counting the vibrations while holding it with the tweezers, remembering that the point which is to go in the stud should be about one-eighth to one-fourth of an inch beyond the place where it gives the correct number of vibrations in the tweezers. This is to allow for the effect of the regulator. (This allowance is not needed when my fitting tool is used. See Chapter XVII). The exact distance will be about one-third less than the actual distance from the regulator to the stud, along the coil. Having placed that point over the hole in the stud, while the pivot is in its jewel hole, the outer coil should lie freely in the regulator, and the elbow or end at the collet must occupy a certain position relatively to the stud. Why that position is preferable to any other might be hard to explain, but experience has shown that it secures a better and more isochronal action, and it should therefore be adopted.

(279.) *Pinning in even coils or fractional coils.*—The mode of pinning the ordinary flat spiral spring depends upon the escapement of the watch. If it is to go in a cylinder escapement watch, the spring should be pinned about half a turn short of even coils, *i.e.*, if we draw a straight line through the center of the spring, the elbow or bend at the collet would be in that line on one side of the center, and the stud on the other side of the center. Thus it would generally have from $8\frac{1}{2}$ to $11\frac{1}{2}$ coils. See section (397.) For a duplex watch the coils should be pinned in the same way, (427), but for a lever watch the spring should be pinned in even coils. See Chapter XXVII. For a chronometer, the flat spiral spring is not used. Directions for the Breguet and cylindrical springs are given further on in this Chapter; also see Chapters XXVII and XXVIII.

(280.) *Pinning in even coils.*—For convenience of description, we will suppose that we are fitting a spring for a lever watch, and for any other kind the directions should be modified accordingly. For a lever, then, the elbow (the end at the collet) of the spring should lie in a line drawn from the center of the spring to the stud. If it varies much from this position, the isochronism of the spring will be more or less defective. Although the time shown by the watch at the end of each 24 hours may become correct, by dint of regulating, it will not be correct at any previous period,—nor afterwards, in case the watch is allowed to run over 24 hours before rewinding. It will either gain in the first 12 hours, and lose in the last 12, or the reverse, perhaps making a correct *average* for the entire 24 hours. Such watches must be wound regularly, at precisely the same hour each day, to secure even fair time. And in regulating them they must be timed at the end of each 24 hours, and at no other time during the day, as that would damage the regulation instead of improving it. But no watchmaker who cares for his reputation should let a job go out in this condition. The correction of this error will be fully treated hereafter. See Chapters on Isochronism and Regulating.

(281.) *Manner of pinning.*—But if the spring has been fitted as I have directed, you may proceed to pin it to the stud, with full confidence that it will perform satisfactorily. It should not have been done before, because at that point in the stud there is always produced a bend or crimp, by the pin forcing it to conform in shape to the hole, and if it should afterwards be necessary to let it out and bring the crimp into the acting portion of the spring, that stiff point would interfere with perfect performance. Even filing the pin flat on one side does not entirely prevent this. Hence it is advisable not to pin a spring unless it is reasonably certain that it will answer the purpose, and then it should be so pinned that it will surely be *long enough*, and that any necessary alteration will be made by taking it up, or drawing it further through the stud, not by letting it out. A spring may be selected, fitted and partly regulated in the watch before pinning it in the stud at all. But as springs occasionally need to be shifted, even after they are fitted, it might be a good idea in fine watches to pin them with a flatted pin on each side—unless some inventor can furnish us a stud with a slot instead of a round hole for the hair spring. It has been proposed to make a square steel punch, and hammer the stud upon it till the hole becomes square. If this plan is to be followed, however, it would be sufficient to have the punch square on one side only, leaving the other side of the hole round, as usual, for the pin.

(282.) The spring must be pinned perfectly solid, both in the stud and the collet, so that not the slightest change or yielding can occur. The larger end of the pin should be towards the body of the spring and should not project at all outside of the stud, so that under no circumstances can it affect the action of the spring, as it would do if it extended alongside of it even for a short distance. Enough spare spring must be left, when broken off, to have at least one-eighth to one-quarter of an inch beyond the stud, after the watch is regulated, to provide for future contingencies requiring it to be let out.

(283.) *The Regulator.*—A few words about the regulator are necessary, since even its purpose does not seem to be always comprehended. If we could make the ideal perfect regulator, it would be in effect a movable stud, which would allow of being shifted in either direction as the exigencies of the timing should require, but would then become the *end* of the working portion of the spring, holding it as firmly as the real stud does, and cutting off the part behind it from any influence upon the time of the watch. But since this cannot be practically realized—at least, it has not been done, so far as I know—we should come as near to this ideal as we can, by placing the regulator pins as closely together as possible, without binding on the spring when the regulator is shifted. The most perfect results in time are obtained when the regulator stands pretty well back towards the "slow," *i.e.*, near the stud—and, in fitting in a spring, if it does not give the correct number of vibrations with the regulator standing between the middle of its scale and the stud, the spring should be drawn further through the stud to shorten it, rather than move the regulator further towards the "fast."

(284.) *Position of the regulator pins.*—It may happen that the regulator pins are further from or nearer to the balance-jewel hole than the hole in the stud, and this should be looked into. If it was so, before the spring was fitted, it should have been looked to then. Sometimes, in putting the watch together, the regulator cap or center-piece gets screwed on the wrong way and causes the pins to stand further in than they should. If this is the cause of the trouble, reversing the cap will throw the regulator further out and obviate the need of bending the spring. Perhaps the regulator-pins can be bent out (or in, as required,) to reach the circle of the spring, and then *be made perpendicular* where the spring coil touches them. But if not, the spring must be bent near the stud to bring the outer coil within the circle of the pins as soon as possible, as, throughout the sweep of the regulator, the spring must lie *freely* between the pins, not pressing against either of them, when the balance is at rest. If there is considerable space between the pins, the spring should stand in the center of it. This position of the spring should be tested by screwing down the balance-bridge in its place and moving the regulator each way. If the spring must be bent, the bend should not be too abrupt at the point where the outer coil is made to become concentric with the regulator, but should be made far enough from the stud so that the change of direction it produces in the spring at that point will not be more than about 15°,—never over 25°.

Such an error is proof that there has been some mistake made either in the manufacture of the watch, or in subsequently fitting a regulator in it. The foregoing course will answer for ordinary work. In a fine watch, you should alter either the regulator or the stud, to avoid bending the spring. Which should be changed, may be judged by trying on it a suitable spring having the proper number of coils, and observing the space it requires, and whether it best fits to the stud or to the regulator.

(285.) *Testing the freedom of the spring.*—When it is correct, take the balance-bridge off, and lay it bottom upwards; having taken the stud out of its hole, place the pivot of the balance in its jewel, and hold the staff nearly upright with the tweezers. Then the spring should lie naturally in the regulator-pins, while the stud must hang freely directly over its hole and must point straight down into it, which will show that the spring is properly pinned and correctly shaped. If it is not as described, it must be made so, for the spring must have exactly the same form when loose as when it is secured in the watch for running, so that it may stand perfectly free from any twist or constraint during its vibrations. This is indispensable to its good performance. When the stud is a heavy bar, the above test cannot be applied, and, instead of that, the collet should be removed from the staff, and the bar screwed into its place, when the collet should naturally come exactly concentric, with the balance pivot-hole. If not, the spring should be bent to bring it so. We often see springs that are too large, with one side spread out, while the other is compressed within narrow limits. Also, springs twisted sideways at the stud, to go over or under a center wheel, and many similar makeshifts. Such jobs may be excusable when the owners will not pay a price for which the watchmaker can afford to do the work properly, but they should be given to understand that good service cannot be expected from them.

(286.) *Taking out the stud.*—In taking out the stud we often see workmen use a knife to pry it up, and, if it should come up more easily than was expected, the knife-blade suddenly slips across the bridge, and off goes the pivot. Tweezers have been made for pushing out studs—also pliers for the same purpose. But as good a way as any is to rest the arm of the bridge upon any convenient square-edged block of metal, say an inch thick, to allow the balance to hang down from the stud, or rest partially on the bench, while you push the stud out from above with a pin-punch of suitable size. As the end of the arm is supported by the top of the block, close up to the stud, which is in contact with its side, it is very easy to hold the bridge level under any amount of force required for pushing out the stud, without the slightest risk to any part. In Fig. 20, *a* is the block; *b*, the arm of the balance-bridge, and *c*, the stud.

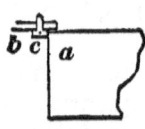

FIG. 20.

(287.) *Putting in beat.*—Putting the watch in beat is an operation that frequently troubles beginners, and sometimes those who are very far from being beginners. I will therefore give directions for so much as relates to the hair spring. Errors in the escapement, etc., will be treated in their proper places. When the power of the movement is cut off and the balance at rest, the position of the parts should be as follows:—

In the chronometer, the unlocking jewel should stand just on the outside of the unlocking spring, *i.e.*, not on the same side as the escape-wheel, or the unlocking side, but on the opposite side. See Chapter XXVIII. In the duplex, the slot in the roller-jewel on the staff should be between the point of the locking tooth resting against it and the line of centers. See Chapter XXVI for full information about the duplex. In the detached lever watch, the ruby pin should be in a line between the centers of the balance-staff and lever-staff, *i.e.*, on the line of centers. When the hair-spring stud is fixed to the balance-bridge, turn the regulator so that it will point to the lever-staff, while the bridge is screwed in its place in the watch, and you can use the regulator as a guide when the bridge is taken off and turned over. Then the ruby pin is easily put in line with the regulator while the balance-bridge is lying bottom upwards on the bench and the balance-pivot in its hole, and got very close before the spring is put into the watch at all. Then it can be tested by "sighting," or by placing a blunt screw-driver against the fourth wheel, or the one which carries the seconds-hand, and moving it very slowly so that the balance will vibrate as far in each direction as the lever carries it, but no further. Notice the position of the arm, or a screw in the rim, at each extreme, then turn the collet so as to cause it to stand at a point midway between them when at rest, and it will be in beat.

(288.) *In the horizontal or cylinder escapement*, the stud should be in line with the two impulse lips of the cylinder. But if the mechanism is not in its normal condition, and the watch does not prove to be in beat, upon trial, take your oiling-wire or a stiff bristle and with it move the balance very slowly each way till the escape-wheel tooth drops, but no further, noticing the position of the banking-pin on the rim, at each drop. Then place the pin halfway between these two drop-points, and hold the balance there while you "sight" a line through the center of the stud to the cylinder-pivot, and identify the point on the rim of the balance which is in that line, by means of some mark or stain, etc., or its distance from one of the arms, or in any other way. Then take off the bridge, remove from it the balance and stud, and turn the collet so that the stud will hang naturally in that line from the mark on the rim to the cylinder pivot, when the balance is held horizontally (385), and the watch will be in beat when put together, provided the spring is not forced out of its normal shape when the stud is fastened in its place. Full instructions for getting each kind of escapement in beat are given in the Chapter devoted to each one in Part Fifth.

(289.) *Turning the collet.*—Most workmen use a screw-driver or a knife-blade to shove the collet around with, and unless they move it very carefully it will slip off and "jab" into the spring; or it will pry open the cut and loosen the collet, rendering the watch liable to be thrown out of beat by jars, or even by running, making it unreliable for time and likely to stop. A tool can be made in a few minutes which will turn the collet without trouble or danger. Take a thin piece of steel, say a piece of the mainspring of an English lever watch, one-eighth of an inch broad, and hollow out the end into two claws or prongs—a long one on one side, and a short one on the other, as shown in Fig. 21. The latter should point towards the end of the former, and be so formed as to hook into the cut in the collet, while the former rests against the side of the collet. It is used by placing it flatwise on the spring, pressing it lightly against the collet, and *pulling*, not pushing, with the short claw in the cut. Mount it in a light handle, and keep the short claw in a good condition and a little under-cut.

FIG. 21.

The collet can be easily raised or removed by a small tool made of thin flat sheet steel, shaped like a very tapering screw-driver, with a slot filed in the center to receive the balance-staff. This tool being secured in a handle, the thin edge is inserted under the collet and pressed in, and moved to and fro sideways till the collet is lifted sufficiently.

The remaining portion of the fitting of hair springs is given in the next chapter.

CHAPTER XIX.

ON POISING.

(290.) *Poising the collet.*—After the watch is put in beat and is fitted for running, we must know if the balance (with collet and spring) is perfectly in poise, for if it is heavier on one side it can never give reliable time. The poise cannot be finally tested until now, with most watches, because they generally have an open cut in one side of the collet, making it lighter on that side; and it would be useless to finish the poise till the position of that cut had been fixed, as any turning of the collet for the purpose of putting the watch in beat would bring the cut into a different position and throw the balance out of poise again unless the collet itself has been poised. In good watches that should be done, as is done with chronometers. After the balance is perfectly poised, put on the collet, with the pin in its hole and also a piece of hair spring long enough to project $\frac{1}{16}$ inch out of the pin hole. If not in poise, file off the heavy side enough to make it so. A collet with a very wide cut should not be allowed in a fine watch, but rejected and a new one made with the cut closed.

(291.) *Poising the balance.*—If the balance has movable screws in its rim, the perfecting of the poise may be done by drawing out one of these screws a little. If much correction is needed, two or more screws should be drawn, so that their position would be altered but little, and nearly alike. But this mode of correcting the poise is not allowable with a cut balance, which is adjusted for heat and cold, but only for uncut or unadjusted balances, in cheap watches.

In a compensation balance there are generally four screws called "quarter-screws," or mean-time screws, which may be moved to perfect the poise, one at each end of the center-bar, and another pair midway between them on the rim. But the latter pair should only be moved very slightly, as it is likely to disturb the compensation for heat and cold; while the former pair will affect only the rate, and even this may be avoided by moving both screws to poise the balance,—one of them in, and the opposite one out, which of course maintains the *mean* distance of the two from the center of the balance the same as it was before, and does not affect the rate. See also (346). Plain balances are poised by filing away metal on the heavy side or adding weight on the light side, as by tinning, etc., (332, 333).

(292.) It is, of course, desirable that the balance should be in poise before the spring is put on, as that facilitates the final poising. Besides that, the parts then on the staff are considered fixed and permanent, but the collet and spring are movable; therefore the fixed parts, as a whole, should be poised, and then the movable parts prevented from destroying that poise. Inasmuch as our object is to get the balance in poise while running, it must be plain that it should be in poise with everything on it *exactly as it will be when running*. That is, the roller table, the hair spring and the collet, and all other parts should be on the staff; and if the collet or any other piece is not perfectly poised in itself, its final position must be determined before the poising is finished. In chronometers it is common to drill a hole in the roller-table, opposite the impulse jewel and notch, to make up for the metal there cut out and balance its weight; and a similar course would be desirable in fine lever watches, not only with the rollers, but also with the collet, as described in the preceding section.

(293.) *Poising the hair spring.*—By poising the collet in the manner stated, with a short piece of spring in the hole with the pin, as the hair spring will finally be, we get everything in poise except the hair spring itself. That cannot be poised with certainty. When the spring is finally pinned in the collet, we can tell whether it is approximately in poise by its concentricity. It is impossible to tell precisely how much of the outer coil or coils is supported by the stud. It may be just enough for the remainder of the spring, the weight of which is supported by the balance axis, to be just in poise—or it may be more, or less, according to the manner of pinning in the stud. The best we can do, therefore, is to poise everything that is rigid and can be poised with certainty, (290 to 292), then get the spring pinned *concentric*, as accurately as possible, when on the balance staff. Further observations on this point will be found in sections (294) to (297).

(294.) *Rule for poising the flat spiral.*—If the balance and the collet have been poised, (290, 292), and the hair spring fitted on as previously described, evenly and truly coiled and concentric with the balance, (277), and the inner end of the spiral reaches to the elbow at the pin, it will be unnecessary to do any more—in fact, very little more can be done with any certainty. But in fine watches, if the inner part of the spring is more open at the collet than directed, the collet should be poised with a piece of spring pinned in, corresponding in length, shape and weight, to all that portion of the spring (at the inner end) which deviates from the true spiral form. Examine the spring to find where it begins to deviate from the spiral form, towards the collet, and from that point to the end in the collet is the portion which should be poised with the collet, by pinning in a piece of spring as near like it as possible, correcting the poise by filing the collet (290.) It is then supposed that the truly spiral portion of the spring will, by itself, be practically in poise. Some workmen merely poise with the spring finally pinned in the collet, and call it right if an allowance for the waste end beyond the stud will make it in poise. But most workmen are content to poise the balance, then the collet, and fit the spring on concentrically without poising it at all.

(295.) *Difficulty of poising the hair spring.*—In Fig. 22 we have one coil of a spiral A, compared with a circle which coincides with the middle point of the spiral at d. The ends a and b are equally distant from the circle, and if we should poise it in the position shown it would be nearly in poise, because *a* is as much nearer the center as *b* is further from it; but the outer side, *e*, *b*, would be slightly the heavier, and with *a c* it would overbalance the part *c d e*. If we poise it with the *d a b* vertical, the outer half, *d e b*, will still further overbalance *a c d*, because the former is longer and also further from the center. It is evident, therefore, that the outer half of every coil will slightly overbalance the inner one. A spiral spring is composed of a number of such coils.

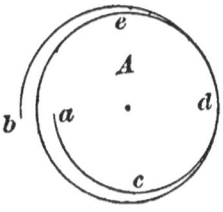

FIG. 22.

If the spring is pinned in even turns, as *B*, in Fig. 23, the lower halves of all the coils will be heavier than the upper. If there is a fractional part of a coil, as *C*, in Fig. 24, the frac-

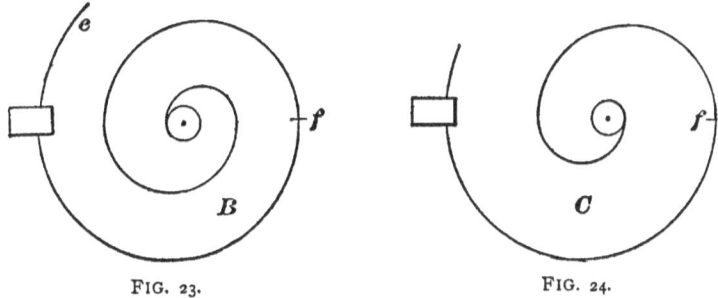

FIG. 23.   FIG. 24.

tional part, (from the stud to *f*,) will overbalance the outer halves of the complete coils.

(296.) *Disturbing effect of the stud.*—But even if it were possible to make any reliable calculations of the poise of the spring by its coils, the action of the stud would render them valueless. In Fig. 25, we have a spiral properly pinned in the stud and collet, *a* being the stud, and *b* the regulator pins. Now, how much of the spring is supported by the stud, and how much rests on the balance pivots, in the position shown? If the spring stands perfectly concentric and free at the center, more of the spring will rest on the pivots when the point *e* or *a* is uppermost than when *c* or *d* is at the top, because the spring yields more easily when the curve is opening or straightening than when closing. This shows that even if we could get the spring perfectly poised in one position, it would not be in poise when in a different position. So far as concerns the poise, the outer end of the spring is virtually at the point where the stud *ceases to support the coil.* And as that point is constantly shifting, we never can tell where the virtual end is, nor which half of the coils is the outer half, nor whether we ought to poise for complete coils or for a part of a coil.

(297.) *Effect of excentric spring.*—But as the spring is seldom pinned so perfectly that it is truly concentric, but is generally

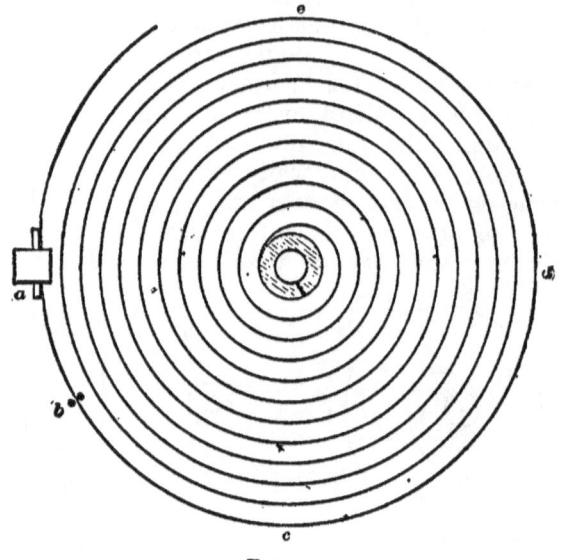

FIG. 25.

sprung to one side, that causes still greater variation and uncertainty, for the stud may in such cases support anywhere from one to half a dozen coils. The poise is not only uncertain, but its effect is so much smaller than that of the side pressure on the pivots as to be of comparatively small consequence. In watches, the weight of the spring is so trifling, and so near the balance axis, that, if the spring is pinned concentrically in the collet, (277), there cannot be a poise-error of any consequence in the spring, and if there is any such error found by timing, we may conclude that it arises from the spring not being pinned concentrically at its outer end, and not from imperfect *poise* of the spring. These explanations will show the correctness of the statement in section (294) that, if the spring is properly fitted in as there described, it is not only useless but impossible to poise it any further.

(298.) *Poising the Breguet spring.*—All that can be done is to have the balance, and then the collet, in poise, so that the collet can be turned in any position without disturbing the poise.

Whether it will then be in poise when running will depend on how much of the spring is supported by the stud, and can only be told, if it can be told at all, by testing it while running, as in section (302).

(299). *Poising the cylindrical spring.*—The balance should first be poised with all its fixed parts in their proper positions, (or, what is better, with each roller separately poised,) but without the collet bar. Then the spring, with its inner terminal curve formed, (but before the other curve is bent up,) is properly pinned in the collet, and poised to see if the body of the spring is concentric with the balance. In doing this, if the spring is not in even coils, *i.e.*, if there is a fractional part of a coil, counting from the collet end, there should be a preponderance of weight on the side where the outer end is, corresponding to so much of the spring as exceeds the complete coils. This allowance is judged as to its correctness by the judgment of the experienced workman, or is tested by hanging an equal length of similar spring wire on the opposite arm of the balance and at an equal distance from the center. If that does not balance it, the body of the spring is probably not concentric with the balance axis, and should be changed by bending at the collet end or curve, till correct. Some workmen merely poise with a duplicate of the inner terminal curve pinned in the collet bar, as for the flat spring (294), making the correction by filing the collet, and get the body of the spring concentric by eye, by whirling the balance in the calipers or turns. In either case the final test is by running it in positions (302). It is generally supposed that, if the terminal curves are properly formed, the center of gravity of the entire spring will be on the balance axis when running. But that is an error. Springs with terminals require poising as much as any others.

(300.) *Poising tools.*—There are two kinds of poising tools, the notch and the straight-edge. It is best to do the main portion of the poising upon the notch tool, using the straight-edge for the final tests only, as much time will be saved thereby. The poising tool consists simply of two jaws or pieces of hard metal, whose distance apart can be changed to suit the length of the piece being poised. By making suitable notches in a straight-edge tool, you have both kinds in one. The jaws may be of either brass or steel, with the edges perfectly straight, smooth, polished and thin, like two knife blades, parallel to each other and with the edges upwards. At each end of the jaws may be made a pair of notches—one pair fine, the other larger. The notch should be about the depth and a little *wider* than any pivot that is to go in it, the bottom semi-circular in form, and the edges filed very thin so as to present almost a knife edge to the pivot, and must be kept clean and polished.

(301.) The staff should be so placed in the notches that they will not rub on the shoulders of the pivots. If the balance seems to be correct and does not turn of itself, whirl it with a bristle, and if it stops with all sides up, indifferently, it may be placed on the straight edges, which should be levelled and made horizontal so that there will be no tendency for it to roll. It is not necessary to whirl the balance here, but simply place it with different sides up, and if it shows no disposition to change its position it is in poise, for there is no friction on the pivots to prevent it rolling over if there was the slightest tendency to do so. Whirling the balance will inevitably cause one or the other of the shoulders to bring up against the jaws, and necessitate another test. But a well fitted notch leaves little to be desired, or accomplished by the straight edges.

(302.) *Testing the poise.*—The poise may be tested after the watch is running, by timing it for 3 or 6 hours each in the four vertical positions, *viz.*, with figures XII and VI, III and IX alternately upwards, and if the times are the same in the different positions, the balance is supposed to be in poise. Rules for correcting the poise will be given in the Chapter on Adjusting for Positions. But if the foregoing directions are carefully followed, we may safely say that any error of poise will not be due to the spring. But in order that this test should be trustworthy it is necessary that the balance jewel holes be well fitted to the pivots, the escapement in perfect order, and the lever poised, so that there may be equal friction in each position; and the watch must be wound up an equal distance for each test, so that the motive force may be the same in each position. Otherwise, errors due to unequal friction or action, imperfect fitting, or lack of isochronism in the spring, may be erroneously ascribed to want of poise in the balance.

(303.) *Oiling the escapement.*—When everything is done, so that you are sure you will not have to take the balance out again, a little oil should be put to the jewel holes, they and the pivots being, of course, perfectly clean. Put in barely enough oil to fill the *holes* but not stand at all in the oil-cup or concavity of the jewels. If it seems to be soon drawn away by capillary attraction between the hole-jewel and the end-stone, put in a little more. But put no oil on the pallets of a verge; a very little only on the long impulse-lip and the escape-wheel teeth of a cylinder; a very little on the pallets of a lever watch, but none on the ruby pin nor in the notch of the lever; a little on the roller-jewel of a duplex staff, but none on the impulse pallet; none on either the unlocking- or impulse-jewels of a chronometer, none on the detent-pallet, and but little on the balance-pivots. Use none but the very best watch-oil to be had at any price. Keep the bottle closed and in the dark; keep your oil-cup perfectly clean and covered; put but little oil in it at a time, and fill it often with fresh, wiping it perfectly dry and clean with paper every time you fill it. Make an oiling-wire by taking the temper out of a sewing-needle, file it tapering to a point as fine as a hair, then turn over the extreme end, and make the smallest possible loop or ring, so close that you can see no hole in the center, and mount it in a light handle. This loop will take up all the oil that any ordinary hole ought to have. Keep it away from soldering fluid, water or dirt, and keep it out of your mouth. Of course, if the balance, spring, etc., are at all greasy or dirty, they should have previously been hung on a wire hook and moved about in a bottle of benzine for a few seconds, then dried by exposure to the air.

(304.) *Regulating the watch.*—The spring being properly fitted, everything poised, in beat and oiled, nothing remains but regulating, unless the spring is to be adjusted for isochronism. Full instructions for timing the watch quickly are given in Chapter XX; for regulating generally in Chapters XXI and XXII, and for fine timing or rating in Chapter XXIII. The isochronal adjustment of the spring is treated in Part Sixth. Although I have dwelt upon a large number of details, the workman should remember that it will take but little more time to do his work rightly, if he understands how it ought to be—and it has been the object of these explanations to clearly show the proper method, so that when his work is done it will be correctly done.

CHAPTER XX.

Quick Ways of Bringing a Spring to Time.

(305.) *By comparison of balances.*—Take as the standard a movement giving the same number of vibrations as required for your trial watch, and which is very closely regulated. Arrange it in a movement box or otherwise so that its balance can be plainly seen. Start the balance of the trial watch to vibrating synchronously with the timing balance, *i.e.*, starting at the same instant and in the same direction. Watch them closely, and, as soon as the trial balance perceptibly gains on the other or falls behind, you move the regulator of your watch to correct that error, and start again. Do this till your balance does not vary perceptibly in one minute, and it is regulated within about one minute per day. If it does not vary perceptibly in five minutes, it will run within 15 or 20 seconds per day. Of course, it is not necessary to watch it all the while, but merely look at it occasionally, to detect the slightest variation. You could be regulating a number of watches at the same time. This is the quickest method known for regulating a watch in a few minutes.

(306.) *By opposition of balances.*—Some are not quick enough to follow the foregoing method with certainty, and they should wait till the two balances get in opposite phases of the vibration, *i.e.*, one will be moving at its greatest speed while the other comes to rest and begins its return vibration. If this can be clearly seen, so as to know that each balance stops just at the middle of the vibration of the other, this variation will mean a gain or loss of half a vibration on the other balance. If you know how long the time is since the start, say one minute, that would be varying $\frac{1}{10}$ second per minute, in an 18,000 train, and would show you how much to move the regulator. But it is not necessary to know the time. You only need to know positively whether the trial balance gains or loses, and that shows how to move the regulator.

(307.) *By reversal or coincidence of balances.*—If you do not find it easy to decide when the balances are in opposite phases, you can wait till they move in opposite directions, which means that the trial balance has either gained or lost one vibration on the other. This is easy to see, in most cases; if not, let it go a while longer till it vibrates in the same direction and starts at the same time as the timing balance, which indicates a gain or loss of two vibrations, or $\frac{2}{5}$ second, in an 18,000 movement. These methods do not require any counting or observation of time, although the process of regulating would be made more definite and certain by observing the length of time the trial has lasted. But even that does not require to be done so closely as is necessary by other methods of regulating.

(308.) *Long trial by comparison of balances.*—When you have your watch so closely regulated that there is no perceptible difference between the balances, you can make a long trial, by starting your watch exactly with the other, then hang it up, examining it, say, every ten minutes, till you see a variation. Turn the regulator to suit, start again, and try it for an hour. If your balance has only gained or lost perceptibly (305) in an hour, (say, ¼ of a vibration,) that would be only about one second per day. In this way, or even by one of the other methods described, you can regulate a watch closely in a few minutes, while being also engaged in other work, merely watching it enough to see when the vibrations are in opposition or reversed.

(309.) *Regulating to a fraction of a second per day.*—In rating a fine watch, this method gives the closest results of any that can be followed outside of a well-equipped observatory. After getting your watch so closely regulated that you can see no difference between the two balances after running it for an hour, as described in the preceding section, you try it for a day in the same manner. For the sake of being sure that you are right, you compare the balances every two hours during the first half of the day, and if, at the end of the twelve hours, you can see no perceptible difference between them, you continue the trial over night. In the morning, you first compare their seconds-hands, to be certain that both watches are still giving the same vibration, *i.e.*, if both of them pass a division on the dial at the same time. If your watch was a beat or two before or behind the division mark when the other was just on it, yours has of course gained or lost so many beats. But if both strike the mark at the same instant, and their jumps or movements exactly coincide, you will know that they only differ by a part of a vibration. You then compare the balances, to find what the difference between them is, and whether your trial watch is ahead or behind. If the balances are in opposition, *i.e.*, one is reversing while the other is in full motion, the difference is half a vibration, or, in an 18,000 train, $\frac{1}{10}$ second for the 24 hours since the trial began. If more, or less, you can tell what it is by sections (305) to (307). Also, see sections (215) to (222). Of course, you require a very accurate timing watch for such regulating. A box chronometer specially adjusted to positions, with a glass over the movement, would be better yet. But if you have a first class timepiece to compare with, there is no difficulty whatever in following this method, except that you must be quick-witted in comparing the balances.

(310.) *By counting the vibrations by ear.*—This is the quick method usually followed, and may be adopted by those who cannot well use the preceding methods. When the watch is cased, hold it to the ear with the left hand, having the pencil in the right. After getting the ear well accustomed to *the period* of the ticks, begin counting them as the regulator seconds-hand touches 60, marking down every 10 beats, till the end of the minute. If there were more (or less) than the proper number of beats given, move the regulator to slow (or fast), and try it for another minute—and so on till you get the right number. Then you can keep on counting for 2, 3, or 5 minutes, if you wish to get it very close, immediately. One beat in 5 minutes would (in an 18,000 train) be 12 seconds in 5 hours, or about one minute per day. Instead of the regulator, the seconds-hand of a box chronometer or good watch will answer.

(311.) *Same, if movement is not cased.*—The easiest way is to get the image of the regulator seconds-dial in a mirror before you, (see Chapter XII, sections (172 to 174),) so that you can keep both it and your trial balance in the eye, count the vibrations as before, and proceed as there directed. By getting the period of the vibrations well in mind, and especially by nodding the head in unison with them, you can look at the image of the seconds-dial long enough to know the exact beginning and end of the minute without losing the run of the vibrations. Both the nodding and the counting aloud greatly assist in keeping track of the vibrations and the number. The reader will do well to frequently consult the Chapters on counting vibrations, to find points which he can adopt with advantage. By either of the above methods he should remember that a chronometer gives only one *tick* to two vibrations, and he should double the number of beats counted to get the number of vibrations. He can perhaps think of some *combinations* of the methods given, which might be specially convenient for him—say, by the use of a vibration marker, mirrors, counting backwards, etc., with parts of the above, *i.e.*, using a part of one method and another part from another method, to make up a complete working method. That is not necessary, however, as some of the methods given are sure to meet any case that can come up.

CHAPTER XXI.

REGULATING WATCHES.

(312.) *Regulating, as distinguished from rating or timing.*—Strictly speaking, regulating would come under the head of timing; but practically, regulating is the coarser branch of the work. It has no reference to any trials for or tests of isochronism, positions or compensation, but consists merely in moving the regulator or changing the length or strength of the hair spring to bring the watch to time under ordinary conditions of usage. Anything which varies to exceed half a minute per day is not being rated, but regulated. It is not in fit condition to be rated. The term regulating also applies to watches which have been cleaned and repaired, but nothing has been done connected with the adjustments.

(313.) Another and perhaps plainer distinction is this: We may call it regulating when it is not necessary to go by seconds, but is sufficiently close if we only need to set the watch by its minute-hand. Thus defined, this Chapter will apply to all ordinary watch repairing, including at least nine-tenths of the hair springs and other jobs done by the trade. Consequently, while not a part of the adjustments, it is a part of the springer's work, and therefore entitled to an honorable place in the MANUAL, since the adjustments cannot be made satisfactorily till *after* the points included in this chapter have been conscientiously attended to. Although not fine work, it is very essential and important, and the reputation of the watchmaker in the community depends far more upon his skill and thoroughness in regulating than in adjusting. It will be for his advantage to bring his regulating as near to being adjusting as he can afford to do, and to habitually employ as many of the methods and means used in the adjustments as can be easily adapted for the purposes of regulating. With this principle in view, I have included in this chapter several points—particularly those on regulating Breguet springs—which would ordinarily be treated under the head of Rating.

(314.) *Put everything as it was before.*—Regulating a fine watch is an operation which but few workmen are capable of doing properly, or, indeed, without injuring it. And even with the cheaper grades of time-pieces, there is more in it than many suppose. When a watch is merely cleaned, or the repairing of it does not require any alteration of the hair spring, the greatest care should be taken, especially with fine work, that it be put together precisely as it was before. The regulator should be at the same place, and the hair spring should occupy the same position between the regulator pins, as before it was taken down. To insure this, a careful examination should have been made, with the balance at rest, free from the motive force of the mainspring, and the position of both the regulator and hair spring noted down—for in a fine watch both of them have probably been carefully adjusted, and changing either of them or opening or closing the regulator pins might seriously damage the adjustment. Even in cheap watches, following this rule will frequently save several days in bringing them to time. Also, count the number of vibrations per minute and note it down. If the number is correct, it will assist you in regulating; if not correct, *i.e.*, not the number the train was designed to give, (Chapter XIV,) it will put you on track of some fault that should be remedied.

(315.) *Pre-requisites of the timing.*—But if a watch does not perform satisfactorily on trial, or if the workman is sure from inspection that it will not do so, the defective conditions must of course be changed and corrected. I have already stated how the hair spring should be pinned in the collet (273 to 277), and stud (282); that it should be perfectly free from constraint when fastened in the movement, (285); that the outer coil should stand perfectly free between the regulator pins as they are moved through the whole of their sweep from "slow" to "fast," not moving nearer to or against either pin at any point in the sweep; and that the regulator should stand pretty well back towards the "slow" when the watch is regulated. The pins should both be tight in their places, so that they cannot yield any when the spring presses against them. If one of them has a foot to close the bottom of the opening between them, the spring should be entirely free from it, nor should any dirt be allowed to accumulate there and touch the spring.

(316.) *The regulator.*—As a general rule, the regulator pins should be as close together as possible and yet leave the spring free between them, (586). But if they are found otherwise, they should not be closed without good reason, for they may have been so opened for a purpose, by some one who fully understood the effects of so doing. But wide pins may justly be regarded with suspicion. The effect of having the pins very open is not only to render the spring less susceptible to control by the regulator, but also to cause sudden and violent checks to its motion, making uniform progression of force difficult, if not impossible. Moreover, the spring vibrates upon the pin against which it rests, as a fulcrum or pivot, moving in one direction on one side of the pin, while back of it it yields in the opposite direction. Sometimes the spring will even slide along the pin with every vibration. In either case, an irregularity of motion results which is injurious to its proper action, and should be avoided whenever the position of the regulator pins comes within the scope of the repairer's duty.

(317.) *Time of winding.*—Many watchmakers do their winding and regulating at night. This is all right for watches known to be in perfect order, and therefore needing nothing but regulation. But for custom watches, the preference is to do it the first thing in the morning, so that if any alterations or examinations are needed they can be made at once. If a watch is found still, or acting strangely, at night, it may start on before morning, and every workman knows that the best time to examine into any trouble is while that trouble is yet in operation and can be seen, but it may escape notice or require a long search if allowed to pass on. Besides, this work is a good preparation for the more serious labors of the day. No one feels like sitting down to the bench in the morning and plunging right into some delicate job the first thing, but after winding he is ready to take hold of anything that is waiting for him. Use always solid-pipe, well-fitting bench keys for winding. Careless workmen ruin more winding-posts and bend more teeth by not following this rule than their heads are worth. When winding, turn the key, but hold the watch still. Many persons twist the watch as much as they do the key, at the risk of overbanking, breaking off the ruby pin, stoppage, etc.

(318.) *Proper order in regulating.*—In regulating, there is a certain order to be followed. Workmen often find watches stopped, and after cautious examination and perhaps much loss of time, discover that they had forgotten to wind them; or they find a watch more out of the way after regulating than before, and cannot tell whether they had set it or not, after turning the regulator; or they will wind and set, but forget to regulate it. The proper way is first to change the regulator, the hands remaining as they were, so that no mistake can be made about the correct change required. If you should forget, or be called away for a moment, the hands are still as they were, so that you can see what the error was. Next wind the watch, lastly set it. After winding always give the watch a little shake, or be sure that it is going, as cheap watches often stop from winding or turning the hands backwards, etc. After winding all your watches glance over them, and if every one is properly set to time, you may be sure that they are also regulated and wound. Otherwise, you cannot be certain. By following the above rules *invariably*, you will never have any doubts or mistakes. In regulating fine watches, either keep a memorandum book, or attach a tag to each, and note down the error and the date, thus: "Aug. 10, 45 s. fast," "Aug. 12, 52 s. fast, Reg. and Set." Or the foregoing can be abbreviated into " 12. 52 s.f., R. S." In this way you will know how long a time the watch has been in making the error, and what effect your previous alterations had; also whether the rate was regular or varied. Always turn the regulator too little rather than too much, and in fine alterations use the eye-glass to observe the amount of movement it has received, especially if it has a tendency to spring back. For further instructions see Chapter XXIII, on Rating.

(319.) In *setting the hands* of a lever or cylinder, if they do not turn hard and the movement is in good condition, they may be moved either forward or backward,—the way which will require the least turning. But if they move at all hard, and the lever is short, they should be turned forward only, or the balance pivots may be bent or broken, or the watch stopped. Chronometers and duplex watches should commonly be turned forward only. (See Chapter XXII, sections (341) to (343). Repeaters, alarm watches, and all complicated movements should always be turned forward, by the customer, and by the workman also, unless he is perfectly familiar with the requirements of the movement in hand. If the hands move quite hard, they should not be turned at all, as damage is almost sure to be done, but the difficulty should be ascertained and remedied immediately. See Chapter II. All of the foregoing and any other defective points in the movement should have been examined while taking it apart, and all repairs made either at once or at least before cleaning. But I have mentioned them here, because they are among the pre-requisites of the timing.

(320.) *Setting to seconds.*—In setting your watch to seconds, do it by stopping the balance. I have seen those who claimed to be fine workmen twisting the seconds-hand forwards and backwards as if it were merely an ornament to the dial. The seconds-hand, when properly placed, should be firmly secured upon its pivot, so that it cannot be accidentally shifted. If it is loosened up for setting, it must be afterwards pressed down again, which will frequently cause an error of one or two seconds, and perhaps the watch is stopped, or the upper fourth-wheel jewel cracked. Or, it may go on too far, and must be pried off again, making another error, etc. The quickest and best way is to stop the watch when the seconds-hand is just on the 60, by placing the bristle on the balance, which should be drawn around far enough to start instantly with a good motion when the bristle is raised. Then set your minute- and hour-hands.

All trials and observations should begin and end when the seconds-hand on your regulator is at the 60, unless the seconds-dial of your watch is imperfectly spaced off; if so, then at the nearest 60 upon that.

(321.) *Variations in running.*—In regulating a watch, the workman should remember the distinction between an error in the rate and one arising from its not being in good condition. Having set it accurately, we examine it at intervals and compare its time with the standard. If it gains or loses an equal amount in each six hours after being wound and set, and four times as much at the end of the twenty-four hours as at the end of the first six, or even if it gains or loses the same amount in the last twelve hours as in the first twelve, the error is one of rate, and can be corrected by the regulator. In such case, we say it "gains," or it "loses," so much per day. But if it gains in the first twelve hours and loses in the last twelve, or the reverse, then we say it "varies," and the fault is not in the rate but in the condition of the mechanism—generally a non-isochronal hair spring, (280, 517), and a variation in the motive force. The only remedy for this is to remove its cause, as directed in the Chapters on Isochronism.

(322.) *Regulating a varying watch.*—Such a watch can only be regulated to produce a correct *average* at the *end* of each day, (280) and the customer must be impressed with the importance of winding it at precisely the same hour every day. It does not matter much what hour that may be, only he should choose one in accordance with his habits and which he will be sure to remember. Furthermore, he must compare its time with the standard regulator at the same hour of the day, for if he compares it in the forenoon at one time, and in the afternoon or evening the next time, regulating and setting on each occasion, his watch will soon keep no time at all. He may even set it in the forenoon, and in the afternoon of the same day find it a minute or two out of the way, while it may be right again the next forenoon, twenty-four hours after setting, if it is not disturbed. A workman who fully appreciates this point may make quite inferior watches give tolerable satisfaction, while if he alters the regulator for the customer whenever he happens to come in the shop, or allows him to do it himself, his reputation as a workman will soon "peter out."

(323.) *Proper care of watches.*—When watches are hung up they should not rest against a hard backing, as a plastered wall, etc., nor be allowed to swing upon their hooks. Nor should they be subjected to any jarring or trembling of the supports to which they are attached. Especially to be avoided is a regular or periodical jarring or thumping, whose intervals may be in unison with the vibrations of the balance, whether exactly so, or coinciding alternately, or in any similar way. They should also be protected from both cold and heat, moisture and dust, and the customers must be instructed not to lay them on marble, metal or other substance that will rapidly abstract their warmth. Watches should not be opened where the air is much warmer than they are, as the moisture of the air is condensed by contact with the cold movement, causing rust of the steel parts on which it settles. The workman must keep the watch as nearly as possible at a uniform temperature while *regulating* it. If it is to be compensated for heat and cold, that is a separate adjustment, which has nothing to do with the rating.

(324.) *Position at night.*—If watches are hung up during the day, while regulating, they should retain the same position at night; and if laid down days, they should also be laid down nights. A common watch will vary in different positions, but you are not to attempt to correct that error by regulating. After it has been closely regulated for hanging, in the shop, the finishing touches should be given while it is in actual use, and subjected to the regular treatment customary with its owner, who *should be instructed to follow precisely the same routine every day.* If he carries it during the day, and hangs it up at night, he should hang it up *every* night. If he lays it down at night, it should invariably be laid down, horizontally, and with the same side up, and protected as directed in the preceding section. Fine watches vary less from such causes, but they are also expected to run more closely than others, so that these rules are beneficial in all cases. It is by attending to such little matters that satisfaction is given, and it cannot be done without.

(325.) *How to carry a watch.*—If the watch cases are thin, they should be carried where no undue pressure can come upon them, to force them down upon the end of the center post, and stop the hands or the watch itself. Always examine the inside of the case to see if there are any marks of touching. If so, the post must be shortened or otherwise protected. Ladies' watches often run very irregularly, or stop, from being squeezed too tightly in their belts. But it is not much better to carry them in their bosoms, as they are kept too warm and moist. The best place is a pocket in the dress-skirt just below the belt, made of a size to fit the watch. The pocket should not be too low. As for chatelaine watches, the workman should never promise that they will keep good time, for it is impossible for them to do so—swung and flopped and jerked and knocked about in the way they are. The best place, for a man, is a pocket in the pants, where the watch will rest upon the abdomen, and be less affected by pressure and blows, than if resting against the unyielding ribs.

(326.) *How to correct errors.*—If we find that the error in the rate of our watch is so great that the regulator will not correct it, or if the regulator is already at the limit of its sweep, our course must be guided altogether by the circumstances of the case. Certain remedies may be justifiable in cheap watches, which would not only be utterly inexcusable in fine work, but would render the workman liable to prosecution for malpractice and payment of damages for the injury done. We will first consider the treatment of common watches, reserving the questions connected with the regulation of the finest movements, without injuring any of their adjustments, for subsequent treatment, as there is considerable to be said on that subject.

(327.) *Altering the hair spring.*—If the watch loses time, we can take up the hair spring enough to approximately correct the error, and finish by the regulator. Before taking off the balance-bridge, see if the watch is in beat. If not, notice in which direction the error is, and how much. An over-sprung watch, and some others, can often be put in beat without taking out the balance or stud, (removing only the balance-bridge,) by the use of the tool named in (51). But it is safer, generally, to take the balance out. First note the distance of the stud from the nearest arm of the balance, or from some screw in the rim, or other mark, and also the distance required to place it in beat, which will show what position the stud should have when in beat. Now draw the spring through the stud the proper distance, and pin again. Next loosen the stud and take out the balance, bend the spring, if necessary, to bring it into proper shape (284, 285,) and move the collet around till the stud takes the correct position as noted above. See also (287). If the watch gains, we let out the spring in the same way. ⚹

(328.) *Grinding the hair spring.*—But if it gains and we have no spare spring to let out, we have three remedies, besides fitting a new spring. First, we can grind the spring on its under edge, till we reduce its breadth and weaken it sufficiently. To do this, take a flat piece of soft cork, considerably larger than the spring and half an inch thick. Make one side very flat and smooth, then cut a hole in the center to allow the collet to be forced in with one or two central coils while the grinding is going on. In a watch of any value, the collet should be taken off the spring. Spread the spring evenly on the cork, which should first be oiled a little to secure its adhesion, then lay the cork carefully down on a clean, sharp oil stone, or a ground glass plate smeared with oil stone dust and oil. Before moving the cork at all, press it down hard, to slightly imbed the coils in its surface, and cause them to retain their position while grinding, then rub it over the stone in circles in all directions, so as to grind the spring as evenly as possible. Keep the stone well oiled, (or the glass well supplied with oil-stone dust,) don't grind too fast, press the cork down flatly by the finger on its center, do not move the cork without pressing it down nor lift it up till you have finished. Then take it from the cork, absorb the oil by paper, and finish by soaking in alcohol, dry, replace the collet on the balance-axis, pin in the stud, put in beat and try.

(329.) *A better way.*—A more perfect way, when the spring needs much grinding, is to remove the collet and cement the spring with shellac on the plate used by workmen for flat polishing, make the cement perfectly liquid by heat, press the spring down to the metal to get it flat, and hold so till cold. Adjust the leveling screws so that the spring will bear evenly on the polishing surface, then grind as much as thought necessary; heat the polisher enough to remove the spring, and remove the shellac in boiling alcohol. Should the spring be soft, or from any other reason there should unfortunately be a "feather-edge" of metal on the coils, it must be removed by dipping the spring in acid, (330.) I have sometimes found springs on which the workmen had left long fibres like hairs, caused by this feather-edge splitting off, and preventing any proper motion of the spring.

(330.) *Weakening with acid.*—To weaken a spring with acid, it should first be cleaned from grease, etc., so that the action of the acid will be all over alike. This may be done by soaking it in absolute alcohol, or in a warm solution of caustic soda in water—such as is used to clean articles for electroplating. If the latter method is adopted, it should afterward be soaked in clean water, then in alcohol. It is best to remove the spring from the collet during this process, but if it is not, after drying it off, put a very little oil at each end of the hole in the collet, to fill the hole, and keep the acid out, or fill it with thick shellac and alcohol. The acid is made by mixing in a watch-glass five drops of water and one drop of the strongest sulphuric or nitric acid, or more in the same proportion. Or use chemically pure muriatic acid 1 part, and water 2 parts. This is best, as it does not blacken the spring like the others. Mix well with a bit of glass, and immerse the spring for a few seconds, or until it becomes black. No time can be specified, as it depends on the strength of the acid, size of spring, and amount of action wanted, but great care must be taken not to eat the spring too much.

(331.) Rinse the spring thoroughly in water, and soak it in the soda to completely neutralize the acid, then in alcohol, and finally dry it off between folds of tissue paper. If you have no caustic soda solution, a moderately strong solution of cyanide of potassium in water will do to neutralize the acid. If the effect is found to be not sufficient, the operation can be repeated. This process, if carefully performed, is safer than grinding, and more equal in its effects, but it blackens the spring, while grinding does not produce any change of appearance that is visible while running. To clean the spring from the black, put it in the muriatic acid solution above mentioned, which will leave the spring white, after which it can be blued, and its appearance be made as good as when new. See section (60). Or if the muriatic acid is used for weakening the spring and the cyanide for neutralizing it, the spring will not be blackened, but left white. And probably the acid process will least injure the isochronism of the spring,—a result which must in *some* degree follow every effort to alter the strength of a hair-spring, no matter how it is done. For this reason the following process may be preferable, as the hair-spring is not disturbed at all. But whenever any change is made, it should be as nearly equal as possible throughout the whole length of the spring.

(332.) *Making a plain balance heavier.*—The third method is to make a plain steel, gold, or brass balance heavier, by tinning it. The spring and all parts that would be injured by heat must be removed, the lower surface of the rim scraped to get a perfectly clean surface, but the edges must not be scraped, lest the tin should run up on them. Then rub over the scraped surface a little soft-soldering-fluid. Now take a strip of thick sheet tin, $1\frac{1}{2}$ inches broad and 3 inches long, bent into the form of a letter Z, only the middle part is nearly vertical. The heat of the lamp is to be applied to the upper part, the middle being between the flame and the balance, and conducting the heat to the lower part, upon which some block tin is melted and spread all over its upper surface. Take the balance in the pliers, at the junction of an arm with the rim, and, when the tin flows freely, rub it on this lower portion of the Z till one-third of the rim is well tinned, then treat the other sections in the same way. No more heat must be used than is necessary to make the tin flow easily, as too much would color the balance. Wash off in clean, soft water, *without soap*, then soak in alcohol and dry, being sure to remove every trace of the soldering fluid, which would rust the balance and other parts of the watch if it remained. To neutralize it, the balance, after washing, could be dipped into the soda-bath, (330,) or in water in which a little common carbonate of soda is dissolved. Then wash again, etc., as above.

(333.) Take off any lumps with the scraper, level the surface of the tin, and poise properly without the spring, etc. Then fit on the spring, and proceed as in section (328). Many workmen do not allow that this operation is workmanlike, but if properly performed, and the change makes the weight of the balance more suitable than before, it would be difficult to raise any valid objection to it. Most certainly no injury, but an improvement has resulted: It must be distinctly understood that I do not justify the two first methods in any but cheap watches, and even then it is hard to see why the workman might not about as well fit a new spring, which he could afford to do for a very little more, and no one could find fault. If he has no suitable new spring, the foregoing methods may be excusable. But the practice of scraping springs is not excusable under any circumstances whatever. It is botch-work and butchery, out-and-out, while the methods just named, if carefully carried out, may give very fair results, and the last one, results that are entirely unobjectionable.

(334.) *When not to regulate.*—When the watch is running closely, do not regulate it too often. If it gains $\frac{1}{2}$ minute in a day, leave it so and see if it has gained one minute, the next day. If so, it will then be safe to turn the regulator. If not, the watch may have been exposed to the sun, or to unusual cold or heat, or kept in a different position, or had different usage. In the same way, when the watch is running closely in the customer's pocket, do not alter it for a slight error, but tell him to remember how it is and try it a little longer. Common watches will vary more or less from the sort of usage they receive, and it is better not to correct each small error, but get them so they will *average* closely, whatever the variation may be from day to day, *i.e.*, they may now be a little fast, and then a little slow, but the mean rate will be about correct. Another cause of apparent error in the rate, which in a cheap watch may amount to as much as one or two minutes, is a want of truth in the marking of the dial. The only remedy for this is to always compare the time when the minute-hand is at the same part of the dial, say at the figure XII. If the dial is not fastened on concentrically with the main plate, *i.e.*, the cannon pinion is not in the center of the circle of the dial figures and spaces, there will be an apparent error of rate, even when the watch runs correctly and the dial is perfectly spaced off. For instance, if the figure XII is too near the center post, the watch would be correct at XII and VI, but will appear to be fast at IX and slow at III. The error may be as much as a minute, and will diminish gradually in amount in each direction from those points, till the minute-hand reaches XII or VI, when it will disappear, to reappear as the hand goes beyond those points. This defect may be detected by training the point of the hand to run close to the dial, and turning it through one revolution; the points which are nearest and furtherest from the center post, are the places where the watch should be compared and regulated. All watches with any such defects should be put in a corner of the board by themselves, to insure their receiving the special treatment they require. Also see sections (369, 373).

(335.) *Effect of running down.*—In conclusion, I may mention a fact not generally known: that if a watch which has been closely regulated is allowed to run down, its rate will almost invariably be different when again wound and set going— generally, it will gain. Whether the change of rate is due to the relaxation of the mainspring when relieved from tension, or whatever the philosophy of it may be, we may derive from the fact a useful practical lesson,—not only to guard against such a mishap while regulating our watches, but, when it does occur, to avoid moving the regulator to correct the error. Many watchmakers allow their watches to run down every Sunday, to save the trouble of winding on that day. This is a great mistake, for it generally takes them several days to fully recover their former or permanent rate, and if the regulator is changed before this takes place, it is evident that an injury is done which will have to be undone again when it has returned to its normal condition. It is well to keep customers' watches running till they are called for, unless they are left for an unreasonable length of time. So, also, sale watches which have been closely regulated, and from which purchasers will expect fine performance, should be kept running. But if they have been allowed to lie still for a while, no account must be made of their rate for the first week after rewinding—simply giving that time for them to settle down again. At the end of the week, set them, without changing the regulator, and they will generally run the same as before. If they do not, it will then be safe to move the regulator, and bring them to time in the usual way.

CHAPTER XXII.

Regulating Fine Watches.

(336.) *Regulating fine watches.*—We will now consider the regulation of fine watches, in which it is not expected, of course, that any great change will be necessary, as in that case a new spring would be fitted. Supposing that we have *an isochronized hair spring*, it must not be let out nor taken up to change the rate, but we must alter the balance. Even if the watch has a regulator, it should be moved but very little, as by so doing we virtually change the length of the spring, and injure or destroy the isochronism. After moving a regulator to change the rate to the extent of half a minute per day, or more, the isochronism should be tested, and if it has been injured by the change, the regulator should be replaced where it was, or where the isochronism will be restored, and the rate be corrected by the balance. This is important in all cases, but particularly so in springs with terminal curves. Of course, in watches without regulators, the rate is to be corrected by the balance only, according to the directions given in the chapters on Rating. But as most watches have them, the greater portion of this chapter is devoted to them.

(337.) *The proper fitting of the seconds-hand* is an important point in timing fine watches. It should fit the pivot closely enough to avoid any risk of accidentally changing its position by being touched, but not be really tight, as the pivot is liable to be bent or the jewel cracked by getting it off, and the cock loosened or sprung or jewel injured by pushing it on. The dial hole must be large enough to render it *impossible* to touch the socket of the hand or for a little dirt or fuzz to clog between them. The upper end of the dial hole should be a little countersunk for safety. The rule is to BE SURE *nothing can affect the seconds-hand;* give too much clearance, rather than not enough. In the duplex, center-seconds watches, etc., be very particular that the outer surface of the seconds-hand socket shall be perfectly free. When the pipe is long, it is customary to broach it out to fit loosely on the pivot, then squeeze it in at the middle, to fit snugly. That is wrong, for the pipe is generally split thereby, and even if it is not, it will seldom stand truly on the pivot, but one side will stick out, and is almost sure to rub somewhere; the index part is also out of level. The proper way to fit a long pipe is to broach it equally from each end, so that it will fit the pivot from the lower end to the middle. Then if the pivot is vertical the hand will clear the dial equally all around. If you are fitting the hand on a chronometer or duplex which is together, put a slip of paper under the balance (when at the point of rest) to hold it still while you are doing the job. But the proper time to fit a seconds-hand is while the fourth wheel is out of the movement, or, at least, the escape wheel is out. Let no oil get on the pipe or socket, or in the dial hole, while the watch is together.

(338.) *Positions of the hands.*—The dial must first be fastened so that it not only cannot move about and change its position, but will not work loose in a little while, even when the watch is roughly used. *Be sure* about that. The dial should of course be concentric with the plate, and so that the hands will all come in the centers of the dial openings, and be free (20 to 22). But if the dial openings are not central with the graduated circles, the hands must be at the centers of the circles. In doubtful cases, watch the point of the seconds-hand once around.

(339.) *The dial.*—Fig. 9, section (165), will show the necessity of correctness in a fine watch. The fourth wheel pivot is shown out of center—at the left side of the opening. The two lines passing through the figures show the divisions of the dial. If the seconds-hand points to 60 at the beginning of the minute, it will point to *a* in 30 seconds, (half a revolution of the wheel,) showing more than 30 seconds on the dial; and at the quarters it will point to *b* and *c*, instead of *15* and *45*. Fig. 8, section (165,) shows the pivot in the vertical center of the circle, but above the horizontal center. The hand would be correct at 60 and 30 seconds, but nowhere else. At the quarters, it would point to *e* and *d*, instead of *15* and *45*.

(340.) *Testing the dial.*—A good way to test the position of the pivot, is to lay a straight edge of brass, or even paper, across the dial between 60 and 30. If the center of the pivot is exactly on this line, it is in the vertical center. Then lay it across between *15* and *45*, to see if the pivot is in the horizontal center. If not correct either way, it should be made so. When right, if there is any doubt about the equality of the marking, cut out a small paper circle to fit inside of the dial circle, prick a fine hole at the center, slip it on the pivot, and mark on its edge the exact positions of the 60, 5, 10 and 15 of the dial. With this gauge test the other quarters of the circle. The equality of the seconds marks can be told closely enough by inspection. An imperfect dial makes rating or fine timing much more difficult, as will presently be seen.

(341.) *To set a chronometer to time.*—The only perfectly safe way is to stop the watch, and start it again when its seconds-hand agrees with that of the regulator. It is not safe to force the seconds-hand ahead, nor back, nor even to hold it still (510). Stop the balance at the point of rest, so that it will remain still till you start it. Stop it with the seconds-hand exactly on the 60; that is the best way, although either of the quarters will do, if the dials are perfectly divided off. To get the hand exact, stop it a second or two too soon, then with the bristle move the balance each way far enough to escape and lock, and look at the hand. If necessary, repeat it—each time bringing the balance to the point of rest before freeing it. When the seconds-hand stands exactly at the 60, you start the watch at the instant the regulator hand strikes its 60.

(342.) *To start the chronometer on time.*—You can do this either with the bristle, or by shaking. If you choose the latter, you hold the watch so that you can give it a circular twist by a motion of the wrist, and keeping your eye on the regulator, at the instant its hand comes to 60 twist the watch and start it. A little practice is necessary, to start them exactly together. The watch must be twisted in such a way that the balance makes its *impulse vibration*, (485,) not the dumb vibration—and it begins to move immediately. Remember that *the balance stands still* while you twist the watch, and thus move the escape wheel around the roller, instead of the balance and roller revolving. Only the one twist is necessary—more than that would be liable to cause tripping or over-running. By the other way, with the bristle, you simply move the balance one-quarter turn from the point of rest, (the dumb vibration,) and hold it still till the regulator hand touches the 60, then lift your bristle and let the balance make its first *impulse vibration.* Some practice the following method.

(343.) *To set a chronometer forward or back.*—Stop it the proper length of time, then start it again. If it is 10 seconds fast, stop it with its seconds-hand on its 60; and 10 seconds later, when the regulator reaches 60, you start it again, either by shaking or twisting, as before described. If it is only a few seconds fast, say 3 seconds, you can get the motion of the balance in your mind closely enough to count the proper number of vibrations while you are holding the balance still, then let it go. With an ordinary 18,000 movement, 3 seconds would take 15 vibrations,—or a little over 7 pairs, if you count only each alternate vibration. Holding the watch in convenient position, you begin counting by saying "one" as you lower the bristle upon the balance, which you hold till you reach 15 (or 7), then lift the bristle and look. It is always safer to start it a little too soon, than to hold it too long, for it is easy to stop the motion for an instant (one or two vibrations) and so get the hand exact. The only safe way to set the hands forward, is to stop the watch and get the seconds-hand correct, as above, then set the minute-hand forward one minute—or more, if required. Many workmen practice the following method with the chronometer, but it is not safe.

(344.) *To set a duplex to time.*—It is not safe to twist the seconds-hand around on the pivot, but there is little risk in holding it still by means of a key on the center or setting post, till the regulator seconds-hand comes to the same point—preferably the 60. But if the watch hand is slow, it should be held still and made slower yet till it agrees with the regulator, then set the minute-hand correctly, as described for the chronometer (343). A better way is to follow precisely the method there given, for setting the hands either forward or back. When the duplex is only a few seconds slow, many workmen give it a twist and make it "overrun" (498) a few vibrations to catch up, but that is a rather rough way of doing it. Besides, it may overrun too long, and get too far ahead, unless you stop the balance frequently and compare.

(345.) *Setting the cylinder or lever to time.*—It does no harm to set these watches backward, if in good condition. But it is seldom advisable to disturb the seconds-hand after it has been perfectly adjusted on the pivot. It is better to get the hand back (if too fast) by holding the escapement still with a key on the center post, till it agrees with the regulator. Or else press the center (or fourth) wheel backwards with the screwdriver till the seconds-hand has been sufficiently delayed. But the best way is to hold the watch so you can see the dial in a mirror underneath, stop the balance with the seconds-hand just on its 60, hold it there (drawn partly around) till the regulator hand comes to 60, then lift the bristle and let the balance go, and set the minute-hand. If only a second or two too fast, touch the balance with the bristle long enough to stop it for two or three vibrations and compare, then repeat as needed. If the seconds-hand is behind time, stop the balance till the seconds hand agrees with the regulator, then liberate it, and set the minute-hand ahead. Some stop the seconds-hand by putting the end of the bench key before the point, hold it till it gets with the regulator, then start as before.

(346.) *Regulating by the timing screws.*—In genuine chronometer or compensation balances adjusted for temperatures, there are generally four mean-time screws,—two at the ends of the center-bar, and two others midway between them on the rim, being thus a quarter of a circle apart, and hence also termed "quarter-screws." The office of these timing screws is to adjust the rate of the watch, by screwing them further in, and thus by carrying their weight nearer to the center of the balance, to make it virtually smaller or lighter, and cause the watch to gain; or turning them out further from the center, to make the balance virtually heavier, and lose. Any alterations should of course be made equally on the two opposite screws, to preserve the poise of the balance. This can be done by noticing the slits in their heads and giving each one exactly the same angle of turn. If there is any doubt, the poise should be tested. Should it be found incorrect, the two screws must be made to restore it. But inasmuch as all watch manufacturers do not use four mean-time screws as above, it will be safer to alter only the *two* at the end of the center-bar. In any case, the other pair must never be changed more than a mere trifle, because any change of a screw upon the cut section of the rim, by moving it either in or out, must infallibly disturb the compensation for heat and cold. Even if a cut balance is not adjusted, it is not advisable to alter the screws near the ends of the sections, but only those near the center-bar, where their effects upon the compensation, or the errors caused in different temperatures, will be less in amount, although the effect upon the regulation will be just as great.

(347.) *Chronometer balance.*—Not all cut balances, even when they are genuine chronometer balances, are compensated; and whether any particular balance is adjusted or not can only be certainly known by trying it in different temperatures. There are very few makers whose stamp, "adjusted," may be fully trusted without trial. A cut balance that is not adjusted may be either better or worse than an uncut balance; as it may happen to be very near correct, or, on the other hand, the position of the screws and the action of the sections of the rim may be so unsuitable to each other as to cause the balance to "act like the devil," when exposed to changes of temperature. As the adjustment of the compensation balance for heat and cold is a special subject by itself, I shall not consider it here, but merely observe that it is important to keep our watches at a temperature as nearly uniform as possible while regulating them, in order to eliminate from our task all the irregularities which would otherwise be mixed up with the action of the hair spring.

We can regulate a watch in one temperature, but we cannot, if we try, make the regulation cover the compensation for temperatures, and by trying we shall not only fail in that, but injure our regulation besides. This rule is especially important with cheap watches. And the best are always *regulated* in *one* temperature and *compensated* in *different* temperatures.

(348.) *Screw balance.*—If we have an isochronal spring with a screw-balance which is not cut, we can alter any or all of the screws in the rim indifferently, so long as we do not destroy the poise. If the watch loses, we must make the balance either actually or virtually lighter. If the screws cannot be turned in, we may either file off the heads a little, taking care to do this squarely and in a workmanlike manner, or we can drill out in the center of the heads, leaving the exterior appearance unchanged. Some workmen file out the slots wider and deeper, in the heads, when only a slight alteration is needed. Or we can take out gold screws and substitute lighter ones of brass, or smaller gold screws. Or, if change enough is required, we can remove an opposite pair of screws entirely. On the other hand, if the watch loses, we can turn out one or two opposite pairs a little. If that is not sufficient, turn others equally far out, being careful not to draw out either of them more than the rest, and drawing out more screws rather than move a few too much. We can also put gold washers under the screw heads, or substitute gold or platinum screws for those of lighter metal, or substitute larger screws, or put in an additional pair to increase the weight of the balance. These changes of weight, if considerable, will slightly disturb the isochronism of the spring, which must be readjusted as hereafter directed. If the watch has a regulator, the isochronism can generally be restored by opening or closing the pins, (585,) or, in the case of a terminal curve, by slightly altering that, after the watch is closely regulated for time. But the isochronism should never be corrected by the regulator pins with any but the plain flat spiral springs, and not then, if a better method can be followed.

(349.) *Making a plain balance lighter.*—If, instead of a screw balance, we have a plain one, whether of gold, brass, or steel, the best way to make it lighter is to hold it by the exterior of its rim in one of the step chucks of the American lathe, or any similar way, and turn out a very little with the graver, on the under side, being careful not to cut away too much. In this way, with due caution, the poise will not be disturbed. Others simply file a little from the inner edge of the under side of the rim, equally in three different places, to preserve the poise.

The only way to make a plain balance heavier is to tin it, (332).

(350.) *The effect produced upon the isochronism of a hair spring by moving its regulator* is, in general, greater in the short vibrations than in the long ones. Turning the regulator towards the "slow" makes all the vibrations slower, but the short ones proportionately more so than the long ones. And, *vice versa*, turning the regulator towards the "fast," not only makes the watch gain, but also causes the short arcs to gain on the long ones. If the spring is isochronal, and the watch gains or loses but little, the error of rate should be corrected, not by the regulator, but by altering the balance. But if the balance has no screws, such alteration would be troublesome, and we may prefer to move the regulator to correct the rate, and then restore the isochronism by opening or closing the regulator pins a little. This course is more often allowable when the required motion of the regulator is towards the stud than when away from it. But when the error of rate is considerable, we must move the spring through the stud, bearing in mind the requirements of isochronism, in the flat spiral spring, (the Breguet spring will be specially noticed) as to maintaining the relative positions of the points of attachment, etc. That is to say, after taking up or letting it out, we must restore their previous relative position, (if correct,) by altering the central coil. If that alteration of the spring, etc., is not allowable or practicable on account of destroying the correct proportions of the central coil, (275, 276,) or for any other reason, then we must change the weight of the balance to the required amount as already described, or, if too much change is needed, a new spring should be fitted; for we must perform the regulation in such a way as not to destroy either the harmonious proportions of the movement or the isochronism of the spring, and to improve both if possible. Also, see Chapter XXIII.

(351.) *Duty of the workman.*—But it is always a grave question for the workman to answer to his own sense of right, how far he is justified in permanently altering a watch by changing the weight of the balance, to save himself the trouble of fitting a new spring. Even in cheap watches he would require a strong excuse for removing or adding a pair of screws, or very much changing the weight of a balance by tinning or filing it; and in good watches it could only be allowed on the supposition that the weight of the balance did not bear a correct proportion to the motive force of the mainspring. If this proportion was correct, then his duty would be to conform the strength of the hair spring to the weight of the balance, so that the balance and hair spring, as an entirety, would be suitable to the movement. The altering of the balance to conform to the strength of the hair spring, in such a case, would destroy the correct proportions of the entire movement, and such a practice should only be followed within very narrow limits.

(352.) *In watches with regulators*, the adjustment of the isochronism becomes more difficult as the distance of the pins from the stud increases. So much so, that many high authorities have claimed that a spring cannot be isochronized at all with a regulator, probably because, in bringing the watch to time, they had got the regulator too far from the stud. There is no denying that, theoretically, the action of the pins renders a perfect progression in the increase of elastic force impossible, —since the spring cannot vibrate as it would if it ended at the regulator, nor as if its action extended to the stud uninfluenced by the regulator, but there will be a mixture of the two, varied by the effect of the pins, and further complicated by the reverse action of the portion of the spring between the pins and the stud. But, practically, if the spring has been fitted in accordance with the instructions heretofore given, and the pins are near the stud, we can so add to or take from the composite action resulting from all these different influences, as to secure a correct progression of strength, and consequently isochronal vibrations. The workman should endeavor, in regulating his watches with flat spiral springs, to keep the regulator as near the stud as possible, not only for the sake of the isochronal perfection of the spring's action, but because even the regulation to time is more easily and closely effected by so doing. It should also be remarked that the effect of opening or closing the pins increases as they are nearer to the stud, so that the isochronal adjustment is more easily made, or restored, when disturbed by moving the regulator. If the regulator cannot be got within $20°$ or $25°$ from the stud when the rate is correct, it is well to move it to different positions, and test the isochronism in each, to find the best place—paying no attention to the rate till the point is found where the isochronism is nearest correct, then bring to time by the balance screws. But if this will take the regulator more than $45°$ distant from the stud, it is better to take up the hair spring, to bring the regulator back, then adjust the isochronism.

(353.) *With complete or fractional coils.*—Many workmen claim that when the regulator is more than $20°$ or $25°$ from the stud, the even coils should invariably be reckoned from the point touching the collet to the regulator pins instead of to the stud, (566.) And if the watch does not give correct time with the regulator in that position, the balance screw should be altered. It should also necessarily follow that if the hair spring has to be taken up or let out, the regulator should be moved correspondingly, in order to retain the whole coils; and when the isochronism is correct, if the rate is not, then the latter should be corrected by the balance, not by moving the regulator, as that would again destroy the isochronal adjustment. If these views were correct, then any change in the length of the spring which might be required to secure isochronal vibrations, could be made by simply moving the regulator in the proper direction and distance, afterwards restoring the rate by the balance screws. But they are not correct, as a rule, although they are, to some extent, in many cases; as, for instance, when the regulator is altogether too far from the stud, say from one-quarter to one-half coil distant. In such a case the isochronal action would probably be better if the even coils were taken from the collet to the regulator pins than if to the stud. But in neither case would the action be as good as if the parts were all in the positions we have before recommended. It has elsewhere been stated that the theory of even coils is merely approximative in any case, (565,) and the actual position of the isochronal point in the spring must be found by trial. So that, even when their views are in the main correct, they must be followed with this qualification.

(354.) *Regulating a Breguet spring.*—It has already been stated that, before taking down a watch with an isochronized hair spring, the workman should examine and make a minute of the position of the regulator, the position of the spring between the pins, and the width of opening, in order to restore everything to precisely the same condition when done. This is especially important with a Breguet spring, for reasons before given. But when an error of rate requires the *status* to be changed, there are certain points to be observed in the regulation of the Breguet spring different from that of others. We first ascertain whether the terminal curve extends to the stud, or only to a concentric arc or portion of a coil, which is pinned to the stud, *i.e.*, whether the concentric arc is a part of the terminal curve, or is separate from it. In the latter case, the over coil is a combination of a terminal curve with a concentric arc; in the former, it is all terminal curve. This can be told by moving the regulator, if it is concentric with the balance. So far as the spring retains the same position between the regulator pins, the coil may be considered concentric. But if the spring, from being free between the pins, soon presses against the outer pin, as the regulator is moved away from the stud, the point where this outward divergence begins may be considered the end of the terminal curve, from which point it sweeps gradually outward till it reaches the normal spiral form at the exterior coil of the spring. When the regulator is concentric with the concentric part of the spring, however, and *not* concentric with the balance, it shows that the terminal reaches to the stud and should be regulated as in the former case. This can generally be told by holding the balance cock up to the light and looking through the end stone—or removing the latter. If the center of the regulator is not over the jewel hole, it has been made concentric with the spring, instead of with the balance.

(355.) *With terminal curve to the end.*—If the former is the case, or the terminal curve extends to the stud, the workman should conduct the regulation to time with the aim to get the regulator as near to the stud as possible. And to this end, he should make the watch go slower by moving the regulator towards the stud; but he should not move it from the stud in case the watch must be made to go faster, but, if practicable, produce that alteration by means of the balance, (769.) If he was able, without much change in the weight of the balance, or alteration of its screws, to cause the watch to gain sufficiently to allow of bringing the regulator entirely to the stud, it would certainly be wise to do so, for he would obtain the very best conditions for the perfect action of the terminal curve—simulating a spring without a regulator. The more closely to the stud he can bring it, the more nearly will the curve be free from restraint, and able to produce the legitimate effect sought for by its form. When springs whose curves reach to the stud are provided with regulators, every shifting of the regulator must be accompanied by a bending of its pins whenever necessary to make it conform properly to the spring in its new position; but *the spring must never be bent to give it freedom between the pins and the regulator*, as that would at once destroy the correctness of the terminal curve.

(356.) *With concentric arc at the end.*—On the other hand, if there is, between the end of the terminal curve and the stud, a concentric arc, (354,) distinct from the terminal curve, then his aim should be to bring the regulator to the point where the spring changes from a concentric to a divergent form. When the watch loses, he should move the regulator from the stud towards that point, and when it gains, he should not move the regulator back, but draw out the screws of the balance. When the watch keeps time with the regulator at that point, and with the pins well closed together, the position of all the parts is the one most favorable for securing isochronism that the spring, in its then shape, is capable of giving. If the isochronal action is not satisfactory, the curve should be altered. When the concentric arc is a part of the curve, as explained in section (354), regulate as for a curve reaching to the stud, (355.)

(357.) *With too long concentric arc.*—But the preceding section is correct only when the concentric portion is within certain limits. If its length exceeds 45°, it is evident that the supplemental coil has not been formed with proper regard to the requirements of isochronism, and we shall obtain better results by modifying the course taken in section (356). If the watch loses, the correction should not be made either by the regulator or by the balance, but by drawing the spring through the stud; while, if it gains, the balance screws should be drawn out. If, by taking up the spring and drawing out the balance screws to a reasonable extent, we can bring the end of the terminal curve (and the regulator pins) within 45° from the stud, or less, we may hope for fine action of the spring. But if that point is more than that distance from the stud, even though we have the regulator pins at the end of the terminal curve, we cannot expect perfect isochronism. The regulator should never be moved beyond that point, and on the terminal curve, to make the watch go faster, but either take up the spring or turn in the balance screws to cause the gain in time. Nor should the spring ever be let out to produce a slower rate, if that alteration would carry the ends of the curve more than 45° from the stud, but we should draw out the balance screws for that purpose.

(358.) *Recapitulation.*—Lest this subject should seem complicated, I will recapitulate briefly. 1st. If the terminal curve of a Breguet spring reaches to the stud, the object should be to conduct the regulation or alterations so as to bring the regulator as near the stud as possible; and rather than move it *from* the stud, the balance should be altered. 2d. If there is a concentric arc at the end of the spring, distinct from the terminal curve, the aim is to bring the regulator to the junction of the concentric and divergent portions of the spring, and all alterations should be made to favor that purpose. But if the concentric arc is *a part of the terminal curve,* (shown by the regulator not being concentric with the balance,) the aim should be as stated under the 1st head. 3d. But if its junction is over 45° distant from the stud, the chief obejct is to reduce that distance to 45°, or less, and the next is to bring the regulator to the junction; and all changes must be made so as to favor the first object, *if at all possible*, and if not, then to favor the second. Whenever any of these changes disturb the isochronal adjustment, it should of course be restored, in the most convenient way.

(359.) These directions are based on the supposition that the workman is willing to take a little extra trouble for the sake of improving the isochronal action when it is not perfect. But if he cares for nothing but to bring the watch to time in the easiest way that will do no harm, or as little as possible, he should make his corrections of the rate principally by the balance. But whether he does or does not observe these rules, he will at least know how he may secure the most perfect results, if he so desires, or how to avoid injuring the timepieces in his care, when he has the choice of modes in which to make necessary alterations. If he only travels a little way in the paths recommended, or even only avoids taking wrong ones, that will be much better than working in the dark, not knowing whether he is improving or ruining his jobs.

(360.) There are different degrees of excellence in Breguet springs, represented by the three preceding classes, in their order. Yet even the third and lowest degree, with a concentric arc greater than 45° and the regulator far from the junction, is without doubt much better than a plain flat spiral not isochronized at all, because the outer coil of the former can contract and expand more evenly on all sides of the balance axis. But we should not be contented without doing in every case the very best we are capable of doing. If we are fitting a spring, let us fit it in the manner that will give the best action; if we are only regulating a spring already fitted, let us strive to obtain the best results which the form of the spring can yield. Only thus can we improve in our art, impress upon our memory the maxims which lead to perfection, familiarize ourselves practically with the finer manipulations, and gain the delicacy and dexterity which we should need if we were called upon to do a perfect job, but which we could not possess unless we had obtained experience by following the above course in our work, even upon cheap jobs or those in which we get no pay for our extra care.

CHAPTER XXIII.

Rating.

(361.) *What is rating?*—The term timing includes all operations for bringing the watch to time, while rating relates to the finer classes of timekeepers which, either naturally or by special adjustment, are more or less perfect isochronally, in positions and in different temperatures. Strictly speaking, rating is *ascertaining* the regular gain or loss of a watch in certain conditions, but in practice the term is also applied to the perfecting of the adjustment and the reduction of the errors to the smallest possible amounts. That being done, the error which remains is said to be the rate.

(362.) *The daily rate* is the amount the watch gains or loses in a day, as compared with the correct time. If it gains 2 seconds in a day, we say the daily rate is $+ 2''$; if it loses $2\frac{2}{5}$ seconds, the rate is $- 2.4''$. If it gains at times, and loses at other times, but never gets more than 3 seconds out of the way, the daily rate is $\pm 3''$, *i.e.*, it may be either fast or slow $3''$.

(363.) *The mean daily rate* is obtained by adding together the gains and the losses in a certain time, and the excess of gains over losses, or the reverse, divided by the number of days, gives the mean daily rate. Thus, if it gained 7 seconds on 4 days and lost 22 seconds on 6 other days, the net error in 10 days would be a loss of 15 seconds, or a mean daily rate for the 10 days of $- 1.5''$. If that excess was a loss of 1 second, the mean daily rate would be only $.1''$—which may be a very deceptive way of stating the error unless one takes care to notice whether the word "mean" is used.

(364.) The operations which constitute the adjustments for isochronism, positions and temperatures will be treated under those headings. We shall here deal only with the means and methods of observing and comparing times, detecting errors, and deciding upon the proper remedy. The first requisite, of course, is a regulator (or other timekeeper) which keeps as nearly perfect time as possible. We of course do not recommend any particular kind or maker, but merely suggest that the workman who aspires to do fine work should get as good a regulator as he can afford. We have already stated some of the requirements, and how it should be used to obtain good service from it, in Chapter XII; also the other conveniences for timing. Be sure to always have a pencil and pad handy on the bench.

(365.) *Comparing the watch with the regulator.*—The best method available to the ordinary watchmaker is by using the chronograph, as directed in Chapter XIII, as he then has a record of the difference of time between them exact to $\frac{1}{5}$ second, which he can examine at his leisure and ascertain the precise amount. That is closer than he can compare them by eye with any certainty, and it is evidently important to find the error as precisely as possible, especially in making the adjustments. In a 6 hours' trial the whole error may not exceed 1 or 2 seconds, and a difference of half a second in comparing times would be a large proportion of the whole error.

(366.) *Comparing by vibrations of balances.*—Those who are quick of perception can compare with equal, or even greater closeness, by using a closely regulated watch and comparing the vibrations of the two balances, as directed in Chapter XV. By this method it is necessary, (unless you watch the trial balance closely enough to know that it has not gained or lost one or more *whole* vibrations, as well as the fractional part which you are comparing,) not only to set the two balances to vibrating synchronously, but to set the seconds-hands so that each will indicate the same number of *beats on their dials.* You first compare the seconds-hands, to see if they both strike a certain division mark exactly together, or if your watch is one or more beats (movements of the hand) before or after the timing watch. Each beat indicates an entire vibration (in the chronometer, it indicates 2 vibrations) gained or lost, besides the whole seconds, if any—in addition to the difference you may now discover in the phase of the balance vibrations. But as before stated, the principal value of this method of comparison is when the difference of phase is the only difference there is. In such cases, it is the closest of all methods of direct comparison.

(367.) *Comparing by seconds-hands* has just been described, when two watches are compared. In comparing the trial watch with the regulator, you must of course set the watch so that its seconds-hand strikes a division mark at the same instant that the regulator hand does, and you can then find the error of your watch in seconds and beats, *i.e.*, in an 18,000 movement, in seconds and fifths of a second. If the seconds dial is evenly divided and the hand central, (334, 338,) this comparison of beats can be made anywhere on the circle. If not, it should be made near the 60. The same rule governs in the comparison of seconds, and minutes. The method differs a little when the watch is slow or fast, as follows.

(368.) *Comparing times when the watch hand is slow, i.e.,* in case the seconds-hand of the watch is between 30 and 60 when the regulator hand strikes its 60. This is the usual way, and is described in Chapter XV, especially in section (198), and also under the head of timing bells (209). Getting the swing of the seconds pendulum, or the jump of the clock hand, well in mind so that you can nod your head in unison with it without looking at it, you begin to count the seconds backward at 55 seconds, following up the watch hand with your finger-nail on the glass, saying "Five—Four—Three—Two—One—Naught"—the "Naught" being at the instant the regulator hand strikes its 60, and at the same instant you begin to count the beats on your watch till its hand reaches the next seconds mark after the "Naught." Hold your nail there, till you have ascertained how many seconds the mark is before the 60. If it is 11, and you counted two beats after the "Naught" before the seconds-hand reached that mark, your watch is $11\frac{2}{5}$ seconds slow.

(369.) *The same with imperfect dial.*—If the watch seconds-dial is poorly spaced off, you should only compare when its hand reaches its 60, by observing how many seconds that occurs after 60 on the regulator dial. Get the period of the jumps or motions of the watch seconds-hand well in mind, so that you can nod your head in unison with them while you close your eyes a moment, or lift them to look at the clock, and can find the nods still in unison with the jumps when you look at the hand again. As your seconds-hand gets up near the 60, you can count the number of beats it gives *after* the clock hand strikes a seconds division and before the watch hand strikes its next seconds mark. That gives you the *fraction of a second* that your watch is slow. You then keep the edge of your finger-nail just in advance of the mark the clock hand is at, drawing it back at each second to correspond, *i.e.*, you mark on the watch dial with your nail, at each second, the position the hand occupies on the clock. This is in order that you can have a sort of *record* of the position of the hand, so you may count up the number of seconds with certainty, at the end of the trial. You can do that on the minute circle of your watch, when the marks are plain and wide apart.

(370.) *Ascertaining the difference.*—As your watch hand gets to 55 seconds, place your nail on the mark (on the watch), when the clock hand is at that second. (Some workmen put the nail 5 seconds ahead of that, *i.e.*, where the clock hand will be, when the watch hand strikes its 60, and hold it there.) As the watch hand strikes each successive seconds mark, draw the nail back 1 second to correspond, and at the instant the watch hand strikes 60 you say "one, two," etc., looking at the clock and counting the beats till the clock hand reaches the next seconds mark. Then hold your nail there and count the seconds from *the previous* mark back to the 60. If that was 17 seconds, and you had counted 3 beats, your seconds hand is 17¾ seconds ahead of the clock hand.

(371.) *Comparing times when the watch hand is fast, i.e.*, in case its seconds-hand is after the 60 when the clock hand is at its 60. The usual way is similar to that described in section (368), except that in this case you place the nail just *before* the watch seconds-hand, and draw it back as the hand approaches, till the clock hand strikes its 60, then hold it still, and the number of seconds between the 60 and that mark on the watch dial shows how many seconds the watch hand is ahead of the other. You count the beats from each seconds mark (on the watch) to the next, then repeat. In an 18,000 movement, you would say: "one, two, three, four, five," and repeat it each second, looking at the clock hand to see which number you pronounce as the clock hand strikes its seconds marks. If it does so just as you say "three," each time, that shows that your watch seconds are three beats earlier than the clock seconds.

(372.) *To find the number of seconds.*—Then find the seconds by counting from the 55 seconds backwards, as described in section (368). Keeping your nail just before the watch seconds hand, as you say "Naught" (and the clock hand touches 60) you begin to count the beats till the watch hand reaches the next mark, then hold your nail there till you have fully satisfied yourself of the number of that mark. If you counted 2 beats from the "Naught" to the next mark on the watch, that will show that your previous count of 3 beats from the watch mark to the next clock mark was correct, for $3 + 2 = 5$, the number of beats per second. Therefore, if that mark was the 13th second, your watch would be 12⅗ seconds fast. Some workmen omit this counting of the beats the last time, and on saying "Naught" hold the nail still. The last previous mark gives the number of seconds, to which they add the number of beats before counted. But the result is more certain by counting twice, as just described.

(373.) *The same on an imperfect dial.*—In that case, it will be necessary to take the time on the clock dial when the watch seconds-hand strikes its 60, as described in section (369). Suppose the regulator hand stood at 44 seconds, and there were two beats after that and before the watch hand touched 60, your watch seconds-hand is 16⅔ seconds fast of the clock hand.

(374.) *Attention* should be paid to the fact that sections (368, 369,) and (371, 373) refer to cases where the watch seconds-hand is on the right or left side of the 60 when the time is compared, *i.e.*, it is ahead or behind that of the clock. But the watch itself may be fast, (say, 45 seconds fast,) although its seconds-*hand* is on the left side of the 60, or it may be slow (say, 45 seconds slow) while its seconds-*hand* is at the right of the 60. The rules are simply for securing an accurate comparison of time when the hands occupy certain positions.

(375.) *Comparing times with the aid of an assistant.*—Many workmen find it almost impossible to compare a watch with the regulator as described, with any certainty, within 2 or 3 seconds. Such will be able to follow the directions given if they will have some assistant call out the seconds on the regulator while they keep their attention fixed on the watch. Everything being ready, the assistant begins at the 55th second and calls "Five—Four—Three—Two—One—Naught," pronouncing each number exactly at the instant the regulator hand strikes each second, and the "Naught" exactly at the 60. Any bright boy can do this properly after a little training, and the workman should then be able to count the beats on the watch and time it to $\frac{1}{5}$ second. By this method, he knows exactly where the regulator hand is, and has constant warning of its approach to the 60. It is equally useful in helping to set the watch exact with the clock.

(376.) *Same, when the watch hand is at the 60.*—When it is required to compare the time when the seconds-hand of the watch is at its 60, which we have seen is sometimes necessary, the workman begins at the 50th second and calls out "Now" at each second on the watch, till the 54th, saying that very loudly. The assistant begins at the next second on the clock, (being warned by the loud call,) and calls out the numbers backward (as in the preceding section), taking notice of *the number* of the second on the clock when he says "Naught." At the same call the workman begins to count the beats on the watch, between the call and the arrival of the hand of his watch at the 60. If he counted 3 beats, and the assistant reported 22 seconds at the "Naught," there would be $22\frac{3}{5}$ seconds difference between the watch and the clock, if the clock hand was ahead. If it was behind the watch hand, *i.e.*, between the 30 and 60, say, at the 44th second, that would of course make the difference $16\frac{3}{5}$ seconds.

(377.) *Rate book.*—When we are merely regulating, we correct the observed error each time, without any special reference to what the watch has done before. But in rating, we make some record of its performance at each observation, and the proper correction is decided upon after considering its errors at previous times, or under different conditions. A rate book is therefore a necessity in rating watches, (or, at least, rate sheets of paper,) and in it should be recorded the exact details of each observation, for future reference. The owner's name, and a brief statement of the kind of watch, and its number, should head the page, which should be ruled off in columns to suit the tests or observations made. In all cases, the first column should give the date of the observation; it is also advisable to add a column for the hour, as it may often help to trace out some error, or, at least, to explain the circumstances. The next column gives the observed difference between the watch and the regulator, preceded by the mark + to indicate a gain, and — for a loss; it is well to add a column for the number of days that have elapsed since the last observation. The next column gives the error per day, since it was last regulated and set, ascertained by comparing the difference from the clock this time, and the last previous time, and dividing the difference by the number of days, (col. 4.) Column 6 states whether the watch was then regulated (R), or set to time (S), or both. If you are doing thorough first-class work, you should add column 7, showing the mean daily rate (363), and the number of days during which it averaged that amount should be stated in column 8. Column 9 gives the temperature (or average) since the last observation, or if the watch has been exposed to the sun, or any unusual heat or cold. Column 10 gives the position, in the shop; or states if it is being carried, or anything special which has happened to it since the last observation, or if any alteration of the mechanism was made.

(378.) It is important that all the facts which affect the rate should be known, and as the workman cannot be expected to remember them, they must of course be recorded. In noting, mark the hours by the letter "h," or simply by the number, the minutes by one dash after the number, and the seconds by two dashes. Thus, 10 minutes and 45 seconds after 9 o'clock in the forenoon would be written "9—10′—45″, A.M." Always mark the time with A. M. or P. M., to prevent any possibility of mistake, for you might compare times at 9 o'clock either in the morning or evening. In the observatories, they count up to 24 o'clock, from midnight to midnight, and therefore do not use A.M. or P. M. to designate the hour, but watchmakers follow the usual custom.

(379.) A page of the rate book, or of the rate sheet, would be ruled off about as follows:—

JOHN W. JONES.

GOLD ENGLISH LEVER. DENT NO. 25,502.

DATE.		DIFFERENCE FROM REGULATOR.		Daily Error.		Mean Daily		Temp. Fahr.	Position and other conditions affecting the rate.
1894.	Hour. h. m.	m. s.	Days.			Rate.	In Days.		
Mch. 29	10.10′ A.M.	+ 1′ 27⅗″	3	+ 29⅕″	R.S.	+ 43⅕″	5	88°	Hanging.
" 31	11.15′ A.M.	+ 53⅕″	2	+ 26.3″	R.S.	+ 38.5″	7	85°	"
Apl. 3	10.30′ A.M.	+ 36″	3	+ 12″	R.S.	+ 17⅘″	5	70°	Let out hairspring.
Apl. 4	10.15′ A.M.	− 14″	1	− 14″	R.S.	+ 12½″	6	75°	Hanging.
Apl. 6	10.15′ A.M.	− 51⅕″	2	− 25⅗″	R.S.			80°	Carried in pocket.
Apl. 9	10.30′ A.M	− 21⅗″	3	− 7⅕″	R.S.	+ 0.2″	11		Carried.

(380.) The first six columns, and the last one, are really necessary. The other three can be dispensed with, although they are useful when doing fine work. The form given is adapted for regular rating or regulating. For adjustment tests, the rate sheet should be ruled off to suit the work. The watches should be hung on the rack in the same order that they come in the rating book, so that it will not be necessary to spend any time in looking up the right page. It will take but a moment to write down the items. You would want to make some memorandum of the error, even if you kept no rate book—and by having it in a permanent form it will be a valuable record, from which you may learn some very practical facts. For instance, it would help you to detect an acceleration in the rate.

(381.) *Acceleration of rate.*—In regulating a new hair spring, allowance must be made for a peculiar action which has been noticed in newly made hardened and tempered springs, (23,) viz., that they accelerate on their rate for the first few weeks or months, and then, having attained their highest degree of pliability and elastic force, become constant. For this reason, the watch or chronometer cannot be regulated immediately after fitting such a spring, to maintain a perfectly uniform rate for a long period. But after bringing it closely to time, the mean-time screws may be drawn out to cause a loss of a few seconds per day, (two to five, generally,) by which means it will take nearly a correct rate after the accelerating process is ended.

The amount is, of course, a matter of guess work, but a moderate alteration will make the final rate nearer correct than if there had been no change. Where the precise permanent rate must be known, as in marine chronometers, whose error of rate is a vital element in the calculation of longitudes, etc., it is necessary to await the completion of this acceleration before a trustworthy rate can be got. Cases occasionally occur where the spring continues to change for several years, but generally they do so only for a few months.

(382.) *Cause of the error.*—Some attribute this to the spring, others to the balance. But it has been found that if a spring has been bent out of shape and then restored, it will accelerate like a new spring; also, that a balance which has been similarly injured will accelerate. It would seem probable, therefore, that the action was due to the metal of either the spring or the balance, or of both, acquiring its permanent condition, or at least acquiring a condition different from the original one. The fact that bending will cause the acceleration to occur *again*, would seem to confirm this. The practical lesson to be derived is, that one should be very careful in handling both springs and balances, or he may render it impossible for him to obtain a uniform and permanent rate for the watch. It is claimed that a spring hardened at a low temperature is not so liable to gain as one hardened at a higher temperature. But it does not gain in proportion to its hardness. A very hard spring is no more difficult to time than a softer one, is more stable and lasting, and the acceleration disappears after a short time, as before stated. Palladium hair springs accelerate somewhat less than steel, and no allowance need be made in the rating for the acceleration.

(383.) *Loss of rate in soft springs.*—While a hardened and tempered spring will gain on its rate, one that is not hardened and tempered loses. Not having its molecular condition changed by fire-hardening, but being merely stiffened by wire-drawing and rolling, the constant bending to and fro of the soft metal probably extends or gradually lengthens it, and may be considered as a deterioration of condition, as it generally continues to lose until it finally becomes "exhausted" and useless. In rating fine watches with such springs, allowance must be made for this. After getting as close a rate as possible while in the shop, then cause the spring to gain a certain amount—varying from 4 to 10 seconds daily, according to the watch, which will bring its permanent rate nearly correct. But it is better to fire-harden the spring, as directed in section (263), and avoid this.

trouble. Of course, in low grade watches, this error is less important.

(384.) *Middle temperature error.*—In compensating for heat and cold with the compensation balance of ordinary construction, if they are correctly adjusted for the two extremes, they will gain at the mean temperature 2 seconds per day, on an average, in marine chronometers. In pocket watches, this error may sometimes be as much as half a minute per day; but when it exceeds a few seconds it must be considered as evidence of either a poor adjustment or an imperfect balance. On the other hand, if the watch is correctly rated at the mean temperature, it will lose as the temperature rises or falls, and will lose 2 seconds daily (in chronometers) at the extremes. It is customary to rate the watch or pocket chronometer at the temperature in which it will ordinarily be kept, and locate the error in the other temperatures, to which it will only seldom be exposed. See section (766), in the Adjustment for temperatures. With marine chronometers, it is customary to compensate so that the rate will be correct at the two extremes of heat and cold, to which it will be exposed, and it will then gain as the temperature approaches the mean, and lose as it goes outside of the extremes. The loss is stated as $1\frac{1}{2}$ seconds in 24 hours for a temperature 15° above or below the extremes for which the watch is adjusted. The above shows that in closely rating a chronometer or fine watch, it is necessary to know (approximately, at least,) whether it has been adjusted to time at the mean or the extremes, and at what temperatures. This can be found by testing. But if not known, it will generally be safe to assume that it has been adjusted at about 45° and 90°, and make the proper allowance for a middle temperature error at 65° or 70°, Fahr.

(385.) *Duration of trials.*—A close rating requires considerable time, as, after the first few days have shown that the watch is running closely, the trials have to be for longer times in order to get trustworthy results. Even in observatories, (as at Yale,) where they have apparatus for detecting errors to $\frac{1}{100}$ second, watches which are entered for first-class certificates are tested for 45 days; second class, 29 days, and third class, 16 days. The first and second class trials are for temperatures and positions, the third class for positions only. The Greenwich observatory trials are much longer and more severe, being mainly for marine chronometers. The trials last 29 weeks, and the temperature range is from 37° to 103° Fahr.

(386.) *Testing the isochronism.*—But the watchmaker should in all cases make an additional trial for isochronism, *i.e.*, see whether the rate is the same in the long and the short arcs of vibration. If not, as already stated, the watch cannot be rated except at the same hour each day. Such a fault is a vital one, and should not be allowed to pass in a first-rate watch. The method of making such a test is fully explained under the head of Isochronal Adjustment.

(387.) *Errors in the rate.*—In the trials at the Kew observatory, (class A,) change of temperature must affect the daily rate *less* than $\frac{1}{3}$ second for each degree, Fahrenheit. The daily rate must not exceed 10 seconds. The mean difference of daily rate between any two succeeding days, during each period of comparison, (5 days,) must not exceed 2 seconds. The difference of mean daily rate between pendant up (hanging) and dial up (lying down) must not exceed 5 seconds. The difference of mean daily rate (of a 5 day period) between pendant up and any other position must not exceed 10 seconds. In the second grade (B) trials, which are for ordinary deck watches for ships, the position tests are limited to pendant up and dial up, and the variation must not exceed 2 seconds in either position, nor exceed 10 seconds between hanging up and lying down. Temperature limit as before. Class C is for positions only, limits as in class B.

(388.) *Excellence marks.*—In class A, marks, showing the exact excellence of the performance, are given in the certificates. They are calculated as follows: If the error of the watches is just the amount stated as the limit, it gets no marks, but barely passes, with a certificate. In the trials for daily rate, the limit, 10 seconds, is divided into 40 parts, of .25 second each; for each .25 second less than 10 seconds, the watch gets 1 mark, and, of course, if its rate was perfect, it would get 40 marks, which would indicate no error at all. The position limit of 2 seconds is divided into 40 parts, of .05 second each, and each .05 second that the error is less than the limit gains 1 mark. The temperature error is divided into 20 parts, of .015 second each, and each .015 second that the error is within the limits gets 1 mark. If the watch got 100 marks, it would indicate perfection. If the watch gets 25 marks for mean difference of daily rate, and the other errors noted in section (387) for daily rate, positions and temperatures, are less than half the limited amounts, it is marked "especially good" in the certificate. The foregoing details will show the workman what performance is considered good, and what errors are allowed to pass by good adjusters.

PART FIFTH.

SPECIAL AND "NATURAL" COMPENSATIONS.

CHAPTER XXIV.

THE FOUR PRINCIPAL ESCAPEMENTS.

(389.) *Require different treatment.*—As will be seen from the following chapters, the different escapements require entirely different procedures, as regards the length of the hair springs, the number and openness of the coils, the mode of pinning them in complete or fractional coils, in the size and weight of the balance, the size and closeness of fitting for its pivots, the strength of the motive force, the mode of oiling and the kind of oil, and numerous other vital points of detail, besides the proper design and construction of the escapement itself. Some require isochronous hair springs and compensated balances, and others are better off without them. These are some of the points in which each escapement needs special treatment adapted to its peculiarities and requirements, but the details on such points are not needed in the general directions, and if inserted there would only encumber them and confuse the inexperienced workman who was in quest of information.

(390.) *New departure.*—I have therefore thought it desirable to take an entirely new departure in the manner of treating the subjects of timing and the adjustments, to deal with each escapement by itself, so far as it needs special handling, and to separately explain the merits and the weaknesses of each, its peculiarities and requirements, what it can do, and what it is unsuitable for, without being mixed up with general directions and rules which do not apply to it, and which if followed would be detrimental to its performance. Only in that way can the workman obtain a clear and correct idea of the nature and needs of each escapement.

My task has been to sift out from the mass of different and contradictory opinions, experiences and results before the trade, published and unpublished, those which relate to each different kind of escapement, and to state the best method to follow with each one of them, and in different circumstances. That has never been done before, and to do it has involved ten-fold more labor and time than to have merely stated either my own experiences and opinions, or those generally held by the practical men in the trade.

(391.) *Merits of different escapements.*—Charles Frodsham has well stated the truth about the different escapements as follows:

"The true seat of the time-keeping principle in every watch or chronometer resides in the union of a perfectly hardened tempered balance-spring and a perfect compensation balance, the weight and diameter of the balance being in just proportion to the motive force. The special value of particular escapements and of escapements in general is very much overestimated; for, when each of the three well-established escapements, the Arnold for chronometers, the duplex and lever for watches, are equally well made, and tried with the same balance and balance-spring, the result of their performance is not so marked as is generally believed, nor is the superiority of the one escapement over the other so evident as many persons have been led to imagine. The Arnold escapement is undoubtedly the most accurate and the most proper escapement for marine chronometers. The perfection of every watch or chronometer lies in the talent and ability of the watchmaker to combine the several parts into one harmonious whole."

(392.) While that is undoubtedly true so far as regards the principle of the escapement, in practice that escapement is preferable in which the proper harmonious relation of the parts can be most easily and surely secured by the maker, and retained or restored by the repairer, and whose performance is least affected by imperfections and injuries. Judged on that basis, the chronometer escapement is very inferior for use in pocket watches. Frodsham himself adds that: "The talent to produce a first-rate reliable chronometer for the pocket falls to the lot of few." It is the special object of Part V to enable the workman to "combine the several parts into one harmonious whole," and he will do well to carefully note and observe every detail of the instructions given.

(393.) *The difference in the escapements.*—The cylinder and the duplex are frictional escapements, in which the escape-wheel teeth rest against the axis of the balance and directly influence its movements. The lever and the chronometer are detached escapements,—the movement of the balance being disconnected from the influence of the escapement or the train during the greater part of its vibrations. These differences are radical, both in their nature and in the consequences involved. By taking proper advantage of them, the two former escapements have what is termed "natural compensation," *i.e.*, they can be so arranged as to compensate for differences in the motive force, the arc of vibration, the frictions, the temperature, etc., by the mechanical action of the escapement alone; while the two latter require to be compensated by special means and adjustments. The directions for "adjusting" watches therefore apply as a general rule only to the detached escapements. The requirements of the "natural compensations" will be given in connection with the two frictional escapements.

(394.) *Mechanical condition of the escapement.*—Aside from the matter of compensation, there are obviously many details of proportion, arrangement and condition of the various parts of the escapements, which must be carefully attended to in order to secure a proper action of the mechanism. Many details regarding the escapement and the train are therefore given, because in the frictional escapements they directly affect the timing of the watch, while in the detached escapements they do so indirectly, by varying the effective motive force, the manner of giving the impulse, the resistances during the temporary connection of the balance with the train, etc. But in the latter cases, the motion of the balance is *comparatively* independent of the condition of the train and the proportions of the escapement—hence only such details are given as do affect the timing or the movement and action of the balance. All faults and imperfections beyond those limits belong more properly to the watchmaker's or repairer's department, and cannot be treated here.

(395.) *Adjusting the different escapements.*—The mechanical manipulations of the escapement to obtain a correct compensation are as truly an "adjustment" as if the same result had been obtained by manipulating the balance or the balance spring. The chapter on the cylinder and the duplex escapements contains all the directions for adjusting them as perfectly as it can be done; while the chapters on the lever and the chronometer escapements give all the special technical details which influence the timing of each, and the reader is then referred to the more general parts of the book, where he will find the subjects of springing, timing and adjusting treated more fully and practically, it is thought, than has ever been done before. As the book is not based upon the studies and opinions of any one workman, however eminent, but upon the results and experiences of all practical men everywhere, so far as publicly known, we believe that the reader will find it complete, accurate, practically useful, and worthy of its title, the Adjuster's Manual.

CHAPTER XXV.

Cylinder Escapement Watches.

(396.) *General characteristics.*—The *cylinder escapement*, also called *lepine* and *horizontal*, is so well known that it will be unnecessary to describe its principle or action, further than concerns the springer and adjuster. It needs neither the isochronal hair spring nor the compensated balance, having what is termed "natural compensation" for temperature and variations in motive force. The good performance of this escapement depends upon a correct proportion between the parts of the escapement, the strength of the motive force, and the size and weight of the balance. It cannot be isochronized unless this proportion exists. But if it does, this escapement is less affected by changes in the strength of the motive force than any other which is used in watches. It can also be so closely compensated for temperatures, isochronism and position, by very simple means, as to answer all ordinary requirements for a low-priced watch. A well-made cylinder escapement therefore needs but little adjustment in order to make it a fairly good timekeeper, and the directions given in this chapter will suffice for that purpose, by indicating what the correct proportion should be, the effect of deviation therefrom, and the proper remedy.

(397.) *The hair spring.*—From 8 to 12 coils are used, many makers preferring from 8 to 10, as being more suitable for a frictional escapement; others prefer 12. They are pinned nearly half a turn short of even turns, as they are found to act better when so pinned, being short and the balance vibrations small. They generally have 18,000 vibrations per hour. Small watches, with very light mainsprings, being very sensitive to shaking, change of temperature, etc., are made to give 19,000 to 21,000 vibrations per hour, and very small watches (from 9 to 6 lines in diameter) have sometimes as many as 24,000 per hour. Even watches of ordinary size, (13 to 20 lines in diameter,) when to be exposed to severe shaking, etc., are made to give 19,000 vibrations per hour. The standard arc of vibration is 270°, or three-quarters of a turn.

(398.) *The balance.*—The good performance of this escapement depends largely on the proper weight and diameter of the balance. If the balance is not correct, it will be impossible to make the long and short vibrations equal by changing the hair spring. If the watch gains when the motive force is increased, the balance is too small and heavy. Some improvement would be secured by making the balance lighter and fitting a weaker hair spring to suit, but the light balance would be more easily affected by differences in the motive force, in the temperature, oil thickening by cold, shaking and jarring, making it unsteady and unreliable. The proper change is to make the balance both lighter and larger, with a hair spring to suit; then the performance is steadier and better.

(399.) A balance too light is too sensitive to variations in the motive force, frictions, change in the condition of the oil, etc. One too heavy is difficult to time, especially in positions. If regulated hanging up, it will gain when lying down; if regulated lying down, it will lose when hanging. This difference is due to the difference in the frictions in the two positions, and it increases as the balance is heavier. The friction of the pivots must be equalized, or a stronger and more suitable hair spring used, if the balance cannot be replaced. But when a rather small cylinder and escape wheel are used, the balance may safely be smaller and heavier, and this combination or proportion is considered to give the best performance which this escapement is capable of.

(400.) *The escapement.*—The usual rule is that the escape wheel should be half the diameter of the balance or a trifle less. Of course, this rule works both ways, and may serve as a guide to the proper size of the balance. Be sure that the teeth clear the slot in its cock when at their highest point of end shake, and that there is no oil or dirt in the slot to clog it; also that the teeth clear the 4th wheel pinion, and that the extremities of the arms carrying the teeth do not rub on the top of 4th wheel, when that is at its highest position.

(401.) *Freedom in cylinder.*—See that there is freedom both when the tooth is inside and outside of the cylinder. In doubtful cases, hold the balance still and test each tooth, in both positions. The teeth should also be free from the cylinder plugs above and below them. If there is freedom when the tooth is outside, the cylinder shell may be too thick; the wheel may pitch too deeply, *i.e.*, the wheel and cylinder planted too close together; the cylinder too small; the escape-wheel teeth too long, or not equal. It is customary to allow more freedom inside than outside, to prevent the heel of the teeth from rubbing, in case the pitching is too deep. The easiest remedy is to "top" the teeth. See Rapping, (411.) If there is freedom inside, but none outside, the cylinder is probably too large, and if the teeth are so formed that "topping" will not cure it, a smaller cylinder should be fitted.

(402.) *The cylinder.*—As a general rule the cylinder should be $\frac{1}{9}$ the diameter of the escape wheel, or the wheel diameter multiplied by .115. The thickness of the shell should be about $\frac{1}{9}$ of the length of the tooth, *i.e.*, of the incline or outside. The shell is cut away for the teeth, not quite half through, its acting part being about 200° of a circle. The two edges or *lips* of the acting part are called the *entering lip* and the *exit lip*. The former is rounded from both sides, the latter from the inside only, making a sort of inclined plane for the teeth. The lips should be smooth, well polished, and free from rust, and the shell both inside and outside free from pitting or cutting. The slot is cut away so that only $\frac{1}{4}$ of the circle remains. See Recoil, (412).

(403.) *Improper cylinder.*—When the cylinder is too large, the friction is increased and the retarding force becomes excessive, the vibrations become sluggish and smaller, and the watch is difficult to regulate. Large cylinders with large escape wheels require stronger mainsprings and lighter balances, and are more sensitive to thickening of the oil and other retarding influences. When the cylinder is too small (relatively to other parts of the escapement), the teeth will be too close in the cylinder, and the balance vibrations will be weak, because the leverage is too short. If the escape-wheel teeth are naturally short enough for the cylinder, (containing a high number of teeth,) the incline on the teeth must be more steep, and the mainspring stronger, in order to get a sufficient impulse for the balance—both objectionable features.

(404.) *In beat.*—When the balance is at rest and free from any pressure of the escape-wheel teeth, the hair-spring stud should be in line with the two lips of the cylinder. To test the beat, notice the dot in the edge of the balance and the three dots on the watch plate. When the watch is made, the dot in the balance rim is set just opposite the middle dot on the plate, and the dots on each side of that indicate the extent of the impulse lift. If the parts have not been disarranged, the beat can be tested by them. Put a pegwood point against the rim of the fourth wheel, and hold it, cutting off the motive force from the escape wheel. When the balance is perfectly free and still, the dot on the rim should stand opposite the middle dot on the plate. Then press the pegwood forward and cause the balance to move slowly each way till the tooth escapes. The distance it moves from the point of rest should be the same in each direction, and at the end of each movement the dot in the rim should be opposite the outside dot on the plate. If the dot on the rim is not in the center of these two extreme positions, move the hair-spring collet to carry the stud towards the side having the smallest motion. When it is corrected the stud should hang in line between the dot on the rim and the upper cylinder pivot, both when in the watch and when the balance and hair spring are out. When the watch has been worked at and the dots are disarranged, make a new dot or mark on the balance rim, and proceed as directed in section (288).

(405.) The foregoing sections give the proper and normal positions, but in some cases the spring is purposely put out of center or otherwise displaced, for timing purposes (277, 694). Hence it is a safe rule when merely cleaning, or repairing some part which does not involve the adjustments nor "putting in perfect order," to *put everything exactly as you found it*, (Chapter I,) unless you are certain it is wrong.

(406.) *The banking.*—The watch being in beat, as described, when the balance is at rest and free the *banking pin* in its rim should stand exactly opposite to the *banking stud*, which is a pin fixed in the balance cock at the other side of the balance. This can generally be tested by "sighting" across the balance from the pin to the stud. A line from the pin through the cylinder pivot should strike the center of the stud. Furthermore, the position of the banking pin is generally a quarter of a circle distant from the beat-dot in the rim, (404) *i.e.*, a line across the balance, from the dot through the center, would be perpendicular to a similar line from the pin, through the center. Consequently, the dot should be midway between the banking pin and the banking stud. The banking is very important, because the balance must not vibrate more than one turn, *i.e.*, half a turn each way from the point of rest, as that is all that the half-shell of the cylinder can allow. If the motion exceeds that amount, on either side, we shall have overbanking (408), and perhaps rapping (411).

(407.) See that the banking pin cannot miss the stud in any position of the watch, (from changes due to the end-shake of the cylinder,) and that it is long enough to hit the stud properly. If the pin is a little short, and liable to get over on the end of the stud, arrange the stud nearer the rim of the balance, (but not too close,) or put in a longer pin. Also see that there is no incline on the stud where the pin strikes it, tending to cause the pin to rise over or under it, and wedge or stick there, instead of striking the stud fairly and squarely. The pin must safely clear the fourth wheel pinion or arbor, the balance cock, the case, etc. The banking pin and stud, as well as the edge of the balance and the arms of the escape-wheel teeth, should be clean, free from oil or other sticky matter, and dry, otherwise the watch may run irregularly or stop.

(408.) *Overbanking.*—When the tooth drops onto the cylinder the balance continues its vibration to the end, or till stopped by the banking pin hitting the stud, and then returns. But if the banking pin is not properly placed and allows the balance to go too far, the point of the tooth slips over the wrong lip of the cylinder and catches, so that the balance is held fast and cannot get back. This is called *overbanking.* To release the balance, move the escape-wheel tooth back a little, just enough to let the lip get before the point of the tooth, then let the wheel go. In rare cases, this is caused by the lips of the cylinder being worn or cut, or having been worked at, till the shell is too small, *i.e.*, the part remaining is barely half a circle, or less than 200°.

(409.) *Remedy for overbanking.*—In the former case, the teeth may sometimes be caused to run on the sound part of the lips above or below the cut; in the other case the proper remedy is a new cylinder. But if the vibrations are small, it is possible to prevent overbanking by putting in another stud at one side of the old one, to prevent the balance coming around far enough to catch. If it catches on both sides, two new studs will be needed. This course may be unobjectionable unless there is danger of "rapping" (411).

(410.) *To test for overbanking*, move the balance around each way till the pin stands against the stud, (the watch being wound,) to see if it catches. If it does, the vibrations are not equal on the two sides, (the banking pin and stud not in the same diametrical line), or the balance is not properly staked on the cylinder, so that the banking pin is not midway between the two lips, (the two diametrical lines are not perpendicular, as described in section (406), on the banking,) or the lips have been so worn or changed that the banking pin is not midway between the two dots (404) showing the extents of the lifts.

(411.) *Rapping.*—If the vibrations are so large that the banking pin frequently hits the stud, great irregularity in time is the result. It may be cured by a weaker mainspring or a heavier balance. If these do not stop the rapping, the impulse may be lessened by "topping" the escape wheel. Arrange it in the turns, and very carefully and evenly take off the heels of the teeth, either by grinding with an oilstone slip or by polishing with a burnisher. Make but little change, and try it in the watch, to avoid overdoing it. Test the smoothness of both the points and the heels; they should not feel rough and scratch on the finger-nail; if they do, they are either rough or too pointed and sharp. This alteration shortens the length of the incline on the teeth, reduces the lift and the impulse, and increases the drops and freedom.

(412.) *Recoil.*—When the banking is properly adjusted, give the balance a large vibration, by pressure on the center wheel, to see if the escape wheel recoils while running. That is caused by the lip hitting against the front of the arm of the tooth. It can also be tested by moving the balance back till the banking pin hits the stud, then try if there is freedom between the lip and the arms of the teeth. If they touch, the passage can be cut a little deeper with a sapphire file or a steel slip and oil-stone dust. The exit lip of the cylinder should pass over the arm of the wheel without touching or coming so near together that the oil can run from the lip to the arm of the tooth, and cause fouling with some other part.

(413.) *Setting.*—If the watch sets and stops, especially when the oil is thickened by cold, the incline of the escape-wheel teeth is probably too high, and a larger cylinder or a stronger motive force may be required.

(414.) *Escape-wheel pinions.*—If the diameter of this pinion is too large relatively to the diameter of the escape wheel, the balance will not move with sufficient freedom, but will seem constrained. This appearance may direct attention to the cause of the fault. With a large pinion, the fourth wheel depthing must be very correct, as any errors in the depthing will show in the action of the escapement. The escape wheel will probably have too much force for the balance.

(415.) *To straighten a cylinder pivot.*—It is very essential that the cylinder shall revolve concentrically, and the pivots should always be straight and in good condition. To straighten a bent pivot, take a pivot "bush" or bouchon, fit it over the bent pivot, and bring it up into line with the axis of the cylinder. If you have no bush, a hole drilled truly in the center of a hard brass wire may be used. If the hole is drilled correctly and the wire is straight, its length makes it an easy matter to get it vertical, and when the wire is vertical, the pivot will be vertical, too.

(416.) *Natural compensation for heat and cold.*—As oil is used on the impulse planes or rubbing surfaces of a frictional escapement, and the pivots are also comparatively large, the condition of the oil becomes an important factor in the running, and gives the cylinder escapement a sort of natural compensation for changes of temperature. In warm weather, the oil is thin, and there is a quicker action of the escapement; in cold, the oil becomes thicker, produces a more sluggish action of the balance, and counteracts the effects of cold upon the hair spring and balance. In order to secure a sufficient compensation in this way, the oil should evidently not be too liquid, and should become considerably thicker by cold. Hence the modern oils which do not thicken in cold are not so suitable for cylinders, although excellent for detached escapements. Another requisite is that the hair spring should not be too long, as the correcting effects are more marked in short springs, and insufficient in those which are too long. The spring should therefore be shortened to increase these effects, and lengthened to lessen them.

(417.) *Natural compensation for variations in the motive force.*—The cylinder escapement also has a very efficient compensation for changes in the motive force, as, the greater that force is, the greater is the pressure of the tooth on the cylinder to restrain its motion and keep the balance vibrations equal. This compensation it possesses in a greater degree than any other, and it is therefore specially adapted for going-barrel watches of a grade too low to admit of special adjustments. It is necessary, however, that there be the correct proportion between the parts of the escapement already spoken of. If the cylinder is too large, for example, the friction of the tooth upon it is so great that the effect is too much for a correct compensation for changes of motive force, and the watch cannot be regulated.

(418.) *Natural isochronal compensation.*—The compensation by friction described in the preceding section, which keeps the balance vibrations of substantially the same extent, combined with the compensation for the effects of heat and cold on the hair spring and balance, virtually constitute a natural isochronal adjustment, when correct. It is only correct, however, when there is the correct proportion between the parts of the escapement, and when all the influences at work combine to balance and neutralize each other, keeping the vibrations uniform, and in reality doing away with the necessity for isochronal adjustment.

(419.) *Frictional adjustment for isochronism.*—If desired, the isochronism can be adjusted and perfected by varying the relative amounts of the escapement friction and the arcs of vibration, as described in section (570). But it should be remembered that a cylinder watch cannot be isochronized unless there is the correct proportion between the weight and diameter of the balance, the size of the cylinder, and the motive power. And further, the opening of the cylinder and the impulse angle of the escape-wheel teeth must be such as to give, if not the best, at least fully satisfactory, performance.

(420.) *Isochronizing by the regulator pins.*—In watches which have but few coils in the hair spring, and they are well separated from each other, considerable improvement in the isochronal action can often be obtained by opening or closing the regulator pins, as directed in sections (585) to (588).

(421.) *Isochronizing by the balance.*—When the weight of the balance is too small for a correct proportion to the rest of the escapement, it can be made heavier as directed in sections (333, 334). If too heavy, the balance (if a plain one) can be gripped by the edge in a lathe chuck, with the under side out, and a very little cut out in a central groove around the rim. Then poise and test it. This is easier than fitting a lighter balance, but should not be done when the watch needs a balance which is both lighter and smaller. In a screw balance, the screws can be altered as required.

(422.) *Timing in positions.*—The watch being closely regulated in a horizontal position, (dial up,) try it hanging up. If it gains when hanging, take a little off the bottom of the balance; if it loses when hung up, take a little off the top. What is here meant by the bottom and top, is that part of the rim which is lowest or uppermost when the watch is in the hanging position, and the balance at rest, free from the motive force. A vertical line through the pivot or the center of the balance will pass through the top and bottom points of the rim. The metal should be filed from the under side of the rim and on the inner edge. Take off but very little, testing the effect frequently, as it puts the balance out of poise, and too much change should not be made. It should only be practiced on low grade watches, and which do not vibrate over one turn. It is not suitable for watches which are carried in the pocket loosely, so that they may turn and change their positions, as the effect produced would be the reverse of the one desired if the watch should be worn with the other edge up. Of course, the same alteration can be made on screw balances by running the screws out on the side to be made heavier, and *vice versa*, or by filing off their heads, or by removing a screw from one side and not from the other, or by removing it from one side and inserting it in the other side at a point exactly opposite.

(423.) *To test if the balance is too heavy for the motive force.*— The watch being wound, move the balance exactly to its neutral or central position, (as it would stand if at rest, free from the motive force,) and liberate it. It should start going, of itself. If it does not, the balance is too heavy—provided the escapement is correct and in beat. Also notice how long it takes to acquire its full vibration. If it requires 12 or 15 vibrations to reach its full motion, the balance is probably too heavy, or the motive force is too weak; and the reverse is the case if it gets into full vibration almost immediately. But only experience can enable the workman to judge positively from such tests. The timing may also indicate when a balance is too heavy by the difficulty of timing in positions, *i.e.*, to get the same rate hanging and lying down. If the motive force is also too weak for the balance, it will gain while horizontal and lose while hanging up. See section (399).

(424.) *Oiling.*—As the oil plays an important part in the performance of the cylinder escapement, its proper quality and application should be attended to. Oil which is too thin and fluid is not suitable, as has already been explained (416). Another reason is that a very fluid oil has a tendency to spread and leave the rubbing surfaces. For example, it would leave the lip or shell of the cylinder to run on the teeth, and from the teeth it would run down the standards or *stalks* of the teeth and foul in the slot and elsewhere. The American oils which are not too thin will be suitable for the pivots, but for the teeth and cylinder the imported Rodanet oil is preferable. All oils should be kept in bottles tightly corked, and in the dark, and should be kept fresh in the oil box.

(425.) *Applying the oil.*—After putting a minute drop of oil in the pivot holes of the cylinder, run a fine clean pegwood point into the hole, to carry the oil through to the end stone,—(otherwise it may remain at the surface, and the shoulder of the pivot coming in contact will draw it away and leave the inner part of the hole almost dry.) Having done so, then apply a little more oil to the hole. Apply a very little oil to the two lips of the cylinder where the teeth act upon them, rubbing the oiling wire up and down to moisten them. Then apply a little oil on the incline of each tooth. When the job is finished oil the escape-wheel pivots, moving the pivot with the oiling wire to be sure that it enters the hole, but not using enough for any to possibly run down into the pinion.

CHAPTER XXVI.

Duplex Watches.

(426.) *General characteristics.*—The duplex, like the cylinder, is a frictional escapement and has what we have called "natural compensation," (393, 416, to 419.) It does not need either an isochronal hair spring nor compensation balance, and is usually better off without them. But it is very sensitive to variations in the motive force, and hence is not so well adapted for going-barrel watches as the cylinder escapement. In watches not provided with chain and fuzee, stop works should always be used on the barrel, and they should be so arranged as to secure as nearly uniform motive force from the mainspring as possible. The best results are obtained with a somewhat strong motive force—considerably stronger than would answer for the cylinder escapement. The duplex is also very sensitive to shaking and jarring, and is, therefore, unsuitable for very active persons, those who jump about, ride horseback, indulge in violent athletics or sports, and it is impossible to guarantee good performance in such cases,—although duplex watches with very quick trains have sometimes performed well. But for persons of quiet or sedentary habits, or when not worn but left hanging in the house or lying on a table, etc., it is capable of running very closely.

(427.) *The hair-spring.*—The duplex performs best with a rather short hair spring; about 10 coils is usually best. But in watches having very large vibrations, such as were formerly made, and are yet by the French and Swiss makers, a larger spring should be used—up to 12 coils, or even more in some cases. In the duplex, the hair spring is thought to perform best when pinned nearly half a turn short of complete turns. It should not be bent from the regular spiral form at the ends where pinned, but should be pinned without any bending at either the stud or the collet. The latter point is especially important. The coils should be regular in form and equidistant from each other, with uniform strength from one end to the other.

(428.) *The vibrations.*—The duplex generally has 18,000 vibrations per hour, and even more. It should not have *less* than 18,000. When it has only 14,400 or up to 16,000 per hour, with a heavy balance, the motion is so slow and sluggish that the watch is very liable to trip or set. But if the proportion between the escapement, balance, and motive force is correct, it can hardly have too quick a vibration, even up to 24,000 per hour. The usual arc of vibration is 360°, or just 1 turn. But it is often made larger or smaller than that for special timing purposes.

(429.) *In beat.*—When the parts are in their proper relative positions, and the balance is at rest, the notch in the ruby roller should be between the locking tooth resting upon it and the line of centers, (line from the center of the balance staff to the center of the escape wheel), or a very little nearer to the line of centers. Many workmen place the center of the notch on the line of centers, but the previous position is considered preferable, unless the motive force is very strong. In that case, the notch is so placed that the locking tooth is just on the point of dropping into the notch, *i.e.*, the balance moves but little to let the tooth pass into the notch, and considerable to let it out.

(430.) *Sizes of parts.*—The diameter of the ruby roller should be $\frac{1}{3}$ the distance between the points of two *locking* or *resting teeth*, or $\frac{1}{15}$ the diameter of the escape wheel. The sizes throughout the escapement are taken with the escape wheel as the basis. The wheel and teeth must be very accurately cut, and the *impulse* (or upright) *tooth* must be midway between two locking (long) teeth. The wheel must be as light as possible, and accurately poised. The length of the *impulse pallet* or *finger* is governed by the number of teeth in the wheel and the *angle of lift*, or intersection of the impulse teeth and impulse pallet. No fixed proportion can be specified, but the object is to have the intersection deep enough for safety and wide enough to give sufficient lift or impulse. The points of the impulse teeth are generally at two-thirds the distance from the center to the points of the locking teeth.

(431.) *The drops.*—When the locking tooth slips out of the notch in the roller, there is an *engaging drop* on to the impulse pallet; when the impulse tooth passes off the pallet there is another or *disengaging drop*, that of the locking tooth on to the ruby roller. The amounts of the drops are very important. The engaging drop is adjusted by turning the impulse pallet on the balance staff; moving the pallet towards the notch makes the engaging drop greater and *vice versa*, but moving it from the notch does not increase the disengaging drop: that is governed by the length of the impulse finger or pallet, and should be no greater than is necessary for freedom of action, as excessive drop on to the ruby roller is liable to spring the balance staff, loosen or break the roller, etc. The disengaging drop is also varied by getting the balance staff and escape wheel closer or further apart. About 10° of balance movement is usually allowed for the engaging drop, and a little less for the disengaging drop.

(432.) *Examining impulse and drops.*—Bring the balance to rest with the locking tooth resting against the roller. See if it is in beat (429). Move the balance slowly back the (*dumb vibration*), to see if the end of the impulse finger safely clears the impulse tooth behind it, (the tooth which has just left the pallet); let the locking tooth fall into the notch, and see that there is no danger of its point escaping past the other lip of the notch when it falls, nor catch on the corner of the notch; try the freedom of the tooth in the notch in all positions as you move the balance slowly back; go on so till the locking tooth again rests on the outside of the ruby roller, and see if the point of the impulse finger clears the impulse tooth in front of it, trying it repeatedly, to be sure. If there is too much space between them when they pass, it may show that the intersection is too shallow for safety.

(433.) *The engaging drop.*—Now move the balance forward, *i.e.*, in the direction of its *acting* or *impulse vibration*, let the locking tooth again fall into the notch, and very slowly move the balance forward till the tooth slips out of the notch and the impulse tooth drops on to the finger, and hold the balance there; this is the engaging drop. This drop should be sufficient, (*i.e.*, the pallet should be far enough in advance of the tooth,) to enable the point of the tooth to lap on the face of the impulse finger far enough to secure a safe action. If the tooth misses the pallet, or catches on its corner, the drop must be increased, (431,) or the finger lengthened, or the impulse pallet jewel (if there is one on the finger) must be moved outward; or in extreme cases, where only the drop can be increased and would then be too great for a good action, the balance staff and center wheel must be brought closer together. But generally (if the locking action is correct) a new impulse finger would be better. The intersection being safe, move the balance forward, see that the tooth acts on the pallet long enough to give a good impulse, and notice the amount of the drop when the tooth passes off the pallet, again trying the freedom of the pallet when passing the tooth which has just dropped. If the wheel is true, this examination will show the condition of the whole escapement.

(434.) *To test the safety of the impulse intersection.*—When the balance pivots are rather loose in their holes, the play may make considerable difference in the action in different positions, *i.e.*, whether the balance is nearest to the escape wheel or further from it, and a special test is then needed for *the safety*. With the watch wound a little, put a pegwood point inside of the balance rim and press it *towards* the wheel, pass the impulse finger by the tooth, back and forth, to see if they *can* touch, where they should clear. Do this with both teeth—the one which has just acted, and the one that is ready to act.

(435.) Then put the pegwood on the outside of the balance rim, and press it *from* the wheel. Try if the impulse tooth drops safely on the pallet when the latter is advanced very slowly towards the waiting tooth. If it catches on the corner of the pallet, and that is considerably rounded, dressing the face down level to the edge may lengthen the finger sufficiently. (The face must be in line with the balance axis.) If it does not, the pallet should be turned on the staff to make the intersection deeper when contact occurs, (*i.e.*, turned toward the roller notch,) as directed in sections (433, 446). This must also be done if it is found that some of the teeth are shorter than others, and do not catch safely, while the others do. When the teeth are not even, both of these tests should be made *with every tooth*.

(436.) *Examining the escape wheel.*—About the only way open to the jobber is to examine the action in the watch. Perhaps the best way to tell whether the locking and impulse teeth are uniform and at equal distances apart is to repeat so much of the foregoing test as necessary, with each tooth on the wheel. Let the impulse tooth drop off the pallet, and while the locking tooth rests on the ruby roller examine the clearance between the end of the impulse finger and the tooth which has just left the pallet. Hold the movement so you can see the light between them as they pass, holding the balance still at that point. If the clearance is the same for all of the impulse teeth, the wheel may be considered true.

(437.) *To test the locking teeth*, hold the movement so that the line of sight will be along the front of the tooth, and observe how near the edge of the roller the point of the tooth stands. Now let the watch run, observing the position of each tooth. If some are longer, they will stop nearer the edge, while the short teeth will be able to get nearer the center of the roller. As the tooth retains its position during the remainder of the acting vibration (after the disengaging drop) and during the first half of the return or dumb vibration, there is time enough to observe closely. The wheel can be examined in the calipers, by setting the point of the slip or toucher very accurately, to see whether the wheel is out of center, *i.e.*, if some of the teeth reach further from the center than others.

(438.) *Correcting the wheel.*—Try both sets of teeth; the locking, and the upright or impulse teeth. If they are concentric at their points, but some of the locking teeth are bent and irregular, about the only way to get them uniform is to make a templet, one edge of which is so shaped as to rest against the pivot, and also along the front side of the teeth. If the templet rests against the root of the tooth, but not the point, the point has been bent back; if it hits the point, but not the root, the tooth is bent forward. The templet is, of course, fitted to a tooth which appears sound and correct. The impulse teeth can be tested in the same way. The width of the templet at the points of the teeth can be made equal to the proper distance between the points, and will show if the points are evenly spaced.

(439.) *Topping the locking teeth.*—This can be done by inserting the wheel and pinion in a depthing tool, and adjusting an oil-stone slip against the centers of the other jaw, (the one nearest the adjusting screw,) so that it will nearly touch the longest tooth. While rotating the wheel with a very fine hair and weak bow, gently press the jaws of the tool together with the fingers. They will spring enough for the oil-stone to get the points all of equal length. Then smooth the corners with very fine burnisher. The straightening and evening of the teeth must have been previously done.

(440.) *General condition.*—The balance staff should not have much end-shake, or the pivots will wear rapidly; in that case they should be repolished and new jewel holes fitted—at least to the bottom pivot. The balance pivots require to be well fitted. If the holes are too large, every change of position causes errors in the running, because it changes the frictions and the action of the escapement. The duplex does best with a strong motive force and rather heavy balance. When the balance has timing screws in its rim, it should be riveted on the staff in such position that these screws will be in a vertical line through the staff, when the balance is at rest and free, with the watch in the hanging position. This is to admit of adjusting for positions by altering the poise (422).

(441.) *Impulse pallet and teeth.*—The acting face of the impulse pallet should be in a radial line to the balance center, and the front of the impulse tooth should be parallel with it when they meet. Otherwise either the pallet or tooth will be cut and pitted by the corner striking it. In a fine watch intelligently made, the position in which the faces are parallel would evidently be where the maker intended the contact to occur, but in common watches the workman must arrange the drop where he thinks the action will be best. Some recommend that the pallet should be just ahead of the tooth when it drops, while others advise that it be placed considerably ahead of it, so that the tooth will have considerable drop before it reaches the pallet. Perhaps the best way is to arrange each case according to what it requires to give the best performance. A very slight increase of drop on the impulse pallet considerably lessens the balance vibrations; and *vice versa*.

(442.) *Locking teeth and ruby roller.*—If the locking intersection is shallow, there will be straining of the balance staff, by the tooth nearly passing by the roller, with engaging friction or wedging, springing the staff, danger of splitting the ruby roller —also danger of *tripping*, and of *setting*, if the watch is jarred or shaken while the tooth is on the roller. If the notch is wide, there is also danger of the tooth slipping by the corner and tripping; the *recoil* is also greater. The roller must be perfectly concentric with the balance staff. The notch should be no wider than necessary for freedom of the teeth, and the corners should be but little rounded, well polished and perfect. The notch should have sufficient depth to avoid any danger of the point of the tooth grazing the bottom. No rule can be given for the size of the ruby roller. The great point is to have the intersection safe. The custom of jobbers is to have an assortment of rollers, fit on one which seems likely to be suitable, and examine the action, with the balance and escape wheel in the depthing tool. If not good, take another size, till correct.

(443.) *Safety tests for positions.*—The watch being wound, hold it edge up, with the balance below the wheel and falling away from it. Run it long enough to see if there is any sign of catching or irregularity. If so, the locking intersection may be too shallow, (433,) or the impulse finger and pallet may fail to meet properly, (441). Notice the extent of the vibrations, then reverse the positions and have the balance above the wheel, and falling *towards* it. If the vibrations fall off, the locking teeth may not be free in the notch, or the impulse teeth may catch on the point of the pallet as it passes them during the dumb vibration. This latter fault can be heard if the watch is in the case. If there are two locking teeth to each impulse tooth, the roller must be perfectly free when between the double teeth, in this position.

(444.) *Running or overrunning.*—If the balance vibrates too far, (during the impulse vibration,) two teeth will pass at a single vibration, causing the watch to gain. It is generally due to a mainspring too strong or balance too light. If the intersection of the locking teeth on the ruby roller is shallow, the watch is liable to *running*. If this fault is inveterate, it can be prevented by a banking pin in the balance and another in the plate below the balance, arranged to come in contact at the proper time and prevent the balance vibrating over one turn—precisely as in the case of the cylinder escapement (406). But nowadays this contrivance is seldom seen, the error being guarded against by more careful usage by the wearer. Besides, it is liable to cause *rapping*, which is almost as bad as running.

(445.) *Setting* may be due to a balance too heavy, too narrow a notch in the ruby roller, or one whose edges are rough or chipped, or the points of the locking teeth are damaged, too thick, or not vertical, so that they clog in the notch as if they were very thick. In a narrow notch, the thickening of the oil clogs the teeth and increases the liability to set. Setting is also more liable to occur if the engaging drop is too small and the impulse tooth has to impel the pallet too far before it can escape. Similarly, the watch is more liable to stop when it is out of beat, in such a way that the locking teeth have to move the roller around a great distance before they can escape from the notch. If this fault is inveterate, it may be well to place the roller notch on the line of centers. See *In beat*, (429). Then the balance will move an equal distance each side from the point of rest, in order that the locking tooth may enter the notch and leave it. A stronger mainspring is generally advisable, unless the watch is also addicted to tripping or running, in which case the best plan would be to make it red-hot and then pulverize it.

(446.) *Isochronal adjustment.*—If the escapement frictions remain the same, and the arcs of vibration are made larger, (as by a greater motive force, or by a better action of the escapement, making the motive force more effective,) the long vibrations will be slower than the short ones, and *vice versa*. See section (570). Moving the impulse pallet towards the roller-notch increases the engaging drop and makes the vibrations smaller, and the long vibrations will be quicker than the short ones, but this should not be done when the angle between the impulse pallet and the notch is less than about 10°, as that amount is considered necessary. Moving the impulse pallet away from the notch and so increasing this angle, increases the arc of vibration and also makes the long vibrations slower than the short ones. But if moved too far, the impulse tooth will catch on the corner of the pallet, or even fail to hit it at all—the tooth getting past the pallet before the intersection becomes deep enough for contact to occur, (432, 433.) Another way to accomplish the same results is to put the watch out of beat. For instance, to make the short vibrations faster than the long ones, move the hairspring collet on the balance staff so as to make the roller notch stand nearer to the tooth resting on it, when the balance is at rest. But this makes the watch more liable to set, and should not be done except when the motive force is very strong (429). The pinning of the hair spring can of course be varied to improve the isochronism, as with levers and chronometers.

(447.) *Natural compensation for positions.*—When the watch is correctly designed and well made, the proportion between the motive force, the momentum of the balance, and the strength of the hair spring produces a "natural compensation" for different positions and for different arcs of vibration. But when this proportion does not exist, it is useless to expect to correct the errors by changing the hair spring, unless that is the part at fault, when it should of course be corrected. The effect of play or looseness in the balance pivot holes has already been mentioned (434). When the watch is in the position which allows the balance to fall closer to the escape wheel, the long vibrations will be quicker than the short ones, and *vice versa*. If this action can be utilized it will help to perfect the "natural compensation for positions." That would be done by arranging the movement in the case so that when the watch was in the hanging position the balance would be over or under the wheel, according to the effect desired.

(448.) *To time the duplex in positions.*—This is done by changing the poise of the balance. The method of altering a plain balance or an ordinary screw balance, has already been described, and is the same as for the cylinder escapement. See sections (421, 422.) When the balance has timing screws, (440,) and has been riveted on the staff so that they are in the vertical diameter when the balance is at rest, hanging, and the roller notch is in the correct position relatively to the rest of the escapement, the poise of the balance can be changed by moving the timing screws in or out as required. If the ruby roller was set after the balance was riveted on the staff, it should be cemented on in the proper position relatively to the timing screws, which is easily done by marking the direction of the line of centers on the rim. If the balance is too heavy, it will be more difficult to time in positions. And if the vibrations are more than one turn in extent, this method is not suitable, for the effect will be one way with the small arcs, and just the reverse with long arcs.

(449.) *To test if the balance is too heavy* for the motive force, (the escapement being in proper condition,) slowly move it backward till the locking tooth enters the roller notch, then liberate the balance; and it should start to going without assistance. If it does not, the balance is probably too heavy, or the watch is not in beat, (429, 445).

Another way is to see how long a time is required to attain its natural vibration, as directed for the cylinder escapement (423).

(450.) *Oiling the duplex.*—Put oil to the pivots, and a little in the notch of the ruby roller, but none on the impulse pallet or teeth.

CHAPTER XXVII.

Lever Watches.

(451.) *General characteristics.*—The lever is often called a detached escapement, but in reality it is only semi-detached. The action is more or less affected by every detail of construction throughout the entire escapement, and a dozen different faults may convert it into a worse than frictional escapement—for the friction in the latter may serve a useful purpose, in controlling and regulating the balance, while in the lever it would be purely detrimental. For an example, take the rubbing of the safety pin on the roller; its effect is entirely harmful, with the single exception that it prevents the occurrence of something even worse than itself. Nevertheless, when well made and adjusted, it is the best escapement in use for pocket watches, and even the low grades have no rival for serviceability in common or rough usage, except the cylinder escapements. Its performance will be in proportion to the conformity of its parts to the correct standard, more than to the fineness of its finish. It is useless to attempt to closely time or to adjust a movement which is not in good condition. The timing being directly affected by the escapement, and being varied by changing the latter in different ways, many details regarding the mechanical proportions and arrangement of the various parts are necessarily given. It is believed that they will pretty fully cover all contingencies, and enable the workman to detect the cause of any fault he meets and know the proper remedy. For good performance the lever requires both an isochronal hair spring and a compensated balance; and after the special directions in this chapter have been carried out, the "adjustments" may be applied and perfected as hereinafter given, with confidence that the performance of the watch will be worthy of the time and labor expended upon it.

(452.) *Technical names.*—The escape wheel may have *ratchet*, *pointed* or *star teeth*, or *club teeth*. The outer surfaces of the latter are *impulse planes*, the sides are called the *locking* and the *heel*.

On the pivoted *lever staff* or *arbor*, sometimes called the *pallet arbor* or *staff*, are the *pallets* and the long part called the *lever fork*, or *lever*. The ends of the pallets are *arms;* the one the tooth strikes first is the *entering arm*, the other is the *exit arm*. The *belly* of the pallets is between the arms. Each arm has a *pallet jewel* or *pallet stone* for the teeth to act upon. The front surfaces are the *impulse planes* or *inclines;* the sides are the *locking* or *locking face*, and the *exit* or *discharging face*. The *horn* of the lever is the curved part on each side of the *notch* in its end, just behind the notch is the *guard point*, or *pin*, or the *safety pin;* in the double roller escapement, the safety pin or *guard finger* projects forward, under the notch.

On the balance staff is the *table roller*, carrying the *ruby pin* or *impulse pin;* in the edge of the roller, in front of the pin, is the *passing hollow* or *crescent*. The double roller escapement has two rollers; the table roller or *impulse roller* which carries the ruby pin, and a smaller or *safety roller* has the crescent in front, and its edge keeps the safety pin from getting by the roller when the lever is pressed backward.

(453.) *The hair spring.*—Springs with 14 coils are thought to be best, but some prefer 12. When the springs are unhardened and soft, as in cheap watches, a longer spring is necessary, in order to avoid bending by use. But this only preserves them for a time, and in a few years they frequently require re-springing in order to do even decent service. The above refers to the flat spiral springs—the only form, except the Breguet, that is used in lever watches. If the flat spiral does not vibrate over $1\frac{1}{4}$ turns, it can be isochronized very closely. If the vibrations exceed $1\frac{1}{4}$ turns, the Breguet form should be used, and abroad, 20 coils are considered best. (The American watch factories use 14 to 15. See Chapter VIII.) For small watches, a turn or two less will be better, as 12 or 13 coils for the flat spiral, and 18 for the Breguet. If the work is cheap and poor, either watches of ordinary size or smaller ones with quick trains should have shorter springs, in order to get the short vibrations fast enough. The diameter of the hair-spring collet should be rather small, the spring should be evenly coiled, of even hardness and temper from end to end, and the inner end should meet the collet without departing from the spiral form. With the ordinary flat spiral, the outer end should meet the stud in the same way. Both the flat spiral and the Breguet are pinned in even turns.

(454.) *The vibrations* of a lever watch are generally 18,000 per hour, but some English levers are made with 16,200 vibrations per hour. But watches will occasionally be met having all the way from 14,400 up to 21,000 beats per hour.

(455.) *In beat.*—The lever is in beat when the center of the ruby pin is on the line of centers, *i.e.*, a straight line between the center of the balance and lever staffs. The center of the lever notch, of the safety pin or guard point, and of the crescent should also be on that line, and in the double roller escapement, the center of the guard finger must likewise be on the line of centers. When the escape wheel is pressed slowly forward, the balance should be moved an equal distance each way from the central position (or point of rest, when the balance is at rest and controlled only by the hair spring,) in order to escape, and the lever should be securely fixed to the pallets in such position that it will move the balance as described.

(456.) *The balance.*—The diameter of the balance is generally twice that of the escape wheel. But when the wheel is smaller than usual and the motive force is strong, it may be 2½ times as large. This is a good rule for English levers. Another rule is that, in a full plate watch, the diameter of the balance should be half that of the top plate, and, in a three-quarter plate watch, it should be the size of the inside of the barrel for a 16,200 train, and a trifle smaller for an 18,000 train. It is supposed that this will insure the size of the balance being suitable for the strength of the motive force, but it is obviously but a rough rule, although sufficient for the needs of the jobber. The manufacturer would need to make a far different calculation if he expected his products to do him any credit. The balance should be tolerably heavy—considerably heavier than for the cylinder escapement—in order to perform the unlocking without affecting its motion. A light balance is greatly affected by variations in the motive force and by imperfections of any kind in the escapement; there being but little friction at the pivots, there will be but little variation between hanging up and lying down. The heavy balance, having greater friction at the pivots, will vary more in the different positions, besides being more liable to injury by falls, etc. For plain balances, gold or brass is preferable to steel.

(457.) *Oiling.*—The lever is much affected by the oil used on the escapement, and none but the best quality should be employed. It requires cleaning at least every eighteen months, and cleaning yearly would greatly improve its performance. On the pivots of the balance staff, pallet staff and escape wheel thin and very fluid oil may be used, but care must be taken not to apply too much, as it is likely to run off and leave the pivots running dry. A very little oil is also applied to the faces of the pallet jewels. After the wheel has gone around two or three times, apply a very little more, let the wheel go a few times around till each tooth has got its point oiled, then with a pegwood point absorb the oil from the pallet faces, and what remains on the teeth will oil them sufficiently. When the pallets are not accessible, oil the teeth only, as described. For the other pivots and bearings an oil with more body should be used. No oil is applied to the escapement except as above directed—none on the ruby pin, guard pin, none in the notch of the lever, or in the crescent, or on the roller. The escapement should not be oiled till the watch goes together for the last time.

(458.) *General examination.*—There are a hundred possible faults, any one of which may affect the running, render it impracticable to secure a close rate or adjustment, or may even cause stoppage. Some of those we shall mention may seem too trivial to dwell upon, but, trivial though they be, they are important enough to spoil your work and damage your reputation. They *must* be attended to, and therefore we shall specify them, and you will do well not to overlook any of them. Of course, only a few out of the number, or perhaps a single one, will be found in any one watch, but *that one* may be the very thing that ails your watch. Only faults which are liable to occur in the lever watch are here mentioned. For those which might be found in any of the other escapements, see the other chapters of Part Fifth.

(459.) *The pivots, staffs, etc.*—The balance pivots in the lever do not need to be so closely fitted as in the duplex, but more so than in the cylinder. They, as well as those of the lever staff, should be well fitted in their holes, (those of the lever being closest,) but not too closely, as then the thickening of the oil would be too much felt. But if the pivots are too loose, there will be more variation in the different positions. Still, it is better to have them a little too free than too close. If the balance and other cocks do not come off easily, from the steady pins sticking or otherwise, you should always look out for *bent pivots*, especially on the lever and balance staffs. The pivots should always be perfectly straight, round, and of equal size (not tapering) as far as they go in the holes, polished or burnished, with end-shake ample for freedom but no more, and the end-shakes should be *equal* for the balance and lever staffs and the escape wheel. All of them should be perfectly vertical and parallel to each other. In a good watch, the balance pivots should both be of the same size.

(460.) *The jewels, pins, bankings, rollers, etc.*—Examine carefully to see if the pallet jewels, the ruby pin and the hole jewels are tight in their places. For the end stones, see sections (17 to 19). See that the guard pin or finger, and the banking and regulator pins are *tight*, vertical, clean, smooth and dry. See that the roller table and the hair-spring collet are fast on the staff, the ruby pin vertical and parallel with the staff, and that the lever is rigidly fastened to the pallets and moves precisely as they do. Be sure that the ruby pin cannot get on top of the horn of the lever. When the lever banks against the sides of the sink, see that they are vertical and free from oil, etc., and that they have only a narrow edge in contact with the lever. Take the same precautions if the lever banks against a pinion arbor or elsewhere. See that the end of the ruby pin does not graze against the bottom of the sink it revolves in, nor on the point of the screw which holds the bottom end stone, nor on any burr around the screw-hole, nor fuzzy fibres sticking in any hole or corner or held by oil or grease in the sink. In the double roller escapement, raise the lever to the highest position its end-shake will allow, while the ruby pin stands over the guard finger, (in its lowest position,) and see if they come dangerously close. If so, set the ruby pin higher or the guard finger lower till they clear. See that the safety pin cannot get above or below the safety roller. The ruby pin should not be round, as that form gives a poor action in the lever notch unless the depthing is exact. The oval form is better, or a round pin with the front third ground off flat, or a triangular pin, with a flat side outward. Exactness in the points mentioned in this and the preceding section will greatly facilitate the timing in positions.

(461.) *The lever.*—The notch should be square to the bottom

—not tapering, and wider at the outside; the sides should be straight, smooth and polished; the ruby pin should have no play, but only be fully free; the notch deep enough to prevent the pin from bottoming, or from fouling or clogging if a little oil, fuzz, or dirt gets in; its outer corners but slightly rounded off, enough to remove sharpness, and polished; and the inside of the horn should be formed to correspond to the path of the ruby pin while the guard pin rests against the edge of the roller—allowing space enough for the ruby pin to clear it safely while passing towards the notch. In the single or table roller escapement, the lever notch and the crescent are so made that the guard pin enters its crescent at the same time that the ruby pin enters the lever notch, and without touching the corner of the crescent in passing. The slightest grazing in passing would seriously affect the vibrations and timing. In the double-roller, the guard pin passes into its crescent some time before the ruby pin enters the lever notch, but the horn must be wide enough for the ruby pin to be *within* the horn before the guard pin passes into the crescent. The lever (with pallets and everything complete on the staff) should be accurately poised, and in an adjusted watch the escape wheel should also be poised. It should be unnecessary to say that regarding the balance, etc.

(462.) *The wheel and pallets.*—To go fully into the wheel and pallet action would be equivalent to a treatise on the lever escapement, which is hardly within the purpose of this book. I shall suppose that the workman understands how it should be, and will only give a few points. as reminders of faults to be looked for. The wheel must of course be true in the flat, and the teeth true in the round, (*i.e.*, concentric with the axis of the pinion,) all alike or equal, straight and in good condition. The wheel and pallet should be set as closely together as possible. See that the teeth clear the belly of the pallets, and cannot rub up under the lever, nor foul with oil or dirt on either of them. Examine the freedom of the teeth. If the lockings are too shallow, and plenty of shake inside, the wheel is too small; if the lockings are too deep, with great freedom or shake outside, the wheel is too large, and may be corrected by topping. (See 439.) Supposing the wheel and pallet action to have been examined, (including the locking, the draw, the impulse, the drops and the freedom,) wind the watch partly up and listen to the tick. If irregular, there may be some teeth thicker or longer than others, or bent. Any grating is also to be looked into. If the tick is regular and clear, we will next examine the most important point, viz. :—

(463.) *The roller action.*—Fold a narrow slip of tissue paper once, and place under the balance rim, so that, in trying to open, it will hold the balance still in any position, but will not have force enough to spring or strain anything. Put the balance in the central position and test (both by feeling and by examining with the magnifying glass,) if the ruby pin is free in the lever notch but without too much play, and the safety pin or guard point is free in its crescent. Move the balance slowly around, constantly testing to see that the safety pin remains free in the crescent and the ruby pin free in the notch till it passes out of the notch and the tooth drops off one pallet and onto the other. Try this in both directions from the central point.

(464.) *The locking action.*—When the tooth drops, as just stated, it should drop onto the locking face, not on the impulse plane. The latter would show a shallow pallet depth, and the watch cannot be timed if the tooth drops on the incline or just on the corner. When the locking is very shallow, try it *with each tooth*. If the teeth are irregular, the fault is in the wheel, which should be replaced. The corners of the pallets may be rounded, or chipped off, causing the tooth to drop on the incline when the locking is really deep enough. If the tooth drops too far up the locking plane, the safety or the banking action may be wrong.

(465.) *The draw.*—Move the balance still further, till the ruby pin is free from the notch, and see if the tooth draws the lever against the banking pin; if not, jar the movement a little, and it should do so. If it does not, the locking face needs to be more inclined, to give it more draw. The watch should have ample draw, in order to keep the lever against the bankings, and prevent the safety pin from being thrown in contact with the roller while running, and so affecting the rate.

Another test for the draw is the reverse of the above. Put the lever against the banking pin and jar the movement to see if the tooth will slide down the locking face and carry the safety pin against the roller. If the lever is poised, that would show that there not only was no draw to that locking face, but that it was inclined the wrong way. Another good test is, while the watch is running, to hold it so that you can see whether the lever strikes the banking pin and *stays there*, or stops short of it, and watch it awhile. Try this on both banking pins. If it occasionally fails to stand against the banking pin, the teeth are irregular, or depthing too shallow, or locking face has too little draw, or possibly the corner of the locking face may be chipped or rough, and catch on the teeth. In the last case, the oil will rapidly become thick, with the powder ground off the teeth. If so, polish both the locking and the teeth.

(466.) *Freedom of the ruby pin.*—Put the paper under the lever, move the balance slowly from the central position, and see that the ruby pin has an equal freedom from the inside (the hollow edge) of the horn of the lever, all the way out. In coming back, keep the safety pin against the edge of the roller, and see if the ruby pin is still free from the horn and if it can enter the notch without hitting the corner. If the safety pin cannot rest against the roller while the ruby pin is passing the horn, the ruby pin touches the horn, which should be altered to give clearance (461), or possibly the safety roller is too small, which is a serious fault and must be corrected. See section (469.) Where it is impossible to see whether the ruby pin grazes the inner edge of the horn, put a very thin coat of rouge (or whiting) in oil on the *front*, only, of the ruby pin, then move it from the central line outward, or the reverse way, with the safety pin against the roller. Do this on both sides. If the ruby pin touches the horn, (or the bottom of the notch,) rouge will be found there. Be sure to clean the rouge and oil off thoroughly, before going further. The space between the ruby pin and the edge of the horn should be more than the play of the safety pin between the roller and the banking. Of course, if the ruby pin (while being of proper shape) is too close to the inside of the horn and bottoms in the notch, that would indicate that it is set too far out, and should be moved further back in the roller.

(467.) *The unlocking action.*—When the ruby pin enters the notch and passes to the further or unlocking side of it, to begin the unlocking, it must not hit on the (unlocking) corner of the notch, but safely on the inside of it. If its widest part hits barely on the corner, it must be set further out in the roller, or put in a pin of such shape that the contact point will be further from the roller center, so as to get a safe contact inside of the notch. When any change is made, repeat the above test, from each side, to the central point, till you are sure that the unlocking is properly accomplished in the notch. The locking (464) and the draw (465) have already been considered.

(468.) *The impulse action.*—Remove the paper from under the lever, and put it under the balance, which is placed at its central position, with the mainspring partly wound, and the lever notch pressing against the ruby pin. Move the balance forward till the tooth drops, and the lever goes to the banking pin, then slowly move the balance back till the tooth is unlocked and the lever flies forward with the other side of the notch against the ruby pin, urging it forward; hold the balance still, exactly in the unlocking position, and see if the first contact is well inside of the horn. If the corner of the horn strikes below (*i.e.*, further from the balance staff) the widest part of the ruby pin, a good motion or action is impossible. The necessity of square corners to the notch will now be evident. They should not be rounded off, but be polished barely smooth, *i.e.*, not sharp. Get the *first contact* correct, and the correctness of the rest of it is already secured. Move the balance forward till the tooth drops, then still further, while noticing whether (1) the notch continues to press the ruby pin forward till the lever reaches the banking, and the ruby pin passes out of the notch without hitting the horn, or (2) the lever stops when the drop occurs, and the ruby pin has to carry it forward a ways in order to leave the notch—perhaps rubbing over the inside of the horn all the way out. The former is correct, but the latter shows a lack of draw or poor locking.

(469.) *The safety action.*—Remove the paper, and move the balance around till the tooth escapes and the lever goes to the banking. The safety pin should then be safely free from the roller edge. If not, the roller is probably too large, and should be freed by polishing off the edge. But if the safety pin has too much play, (between the banking pin and the roller edge), the roller may be too small, the safety pin too short, or not set near enough to the roller. While the lever is against the banking, press the safety pin against the edge of the roller, and the tooth should still remain on the *locking face* of the pallet, when tried with both pallets. If not, it must be made to do so, either by lengthening the safety pin or bringing it nearer to the roller, or by a larger roller, and then, if necessary to give the safety pin freedom, the bankings must be opened. When pressing the lever back, as described, if the safety pin wedges against the edge of the roller, and seems almost likely to pass by to the other side, the safety pin (or point of the lever) must be set forward as above directed. In a double roller escapement the fault would be cured by a smaller safety roller and a longer safety finger.

(470.) *The banking action.*—The primary object of the banking pins is to give the teeth the proper amount of lap or run on the locking faces of the pallets, and no more. If the bankings are too close, the locking may be too shallow, and the whole action of the escapement confined within such narrow limits that the slightest error anywhere or change of conditions will cause stoppage or derange the timing. If they are too wide, the unlocking is made more difficult and the entrance of the ruby pin in the notch more uncertain and imperfect, and the ruby may even pass by the notch and strike the inside of the horn, in which case good time is of course impossible. Anything that affects the proportion between the effective impulse given by the motive force, and the momentum of the balance, affects the rate,—and deeper lockings will evidently have that effect. In fine watches, very little lap is required, and less is needed in the double-roller than in the single or table-roller escapement. But in coarse work, where the teeth may be irregular, the locking faces not properly inclined, the impulse planes too steep or too flat, etc., more lap may be required for safety. Of two evils, too much lap is better than too little, and in all cases there must be enough to make the action of the escapement safe—or else the escapement must be put in better condition. The proper amount can only be told by trial.

(471.) *Changing the bankings.*—If the bankings are pins, they must not be bent inward or outward to alter the width between them, as that throws their contact sides out of vertical, and the lever would have different amounts of freedom when in different portions of its end-shake. It is an invariable rule that the contact surfaces must be straight, vertical and parallel with each other. To open the banking, file away the inside of the pin, being sure to remove any feather-edges and filings, and leave it smooth, clean and vertical. To close the banking or lessen the play of the lever, pull out the pin, broach out the hole, and insert a larger pin, which will stand closer to the lever. Another way is to file away the edge of the lever to give it more play; and another is to insert pins in a new place, at the proper distance apart, to lessen the play. In the former case, the lever must be poised again. As a general rule, the banking pins should allow equal play on each side, but as *safety* is the final test of correctness, they should be changed as required to secure that condition, remembering that the wheel and pallet action is the starting-point to be considered in arranging the bankings, and that in a fine watch the other actions should be made to conform to that, rather than open the bankings any wider.

(472.) *Setting.*—If the watch sets or stops, (when clean, partly wound and in beat,) it may be due to any one among the following causes:—

1. If it sets with the teeth on the locking face of the pallet,

the locking is too deep; or the locking face is too much undercut and has too much draw, *i.e.*, the locking is too strong. Small watches with light balances are most liable to this fault.

2. If it stops or sets with the tooth on the impulse plane of the pallet, the impulse angle may be too great, *i.e.*, the incline is too steep; or the motive force too weak. I do not give directions for altering the pallets, as to do so properly would require many pages, and belongs more to watch repairing than to the adjustments. The work requires much study and experience to understand just what to do and how to do it, and such alterations should be cautiously undertaken.

3. If the teeth set part way up the impulse plane of one pallet, and not on the other, only the former is too steep.

4. If the teeth set on only one locking face, that alone is too deep or has too much draw.

5. The locking may be too shallow, and the teeth can drop on the impulse planes instead of on the locking faces; the banking pin may be bent.

6. There may be too little draw, or none at all, and shaking or jarring may jar the lever from the banking pins against the roller.

7. The motive force too weak for the movement, or weakened by poor depthings or other faults, in the train. The lever escapement requires a rather strong motive force for good performance.

8. Lever and pallets not poised, and jarring or change of position displaces them.

9. The lever does not move with the pallets, not being firmly fastened to them, or on the pallet staff.

10. Pallet jewel loose in the pallet.

11. The lever too slender and springy, allowing irregular wheel and pallet action; or too short, so that setting backward or jars (see number 6) cause rubbing or overbanking.

12. Watch gets out of beat, by loose collet, loose roller, lever loose on pallets, hair spring forced out of place by regulator, or jumps into or out of regulator, etc.,—putting too much lift on one pallet.

13. Ruby pin too loosely fitted in notch, or too closely; not set vertical; loose, and wedges or clogs in notch, or on corner; rubs inside of horn, or strikes inside or outside corner in passing; ruby pin or notch rough; ruby pin grazes bottom of notch, or of sink; or grazes guard finger of double roller; ruby pin too short (or too much end-shake) and gets nearly on top of lever horn, or quite so.

14. Safety pin too short or table roller too small; although not enough so to cause overbanking, yet the friction of the safety pin on the roller checks the motion and causes setting.

15. Safety pin or guard point (or guard finger in double roller) not over the centre of the lever notch, and too close to the roller on one side, while showing the preceding fault when on the other side; pin accidentally bent.

16. Safety pin hits corner of crescent in entering or leaving it, due to lever notch being too wide for ruby pin, giving it and safety pin too much play.

17. The crescent in edge of roller too wide, so that the safety pin enters it too soon (before the ruby pin enters lever notch) and allows inside of lever horn to fall against the ruby pin.

18. Crescent too narrow, or too shallow; safety pin hits on corner or bottom of crescent in passing.

19. Escape-wheel teeth rub on belly of pallets, or up under lever, or oil gets between them and clogs the teeth.

20. Oil between the lever and the banking pins, or sides of sink against which it banks, or dirt filling up banking space.

21. Oil on safety pin and the roller, clogging or sticking them together; in a double-roller, oil between the ruby pin and guard finger.

22. Oil in the lever notch, or between the under side of table roller and the lever horn, or between lever and under side of balance.

23. Lever or other part magnetized, or in the vicinity of a magnet.

(See Chapter III.) The foregoing are only a few of the faults which might cause setting, or so interfere with the action of the escapement as to prevent any close timing. If timing is difficult, look for every *possible* fault. (See Chapters II and XXXVII.) When the movement is in correct condition the various adjustments can be perfected by the methods given in Chapters XXIX to XLI.

CHAPTER XXVIII.

Box and Pocket Chronometers.

(473.) *General characteristics.*—The chronometer is a really detached escapement. If its parts are well made and arranged, the balance meets with only a trifling resistance in unlocking, the impulse is given in an almost perfect manner, and during the remainder of the vibration it is entirely detached and free, while the whole of the return vibration is entirely free, except for the passing of the gold spring, which is so easily done as to be practically unnoticeable. The balance is therefore under the control of the balance spring only, (except during a minute portion of one vibration,) there being practically no other regulating influence acting upon it.

(474.) An isochronal hair spring and compensated balance are therefore absolutely indispensable for this escapement to give even fair performance, and the adjustment for positions is as necessary and useful for the pocket chronometer as for the other escapements. Under favorable conditions it is capable of giving the best performance of any portable time-keeper known. For marine chronometers, for example, where there is plenty of room for all the parts, ample motive force, of practically uniform strength, and they can be kept in one position, it is almost perfect.

(475.) But it is not adapted for pocket watches, except when carried by men who understand how it should be handled and are very careful to use it properly. For the use of ordinary wearers it is not so suitable as the lever. It also requires the very best workmanship in its construction and adjustment. While a very ordinary lever may give fair performance, a chronometer of the same grade might not be worth carrying. As only first-class workmen can do first-class work, the chronometer is more expensive than any other, both in its construction and repair, yet it is well known that the lever can keep equally accurate time, and is far more reliable. Its use in pocket watches is rapidly declining, and it is only a matter of time when it will be confined exclusively to box chronometers and semi-portable instruments of precision.

(476.) The specific objections to its use in pocket watches are, that it is liable to "set," or stop, when exposed to jarring, shaking, jerks or twisting, which lessen the balance vibration; and if they increase the vibration, the watch will trip or overrun; while a knock or shake at a certain time may displace the detent and cause mislocking, tripping or butting. Its heavy balance also exposes it to breakage of pivots. When taken apart for cleaning or repairs, it is not so certain to resume its former performance as the lever, but requires to be newly adjusted and perfected, occupying a long time, and being troublesome and unsatisfactory to the owner, as well as the workman. It cannot start of itself, but requires to be shaken.

(477.) *Number of vibrations.*—Marine chronometers have 14,-

400 vibrations per hour, or 4 vibrations per second. As the vibration in one direction is dumb, there is one beat to 2 vibrations, and they beat half-seconds. Pocket chronometers generally have 18,000 beats, and some as high as 21,000—the quicker trains being less liable to set, and less affected by shaking and carrying.

(478.) *Arc of vibration.*—The balance was formerly made to vibrate 360°, or one turn, but the present custom is to give it a vibration of 430°, or 1¼ turns, for both marine and pocket chronometers, as being less liable to set, and less sensitive to errors in the poise in different positions.

(479.) *The balance spring.*—The cylindrical or helical form is used for both pocket and marine chronometers. The diameter of the coils is one-half the diameter of the balance, or ½ inch in an ordinary 2-day chronometer, and a little under ⅝ inch from top to bottom. For marine chronometers, 11 to 13 coils are used, the highest number being preferred, and the ends are pinned ¼ turn short of even turns—springs so pinned being most nearly isochronal and regular in their action. For pocket chronometers, 7 to 10 turns, preferably the last number, are employed, and pinned in even turns. In the occasional instances when Breguet springs are used, they have about 20 turns, and are pinned in even turns.

(480.) *Oiling the escapement.*—Put *no oil on any part of the escapement*—only on the *pivots* of the balance, the escape wheel, and the pivoted detent.

(481.) *End-shakes.*—The end-shake of the balance staff and escape wheel should be ample for freedom, but no more, so that the parts cannot materially change their relative positions. The pivots should also be sufficiently free in their holes to avoid any risk of the slightest binding or clogging in any position, but not loose. When the balance pivots fit too closely, the thickening of the oil affects the vibrations very sensibly. The pivots of a pivoted detent must also be fitted as directed for the balance staff.

(482.) *The chronometer escapement.*—As many workmen are not familiar with the construction and operation of this escapement, I have inserted Fig. 26, a diagram of the spring-detent form. The detent is supported by a foot b firmly screwed to the plate, and is carried at the end of the spring part g. At its other end is the pipe containing the locking pallet lp, and an extension n, called the nose or point, against which rests the gold spring s, screwed to the detent at m, and shown as just ready to drop off the unlocking pallet up, held in the unlocking roller ur. As

202   THE WATCH ADJUSTER'S MANUAL.

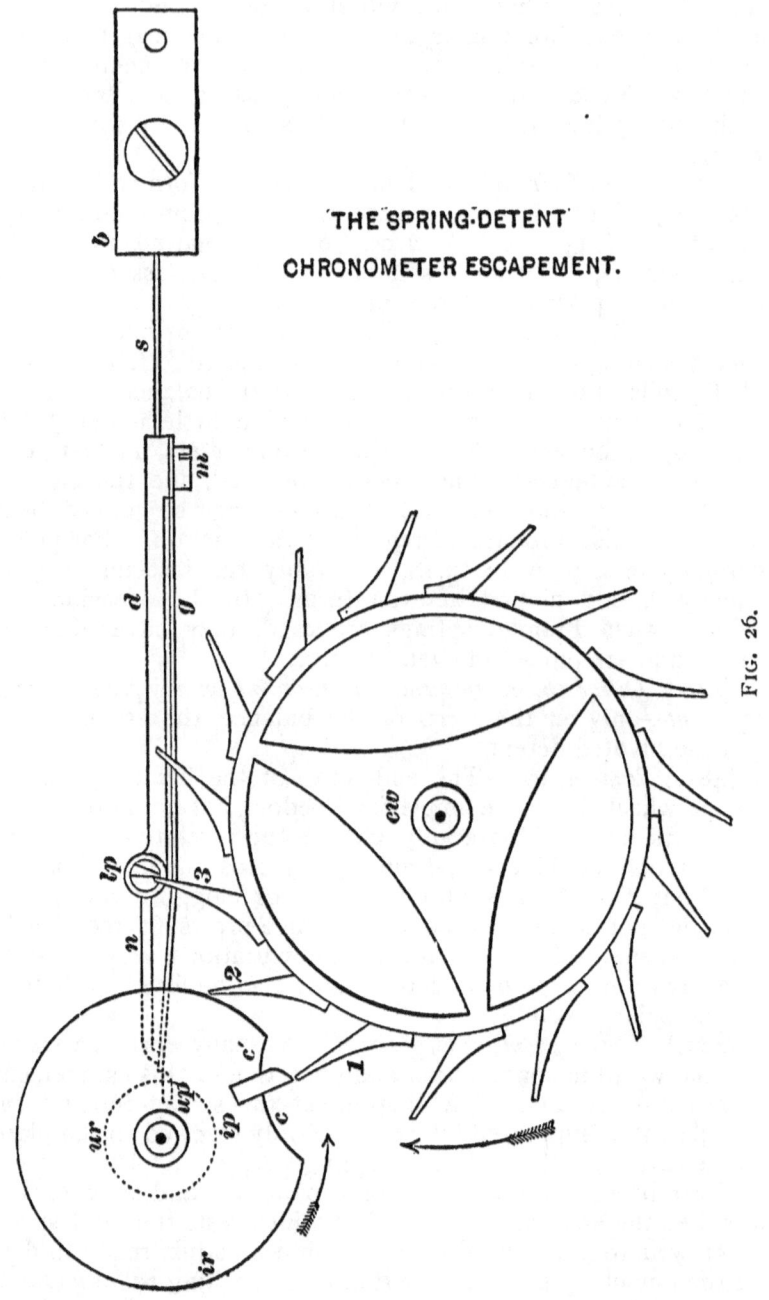

THE SPRING-DETENT
CHRONOMETER ESCAPEMENT.

FIG. 26.

these last parts are underneath the impulse roller *i r*, they are shown in dotted lines. The escape wheel *e w* is shown as locked, by tooth *3* resting on the locking stone *l p*. The tooth *2* has just dropped off the impulse pallet *i p*, and tooth *1* is ready to drop upon the pallet as soon as the wheel is unlocked by *u p* moving the locking stone up out of reach of tooth *3*. *c* is the front, and *c'* the back, of the crescent or passing hollow in the impulse roller. The general principle of the bascule or pivoted detent form is the same, but the detent is carried by a pivoted staff at about *s*, and the nose *n* is kept drawn towards the escape wheel by a small hair spring on the staff. The banking screw against which the pipe rests, and which is adjusted to vary the depth of the locking on the pallet *l p*, would come under tooth *3*, and therefore it has been omitted for the sake of clearness.

(483.) *Technical terms and description.*—The large form is called *marine*, or *box*, or *ship's chronometer;* the small form is termed *pocket chronometer*. The escapement is generally called *detent*, or *spring-detent*, or *chronometer escapement*. When the detent and spring form one piece, as shown in Fig. 26, it is termed the *spring-detent escapement;* when the detent is carried upon a pivoted axis, it is known as *pivoted-detent* or *bascule escapement*.

(484.) The escape-wheel tooth gives an impulse to the balance by impelling the *impulse pallet u p*, held in the *impulse roller u r* on the balance staff, having its *face* or acting surface in line with the centre of the staff. The edge of the roller is hollowed out in a *crescent c c'* to free the escape-wheel tooth while giving the impulse, and the pallet projects into this hollow, about two-thirds of which, *c*, is in front of the pallet face. After the driving tooth has given the impulse and passed off the pallet, it *drops* a short distance, when the wheel is stopped or *locked* by a tooth resting on the *detaining* or *locking pallet l p*, also called *locking stone*, or simply *locking*. This is held in an opening or *pipe* in the *detent*, which may be either a spring, *s*, or a pivoted detent. In the former case it is held against the *banking screw* by its own elasticity; in the latter, by a spiral *recovering spring* around the detent axis, similar to a balance spring, but smaller.

(485.) The balance having reached the end of its *excursion* or vibration, swings back again through the *return* or *dumb vibration*, so called because it gives no beat while moving in this direction; nor does it receive any impulse. It would be entirely free if it did not hit the *discharging* or *gold spring*, *g*, with the *discharging* or *unlocking pallet u p*, held in the *discharging roller, u r*, on the balance staff. This spring is long and thin, and readily yields to the discharging pallet during the dumb vibration, with an imperceptible resistance, and without moving the detent at all. It cannot yield in the opposite direction, because the *horn* or *nose n* of the detent supports it behind, near its point, so that when the discharging pallet hits it and moves it back it carries the detent back with it, and so carries the locking pallet out of the wheel. The impulse pallet also swings past the teeth without touching them during the dumb vibration, at the termination of which the balance begins another *acting* or *impulse vibration*.

(486.) When the discharging pallet now hits the gold spring, it carries that and the detent back, thus moving the locking pallet out of the wheel and letting it advance, and then lets the detent spring back to its place, ready to lock the next tooth. When the wheel was *unlocked*, a tooth *dropped* on to the impulse pallet, *i p*, and gave the balance an impulse as before, then the wheel was again arrested and locked by the locking pallet. The intersection of the gold spring and the discharging pallet is such that the balance moves about 5° to unlock the escape wheel.

(487.) *In beat.*—When in beat, the parts should stand as follows, in the usual construction of chronometer: when at rest, and perfectly free, the balance requires to be turned the same distance in either direction, to enable the unlocking spring or the detent to escape.

(488.) *To test the beat.*—Allow the balance to come to a free rest, with the escape wheel locked. The end of the gold spring should be close to the back side of the unlocking pallet, *i.e.*, the side nearest the escape wheel, and the impulse pallet should stand just opposite the point of a tooth, the faces of both being in a radial line to the balance axis.

(489.) Slowly move the balance back till the gold spring drops off the discharging pallet, note the distance moved, and bring the balance back to the point of rest. Then move the balance the other way till the gold spring (and detent) again drops, note that distance moved, then let the tooth escape. The two distances should be equal.

(490.) *Test by starting.*—If the watch is in beat, it should start going if you move the balance in either direction, as above, and liberate it at the instant that the drop occurs. Test it in both directions. If the distances are equal but the watch fails to unlock when liberated in the first position, the unlocking is too difficult, for some reason, which you should discover and remedy; if it fails to start off when liberated in the latter position, the impulse roller may be too small, the balance too heavy for the motive force, there may be too little drop on the impulse pallet.

Examining the Escapement.

(491.) *The escape wheel.*—See if the points of the teeth are straight, smooth and vertical. See if they are equal, by moving the balance from the point of rest slowly forward till the tooth drops on the impulse pallet, then backward till the tooth drops off, and note whether the intersection is safe, *i.e.*, whether the tooth laps far enough on the pallet *i p*. You can judge somewhat by the distance moved backward to enable the tooth to pass off. If the distance is very small, the intersection is shallow; but if large, while the intersection will be deep enough for safety, it may be so deep as to cause danger of setting (499). Try this with all of the teeth; if some intersect more deeply than others, the teeth are *not equal* in length, or have been bent or injured. If some do not intersect enough for safety, catch on the corner of the pallet, or miss it entirely, the wheel must be corrected or replaced; or, if the error is slight, turn the impulse roller on the staff to bring the pallet a little towards the line of centers (of balance and escape wheel) to get a little deeper and safer intersection.

(492.) *To test the clearance of the escape-wheel teeth.*—The watch being in beat (487) and running, hold it up to a strong light in such position that the balance falls towards the escape wheel, as closely as it can; there should be just visible clearance between the teeth at *2* and the edge of the impulse roller, and between the teeth, *1*, and the point of the impulse pallet *i p* when they are just opposite and nearest together. If difficult to see the latter clearance, hold the balance still with the pallet opposite the tooth and examine. The light should be barely visible between them. If too close, make the end of the pallet jewel more bevelled, so it cannot touch the tooth.

(493.) The clearance should be equal in both places, *1* and *2*. If it is not, knock the foot *b* of the detent towards or from the roller *i p* to make them so. Moving the detent also moves the locking, and so changes the position of the teeth when at rest, or locked.

(494.) If the clearance is too great (more than required for safety) there will be too much drop off the pallet and onto the locking, and the impulse will be wasted; and the drop onto the pallet will be less secure. If the clearance is excessive, the impulse pallet *i p* should be set out further from the roller center to bring it nearer to the teeth at *1*.

(495.) *Correct impulse action.*—When properly adjusted as directed, and running, the impulse pallet will move 5° from its point of rest before the wheel is unlocked, and will have moved still further before the tooth *1* overtakes it to give the impulse. When the tooth reaches the pallet *i p*, the circumferences of the roller and the wheel will intersect sufficiently for the tooth to lap well onto the pallet and give a safe contact. At the other extreme of their intersection the tooth slides off the pallet, and the wheel is then locked with the tooth *2* just clear of the edge of the roller.

(496.) *The drops.*—There are two drops, the drop of the driving tooth *1* from the position of rest till it strikes the impulse pallet, and a small drop, from the position of leaving the pallet at *2* to that of locking. The former is the *engaging drop*, the latter the *disengaging drop*. These drops are very important, as their extents affect not only the safety of the intersection and the useful amount of the impulse, but also the time and the liability of the watch to vary or to stop. When "the drop" is spoken of, only, the engaging drop is meant.

(497.) *Extents of the drops.*—When the arrangement is as described, (487, 492,) the engaging drop will generally be about 10°, and the disengaging drop should be but little more than is required to give the tooth proper clearance. The 10° is the distance the balance has moved, from the instant the tooth was unlocked till it overtook the pallet. In the case of a balance one inch in diameter, 15° would be $\frac{1}{8}$ inch on its rim, and 5° would be a little less than $\frac{1}{16}$ inch. For a smaller balance, the distance would be proportionately less. In any case the distance is small, and requires careful observation by the workman. The total intersection of the circle described by the point of the pallet (by the circle of the points of the teeth) is generally 45° for marine chronometers and about 35° to 36° for pocket chronometers. This is reduced slightly by the allowance for clearance, etc., so that the distance moved by the balance rim through the entire arc of intersection, as in testing the beat (487), would generally be less than $\frac{1}{4}$ inch. If we allow 5° for clearance, 10° for engaging and 5° for disengaging drop, there would be only 15° left for the actual contact while driving, and then supposing the impulse roller to be $\frac{1}{4}$ inch in diameter, the contact would continue through only $\frac{3}{100}$ inch at the edge of the roller, and at the balance rim it is only $\frac{1}{8}$ inch, showing how minute the action is, and the perfection of adjustment required.

(498.) *The engaging drop.*—Some workmen put the pallet more than 5° in advance of the tooth, and some have it less, thus increasing or lessening the drop onto the pallet. If the balance vibrations are large, and there is danger of overbanking or running (499), an increase of the drop will lessen the impulse given, and reduce the vibrations; if the vibrations are too small and sluggish, lessening the drop will increase or strengthen the impulse and enlarge the vibrations. But the drop should not be changed from the correct amount, as stated in (499), without good reason.

(499.) If the engaging drop is too great, the balance vibrations may be so reduced as to be liable to set, especially if the motive force is weak and the balance heavy. If the drop is too short, there is danger of the tooth missing the pallet, or catching on its corner, from the pallet not being far enough in advance to make the intersection of proper depth for safety; or, if the tooth strikes the pallet safely, the balance vibrations may be so enlarged that shaking or carrying will easily cause overrunning. The engaging drop is changed by turning the impulse roller on the balance staff, towards the line of centres to increase the drop, and from it to lessen the drop.

(500.) *The disengaging drop.*—There can hardly be too little drop off the impulse pallet, provided that the tooth *2* after the drop stands far enough from the roller to safely clear its edge and the point of the pallet *i p* during the dumb vibration, (485.) But the drop may be too great, causing waste of the impulse, which is expended upon the locking instead of on the impulse pallet, endangering the security of the locking, causing buckling of the detent, etc. If the clearance is correct and equal (492, 493), the excessive drop can only be caused by the impulse pallet not projecting out far enough, letting the tooth off too soon at *2*. If the pallet clears the tooth properly when at rest (492), but the second tooth *2* is too far from the roller edge, the locking stone and detent may require moving up towards the balance, to bring the tooth *2* nearer to the roller edge. If this moves the other tooth *1* too far from the point of the impulse pallet, the pallet must be set further out in the roller, to get a safe intersection (491.) Possibly a larger roller would most easily secure a safe intersection of pallet and tooth during the impulse and lessen the disengaging drop.

(501.) *Impulse roller.*—In marine chronometers the diameter of the impulse roller is usually half that of the escape wheel, (at the tips of the teeth,) but in pocket watches the roller is larger, to lessen the danger of setting, and to increase the control of the balance by the motive force. Whenever necessary (491, 500), it can therefore be safely enlarged. The point of the pallet comes just to the circumference of the roller, which is set as closely in the escape wheel as will allow a safe clearance (492).

When the roller is rather small there is more danger of mislocking; if it is rather large, there is less danger of setting, but the intersection of tooth and pallet is more shallow and less secure, and the angle of impulse is lessened. The roller edge must be highly polished, vertical, concentric with the balance, and free from rust.

(502.) *Proper size of escape wheel and impulse roller.*—The proportions adopted by an eminent English maker of pocket chronometers, the late Mr. Walsh, were as follows: With a fifteen-tooth escape-wheel, the ratio of the radius of the wheel to the center distance (centers of balance and wheel) was as 65 to 100. By measuring the center distance with the depthing tool, the proper radius for the wheel can be easily calculated. Or, if a sector is used, a circle drawn with the depthing tool after taking the measurement as above can be set in the sector at the 100th division, and the escape-wheel diameter is given at the 65th division. This gives a rather large wheel, which he preferred, as it more quickly checked the balance in case of overrunning, by the pressure on the roller edge. After allowing for drop and unlocking, the escaping arc would be about 43°. Other makers use other proportions, which must of course be followed in working at their watches, but the above will be a guide to show what proportions have given excellent performance.

(503.) *The crescent.*—The crescent should be deep enough to prevent the point of the tooth bottoming in any position. The portion c, in front of the pallet, (about two-thirds of the whole,) should be wide enough to prevent any danger of the tooth hitting its corner when starting to overtake the pallet, but not so wide that a second tooth could get into it while one was on the pallet. The intention in that case is that the second tooth should butt on the edge of the roller to the left of c, and be stopped there. That is very likely to damage the tooth, as it comes so near to passing by, and the engaging friction on the roller tends to wedge and force it by. It would seem better to make the crescent just wide enough to prevent the driving tooth from hitting the corner when starting, and then cut a notch in the roller edge, to the left of the hollow c and beyond its corner, *like another pallet $i\,p$*, of steel. This would save the tooth from injury, and no great harm could be done by giving the impulse upon *it*, instead of on the true pallet $i\,p$.

(504.) The portion of the crescent behind the pallet, c^1, is intended to catch the tooth if it slips by the pallet, and prevent it getting through. But that does no real good, and is likely to damage the point of the tooth. It would seem better to form that corner *i p*, with an upright or radial face, like another pallet, to save the tooth from injury, and it would also get the impulse nearly as well as on the pallet *i p*. The faces of these two false pallets should of course be radial and well polished. In case the wheel was accidentally unlocked either one or the other of them would be pretty certain to catch the tooth, and without danger of injuring it.

(505.) *The locking.*—Locating the locking stone properly is the most important point in setting out the escapement. The face of the locking should have a perceptible draw on the tooth, and this is indispensable in the pocket chronometer, for if the draw is not sufficient to keep the locking to its place the watch will be utterly unreliable for carrying. It serves to keep the spring detent from being jarred off the banking, and the pivoted detent from leaving it by rebounding after striking it. But of course it must not be so great as to make the unlocking difficult. The angle of draw should be about 10° in marine chronometers and 12° to 15° for pocket watches, or even 18° when the detent does not remain securely against the banking (509.) The security should not depend altogether on the draw, but be aided by the stiffness of the detent spring, and by the tooth having a safe *depth* of locking on the stone. When the face of the locking stone is much inclined it should be observed that turning the banking screw to adjust the depth of locking will also alter the clearance of the teeth at the impulse roller, (492,) and the clearance should afterwards be examined.

(506.) *The detent.*—The spring detent is considered best for marine chronometers, but many workmen prefer the pivoted detent for pocket watches, with quick trains. The spring should be stiff enough to bring the detent to its place against the backing in time to catch the next tooth, but not so quickly that the pipe will hit the point of a tooth before it has had time to get out of the way after unlocking. To prevent this, it is customary to carry the locking stone as far *out* of the wheel as it moved to unlock the wheel, *i.e.*, as far as it has moved *into* the wheel to lock it, making double the actual unlocking distance. If the spring is stiff, or the detent light, that may be necessary; in other cases a less distance might answer. The further a detent needs to be carried back in unlocking, the stiffer its spring must be in order to bring it back to its place in time. The detent itself must not be too slender and liable to bending; the longer it is, the heavier it must be to give it rigidity, and the spring must be stiffer to move it quickly—both of which are objectionable.

(507.) *The pivoted detent* should be very carefully poised. Its recovering spring is a spiral, similar to the balance spring, but having only three to five coils. Its stiffness can be adjusted by turning the collet on the detent staff, or by moving it through the stud, till it controls the detent briskly enough. The banking must be very carefully adjusted with a pivoted detent. Examine to see if it rebounds from the banking instead of remaining against it, especially if the detent is light, or is so slender that it springs and trembles. Get the light so that you can see any interval between the detent and the banking, use a powerful glass, and run the watch with the mainspring fully wound up to get the heaviest blow of the tooth on the locking. Also try this, held so that the spring-detent falls *from* the wheel. If there is a marked interval between the banking and the detent while the tooth is locked, it may be due to the recovering spring being too stiff, the detent carried too far out in unlocking, not enough draw, lack of poise, the detent too slender for the blow of the teeth, springy, etc.

(508.) *Examining the detent action.*—Examine (both pivoted and spring detent) while the watch is running, to see that the detent spring S or the detent itself does not yield under the blows of the teeth and bend, buckle or tremble, nor spring and vibrate when it flies to the banking, nor fail to rest safely against it (507). See that it acts lively, and gets back to its place in time. This might be tested in very important cases by sticking a slip of card or thick paper on the face of the locking stone. If the tooth locked safely on that, it would show that the locking stone got to its place considerably before the tooth. See that the tooth locks far enough on the face for safety, but not too far, for that would make the unlocking difficult. This can be tried as directed for the "test by starting" (490,) or in any of the other ways mentioned.

(509.) *Testing the safety of the locking* with spring detent. If the detent is long or heavy, or the spring weak, hold the movement so that the detent is *below* the escape wheel and tends to fall from it, then jar it while running, to see if you can shake it from its place and unlock at the wrong time. In doubtful cases, try this repeatedly, with the balance still, to see if the locking stone can be shaken from under the tooth, or partly out. (If shaken out, the watch will probably start.) If so, the detent may be too heavy, or have too little draw on the tooth, or the point of the tooth may be bent or injured so as to neutralize the draw, or the locking of the tooth may be too shallow on the stone lp. The spring must not be too stiff, nor the draw too strong or the locking too deep, as it would make the unlocking hard, and both affect the timing and promote setting (570).

(510.) *Setting the hands back* is very objectionable, and even dangerous, with the chronometer. The tooth 2, which has just dropped off the pallet, may catch in the crescent, behind the pallet, during the dumb vibration, and butt, marring the point, or bending the tooth, or even breaking off the balance pivot; or if the tooth rests on the roller edge and the intersection is rather shallow, or if it hits on the end of the impulse pallet, the same result may follow; and the greater the force with which the hands are moved, the more risk of injuring something. This applies not only to setting the minute-hand, but also the seconds-hand. Even stopping the seconds-hand by putting something before it, on the dial, and holding it till a certain instant, for the purpose of setting the watch, is equally dangerous. Aside from the probability of pushing it backward in spite of all your care, is the risk that when the hand is liberated the tooth may meet the roller edge or crescent or pallet in such a position as to damage something as already described. For instance, suppose that when you let loose the seconds-hand, and the tooth jumps forward, the balance is making its impulse vibration, *i.e.*, both the balance and the wheel are moving in the same direction, at full speed, and the point of the tooth happens to land on the end of the pallet, or at a shallow point in one end of the crescent, say, at the left end of c, or right end of c', a bent or blunted tooth is certain, and a bent or broken pivot very probable. If the truth was known, the poor performance of many a good watch, after being repaired by a good workman, could be traced to this very cause.

(511.) *Taking off or putting on the hands,*—and especially the seconds-hand, of a chronometer, is also an operation which must be properly performed, or injury will be done. In either taking the hand off or putting it on, there must be no pressure forward or backward, but it must be lifted directly upward or pressed directly downward. If it is twisted backward, the results named in the preceding section will follow; if twisted forward, the pressure on the locking pallet may bend the tooth, loosen or break the pallet jewel, bend, twist, loosen or even break the detent. If the pallet lp was not very firmly secured in the detent pipe, the pressure may tear it loose and turn it in the pipe, so as not only to take away the draw, but even to incline the locking face the wrong way. Then the wheel gets the habit of slipping off the locking and catching on the impulse roller, and may soon be ruined; or, if the fault is not quite serious enough for that, the watch is unreliable for time and condemned as "no good," when there may be really nothing wrong except as above described.

(512.) *Tool for putting hands on.*—In putting on a seconds-hand, *bring the balance to rest*, with the tooth locked to hold it still; put the socket of the hand on the pivot just far enough to stay as you place it, but not at all tight, adjust it to point exactly to the mark at 60, and then with a long mahogany slip press it down a little—all without starting the watch. If not far enough, press it on a little further; not enough to be too tight, but so that you can press the extreme end forward a little without displacing it—just tight enough not to be loose. The mahogany slip should be six inches long, to give a good handle to hold it by, with the other end tapered down to $\frac{1}{4}$ inch wide and $\frac{1}{16}$ inch thick, bevelled off from the top surface. Grasping this securely in the hand, rest the edge of the movement or case against the thumb and forefinger as a fulcrum, and press the end on the socket of the hand. In this way a direct downward pressure without twist is easily obtained—the length of the handle preventing any twisting at the working end. To take the hand off, a long-handled tool like a tack lifter should be used in a similar way. Of course, any other means will do which will secure equal safety, but those described will be found easy to make and as good as any. (See *Hands* and *Dial*, in Index.)

(513.) *Other points.*—This chapter does not give all the faults which may be present, but it will give the workman an idea of how the parts should be, the effects of errors and of changes, and how to secure any desired results. He will not need to make so many separate tests as are described, but each one has been treated by itself in order to make the object in view perfectly clear. In practice, a single observation may answer for determining a number of different points. But it would be better to make each test described, and many others, than to overlook some point in order to save time. The thorough way is the only safe one, and is generally also the quickest.

(514.) *Further details* will be found under other headings appropriate to the chronometer. Details of making, fitting and testing cylindrical hair springs of course refer to the chronometer; as regards the compensation balance, they apply to the chronometer equally with the lever; also, the chapter on magnetism, etc., and the portion of the book treating on the various adjustments.

PART SIXTH.

THE ADJUSTMENT FOR ISOCHRONISM.

CHAPTER XXIX.

ISOCHRONISM.

(515.) *The isochronal adjustment.*—We now come to the final adjustments of the hair spring for the purpose of insuring that the vibrations of the balance, whether they be great or small, shall always be accomplished in equal times, when the spring is said to be isochronized or adjusted for isochronism. I have already given general directions for fitting springs, which, if followed, will prevent any very great errors of time from varying arcs of vibration, and which, moreover, must be attended to before the last finishing touches, presently to be described, can be proceeded with. The isochronal adjustment of the hair spring is, without doubt, the most delicate and least understood operation the watchmaker is called upon to perform. Many who talk and write most glibly about it do not appear to know even the meaning of the term. And upon considering their ideas we are forced to the conclusion that unless their practice is better than their theories, it is not worth much; or else, if they do really understand the subject, they are purposely trying to lead others off upon a wrong tack, in order to keep their knowledge to themselves. But to this there are, of course, honorable exceptions.

(516.) I do not propose to advance any new theories, but to regard it in a very practical light, as a merely mechanical problem, requiring no profound knowledge, either scientific or mathematical, but which may be satisfactorily solved by any watchmaker of ordinary skill and patience. And I shall endeavor to give all necessary instructions for doing so. Even if the workman does not intend to undertake the isochronal adjustment, it is important that he should know how to discover whether the watches he buys and pays an extra price for as isochronized, are so or not, for there is as much swindling of ignorant dealers on "isochronal hair springs" as on "compensation balances, adjusted for heat and cold," of which not one out of a hundred so called are adjusted at all.

(517.) *Action of non-isochronal springs.*—If the hair spring is not isochronal, the watch will vary from correct time whenever the extent of the motion of the balance, or the "arc of vibration," as it is termed, is changed. In a watch having a going-barrel the vibrations are largest or longest when first wound up, and become smaller as the motive power becomes weaker, so that during every hour of the 24 the watch may keep a perceptibly different time. Some springs perform the short vibrations in less time than they do the long ones, while others do the reverse. A well made and well fitted spring will not vary much from uniform time, while a spring that is misshapen, crooked, out of center, unevenly coiled or tempered; that has been scraped, ground, much bent, or is very soft, will vary sometimes several minutes during the day, although it may be somewhere near right at the *end* of the day. Every change of the arc of vibration caused by jarring, carrying, keeping it in different positions or different temperatures, irregular winding, poor oil, dirt, etc., causes it to vary, so that for accurate timekeeping it is valueless.

(518.) In duplex and cylinder escapements the resistance to the momentum of the balance caused by the pressure of the escape wheel upon the roller or cylinder, is greater or less in proportion to the greater or less motive force, and therefore these escapements are in some degree self-compensating for irregular motive forces. Yet they generally do vibrate further when first wound up. In English levers and chronometers the fusee and chain are employed to equalize the motive power. But, to do this accurately, the fusee must be cut in conformity to the varying strength of the particular mainspring used, which is seldom done, as is shown by the varying arcs. When that mainspring breaks or another is substituted, whose strength increases in a different ratio, the fuzee cut for the original spring does not suit this one, and does not equalize its force. But were it so, the friction upon the balance pivots *in different positions* is another disturbing influence in all watches. And even if the watch is adjusted for positions, the thickening of the oil, accumulation of dirt, etc., by running, causes the vibrations to gradually diminish.

(519.) As it is practically impossible to prevent the arc of vibration from varying more or less, it is necessary in fine watches, after reducing that variation to the smallest possible amount by mechanical means, to adjust the hair spring within those limits, so that no error of time shall result from such unavoidable changes of the arcs of the balance. This adjustment or isochronizing of the hair spring can be done in different ways, which we shall consider at some length. But before undertaking this, and even before we can safely test our spring to see what and how much adjustment it requires, there are certain other points to be attended to.

(520.) *Requirements of isochronism.*—Besides observing the instructions already given for the correct forming and fitting of the spring itself, the balance and the lever must be perfectly poised; the balance, spring, lever, and all other parts in the watch, even the springs in the case, must be free from magnetism; the movement must be in good condition to transmit the motive force uniformly to the balance; the escapement particularly must be as perfect as it can be made; the end-shake of the balance, lever and escape-wheel no greater than is necessary to give freedom of motion, so that there can be no material change in their relative positions; the pivots of the lever and balance staffs well fitted to their jewel holes; the lever pivots well polished and free from any "binding" in any position of the movement; the balance pivots straight, hard and round, well polished, as small as is consistent with strength, their shoulders well clear of the jewels, and the balance not running too near the plate, bridge or any other part; the hole jewels thin and the holes round and finely polished; the holes not perfectly cylindrical, but a little rounded out or enlarged towards each end, to diminish the extent of surface in contact with the pivots, and prevent any possible binding by either the jewel or pivot not being set exactly true, as well as to lessen the adhesion of the oil to the pivot; and in lever watches the ruby pin must be perfectly firm in its place and vertical, or parallel to the balance axis, and the slot in the end of the lever polished and well fitted to the ruby pin. Full details of the special requirements of each kind of escapement are given in the chapters devoted to that subject. (See Part Fifth.)

If all this is not the case, it should be made so as nearly as possible, after which there is a certain order to be observed in our further proceedings.

(521) *Common notions about isochronism.*—Most workmen have an idea that isochronism is some mysterious property of the spring which will enable it to overcome irregularities and difficulties and make the balance "come to time" in spite of them. Now that is just as incorrect as to say that it is one of the prop-

erties of a pivot to fit its jewel hole. It will fit the hole after it is made to fit, and not until then. So, a hair spring is isochronal after we have isochronized it, and not before. That is to say, after we have adjusted the length and shape of the spring, so that, under the effects of all disturbing influences acting upon it while the watch is going, it will make unequal vibrations in equal times, it is isochronized, or isochronal. Just as we say, after we have fitted the pivot, "it fits." But the fit is not a "property" of the pivot, nor is isochronism a property of the hair spring. It is simply a term representing a certain *condition* of being adjusted to act in a certain way under certain circumstances. But if those circumstances are changed one iota, there is no property or power in the spring to vary its action to suit that change, or correct its effects. Whatever peculiarity of action it may have as the result of our manipulations, that action is unvarying. If we want it to overcome certain difficulties, we must alter it till it does overcome them. Hence the spring should be isochronized with the frictions and all other influences, good or bad, which it is desired to neutralize, acting precisely as they will when the watch is finished and passed over to the customer.

(522.) *Testing the isochronism.*—Premising that all previous requirements have been properly attended to, we are ready to test our hair spring to see whether it is isochronal, and if not, in which direction it errs and how much. This is done by causing the arcs of vibration to vary considerably, in the manner that is most convenient, and accurately observing the rate of the watch for an equal period with the long and with the short vibrations.

The various methods of varying the amplitude of the vibrations will be described in Chapter XXXVI, sections (671–673.) But in whatever way they may be changed, if we find that the watch keeps the same time while running 4, 6 or 12 hours with the long vibrations, as during the same period with the short ones, the spring is already isochronal. But generally the watch will run slower with the long vibrations than with the short ones. In some cases the difference may be only a second or two—barely perceptible; in others, it may be several minutes. If the variation is considerable, it is better to repeat the test before making any change in the hair spring, to ascertain whether it is not due to some irregularity in the action of the movement. For it is useless to attempt to isochronize the spring unless the movement is in good condition.

(523.) During these trials the watch should be kept in the

same position, (generally dial up,) and at the same temperature, as otherwise the effects of changes of position and of temperature would be confounded with the normal action of the spring in different arcs, and mislead the workman. The compensation for heat and cold is no part of the duty of the hair spring, but, on the contrary, the adjustment of that compensation must counteract the effects of heat and cold upon the spring. It must therefore be kept at a uniform temperature while being isochronized.

(524.) *Quick test for isochronism.*—Just here I will mention a "quick and easy method of testing the isochronism of a spring," widely taught and highly indorsed:—" Insert four pins in the rim of a balance, about a quarter of an inch long and equidistant from each other. Then fix a temporary detent by the side of one of the pins when the spring is free. Then turn the balance one quarter around, and let the next pin rest against the detent, and find the weight that will just balance the force of the spring when placed on the pin. Turn the balance another quarter around, and if the weight that pin will sustain is just double the former, the spring is isochronal. Turn the balance to the third pin and the weight should then be three times the first. If the spring will not sustain that weight, it will be too slow in the long vibrations. If it sustains more than that, it will be too fast in the long vibrations," and so on.

This is substantially equivalent to the "elastic balance" devised by le Roy and used by all of the older horologists for measuring the force of balance springs and their divergence from a uniform increase of strength.

(525.) *No true test except timing in the watch.*—Such a test is only approximately true in theory, and worthless in practice. There is no practical method of testing the isochronism of a spring except by testing it in the watch, in the precise circumstances for which it is required to be isochronal, by timing it as already described. Were the strength of the spring the only factor to be considered, this test would be theoretically correct for a perfect spring. But since all escapements do in some degree disturb the oscillations of the balance, and different escapements do this very differently, it must be impossible to isochronize a spring independently of the escapement, *i.e.*, otherwise than in the watch to which it belongs. And this conclusion is the more evident when we consider the many other disturbing influences, of which we cannot foresee the nature, degree or manner of their occurrence, but which must necessarily be provided for. The principal use of the elastic balance and spring gauges, in connection with isochronism, is to find whether a spring, by itself, increases in strength in proportion to the angle of flexion. Any irregularity would indicate some flaw in the metal or other fault, and the workman would be saved from expending labor and time on a worthless spring by thus discovering the fault at the start.

(526.) Even were it possible to secure certain and definite conditions, and to know the exact form and strength of the spring adapted to them, the above test would be practically worthless from its clumsiness. A watch makes, we will say, 432,000 vibrations in 24 hours. Now does any one suppose that, by the above or any other weighing process, it would be possible to detect a variation from the proper *progression* in the strength of the spring, so slight that, after multiplying the effect it produces on a single vibration 432,000 times, it only causes an error of a few seconds more or less? It must be remembered that the isochronal test has nothing to do with the actual strength of the spring, (which concerns only the rate,) but only with the correctness of the *ratio* in which it increases. The above "test" might possibly detect errors amounting to several minutes in a day, but such errors cannot occur if previous directions for selecting springs have been followed, and any good workman would know that such a spring was unsuitable or defective, without any test at all.

(527.) *Comparing the results.*—We will suppose that we set the watch at 9 A.M., and on running it for 12 hours with the long vibrations, its hands show 8 hours, 59 minutes, 45 seconds—and after setting again, it shows for the 12 hours with the short vibrations, 9 hours, 15 seconds, *i.e.*, 15 seconds after 9 o'clock.

Then there is a difference of 30 seconds—the long vibrations being slower than the short ones, or taking longer time to accomplish them. This point must be clearly understood, to prevent blunders and improper alterations. Whenever *the watch gains*, it is because more than the proper number of vibrations have been made in the given time, therefore they are shorter and quicker than they should be. When the watch loses, less than the proper number are made, because each one takes longer than it should and the hands are not moved so far as they should have been. But it does not matter whether the times kept by the watch are faster or slower than the correct time, nor if our alterations make both of them faster or both slower than they should be. All that is necessary for these tests is to compare the two times *with each other*, to see whether the short vibrations are quicker or slower than the long ones. And the only use of correct time, at present, is to enable us to compare the two results and know the exact difference.

(528.) *What is isochronism?*—The question naturally arises why the long vibrations are slower or quicker than the short ones, when the length of the hair spring is exactly the same in each case. The prevailing theory is that the isochronism of the spring depends on its being of a certain length in proportion to its strength, and if it is longer than that it will lose in the long vibrations, but if shorter, it will gain in the long vibrations. This theory is credited to Pierre le Roy, and has the indorsement of a host of other eminent authorities from le Roy's day to this. Yet it is not true, for a spring will have *several* different isochronal points or lengths, while it is not isochronal at any intervening points. In fact, there appears to be an isochronal point somewhere in every coil, provided that its length is not so great or small as to interfere with its free and proper action. The theory has the appearance of truth, because, when the isochronal point is found for the particular spring, if it is then lengthened it will lose, and if shortened will gain, in the long arcs. But that isochronal point depends upon many other conditions besides the proportionate length and strength of the spring. The number of coils and manner of coiling, the mode of attachment to the stud and collet, the shape of the terminal curves at the ends, are among the conditions in the spring itself which may either improve or destroy its isochronism. And outside of the spring are many others. The truth is that a spring which has been perfectly isochronized is so only for the precise conditions for which it is adjusted.

(529.) Another definition of isochronism as follows: "Isochronism is a certain correspondence or relation between the proportions of a hair spring and of a balance, and such that under proper conditions the spring will move the balance through greater or smaller arcs in equal times." This is very good so far as it goes, but it takes into consideration only the spring and the balance. But, as already shown, there are many other points which theoretically and really are concerned in bringing about the complete result we call isochronism.

(530.) *Modifying influences.*—It would be interesting to go fully into the theoretical consideration of the conditions of isochronism, the effects of all the modifying influences upon the extent and the time of the vibrations. But to do so would require several chapters, and I will content myself with a brief classification of a few of the more prominent influences and their practical effects. The first class comprises any friction or retarding influence which is equal and continuous throughout the whole or nearly the whole of the vibration, as the friction of the pivots, thickening of the oil, pressure of the duplex or cylinder escape wheel against the balance axis, and the like. The effect of these may be to make the short vibrations either quicker or slower than the long ones, according to the conditions in each case, but generally they will be slower.

(531.) There is another class of influences, the principal and type of which is the resistance of the air to the motion of the balance. This depends on the construction, weight, specific gravity and exposed surface of its parts, and it increases with the increase of the arc of vibration in the proportion of the squares of the velocities. That is, if one balance vibrates twice as far as another, and in the same time, the resistance of the air to the motion of the former would be four times as great as of the latter. But as the momentum of the balance also increases as the squares of the arcs, they therefore increase and decrease uniformly. Of course a smooth, heavy balance will meet with less resistance than a large and light one, with numerous screws, etc. But whether that resistance be great or small, whatever the amount may be, it will increase and decrease as the squares of the velocities. The effect is therefore greater as the amplitude of the vibrations increases, and makes them quicker.

(532.) Thirdly, different escapements affect the time of the vibrations, because they interfere with the normal time which the spring alone would give, by breaking in at a certain point and giving the balance a push, thereby hurrying up its motion while in contact. So that the length of the time of contact, or angle of impulse, becomes a factor in the problem, as well as the frequency of these contacts—whether occurring at each vibration, or only alternate ones, as in the chronometer and duplex; and whether there is any recoil in the escapement, as in the duplex and cylinder escapements under certain circumstances. The power required to unlock the escapement, giving more or less of a check to the motion of the balance, is another factor; the fall or "drop" of the escape-wheel teeth against a cylinder or balance staff, urged on by the entire motive force, must at the instant of impact exert a checking influence. In the cylinder escapement the side pressure upon the balance axis is removed during the arc of escape, at the middle of the vibration,—another point to be considered. Escapement frictions retard the short vibrations more than the long ones.

(533.) Lastly, there are the irregular influences, among which may be mentioned unavoidable imperfections in the metal or form of the spring, unequal hardening or temper, imperfections in the balance, pivots, escapement, and others already mentioned. A soft spring cannot be isochronized, and if it could it would not stay so. Even the mere bending of a spring, although it may have been restored to its former shape, produces an unevenness of texture at that point, and the lower the temper of the spring the great is the effect of such treatment. If these spots are stiffer than the remainder of the spring they do not bend with the other parts, or not equally, and throw the spring out of shape; if they are not so stiff, they bend too soon and the same result follows. If a spring is let out at the stud, the crimp made where it was pinned will produce a stiff spot and interfere with uniform inflexion of the spring. A beginner will frequently render a spring worthless for isochronal adjustment by numerous changes and corrections. It should be bent as little as possible, and when necessary it should be done a little at a time and repeated, rather than bent too much and then have to take back a part. Many other disturbing influences are mentioned in Chapter XXXVII, on Position Faults.

(534.) This class of influences no foresight can entirely prevent, nor can we know in what part of the vibration they will occur, or how great they will be, until we ascertain by actual test. No theory can avail against their occurrence nor do away with their effects. This can only be done, if done at all, by proceeding at once to *adjust the spring*, in the direction indicated by the test, until success is attained or found to be unattainable. And, from what has already been said of the first three classes, it must be plain that, for all practical purposes, the workman will find that nothing further is necessary in the isochronal adjustment than to secure the mechanical correctness of the different parts, and then to govern his proceedings entirely by the *extent* of the vibrations, and the *times* given during his trials, while actually adjusting the spring in the watch, to counteract the errors caused by frictions and all other disturbing influences.

CHAPTER XXX.

Why Springs are Isochronous.

(535.) *On what does isochronism depend?*—As we have seen, a great number of influences affect the isochronism of a spring. Some make the short vibrations quicker than the long ones, others have the contrary effect. A spring which is adjusted and made isochronous with one kind of escapement will not be so with a different escapement, nor with another watch having the same kind of escapement but made differently, nor even when made the same, with the exception that the balance has different dimensions. On the other hand, if a spring of a certain length, shape and temper is isochronous, we may substitute for it another spring exactly like it except that it is wider, and the latter will also be isochronous for the same arcs of vibration. It will be stronger than the former, in proportion to its greater width and will carry a balance which is heavier, but in other respects like the one carried by the former spring.

(536.) *Different opinions of the cause of isochronism.*—It was formerly thought that if the strength of a spring increased in proportion to the angle of flexion, it would be isochronous. But it was soon discovered that that would secure theoretical isochronism, of the spring by itself, but not practical isochronism in the watch. The best authorities of the present day differ widely in their opinions as to the cause of isochronism. I have taken the trouble to bring their various ideas together for instructive comparison, while refraining in most cases from mentioning names.

(537.) The original theory put forth by Pierre le Roy was that in every spring of sufficient extent there is a certain length where all the vibrations, long or short, large or small, will be isochronous, and that when this length is found, if you shorten the spring the large vibrations will be made in less time than the small ones, or, if you lengthen the spring the long vibrations will be slower than the small ones.

(538.) Coming down to modern times, one school of adjusters claim that isochronism does not depend on the length of the spring, but is obtained by pinning it in even or complete coils, and avoiding fractional parts of coils between the collet and the stud. Another school holds that isochronism does not depend either on the length or method of pinning, but on giving the proper curvature to one or both ends of the spring, (*i.e.*, on terminal curves,) and that mere length has nothing whatever to do with isochronism.

(539.) Another insists that length has everything to do with it, and that a spring which is too short will make the short vibrations in less time than the long ones, and *vice versa*, regardless of its form. Another claimed that every coil had its isochronal point, and that if the spring was pinned there, the vibrations would be isochronal. Another holds that the length is the essential point, and that different lengths were required for different escapements,—a length which would be suited to one escapement would be quite unfit for another. Another explains that the different length of the spring has of itself no influence in correcting errors in isochronism, but the effect is due to the mechanical relation of the collet and stud being changed, *i.e.*, the relative positions of the two ends of the spring are better adapted for causing it to vibrate synchronously. SAUNIER says, however, that it makes absolutely no difference what their relative positions may be; one may be over the other, or be at any angle whatever with it.

(540.) Many practical springers and adjusters secure isochronism by putting the balance out of poise in such a way as to assist or retard the spring at the ends of its vibrations, while others correct errors of isochronism by putting the spring itself out of center, or making it excentric, instead of concentric, as others insist that it must be. So it goes. Every one of these methods secures good results in certain cases, adapted to it, but none of them succeed in all cases.

(541.) *The Phillips' theory of the terminal curve.*—If there is any one theory regarding isochronism which is more generally regarded with respect than others, it is probably the theory of terminal curves put forward by Prof. Phillips of the Polytechnical School, in Paris, in his treatise *Sur le spiral réglant.* Prof. Phillips is a very able mathematician, and has developed his theory in detail, in accordance with mechanical laws—with such ability, in fact, that the most eminent horologists, as well as practical men everywhere, tacitly accept it as being unquestionably true. It will therefore be worth our while to examine it carefully, so far as may be necessary to understand it.

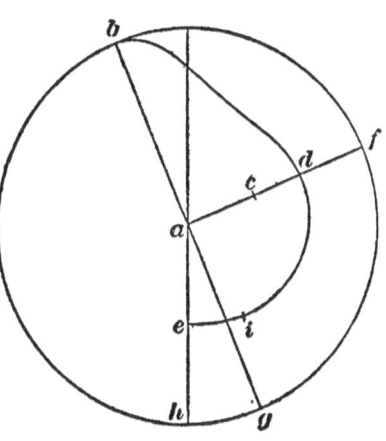

FIG. 27.

(542.) *Diagram of a Phillips' curve.*—Fig. 27 is substantially the diagram given in his treatise. The circle represents the outer coil of the spring; the terminal curve leaves it at *b*, and curves through *d* to its end at *e*. At *a* is the center of the spring, and the position of the axis of the balance; *ba* is a radius drawn through the beginning of the curve, and *ah* is one through its end.

(543.) *The conditions of the Phillips' theory* are: (1) that the center of gravity of the terminal curve *be* must fall upon a radius which is at right angles to the radius passing through the beginning of the curve, or *ba*. The center of gravity of the curve must therefore be somewhere in the radius *af*, (which is at right angles to *ab*,) and, for the curve shown, the center of gravity is at *c*. (2) The distance *ac* must be to the distance *ab*, as the length of the radius *ab* is to the length of the curve *bdie*, a proportion which we write thus:

$$ab : bde :: ac : ab,$$

which gives us the distance $ac = \dfrac{(ab)^2}{bde}$. This condition was expressed in the treatise in a different way, viz.: that the distance *ac* must be a third proportional to the radius *ab* and the length *bde* of the curve. But the reader who is not versed in mathematics will understand it better when expressed the other way.

(544.) *Properties of a spring with such a terminal curve.*—Prof. Phillips states that a spring having its ends formed into two parallel curves which satisfy the above conditions will have the following properties:

1. The center of gravity of the spring will always be on *a*, the axis of the balance.

2. The spring will remain perfectly cylindrical and concentric with the axis *a* while coiling and uncoiling, and its strength will increase in proportion to the angle through which the balance is turned.

3. The spring will never cause any side pressure of the balance pivots in their holes.

It will be observed that this theory is intended to apply more especially to cylindrical springs having a terminal curve on each end, and I will examine it first on that basis.

(545.) *The center of gravity, with two curves.*—Prof. Phillips says the center of gravity of the spring will be on the balance axis, if it is provided with "two parallel curves" such as described. Taking that statement literally, it is evidently an error, for if they are parallel, and one over the other, (as they must be if parallel,) the center of gravity of *both* of them would be at *c*, and *not* on the axis *a*. There are only two conceivable cases in which that statement can be correct: (1) The two curves *not* parallel, but exactly opposite. Fig. 28 illustrates this. In order that the center of gravity of the entire spring should be on a, the centers of gravity of the two curves must fall in radii af and af^1 which are exactly opposite, (*i.e.* in the same diametrical line,) and at points c and c^1 which are at the same distances from a; in that case the center of gravity of the two would be on a. This would require that one curve should begin at b, and the other at b^1, exactly opposite, and the lengths of the two curves must be precisely the same. It is very doubtful if any spring was ever made in that way. The distances ac and ac^1 may be unequal, however, if the lengths of the curves are inversely modified, *i.e.*, if the length of the first curve multiplied by ac is equal to the length of the other curve multiplied by ac^1. The center of gravity of the weights at c and c^1 would then be on a. It is stated that the two curves may be crossed or inclined at any angle to each other—but that would not be in conformity to Phillips' theory. (2) If the centers of gravity of the two curves do not fall on radii exactly opposite, as is shown in Fig. 28, the center of gravity of the spring cannot fall on a unless the distance ac or ac^1 is nothing; and according to the proportion given in section (543), if ac was nothing, ab must also be nothing, *i.e.*, the diameter of the spring would be nothing, which is impossible.

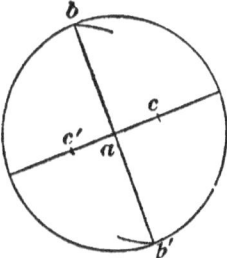

FIG. 28.

(546.) *Center of gravity, with one curve.*—Breguet springs are often provided with curves similar to that shown in Fig. 27, and called Phillips' curves. The reader will also bear in mind that when the watch is running, one curve of the cylindrical spring is *supported by the stud*, so that the weight of only the other curve rests on the pivots. I will therefore consider the center of gravity of a single curve, supposing the body of the spring to be concentric and in poise. In the case of the Breguet spring, it does not matter where the center of gravity of the curve may be, because it is supported by the stud. The curve of a cylindrical spring the weight of which rests on the pivots cannot possibly have its centre of gravity on the axis a, (see Fig. 27,) if its length does not exceed a half turn, and in any of the forms ordinarily used it cannot be on the axis at all. Mere inspection of Fig. 27 will satisfy any one of that fact. This shows the propriety of the rule given in section (299), that the collet bar and *the curve* of the spring should be poised in position on the balance staff. It will be seen, from the foregoing considerations, that in forming terminal curves it is perfectly useless to pay any regard to their centers of gravity.

(547.) *Securing concentricity and regular progression of force.*— Prof. Phillips states (544) that a spring having two parallel curves which satisfy the conditions in section (543) will remain concentric, will exert no side pressure on the pivots, and will increase in strength in proportion to the angle of flexion. If so, it is important. Suppose we modify the form shown in Fig. 27, as indicated in Fig. 29, in dotted lines. The original curve is *b 1 d 4 e*. One modification is *b 2 d 5 e*, the other is *b 3 d 6 e*. The center of gravity of each one is at *c*, and each satisfies the conditions of Phillips' theory. Is there any reason for believing that either modification would cause the body of the spring to remain concentric, avoid side pressure, and increase in strength in proportion to the angle of flexion. If not, it follows that springs made in accordance with that theory are *not* invariably or necessarily isochronous. Even if they possessed the regular progression in force, that would only secure a theoretical isochronism of the spring by itself, which is valueless, as only a practical isochronism which covers all peculiarities of the entire watch in action is of any real importance.

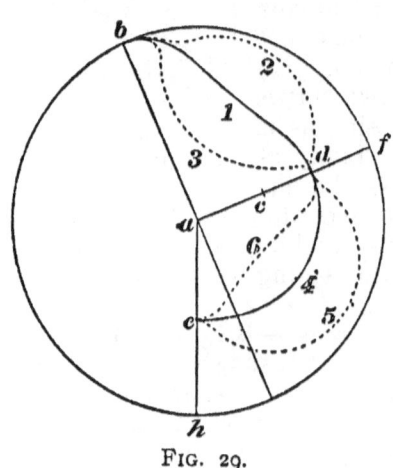

FIG. 29.

(548.) *So-called Phillips' curves in use.*—It appears, therefore, that the most of those who use so-called Phillips' curves, are blindly following a theory, they know not why, and without getting any benefit from it. They speak of "the Phillips' curve," and of it being "always the same," not knowing that there is no such thing as "the Phillips' curve," in the sense implied, of it having one particular shape. There are dozens of curves, having the most dissimilar forms, each of which is "*a* Phillips' curve," because it is made according to the Phillips' theory. But there is no one particular form which can be correctly called "*the* Phillips' curve." Those who are using "the Phillips' curve" are merely imitating the form chosen by him as most convenient in illustrating his theory, and which I have reproduced in Fig. 27. But neither that *nor any other form* will suit all cases; it must be changed and "adjusted" to make it provide for all the peculiarities of the movement containing it. Hence all such fancy forms merely cause useless trouble in making and adjusting. A more regular form would be far better. The English, with their practical, common-sense methods, recognize this, and use more direct, simple and serviceable shapes for their curves. The perfection of their results affords ample evidence that they are correct in doing so.

(549.) *Old and new forms for Phillips' curves.*—Twenty-four different shapes were originally shown, each of which would satisfy the conditions of Phillips' theory. On looking them over, we find almost every form, from the most regular to the most irregular. Some make a half turn, and others are from that up to a full turn. In some, the end of the curve is at the center of position of the spring, and in others at the outer circle; others at $\frac{1}{3}$ the distance from the center to the outside, or at $\frac{1}{2}$, $\frac{2}{3}$, $\frac{3}{4}$, $\frac{4}{5}$ that distance. In some, the curve starts very gradually from the outer circle, in others abruptly, both kinds having the same length, $\frac{1}{2}$ turn. The outer ends are generally pinned at a tangent to the radius passing through them, but some curve inward of the tangent, and others outward. It is stated that the curves at the two ends of the spring need not be alike, and they may stand at any angle with each other. I had intended to show some new forms which would satisfy Phillips' theory, and among them curves for pinning at one-half the radius of the spring and others to pin *outside* of the circle of the spring, as is done with the flat spiral. But the reader who has fully understood the foregoing descriptions can easily do that for himself. Those who feel interested can obtain Prof. Phillips' treatise for two francs, (in French,) and study it at leisure. What may be called the English curves will be treated in the chapters devoted to making terminal curves.

(550.) *Contradictory methods of securing isochronism.*—As is well known, we can secure isochronism by means of terminal curves, and equally well without any curves at all—merely using a straight piece of spring at the stud end, (called the isochronous stud (559,) or even without that—as in the flat spiral spring; by pinning in even coils, or in fractional coils; by a certain length, and without regard to the length; with the balance in poise, and out of poise; with the spring concentric, or excentric; by the regulator pins, and without any regulator; by pinning the stud end of the spring outside of the circle, or at half its radius; by changing the weight of the balance; by changing the shape of the screws in its rim; by changing the average motive force;

by changing the action of the escapement; by changing the size or the shape of the balance pivots; by changing the size of the collet; by changing the form of the inner end of the spring; by changing the direction of the spring as it leaves the stud; and in still other ways, as indicated in Chapter XXXI.

(551.) *The law of isochronism.*—In view of these facts, the question again arises, on what does isochronism depend? What is the action or principle or means which is really useful and indispensable? The law which evidently includes all conditions and all forces affecting the result is the mechanical principle that "the movements of a vibrating balance will be isochronal when the sum of all the forces impelling or retarding it increase in proportion to the angle of oscillation." This covers every force acting upon it, either to advance or retard it: the momentum of the balance, and any lack of poise, or of truth in form or centering; the frictions of pivots, air, etc.; the action of the oil, and of dirt; the effect of the escapement; the action of the hair spring, whether correct or otherwise, and all other influences. Some of them urge the balance forward, at the same time that others resist it. But the net result of all of them combined must be a force proportional to the extent of the vibration. When that is secured, this joint force will be doubled to propel the balance through double the angle of rotation, from the point of rest, and so with any other proportion, and the strength of the spring must be doubled to bring the balance back to the point of rest in the same time as before.

(552.) *The force of the hair-spring.*—At the end of the vibration, the spring draws the balance back; while inertia, the various frictions, etc., resist it. The spring is the only force then acting to produce the vibration, and it must overcome all other influences. But, as the balance moves towards the center or point of rest, some of the opposing influences become less or disappear entirely, while others make their appearance, and then the disturbing influence of the escapement comes into play. Fortunately, the balance (if it has the correct proportions) is not controlled by these several influences. It acts as a storehouse of energy; whatever influence impels it onward is added to the force already stored in its mass; whatever resists it is subtracted therefrom, and the remainder is the net or active impelling force producing the vibration.

(553.) *Isochronal vibrations.*—When the retarding and the propelling influences are practically equal, or when these irregular or disturbing influences are extremely small in amount as compared with the regularly progressive force of the spring, or when that progression is not regular but is properly modified to counteract the disturbing influences, we have nearly or practically isochronal vibrations. The foregoing explanations will show why the hair spring is but one factor, although the most important one, which has to be taken into consideration in securing isochronism, and why a spring which is perfectly isochronous by itself, or even when attached to a balance, may not be isochronous when running in the watch. It also shows that there *cannot* be any one form of spring, or any theoretical method of procedure, which will invariably secure isochronism, but the different escapements and the peculiarities of each movement must be allowed for. It is only after that has been done that we can have really isochronal vibrations. And even then it must be remembered that while theoretical isochronism is perfection, practical isochronism is a compromise, and therefore only approximate.

(554.) *Summary.*—After we have considered all theories, all principles and laws, all influences affecting the result, and all the conclusions which have been arrived at by different persons, so far as they are generally known, what have we learned from them? Simply this: 1. That there is such a condition as theoretical isochronism, which exists when the strength of the spring increases in proportion to the angle of flexion. 2. That theoretical isochronism is of no value or use whatever to us in adjusting a watch for isochronism. 3. That what we require is practical isochronism, *i.e.*, isochronal vibrations when the watch is actually running. 4. That the only way yet known for securing practical isochronism is to adjust the spring by certain empirical methods, derived from experience, until the vibrations are found to be isochronal. 5. That the true philosophy of the adjustment, *i.e.*, how or why those methods make the vibrations isochronal, has never been explained. It is not enough to say that they adjust the spring in such a way that the propelling and retarding influences are equally balanced; or that, when the various influences are so balanced, the long and short vibrations will be made in equal times, for that is a sort of explanation which explains nothing. The question is, *why* are they performed in equal times? How does that balancing enable a spring to do that?

(555.) *Theoretical isochronism.*—To make this point more clear, I show in Fig. 30 two arcs: the first from 1 to 2, representing the short vibrations, and another twice as long, from 3 to 4, for the long ones. Let us suppose that the balance vibrates through the lower arc, $1\,b'2$, in one second. It is evident that, if it also vibrates through the arc *3 b 4* in one second, its peripheral speed in the part *1 b 2* will be more than double what it was when making the short vibrations *1 b'2*, of that length. This shows the fallacy of the common idea that it vibrates through the short arc in a certain time, and, when the arc is doubled, it first vibrates through the short arc as before, and then an equal additional amount of force is required to carry it through the additional distance. The fact is, that it not only performs the additional distance, but it also performs the original distance in less than half the time it did before. Now, is that accounted for or explained by saying that the propelling and the retarding influences are equal, or that double the force will carry the balance through double the distance? Not at all, for that is merely theoretical isochronism, of a free spring and balance without friction. In a watch, with its frictions and other faults, that statement would not be true, for double the force would *not* carry it through double the distance, except in very rare cases. The distance might be more or less than double, according to the condition of the movement.

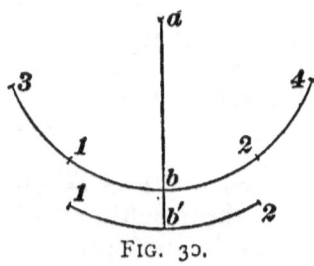

FIG. 30.

(556.) *Practical isochronism.*—The correct explanation of practical isochronism is this: The true (*i.e.*, practically) isochronous spring,—by itself or with the balance, without frictions, etc.,—would *always* perform the long and short arcs in *different* times —*never* in equal times; if it did, it could not possibly be isochronous. For example, let us suppose that we have a spring *theoretically* perfect, *i.e.*, its force increases exactly in proportion to the angle of flexion, and when run in the watch in such a way that frictions, position faults and the like could not affect the vibrations, it would perform the long and short arcs in precisely the same times, (555.) Then we find by trial that the frictions and other disturbing influences, when allowed to affect the motion of the balance, retard it, so that the long vibrations are 4 seconds per day slower than they were before, and the short arcs are 12 seconds slower—these influences being always more felt in the short arcs than the long ones.

(557.) In the ordinary way of speaking, we would say that there was a loss of 8 seconds in the short arcs, because we would take the rate in the long arcs as the standard of comparison, and compare the rate in the short arcs with that. But in reality, both long and short arcs are retarded, as we would find if we could time the spring without being at all affected by frictions, etc. As it is, we cannot do that, and when we take the rate in the long arcs, that rate includes such effects of friction, etc., as are felt in the long arcs; and the loss observed in the short arcs is due to those frictions being proportionally *more* felt in the short than in the long arcs. We then proceed to adjust the spring to correct that loss. How do we do it? Simply by *destroying* the theoretical isochronism of that "perfect" spring, altering it so that it would (alone) perform the long and short arcs in *different* times, causing it to *gain* in both the long and short vibrations, but to gain *most* in the short ones, *till the gain of the spring balances the loss due to the frictions, etc.* Then the rate will be the same in both long and short arcs, the spring will be what is termed "isochronous," and we will have attained practical isochronism.

(558.) *Isochronous spring.*—The proper definition of isochronous spring, therefore, is "a spring whose errors in different arcs and positions are equal to, and the reverse of, the errors caused by frictions and other disturbing influences." When that is the case, the vibrations will be isochronal, the rate will be the same in different arcs and positions, and the spring will be truly "isochronous." The greater the errors to be covered or corrected, the greater must be the contrary errors of the spring, in order to balance them. They cannot be hidden or "corrected" in any other way. If the faults of the movement cause a loss of 8 seconds per day in the short arcs, and we alter the spring so that the watch then loses nothing at all, we have made the spring gain 8 seconds, so that its gain just balances that loss. On the other hand, if the disturbing influences cause the balance to accelerate in the short arc, the spring must be made to lose an equal amount, in order to balance it and secure an equal rate in the long and short arcs. Any talk about causing the spring to increase its force in a different ratio, etc., is simply nonsense. The spring has no occult properties, and it is not necessary to fall back upon such mysterious and meaningless suppositions, when we have a plain, common-sense explanation, which common sense tells us is true.

CHAPTER XXXI.

Methods of Securing Isochronism.

(559.) *Numerous methods.*—A great number of different methods have been proposed for isochronizing a hair spring, of which some are good, some not so good, some good for nothing, and some worse than nothing. I had prepared a list of over forty different methods of securing or varying the isochronal action of the spring, with the intention of describing each one in detail. But as only a few of them are employed in practice, and those which are used are capable of producing any effect which could be produced by the others, it was thought wise to devote the space to matter more generally useful and indispensable. Those selected, however, are treated with all necessary fulness and perspicuity, and will be found all that are required for actual work. For the same reason, some of the methods described in my *Practical Treatise* are left out. Among those which are now omitted, is the isochronous stud, that not being in practical use, because it does not allow the use of a regulator with it. Some ten years ago, I patented a very simple modification of this method, removing that objection, but, owing to certain provisions of the patent law, the patent became void, and I let the matter drop. It is now free to any who choose to use it.— The methods to be described are:

(560.) 1. *Isochronizing by a certain length.*—Springs will only secure isochronism within certain limits. With the flat spiral, it can be isochronous if the vibrations do not exceed $1\frac{1}{4}$ turns. When provided with terminal curves, as in the case of the Breguet and cylindrical springs, the vibrations may be isochronal up to $1\frac{1}{2}$ turns, or a little over that. A spring which is too short, *i.e.*, too thick in proportion to its length, will gain in the short vibrations and lose in the long ones, and *vice versa*. The shorter the spring, the greater the difference of rate in the long and short arcs; and the longer it is, the less the difference, and the less necessary is it to pin it in any particular way. Hence flat spirals and Breguet springs which employ regulators should be long, so that the change of length by the regulator may produce the least difference between the rates in the long and short arcs. The length of the flat spiral (for lever watches) should be at least 14 coils, and for the Breguet spring from 14 to 20 coils. In cheap watches, use shorter springs, to quicken the short arcs. Cylindrical springs run from 10 to 13 turns.

(561.) *Allowance for adjustment or non-adjustment.*—When springs are to be closely adjusted, they may be shorter, as, in short springs, differences in the mode of pinning, in the length, and other influences, produce a greater effect on the rate in different arcs, and consequently we can isochronize a short spring through a wider range, and counteract greater position and other errors by the adjustment than could be done with a long spring. Long springs are therefore better in watches which are not to be adjusted, or not adjusted closely, because the difference of rate in the long and short arcs is less. But for that reason they cannot correct very large position errors, and when such errors are large a shorter spring of the same strength is preferable. In substituting or fitting springs follow the above indications. In altering a spring, shorten it to make the short arcs faster, and lengthen it to make the short arcs slower. See section (630).

(562.) It is also necessary to correct the rate of the watch, which will be altered by thus shortening or lengthening the spring. If the long arcs are only a few seconds slow, take up the spring half the width of the stud, then make the balance heavier to neutralize the effect on the rate, as by putting two heavy screws in place of two light ones; if the long arcs are too quick, let out the spring and make the balance lighter to correspond. The necessity of making two changes renders this method rather troublesome. But the same objection lies against nearly all of the methods except that by terminal curves.

(563.) 2. *By taking up and letting out the spring.*—As the reverse of the foregoing method, we have the well-known rule among adjusters: "If taking up the spring don't accelerate the short arcs, let it out some." This might be explained on the theory that there is an isochronal point in every coil, and that lengthening the spring would carry the end further away from the isochronal point in one coil, while bringing it closer to that in another, but not near enough to be appreciably benefited by it. The change of length may be beneficial or otherwise, according to which isochronal point is nearest. This method is, roughly speaking, merely "feeling around" to find the isochronal point. To prevent the spring being damaged by frequent pinnings in the stud, one of the tools described in Chapter XVII will be found invaluable, as it grips the spring between flat jaws and produces no crimp or injury, no matter how many times the place of holding it is changed. It is not even necessary to remove the stud for the trials, (in the case of watches,) as the coil can be gripped on either side of the stud, which will swing with it and do no harm if it is not too heavy, and if the watch is kept in the horizontal position during the trials.

(564.) 3. *By pinning the spring in even turns.*—This method was at one time thought to be a cure-all for isochronal errors, and all springs were thought to be made isochronous by merely avoiding fractional parts of coils. That is now known to be an error, but that method of pinning has certain advantages which are important. One of them is that the difference of rate between long and short arcs is least with even turns, while it is greatest with half turns, and proportionally great as we change from even coils to the half coil over or under the complete turns. Hence, for watches which are not to be adjusted, complete coils will generally secure vibrations with the least isochronal errors.

(565.) *Principle of the isochronal adjustment by even turns.*— But if the spring is to be adjusted for isochronism, it can be made to cover greater errors (of positions, frictions, etc.,) by pinning it over or under complete coils. For instance, if there was a large loss in the short arcs, due to various disturbing influences, and we could produce an equally large gain in the short arcs due to isochronal error, we should obtain a perfect rate, and the spring would be called isochronous. The isochronal error might be insufficient for the purpose, if pinned in even turns, but it could be made greater by properly changing the spring in the stud, till the necessary amount is obtained for counteracting the effects of friction, etc. The error produced by pinning over or under even turns becomes greater as the spring gets shorter. If the isochronal error in the short arcs is a loss, the loss will (as a general rule) be greatest when the spring is pinned in half turns, other conditions being the same. If the isochronal error is a gain, the gain will be greatest when pinned in half turns.

(566.) This method consists, of course, in bringing the two ends of the spring, or "*points d'attaché*," as they are termed, in the same radius, *i.e.*, a line drawn from center to outside passes through both the end at the collet and that at the stud. But we find in practice that with any given hair spring, the isochronal point would require to be at different places in it, depending upon the construction of the balance, the escapement, etc.,—even changing the size of the coils will cause the isochronal point to vary its position. The most that any method can do is to enable us to approximate to the isochronal point, leaving the corrections to be done by means of testing and adjusting. And, although I have examined a great many fine-running watches for that purpose, I have not yet found one where the spring was pinned *exactly* according to this theory,— the nearest always being a little to one side or the other. Nor have I succeeded in closely isochronizing a spring according to this theory, without resorting to the regulator pins (585) to enable me to complete the adjustment without changing the *points d'attaché* of the springs. But as this mode of pinning enables the workman to fit his spring with tolerable accuracy attended with scarcely any extra labor, it should be generally followed, even when the spring is not intended to be isochronized, as I have already recommended. Even a low-priced job should always be done as well as can be afforded. This method will at least guide us to an eligible starting point, at or near which we may reasonably expect the spring to be isochronal. It should be observed that if the regulator is not very near to the stud, that is to say, within 20° to 25° from it, the whole coils are reckoned from the point touching the collet to the *regulator pins*, instead of to the stud. If the isochronal point is not at the even turn, or if the spring is not pinned in even turns, changing the pinning towards even turns will generally make the long vibrations quicker. Further remarks on this subject will be found in Part Fifth on Rating.

(567.) 4. *By fractional coils.*—As before stated, (561,) the error of rate increases as the pinning is changed from even turns to half turns, and in adjusting we increase the variation from even turns till the isochronal error balances the opposite error of positions, etc. Of course, we produce a loss to balance a gain, and *vice versa*, making the spring shorter to cause a gain in the short arcs, and longer to make them slower. *As a rule, pinning in half turns makes the long vibrations slower.* But in watches with frictional escapements, short springs and short arcs, such as the duplex and cylinder escapement, the least observable error is found, (*i.e.*, the isochronal error most nearly balances the frictional errors, etc.,) when the springs are pinned nearly half a turn short of complete coils. In box chronometers, the result is best when the (cylindrical) springs are pinned about a quarter of a turn short, but in pocket chronometers they are pinned in even turns. Breguet springs are generally pinned in even turns if not adjusted for isochronism. When adjusted, they follow the same rule as all others. Also, see Isochronizing by terminal curves, (589 to 610.)

(568.) 5. *By altering the frictions.*—As a general rule, friction makes the short arcs slower. It, of course, retards both long and short arcs, but being proportionally greater in the short arcs, it retards them more than the long ones. This includes friction arising from rough or poorly polished jewels, pivots imperfect, jewel holes too long, etc. Improving these conditions will of course make the short arcs quicker, or make the loss less. Thickening of oil on the balance pivots, dirt, etc., make the short arcs slower. But if the thickening of the oil is on the pivots of the escapement or train, it makes the short arcs faster. See section (573). The short arcs can be made quicker in either horizontal or vertical positions by lessening the friction in those positions, and slower by increasing the friction.

(569.) 6. *By altering the balance pivots.*—When the watch is held in the vertical position, the side friction on the balance pivots makes the short arcs slower, in proportion to the amount of the friction and the size of the pivots. Hence shortening the holes, and polishing them, will quicken the short arcs. When the pivots are too closely fitted in the holes, the friction retards the short arcs, and any variation in the consistency of the oil produces considerable effect on the rate. Slightly freeing the pivots by hard burnishing will considerably quicken the short arcs. When the balance pivots are rather large the friction increases very rapidly, and reducing the size of the pivots (and of course fitting smaller jewel holes,) will greatly quicken the short arcs. This fault is very noticeable in small watches where the size of the pivots is large in proportion to the size of the balance, and in such cases the short arcs are quickened by using a hair spring one or two coils shorter. This alteration of course quickens all the vibrations, but the short ones more than the long.

(570.) 7. *By the balance.*—The isochronism can also be altered by changing the size or weight of the balance, but the results are so uncertain that the method is not followed by adjusters. See Chapter XXXVII, section (697.) In marine chronometers the long arcs are slow, which is attributed to the rims flying outward by centrifugal force further than in the short arcs. This error is greater when the rims are thin and narrow, than when wider and thicker. It has been proposed to make the long arcs slow in watches having expansion balances, by drilling a hole through each segment, near the ends of the center bar, and enlarging these holes, and thus weakening the segments, till they would fly out in the long arcs sufficiently to make them as slow as required. But this method cannot be considered commendable.

(571.) 8. *By altering the escapement frictions.*—In the duplex and cylinder escapements we may vary the isochronism by varying the relative amounts of the escapement-friction and the arcs of vibration. For instance, if the escapement be changed so as to transmit the motive force more advantageously and increase the impulse-power, without changing the friction upon the roller or cylinder, the arc of vibration will be increased and the long arcs will be slower than the short ones. (So in general, any alteration which increases the arcs without changing the escapement-friction, will make the long arcs slower than the short ones.) But increasing the friction without increasing the impulse-power, will make the long arcs quicker. So in general, any change which lessens the effective impulse-power, without lessening the escapement-friction, will make the long arcs quicker than the short ones.

(572.) 9. *By altering the drops.*—In the chronometer and duplex, the short arcs may be made slower by making the locking spring stiffer, or by giving the escape wheel more drop upon the impulse pallet, both of which operations are highly objectionable. But these methods are of no great practical importance, because it is, of course, not advisable to make the escapement worse off in order to improve the isochronism; and on the other hand, the escapement should be in as good order as we can get it, before we undertake to isochronize the spring. So there is very little margin left for our alterations.

(573.) 10. *By altering the motive force.*—As a general rule, stronger motive force makes the short arcs faster; (see section (571;) and diminishing it makes them slower, because the frictions, etc., are more felt. But this should be done with great caution, for there is a correct proportion between the motive force of the mainspring and the weight and diameter of the balance, which should not be greatly departed from. When the vibrations are very large, in the lever or chronometer, it is allowable to lessen the force of the mainspring, or put in a weaker one, to make the short arcs slower; and the reverse of this may be done to make the short arcs faster, if the vibrations are rather short, and can be safely enlarged. But the above remarks will show how incorrect is the idea that isochronism can depend upon the hair spring alone.

(574.) 11. *By changing the distance between the coils of the hair spring.*—It has been found that the difference of rate between long and short arcs is least when the distance between the coils of the flat spiral is equal, and greatest when that distance is most unequal. If the distance is the same at the center of the spring as at the outside, there will be the least difference in the long and short arcs. If the distance between the coils increases from the center to the outside, the difference between the long and short arcs increases. When the springs are fire-hardened and tempered in the same form as they are wound, the distance is practically equal. Such springs are best for watches which are not adjusted for isochronism, as their isochronal errors are small. But in adjusted watches, the distance between coils should vary, in order that there may be a greater difference of rate in the long and short arcs, so that the isochronal adjustment may be able to correct larger positional and other errors, and secure a more perfect rate. The method by which such springs may be made is given in Chapter VIII. The adjustment is accomplished by changing the place of pinning until all errors are covered by the isochronal action of the spring. See sections (564) to (567,) also Chapter XXXIV.

(575.) 12. *By excentric spring.*—Mr. Kullberg is the principal exponent of this method, which is largely followed, and I give his explanation of the principles involved. He utilizes the normal excentric action of the flat spiral spring while vibrating, which always occurs, even when it is so formed and pinned in the stud that its coils are concentric with the balance axis when at rest. As the balance vibrates in such a direction that the coils open, they open most on the side distant from the stud, because it has freedom on that side, but on the side next to the stud it is prevented from expanding freely. The result is that all the coils become excentric, and more so in proportion as the vibrations are larger. When the balance vibrates in the opposite direction, the result is the reverse of that described, and the spring is excentric on the side next to the stud. It is concentric only when the balance passes the point of rest, the pressure being alternately against one side of the jewel holes and the other, causing the usual error of the flat spiral—the long vibrations too quick and the short ones too slow.

(576.) He remedies this by forming and pinning the spring so that it is excentric when at rest, *i.e.*, it "bulges" towards the stud. When the spring uncoils in vibrating, it expands most on the side opposite the stud, as before. At a certain point in the vibration the coils become concentric with the balance axis, but if the vibrations become still larger, the coils again become excentric, but on the opposite side. In each vibration, therefore, the center of the excentricity travels from side to side, past the balance axis, as before, but the center of the coils comes on the axis at a different time—not when the balance is at the point of rest.

(577.) That time can be varied, to produce the effect required for correcting the error of isochronism. The spring is usually caused to be concentric when the balance has passed through half the distance it usually vibrates, (being held in that position while the coils are bent into concentric position,) but if necessary they can be made concentric at or near the *end* of the vibration. The spring is thus tried and changed till the proper action is obtained. The increased arc of vibration is an indication of a change for the better. The benefit is partly due to equalizing the frictions on the pivots. With the flat spiral there will unavoidably be some side pressure on the pivots, and the shiftings of the spring are to equalize them and neutralize the friction errors. This is the usual explanation of the method, but another and better one is given in sections (633, 634, 660).

(578.) This procedure is only recommended for making the short vibrations quicker and the long ones slower. It is claimed that in this way the flat spiral can be made as isochronous as the Breguet or cylindrical spring. Nevertheless, it is a method which cannot be considered advisable or workmanlike, and is only excusable because it does not produce excentricity when it did not exist before, but only shifts the existing excentricity to different points in the vibration, to reduce its injurious effects on the isochronism. Independent of any adjustment, it is quite common to pin the flat spiral excentric towards the stud, both to lessen the extreme of excentricity and to quicken the short arcs, as a remedy for the retarding effects of the oil in cold, of the dirt, etc. For lever clocks, and the like, it would be useful for making them keep the same rate when wound up or partly run down, especially those running longer than one day.

(579.) 13. *By regulator, on Breguet overcoil.*—There is no more propriety in using a regulator on a Breguet spring for timing purposes than on the terminal curve of a cylindrical spring. The Breguet overcoil is as truly a terminal curve as the other. Manufacturers and others will sometimes form a part of the overcoil into a good terminal curve, and another part in a concentric arc, with the apparent belief that the terminal will perform its functions in substantially the same way, notwithstanding the presence of the concentric arc. How erroneous that idea is will be seen in Fig. 31. Let us suppose that the curve $c\,c'd$ from c to d

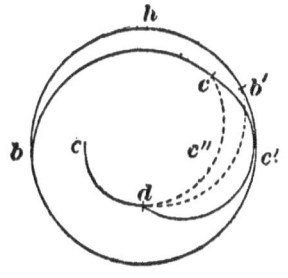

FIG. 31.

(half a turn in length) is what the spring really requires to make it isochronous. To one end of it is joined the concentric arc $e\,d$ for the regulator, and to the other is added the portion $c\,b$, to avoid too great abruptness. The overcoil then has the form $b\,c\,c'\,d\,e$, and it is a true terminal curve having that shape. It is perfectly clear that the portion $c\,c'\,d$ will not act as it would if it alone connected the point b with the stud at e, because it is merely *a part* of the curve $b\,e$; and it is equally clear that the curve $b\,c\,c'd\,e$ cannot possibly be made to have the same action as $c\,c'd$ would have alone. Of course, no springs are made in the form drawn; but it serves to show that, no matter how correct the form of the curve may be, it loses its value when a concentric arc is added, apart from the changes of length produced by the regulator. The directions for regulating a Breguet spring with concentric arc given in Chapter XXII refer to such a spring, *i.e.*, to *a combination* of a terminal curve and a concentric arc, as they are usually made.

(580.) *A better form.*—A better form, if a regulator must be used on it for timing purposes, would be obtained by making a gradual curve, (as shown in dotted lines,) from the end of the concentric arc at d to the spring at b', Fig. 31; or, if a full turn is wanted, make the curve in the form $d\,c''c\,b$. The center of the regulator would then be at a, the center of the spring, and it would have a concentric arc $d\,e$, of 90°, to act upon, while the whole length, from e to b (or to b') should be formed to act as a terminal curve. The shifting of the regulator will, of course, change the acting length of the curve, and in order that this shifting may affect the isochronism as little as possible, such springs should be very long, (560,) should be equally open from center to outside, (574,) and should be pinned in even turns. The overcoil should also be as regular in form and as long as allowable, so that the shifting of the regulator may change its total length and shape but slightly.

(581.) *The best form.*—The concentric arc so made is always more or less objectionable, as not fully meeting the requirements of a terminal curve. I believe I was the first to point out a way to overcome this objection, in the first edition of *The Practical Treatise*, which is to abandon *the combination* (579) and use *only the terminal curve*. Form the overcoil into a regular terminal curve, as in Fig. 32, having the portion $d\,e$ formed as the arc of a circle, whose center is not at a, the center of position of the spring, but at a', which may be located wherever the general form of the curve brings it. Then plant the regulator center at a'. It would have a sweep of 90° on the spring, without necessarily injuring the form of the curve *d c b*. To lessen its effect on the isochronism, the spring should conform to the same conditions as named in section (580.) As regards pinning in even turns, it should be pinned at that or any other point which was found to be least sensitive, *i.e.*, where the isochronal errors caused by moving the regulator would be smallest. The number of coils should also be that which would make the spring least sensitive. Manufacturers could easily ascertain the most desirable arrangement, and adopt it. But this improvement can also be practised by adjusters, and even by ordinary watchmakers.

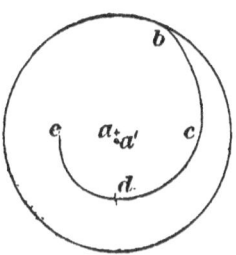

FIG. 32.

(582.) *Isochronizing by regulator, on terminal curves.*—The principal object of the foregoing details about timing by the regulator is to make clear the method of *isochronizing* by means of a regulator, when it is used for *adjustment*, instead of for rating. In that case, the requirements mentioned in the preceding sections would be reversed, and the number of coils, mode of pinning, and length of overcoil should be such as would cause the errors produced by shifting the regulator to be *as great as possible*, (580,) since a less *shifting* would then produce the required effect. The coils should become more open, the distance between the coils being about twice as great at the outside as at the center. The regulator pins should be as close as possible without binding on the spring, and they should be kept near the stud, to prevent the reverse action of the coil between the pins and the stud.

(583.) If these conditions are complied with, the adjustment will be facilitated by the use of the concentric arc, because the shifting of the regulator would be substantially equivalent to taking up or letting out the curve in the stud, without displacing the balance, or requiring the beat to be corrected and the remainder of the curve reformed. But in a fine watch, that should be done in the stud. When the adjustment is finished the rate will, of course, require to be corrected by the balance screws, as in this case the regulator is not available for timing purposes. It should be remembered that shifting the regulator *always* affects the isochronism, even when it is done for timing purposes. Hence it should be kept as near as possible to the stud, as, when it is far from the stud, even close timing by it is impossible.

(584.) 14. *By regulator on flat spiral spring.*—The use of the regulator for isochronizing is seldom advisable, but when it is resorted to, the requirements are the same as described in section (582) for the Breguet spring, except those relating to the overcoil. The length, openness of coils, mode of pinning, form and position of regulator pins should be as there directed, and the rate should be corrected by the balance. Further instructions are hardly necessary.

(585.) 15. *By opening or closing regulator pins.*—Another method is by opening or closing together the pins of the regulator, and is an attempt to secure the same results of changing the stiffness of the hair spring as are secured by terminal curves. It is mainly applicable to the ordinary flat spiral springs. In this method the stiffening of the spring is effected by its contact with its pins; the action of the spring, before stiffening, takes place while it remains free between the pins, and is virtually without any control entirely up to the stud. The idea is that the longer it remains free the slower the vibrations will be, while the earlier in the vibration the pins come into contact with the spring and stiffen it, the quicker the vibration will be. Of course, this effect is produced in both the long and short vibrations, but it is greater in the latter, because the difference produced by opening or closing the pins is in a greater proportion to a short arc than to a long one. Hence, if the watch loses in the short vibrations, it shows that the stiffening of the spring does not commence early enough, consequently the regulator pins are too wide and must be brought closer together. If it gains in the short vibrations, it begins to stiffen too soon and completes the vibrations too quickly. The pins must therefore be opened a little, which increases the length of the slow part of the vibration before the spring comes against the pins, and shortens that part of it in which it is stiffened and hurried up by the contact with the pins.

(586.) At first thought, this appears to be all that could be desired, being easy, quickly done, and apparently meets all the conditions of isochronism. But the objection is that the regulator has its own office to perform in the mechanism of the watch, and for its perfect performance it must be made in a certain manner. Among other things, the pins should be as closely together as possible, while avoiding any binding upon the spring when its position is shifted. Therefore we should not permit any material departure from the form which will best preserve its true functional character, for the sake of accomplishing some other end. But this method is well adapted for all classes of fine clocks, both American and imported, and whether having lever or cylinder escapements. For watches it is not well adapted, except those in which there are but few coils of the hair spring and they are wide apart, to which more room is usually given in the regulator, as will be noticed in a large share of English lever and duplex watches.

(587.) The cylinder escapement watches may also be advantageously isochronized in this way, as their low price generally precludes the employment of the more expensive methods. And it must be admitted that a well-made cylinder or duplex watch, particularly when provided with the fusee and chain, may be adjusted very closely by this method. For this purpose the regulator pins are placed further apart than stated in (586), when fitting the spring, so as to allow of either opening or closing them a little, as might be required by the adjustment.

(588.) But in fine watches, its use, if allowed, at all, should be restricted to the finishing touches, which would require only the very slightest alterations of the pins, which, in this case, I should advise to be placed at the proper distance apart at the start, and only change them by opening them very slightly. Should a still wider opening be required, or if it proved necessary to bring the pins a little closer together, (which, of course, could not be done,) the hair spring should be moved in the stud, according to section (561). In all cases, when the adjustment is completed the two pins should be left parallel, not inclining toward each other, so that, if the spring should play between them at a higher or lower level, it would still find the same width of opening. Some workmen make the short arcs faster by causing the hair spring to press more or less against the regulator. But this practice is entirely wrong.

CHAPTER XXXII.

ISOCHRONIZING BY TERMINAL CURVES.

(589.) 16. *By terminal curves on the spring.*—The method most approved is by curving one or both ends of the spring towards the center, pinning them at half the radius, *i.e.*, at half the distance from the center to the outside of the spring, and giving the curved portion such a length and form as will cause the spring to gain or lose the proper amount for securing isochronal vibrations. (557.) When this method is practiced with the flat spiral spring the curved portion is called the Breguet overcoil, it being raised so that it can curve toward the center over the other coils. The overcoil is generally rather long, varying from ¾ to 1¼ turns. Springs with overcoils are usually called Breguet springs. The cylindrical spring has both ends curved toward the center as above described, and these curved portions are called terminal curves. They vary in length from a full turn, in pocket chronometers, down to less than a half turn in marine chronometers. There is no particular form which has any advantage over others, but both reasoning and experience indicate that it is advisable to have the form as regular, or free from abrupt changes of direction, as possible, because it is more easily changed for adjusting purposes, and a change of length or shape necessitates less labor in making the rest of the curve or spring conform to it.

(590.) *The general functions or effects of a terminal curve* are (1) to make that portion of the spring either more or less rigid than the adjacent portions, as a short or abrupt curvature offers more resistance to bending than a larger or more gradual curve, and *vice versa.* It thus produces a difference of action between the long and short arcs, without changing the rate at the arc of medium extent—the true "rate" of the watch depending only on the *length* of spring in action. (2) To enable the spring to expand and contract more freely and equally in all directions, without displacing the body of the spring and causing side pressure on the pivots. (3) To change the point of greatest strain to a greater or less distance from the end, as may be required to secure isochronal vibrations. In other words, to virtually translate the acting end of the spring from point to point, at different periods during the vibration.

(591.) *The virtual end of the spring.*—In any spring, when it begins to bend as the balance leaves its central position or point of rest, it will bend most where the spring is least curved, and will bend least where the curves or coils are the smallest and most rigid.

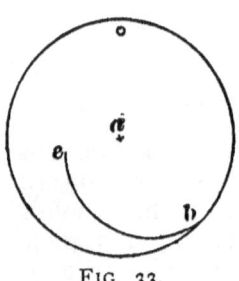

FIG. 33.

In the case of a cylindrical spring, where all parts have an equal curvature, if one end is fastened to the stud and the other to the collet, exactly in the outer circle, the whole of the spring will bend equally. But if the collet end, for instance, is formed into a rigid curve *e b*, Fig. 33, for, say, half an inch, that curve will not bend appreciably until some other portion of the spring has been bent sufficiently to make its resistance equal to that of the curve.

(592.) At the beginning of the vibration or "excursion" of the balance, therefore, the collet end of the spring would virtually be at one end of that curve, at b, instead of at the collet e, i.e., the virtual length of the spring would be half an inch less than the actual length. If this curve was rigid enough to escape bending at all during the short arcs of vibration, they would be very much quickened, for the spring would virtually be half an inch shorter during the short vibrations than in the long ones. If each end of the spring had such a curve as described, the virtual ends of the spring would be half an inch from both collet and stud, and its virtual length during the short vibrations would be an inch less than during the long ones, causing a great difference of rate between the long and short arcs.

(593.) *To make the short vibrations either quicker or slower.*— As a matter of fact, however, the curves do bend a little, even at the beginning of the vibration, and do so more and more as the amplitude of the vibration increases. This greatly reduces the effect of the curve, but the principle still holds good, and it explains how a terminal curve can make the short arcs quicker than the long ones, when the actual length of the spring is the same in both cases. In the foregoing instance, the curve is more rigid than the remainder of the spring, and virtually makes it shorter, during the short arcs.

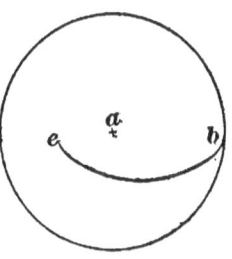

FIG. 34.

But if we make the curve less rigid than the remainder during the short arcs, the spring will virtually be longer, and will lose, during the short vibrations. In Fig. 34 I have shown such a curve, $e\,b$, which would not become as much curved and rigid as the body of the spring till in the last half of the vibration, and therefore would make the long vibrations much quicker than the short ones.

(594.) *The proper form for terminal curves.*—In any terminal curve, that part which is more curved and therefore more rigid than the body of the spring tends to quicken the short arcs, and the portion which is less rigid makes the short arcs slower and the long arcs quicker. This emphasizes what I said concerning the propriety of making a curve regular in form, because if one part is more and another part less rigid than the remainder of the spring, the two parts neutralize each other, and the only virtue of the terminal arises from the excess of one part over the other. Hence the fallacy of such curves as that of Phillips, in Fig. 27, where the part $d\,b$ neutralizes the part $e\,d$, and renders it difficult to tell without trial whether it would make the short arcs quicker or not. When a terminal curve is properly formed, its action can be ascertained by inspection, without trial; if its form does not indicate whether it will make the short arcs faster or the long ones, trial will show that it has but little effect either way.

(595.) *Form and length of terminal curve.*—The greater the curvature of the terminal, the longer it continues to act as described, because the balance will be nearer the end of its excursion when the remainder of the spring becomes equally rigid and brings the terminal into equal action with it. If the curvature of the terminal is greatest at the stud, (or the collet,) and becomes less and less rigid from there to its end or junction, the virtual end of the spring will be at the junction of the spring with the terminal, when the balance excursion begins; but as the body of the spring becomes more and more curved, and its rigidity thus becomes equal to that of a constantly increasing portion of the terminal, the virtual end of the spring will travel along the terminal, from the junction to the stud. The specific action of a terminal increases as its length becomes greater. When the above conditions are reversed, the actions and results will of course be the reverse of those stated.

(596.) *Meaning of terms used.*—In speaking of the beginning and end of the excursion or vibration *in this explanation* of the action of terminal curves, I refer to the flexion of the spring, from the point of rest of the balance to the end of its arc, *i.e.*, I refer to one-half of what is usually called "the vibration," and to that half during which the spring is wound up and becomes more and more rigid. The beginning is at the point of rest, and the end is the limit of its movement. During the other half, in which the spring uncoils or opens, it of course becomes less curved and therefore less rigid, and the action is the reverse of that stated. But for the purpose of explaining the action of terminals, it is only necessary to describe the coiling up of the spring, as the reader can readily see what the action must be in the other half of the vibration. The beginning or end of the terminal refers to the point at the stud or collet, and the "junction" is the point where it meets the body of the spring. I call a terminal which is more curved and therefore more rigid than the adjacent body of the spring *a plus terminal*, because it makes the short arcs quicker. A terminal which is less curved or less rigid than the body of the spring I call *a minus terminal*, because it makes the short arcs slower. A terminal which contains curves or portions of both characters is a mixed terminal or mixed curve.

(597.) *Mixed terminal curves* are those which have portions producing contrary effects, *i.e.*, one portion may be more and another less rigid than the rest of the spring. As before stated, the effect of such a terminal is due to the excess of one kind over the other. In some cases mixture cannot well be avoided. For instance, Fig. 34 is drawn to illustrate a curve less rigid than the body of the spring, and which would make the short arcs slower and the long arcs quicker. But if a curve was actually made as shown, it would evidently cause displacement of the spring and side pressure during the vibration, and to avoid this it would be necessary to introduce a portion with more curvature, to connect the point b with the body of the spring. Another curve at e would also improve it. The curve shown in Fig. 33 would also require to be tested as regards side pressure, and in fact that should be done with every kind of terminal. In making mixed terminals, the different parts should not be nearly balanced, but the portion which produces the desired effect should constitute the major part of the curve, and only enough of the opposite character introduced to prevent side pressure, etc. A good illustration of the employment of mixed terminals will be found in Fig. 37, (617,) which represents the spring and both terminals of a marine chronometer. A poor example is the Breguet curve in Fig. 36, (604) in which from e to i is minus, from i to d is plus, and from d nearly to b is minus.

(598.) *Action of plus terminal curves.*—It may be well to again explain that although the whole of the spring (see Fig. 33) does bend, from the beginning of the vibration, the terminal curve bends *less* than the body of the spring, being more rigid. Its action is the same as if the terminal had retained the original curvature of the body of the spring, but had been shortened sufficiently to bring it to the same rigidity. This virtual shortening is greatest at the beginning of the balance excursion. As the spring becomes wound and bent into smaller circles, it becomes more rigid, there is less difference in that respect between it and the terminal, the latter bends proportionately more than before, its virtual shortening is less, and the spring becomes virtually longer. This change in their relative conditions goes on till the end of the excursion, and the virtual end of the spring constantly comes nearer to the actual end. When the body of the spring acquires a rigidity equal to that of the curve, both will bend equally, and the virtual and actual lengths of the spring will be equal.

(599.) *Action of minus terminal curves.*—When the terminal is less rigid than the adjacent body of the spring, its action is the same as if it had retained the original curvature of the spring but had been *lengthened* to bring it to the same rigidity as it possesses in the terminal. That is to say, it is equivalent to lengthening the spring while leaving it in its original form. This virtual lengthening is greatest at the beginning of the excursion, and the terminal then bends more, in proportion to its length, than the body of the spring. As the balance moves further from the point of rest, both the terminal and the body of the spring become more rigid, but the terminal does so more rapidly than the other part, the difference of rigidity becomes constantly less, and the virtual lengthening of the spring decreases, *i.e.*, the spring virtually becomes shorter and shorter, until their respective rigidities are equal, when they will bend equally and the virtual length of the spring will be the same as the actual length. The shortest vibrations will therefore be slowest, because the virtual length of the spring is then greatest, and the long vibrations will of course be quicker than the short ones.

(600.) *The meaning of gain or loss in the short arcs.*—With a plus terminal the short arcs will therefore be quicker than the medium, and the medium arcs quicker than the long ones. If we take the long arcs as the standard, we shall say that the short arcs gain; if the short arcs are the standard, we will say that the long ones are slow; if the medium arcs are the standard, then we must say that the short arcs gain and the long ones lose, but the gain and loss are only half as much as in the two previous cases, because we now compare each end with the middle of the scale, instead of with the other extreme. It is almost universally customary to take one of the extremes as the standard, because it is so easy to get the long arcs by placing the watch in the horizontal position, and the short ones in the hanging or vertical position; but it is not so easy to get the medium arcs, although that is the proper way to find the true rate of the spring as due to its actual length.

(601.) *Meaning of no loss nor gain in the short arcs.*—This gain or loss is the actual performance of the spring. When run in the watch, however, the rate observed does not depend on the spring alone, but also on the frictions and other influences affecting the motion of the balance. If, with such a spring as that shown in Fig. 33, and taking the rate in the long arcs as the standard, we should find that the rate was the same in the short arcs, most workmen would say that the spring was isochronous and its action was precisely the same in both long and short arcs. But that would be a great mistake. We all know that friction and the like greatly affect the rate, and that such effect is unavoidable. Let us suppose that their effect in this case was to cause a loss of 8 seconds in the short arcs. Reason would tell us, if we found no such loss, that the spring must have been in a condition to *gain* 8 seconds, and that that gain had just balanced the loss due to frictions, etc. It is true that the spring would be isochronous; but it would be so, not because its action had been the same in the long and short arcs, but because it had *not* been the same. If it had, it would not have corrected that error, and the watch would still have lost 8 seconds in the short arcs.

(602.) *Adjusting by altering the length of terminal curves.*—In adjusting, *i.e.*, in altering the curves to produce certain desired effects, we may change either their length, their form, or both. If we adjust plus terminals by their length, we make them longer to quicken the short vibrations, and shorter to make them slower. Fig. 35 is the diagram used from time immemorial to illustrate the alteration of terminals. If the terminal has the form *A*, for example, and the watch gains in the short vibrations, we make the terminal shorter, and bend a portion of it back into the form of the outer coil, as shown by *B*, which is considerably shorter than *A*. On the other hand, if there is a loss in the short vibrations, we quicken them by making the terminal longer, as shown at *C*, by taking more of the outer coil into the terminal.

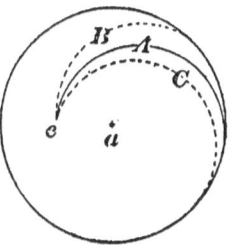

FIG. 35.

(603.) *The philosophy* of the change is plain. The longer the plus terminal is, the further the virtual end of the spring is from the stud (or collet) *e*, *i.e.*, the more of the spring is virtually cut out, at the beginning of the vibration; and the shorter the terminal is, the greater is the virtual length of the spring, at the commencement of the vibration. As examples, Fig. 33 shows a short curve, which could be made longer like *e d b'* in Fig. 31, or still longer like *e d c b* in Fig. 32, which is ¾ turn; or like *e d c" c b* in Fig. 31, for a full turn, and each such change would make the short arcs quicker. If we want to make them slower, a long terminal can be shortened up as required. Adjusting by altering the length is the easiest, most rapid and most certain method.

(604.) *Adjusting by altering the form of the terminal curve.*—If we adjust by changing the form of the terminal, the general principle to be followed (with a plus terminal) is, to make the curvature more gradual, *i.e.*, flatter, to quicken the long vibrations, and more rounding, or in shorter bends, to quicken the short vibrations. In altering the form, it facilitates the work to have the terminal so made that a portion of it can be changed, with a minimum of change in the remainder, instead of having to re-form the whole terminal to suit the part changed. To illustrate, I reproduce in Fig. 36 the curve shown by Phillips, in which the part between b and d can have its form considerably altered, without requiring anything more than a little bending at the points b and d to relieve the rest of the spring from any displacement or strain. This facility of manipulation is its only saving quality, but the length of $b\ d$ should be made much less than $e\ d$, to avoid their being so nearly balanced, and make the terminal more positive in its action. The Breguet spring is used for pocket watches, in which the short arcs are always slow, hence it is a mistake to introduce a minus curve $b\ d$ into the terminal of a Breguet spring, because that only adds to the loss caused by the frictions, etc., and increases the total error to be corrected by the plus part of the terminal.

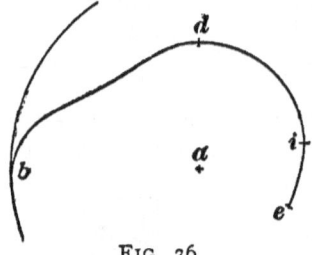

FIG. 36.

(605.) *Adjusting by minus terminals.*—In changing the minus curve, an increase of length increases its specific action, and *vice versa*, as it does with a plus curve; but its specific action being the reverse of that of a plus curve, the effect of the change is also the reverse, *i.e.*, making a minus curve longer makes the short arcs slower, and decreasing its length makes them faster. The reason is, of course, that the longer the curve is, the greater is the virtual lengthening of the spring caused by it, in the short arcs—and *vice versa*. And making a minus curve flatter virtually lengthens the spring and makes the short arcs slower, while making the terminal more curved quickens the short arcs. But the effect of altering the form is much less than that of changing the length.

(606.) *Action of Breguet overcoil.*—The overcoil may be either wholly or partly formed into a terminal curve. If a part of the overcoil continues in the normal direction and position of the outer coil of the spring, with the exception of being raised above the level of the other coils, it still remains a part of the body of the spring, and not of the terminal. The terminal curve includes only that part of the overcoil which is bent out of its normal spiral position or curvature. In forming such terminals, the same rules prevail as with cylindrical springs. The action is the same as there described, and they are adjusted in the same way. The fact that many of the regular coils of the spring are more curved and more rigid than the terminal, does not change the principle involved.

(607.) It is sufficient for us to know that the curve is either more or less curved than it would have been in the normally formed outer coil, and that it will in consequence act differently, and according to the rules already given for the terminal curves of cylindrical springs. If a Breguet overcoil is formed as shown in Fig. 36, for example, the part ed will be more rigid, and db less rigid, than the outer coil, and that is enough to tell us what the action of each part will be. When we consider the inner end of the flat spiral, the inner coils are even more curved and more rigid than any part of the terminal, and this fact undoubtedly affects the isochronal action of the spring, just as a terminal would at that end. Doubtless, too, this matter of the relative rigidity of different parts of the spring has something to do with the isochronal action of springs whose coils become further apart at the outside, of those which are pinned in even or fractional coils, etc. But as that is a theoretical point not necessary to discuss here, and having already exceeded the limits assigned to this subject, I will content myself with saying that the instructions already given are all that are needed for practical work.

(608.) *Experts' opinions differ.*—Before stating the latest and most approved practice in terminal curves and the method of pinning springs having them, I thought it well to consult some of the leading working experts and learn what conclusions their experience had led them to consider as reliable. I did so, with the result—the usual one, by the way—that I got about as many different opinions as there were experts. For instance, in reply to questions as to what *length* of terminal curve in the Breguet spring they had found to be best, one said it should be as short as possible and keep its shape; another, that as a rule the best results are obtained from long terminals. With regard to the best method of pinning the Breguet spring, one said the rule was to pin them $\frac{1}{8}$ over full turns, while another said that they might be full turns or a half turn; and so it went with all the other points asked. Also, see Chapter VIII on the usages in the American watch factories.

(609.) *No one method can meet all cases.*—What inference should we draw from all this? Simply that there is no rigid rule, but that different forms and methods are required in different cases.

Each expert gave rules suited to the kind or class of work he was in the habit of doing. As I pointed out and insisted more than twenty years ago, and repeated in *The Practical Treatise*, perfect isochronism is only to be obtained by a special *adjustment* to suit the peculiarities of each watch. The truth is to-day, as it was then, that there is no rule or method whatever which will certainly secure isochronism in all cases. The most that it can do is to secure a more or less close *approximation* to isochronism *at the outset*, and thus abridge the time and labor of the adjustment. Where great numbers of movements are made precisely alike, as is done by the American watch companies, a minute tabulation of the results given by different springs will enable them to select some particular form, method of pinning, etc., which will, *in connection with similar movements*, secure an approximation close enough for all ordinary purposes. But when the finest time is required, the American manufacturers, like all others, depend upon special adjustment.

(610.) *The result will depend upon the skill of the adjuster.*— While the reader will have before him a carefully considered and classified epitome of all that is known to the trade, stated in form suitable for practical use by practical men, the rules given do not secure perfection. No rule can do that, nor will ever do it, so long as watches and workmen fall short of perfection. But they will enable him to obtain in a few minutes results which otherwise might require hours or days of labor; to do even his cheapest jobs in a thorough and workmanlike manner; and, in fine work, to produce an excellence of performance in proportion to his patience, thoroughness and skill.

CHAPTER XXXIII.

Isochronizing the Cylindrical Spring.

(611.) *Selecting the spring.*—The workman will generally find it necessary to make his own spring, for which instructions are given in Chapter VI, Part Second. Standard sizes are sometimes sold, however, ready made in the cylindrical form—especially the new palladium springs. The proper size, number of coils, etc., are given in Chapter XXVIII, Part Fifth. Having obtained a suitable spring, you cut off the ends that were held during the making, till you find the wire is in perfect condition, and form your first terminal curve on the end, to go into the collet. Having then taken the proper number of coils to the upper end, you also form that terminal curve, taking care to leave some surplus spring. The number of coils may be varied, to secure the proper number of vibrations per minute. If the number to be used is already settled, the spring can be tested, to find whether it will give the correct number of vibrations, by pinning one end in the collet and holding the upper end in the holding tool, Fig. 11, (238,) before that end is bent into form. The upper coil can thus be shifted through the clamps and tried at different points, without marring or injuring the wire, or even bending it until it has been tested both for correct time and for its isochronal action. By following the rules already referred to in regard to mode of pinning, etc., it will be nearly isochronal.

(612.) *Forming the terminal curves* is done by means of the tweezers shown in Fig. 18, (249,) for small springs to be used in pocket watches. The heavier springs of box chronometers require to be manipulated with pliers made in a similar way. As shown in Fig. 18, the tweezers (or pliers) are lined with brass blocks, a convex block fitting into a concave one, and both *turned* in cylindrical form, not filed, for it would be difficult to file the curves true and parallel. If not correct, they would twist the ends up or down, instead of curving them directly inward. Several different tweezers may be used, having different curvatures, to give the terminals the desired forms. One pair having the same curvature as the body of the spring is used to hold it by, while being curved with another. The curves can be bent cold, especially if the temper is a very dark blue, or still lower, but the spring has to be bent considerably more than it is intended to be, as it springs back when released. If the temper is higher, it is better to heat the pliers (or tweezers) and hold the spring in them till the block cools, and the spring will remain in nearly the form so given to it.

(613.) *Heating the tools.*—The heating can be done in the alcohol lamp or otherwise, observing that the heating of the tool in the lamp, and the working of the spring upon it, must not be ventured at the same time. Some workmen use an iron block a couple of inches square, having holes drilled into it for inserting wires of different sizes, changeable as needed. They heat the block on a stove or in a lamp till it turns a dark blue, then put it into a wooden block cut out to receive it, with a cover having holes bored for the forming wires to pass through into the block. This wood casing not only protects the hands from injury, but keeps the block from cooling off too rapidly.

The springing open of the tweezers and the weight of the pliers will secure good contact and speedy heating. The tools are left resting in the block when not in use, so that they are always ready. Screw clamps are sometimes used for bending the curves.

(614.) *Use of the forming tools.*—Whatever tool is used, it must not be too highly heated, as it will reduce the temper of the spring too low, and even ruin it entirely by causing it to curl up out of all shape. It is not absolutely necessary that the heat should be sufficient to even color the spring, although it facilitates both the bending and the setting. Yet the heat may be considerable without affecting the color, as steel may be raised to about 425° Fahr. before a change of color takes place; at 450° the article will take a straw color; at 500°, a brown; at 530°, a purple; at 575° to 600°, the different blues. The forming wire or tool should be of steel, or, if of brass or other metal, a hardened steel screw should be planted in it as a color-piece, (81, 82,) to indicate the temperature. The heat should never be greater than will give the color-piece a dark-blue shade. If the hair spring is of a lighter shade, the color-piece should not go beyond *that* shade, else the terminal curve will be reduced lower than the rest of the spring.

(615.) If repeated heatings are necessary, the color-piece should not reach the shade of the spring, (81). If the spring is a dark-blue, the color-piece should then not go below a purple, either removing the spring at that stage of the process, or taking the forming wire from the block and quenching the whole in alcohol. If the spring is fine, or the heating is done very rapidly, from the block being large, too hot, or any other reason, great care must be used to avoid reducing the temper of the spring too much. The color-piece, or that part of the wire which you brighten up to show the color, should be very near where the hair spring is held by it, and before the spring is put into it at all, the heat should be ascertained. If the color goes beyond the blue, the block or tool must be cooled a little till it does not exceed the proper shade, when it may safely be used. Many workmen are partial to rather high heat, but those who have not plenty of experience to justify them in using it are recommended to *never* use a heat above straw color, as that is ample for all purposes. A spring held over an ordinary round broach at that heat will retain its form when cold. As every different tool requires different management, I will not give more specific directions, but recommend the workman to make the best he can afford, and experiment a little on an old spring, and he will learn more about it in a few minutes than I could explain in several pages. Be sure to compare your spring often with the gauge, see that it fits *without pressure*, using the eyeglass to insure accuracy.

(616.) *Gauge for forming curves.*—Do not attempt to form a curve "by eye." Having settled upon the form it is to have, draw the curve, in its exact shape, size, and position relatively to the outer circle of the spring, upon cardboard, in ink, or upon a thin sheet of brass or copper which is filed down to the outside of the curve on that side—and use that as a guide or templet, comparing the spring with it frequently, by the aid of a strong glass. You first measure the diameter of the spring through the center, lay off that distance on paper with the dividers, set the points to just half this distance, and with this radius mark a circle corresponding to the outer circle of the spring. Draw a line across it, exactly through the center, and another exactly at right angles to it. These are guides in marking the curve upon it, and also in comparing the spring with it when marked. Let the end of the curve be exactly at one of these lines, half-way from the centre to the circle, and also marked where the "junction" is to come, then draw the curve between those points, and file off the metal outside of the curve. Whenever you change the curve, in adjusting, this gauge will show you what you have done. Make every part perfectly clear—the circle, the curve and the lines.

(617.) *The proper forms for the curves.*—It is, of course, impossible to tell beforehand what form is required, except in cases where custom rules. In chronometers of ordinary types, similar curves will be needed in similar movements. For a marine chronometer, with heavy balance, slow vibrations, and

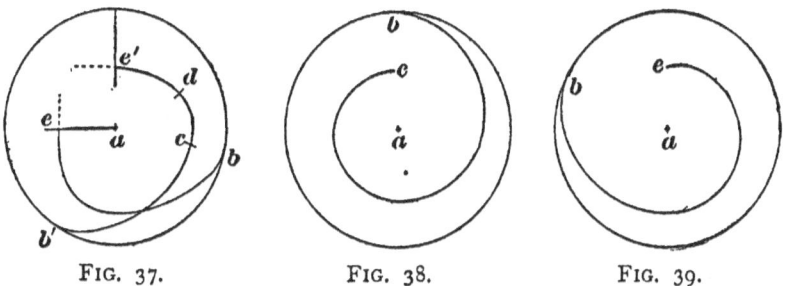

FIG. 37.   FIG. 38.   FIG. 39.

with the short arcs fast, the terminals should be minus curves. Fig. 37 shows a spring with extremely well formed terminals for such a case. The entire length of each curve is minus, except a very short portion at the turn or corner between *c* and *d*, which is plus, while from *b* to *c* and from *d* to *e* is minus. Such a curve could easily be lengthened between *c* and the outer coil, and so made more minus, by making the turn *c d* a trifle sharper. The reverse change could also be easily made. In Fig. 38 is shown the lower terminal, and in Fig. 39 the upper one, of a spring suitable for a pocket chronometer, in which the short arcs will nearly always be slow. It will be observed that the whole of these two terminals is plus, as it should be in such a case, and could easily be made more plus by lengthening them. Both of these springs (four terminals) may be accepted as models of good construction, for the two types of timepieces.

(618.) *Pinning the spring.*—The curves being formed, you broach out the hole in the collet inclining upward, so that it will hold the spring in proper position. Try this frequently, by temporarily pinning in the stud, till it stands true with the broach on which the collet is held. The spring *must not be bent* to get it true, but unpin it and change the hole till it will stand true naturally. Make the pin round, of the same taper as the hole, file away about one-third on one side to go next to the spring, and fix it in tightly. Then put the collet on an arbor, and try it in the calipers to see that the spring stands perfectly true. Drill and broach the upper hole, with the proper inclination and position so that the upper curve will stand naturally and freely in the hole, fitting both the hole and the pin to it with the same care as the lower end, to see that it is *perfectly free* from constraint when tightly pinned at both ends.

(619.) *Lengths of the curves.*—The upper curve should occupy nearly three-fourths of a circle, for a marine chronometer, and the lower curve (collet curve) a little less than a half circle, or two curves of half a turn each for short springs, so that the spring will be pinned in even turns for long springs, or down to one-fourth turn short of even turns when the spring is short. In pocket chronometers the upper curve should generally be about three-fourths of a turn, and the lower one nearly a turn, —the ends being pinned in even turns. These lengths are by no means obligatory; they are used by good makers, but others use very different lengths and modes of pinning. What is best in any particular case can only be told by actual trial. The lengths of *the curves* can be changed as required, and be made longer or shorter as well as changed in form.

(620.) *Length of the spring.*—But it is evident that the length of *the spring* cannot well be changed after the curve is made, because the coil is inclined upward and the end at the stud would then stand too high or too low to come naturally and freely in the hole. By considerable labor, a change of length might be allowed for, but the trouble is so great that the workman should never form the upper curve and fit it to the stud until he has timed the spring sufficiently to be certain that it will run within a few seconds per day—*i.e.*, within limits which can easily be corrected by the timing screws in the balance. This shows the necessity for some spring-holding tool like that in Fig. 11 for timing the spring before the terminal is bent up.

(621.) *Manner of attachment to the collet and stud.*—The ends should ordinarily meet the collet and stud at a right angle to the radius passing through them,—*i.e.*, to the face of the collet or stud—or tangentially. But some makers pin the upper end in a different way, viz: When the short arcs are too quick, in a marine chronometer, the spring is bent a little outward, *i.e.*, the end is bent more outward from the center, to make the short arcs slower. In Fig. 40, *e* is where the end of the terminal meets the stud, and *e b* shows the direction of the end according to the general rule, while *e c* is the inclination given to it as just stated. The pin is then placed on the inside or right. Others do this bending in the opposite direction, in pocket chronometers, where the short arcs are too slow. If *e* represents the end of the terminal of a pocket chronometer, *e b* would be the direction it would usually have at the stud, while *e d* would be the direction given to it to quicken the short arcs.

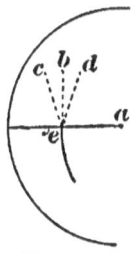

FIG. 40.

(622.) *Effect of changing the direction at the point of attachment.*—If the reader has understood my explanation of the action of terminal curves, he will perceive that bending the portion near *e* to the left makes that part more minus, and that causes the slowing of the short arcs; while the bending of the portion near the stud to the right makes that part more plus, which accounts for the quickening of the short arcs. Both practices are therefore in conformity with the law of terminal curves already laid down. But I cannot consider them commendable, for the same result could be better obtained by changing the length or shape of the terminal. When this method is followed, only *the end* of the terminal is bent, just at the point of pinning.

(623.) *General arrangement.*—The forms of the curves and the relative positions of the two ends of the spring must be such that any tendency to displace the spring in one direction will be counteracted by a tendency to draw it in the opposite direction. Whether these tendencies do balance each other, can only be told by carefully watching the movements of the spring when in action, or by timing it in positions.

(624.) *Changing the curves.*—When the curves require to be changed in the process of isochronizing, the method is the same as for originally forming them. Pliers or tweezers of greater curvature are used to make them more plus, and those of less curvature or flat to make them more minus. The effect of a curve is in proportion to its length, and, in a lesser degree, to its curvature. Hence, to increase its specific effect, increase its length; and increase the curvature of a plus curve but decrease that of a minus curve. To lessen its specific effect, take the opposite course. For example, if a watch loses in the short arcs, make the plus terminal curve longer or more curved; to make the short arcs slower, make its curvature less or the terminal shorter. When a curve is made longer, some of the body of the spring is taken into the curve and its total form made such as will be in harmony with the service required; if a curve is made shorter, a part of it is bent back into the form of the body of the spring, and the remainder made regular and proper in its curvature.

(625.) *Return of form.*—Springs, after a change of shape, have a tendency to return more or less to their previous form, and this settling back must be first gone through with before permanently trustworthy tests of the effect of the change can be made. In the preliminary and coarser alterations, the test may be had at once, but as we approach closer to correctness it will be necessary to wait at least three or four hours, or over night, before testing. The watch should be kept running during the settling-back process, as the vibration hastens the completion of the change in the spring. It is advisable to anneal a spring after it is finished, also, after it is changed in form, to avoid the risk of having it gradually alter its shape and rate while running. It can be annealed in any convenient way, one being to heat it in an oil bath to about $212°$, or the temperature of boiling water, for the final annealing.

CHAPTER XXXIV.

Isochronizing the Flat Spiral Spring.

(626.) *Selecting the spring.*—Taking a spring of the breadth, thickness and temper which the old one had, or which you deem suitable, and of apparently suitable strength, try it for size, by laying it on the inverted balance cock. The size should generally be just right to lie naturally between the regulator pins and in the stud hole, and at the same time be concentric with the balance jewel hole. But if the kind of watch you are working at is known to be addicted to losing considerably in the short arcs, it is better to have the spring a little small, so that it will *not* be concentric at the jewel hole, but its center will come a little towards the stud. That will make the short arcs quicker and so balance the customary loss.

(627.) *Testing the spring.*—Having one apparently suitable, seize the coil which lies in the regulator pins and over the hole in the stud, at a point midway between the regulator and the stud, and mark the point with a speck of whiting and oil. Fasten its centre concentrically to the balance staff with putty powder, and find the number of vibrations it gives, as directed in Part Fourth. If the number of vibrations is correct, after allowing for the amount which will have to be broken out at the centre to fit the collet properly, and holding the outer coil at a point which has the proper position relatively to the collet end, (*i.e.*, even turns or otherwise, according to the kind of escapement, as directed in Part Fifth,) and also such as will give the spring the proper size or freedom, (626,) proceed to fit it properly to the collet and pin it securely.

(628.) *Timing the spring.*—Put the spring and collet on the balance staff, and again try the vibrations more closely, either with the timing balance or in the watch, using one of the spring-fitting tools described in Chapter XVII, or something similar, instead of pinning it in the stud. If the vibrations are within the limits which can be regulated for, put the balance in the watch, (if not already done,) screw the balance cock in place, but hold the spring in the claws of the fitting tool instead of the stud, which should be taken out of the way of the spring. If you have no such tool, you will of course have to pin the spring in the stud. The next thing is to get the rate tolerably close, in the horizontal position which will be employed in the position trials. If the watch is to be adjusted for positions, that adjustment comes next, as already stated, after which the isochronal adjustment should be attended to.

(629.) *Adjusting for isochronism. Effect of form.*—In adjusting the flat spiral spring, there are several ways which may be employed, if necessary. (See Chapters XXXI and XXXII.) The best way is by plus or minus curves. The reader may be somewhat astonished at the mention of terminal curves in connection with the flat spiral spring. But it is a fact that we have what are substantially equivalent to terminal curves, and which I think he will be willing to call by that name after he has read the following explanations: In a spiral spring which is uniformly coiled and curved, any part of it is "minus" relatively to the portion nearer to the center than itself, and "plus" relatively to portions further from the center. Every coil and part therefore acts differently, according to its form and relative rigidity, and the action of the spring as a whole is the joint resultant of the actions of all the parts and curves in its entire length. That result is that there is a certain point in every coil, at which the spring, if properly pinned, will perform large and small vibrations in equal times. That point depends on *the form* of the spring or of its curves, and it can be changed by a change of form, because a change of form is a change of rigidity and of action, and changes the resultant action of the spring as a whole. Whenever any part of the spring is given any unusual form, or bent out of the normal spiral, and even when it is simply taken up or let out at the stud, the effect produced is governed by the law of terminal curves as already laid down. By looking at the subject from this point of view, many seeming inconsistencies, irregularities and mysteries will be found to be in strict conformity to that law, and the methods of isochronizing will become intelligible and clear.

(630.) *Effect of taking up or letting spring out in stud.*—As regards the effect upon the isochronal action of the spring, letting it out is equivalent to putting on a minus terminal of that length, which, being less curved and less rigid than the contiguous part of the coil, makes the short arcs slower than the long ones, and at the same time the additional actual length of the spring makes both the long and short arcs slower, (561.) But if there is a crimp or stiff part in the portion let out, that of course acts as a plus curve, and lessens the effect produced by the letting out. Taking up the spring will obviously have the contrary effect, both in specially accelerating the short arcs, and also making both long and short arcs quicker. Taking up $\frac{1}{4}$ or $\frac{1}{8}$ turn of spring, is equivalent to cutting off that length of minus curve, and, so far as the short arcs are concerned, is equivalent to substituting a plus curve in its place. The difference of rigidity spoken of being small, the isochronizing effect will also be small, but it increases more rapidly than the length taken up or let out.

(631.) *Effect of bending the spring.*—It is obvious that if, after taking up the spring, we *bend* the portion near the stud in such a way as to make it less curved and less rigid than before, that whole portion will be equivalent to a minus terminal of the same length, and will make the short arcs slower. The effect of this bending may easily be to retard them *more* than the taking up of the spring accelerates them—in which case the result would be the reverse of that intended to be accomplished by taking up the spring. This result is so common that it has given rise to the adjuster's rule mentioned in section (563).

(632.) *Effect of bending the spring toward the stud.*—This may perhaps explain why the customary setting of the spring "close to the stud" prevents the short arcs from being slow; also, why a spring too large, in proportion to the position of the stud and the regulator pins, will lose in the short arcs. The spring is made to "set close" by bending the half turn next to the stud, giving it a more rapid curvature, which of course makes it act as a plus terminal and quickens the short arcs. In Fig. 41, the full line shows the natural position and shape of the outer coil, concentric with the axis at a, and the broken line shows how the outer coil would be bent inward, from f to f', in order to throw the spring nearer to the stud e. The fact that it does

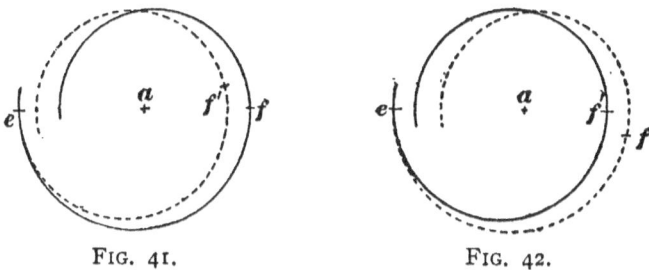

FIG. 41.   FIG. 42.

quicken the short arcs, (575,) notwithstanding that the side friction produced on the balance pivots makes them slower, shows that the effect of such bending is much greater than the contrary effect of the side pressure—doubtless because from e to f is a long terminal. The result is not due to its proximity to the stud, but to the excentricity of the spring, no matter on which side of the center that may be.

(633.) *Effect of fitting the spring excentrically.*—Sometimes the spring is a little small for the stud and regulator pins, and naturally stands close to the stud, without requiring any bending to bring it there,—as shown by the full line in Fig. 42. In such cases the short arcs do not lose nearly so much as they would if the spring was bent to the position shown by the dotted lines, to make it concentric with the balance axis a. Most workmen would say that the spring acted better in the former case (*i.e.*, it lost less in the short arcs,) because it retained its natural form, as well as from it being close to the stud. But according to the principles I have been explaining, the reason is altogether different from that. Let us suppose that the natural form of the spring had been as shown by the broken line, and that we had *bent it* to the form of the full line. It is perfectly clear that the arc ef' would then have acted as a plus terminal, and would quicken the short arcs. Reason tells us that the action of the terminal is due to its length and form, and that it matters not whether it was bent into that form by the spring maker or by the adjuster.

(634.) *Actions of terminals compared.*—Let us now consider these two terminals in Fig. 42, solely from what we know of their actions, the rest of the spring being the same in both cases. As compared with ef, ef' is a plus terminal, and it makes no difference when it received its form. According to established horological laws, we ought to bend it into the form ef, and bring the body of the spring concentric with a, to *make it correct.* If we prefer to use the form ef', the effect will be the same as if we had *bent* it into that form, *i.e.*, it will make the short arcs quicker than ef will. That is the true explanation of the action of excentric springs. As regards the side pressure, there is no doubt that the side pressure compresses one side of the inner coils and expands the opposite halves, but we may probably say that these opposite effects will practically balance each other. At any rate, it is safe to consider such effects as of small importance compared with those of the terminals, inasmuch as the terminals show their characteristic effects over and above those of all other influences.

(635.) *The effects are due to departure from the normal spiral form.*—The effects of different curvatures or forms are due to the forms themselves, no matter whether they were made into those forms by the spring maker or by the adjuster. Disregarding any minor effects due to change in the texture of the metal caused by bending, etc., we may say as a general principle that the action is due *to the departure from the normal spiral form of the spring.* If the normal spiral form in Fig. 42 is ef, the form ef' is a plus curve, no matter how it received that form; if ef' is the normal form, then any variation from it in the direction of ef will act as a minus terminal. If that is true, it follows that any change from the normal spiral form, whether at the outer or inner end, *or elsewhere*, will affect the isochronal action of the spring according to the rules before laid down. This will explain the action of the inner end when it does not leave the collet in the true spiral form. But I will not occupy more space with that point, since it is never advisable, and never necessary, to alter the inner end for isochronizing purposes. That end should always be properly formed and pinned in the collet, letting all isochronal alterations be made at the outer end. But the effect of changes or improper forms anywhere in the length of the spring may be known from the following:—

(636.) *Rules for the isochronal adjustment of the flat spiral.*— Any portion which is more curved, stiff and rigid than it was or would be in the normal spiral form will act as a plus curve, to quicken the short arcs, and *vice versa*. Any increase in the length of such a curve increases its effect. If it is a plus curve, making it longer will make the short arcs faster, and *vice versa;* if it is a minus curve, increasing its length will make the short arcs slower, and *vice versa*. The absolute amount of change produced will of course depend on the conditions in each case.

If the adjuster will keep these cardinal principles in mind, the process of isochronizing the flat spiral should be plain sailing.

CHAPTER XXXV.

Isochronizing the Breguet Spring.

(637.) *The Breguet hair spring.*—What is called the Breguet hair spring is a flat spiral provided with a terminal curve at its outer end, which is raised up by means of an elbow or bend, so that it can be returned towards the center *over* the other coils. As we have seen, all flat spiral springs which are desired to possess isochronism should be as long as possible and closely coiled, as the angle of inflexion of each coil will be thereby reduced, its action will be more uniform and easy, and it will have less tendency to be forced out of center and exert a side pressure against the axis of the balance. This is particularly important with the Breguet spring, which should be broad and flat, the coils very close together and more numerous than for a plain spiral of the same diameter. It is usual to give the Breguet from one-third to one-half more coils than the plain spiral would have in a similar situation. Being so close, the least injury or irregularity in the coils renders the spring worthless for fine adjustments. The American watch companies use the same number of turns as for the flat spiral, namely, about fourteen coils. See (105), Chapter XVIII.

(638.) *Selecting and fitting the spring.*—The process is the same as for the flat spiral. To test it, by finding whether it will give the proper time, which must of course be done before the overcoil is bent up, it is indispensable to have some spring-fitting tool. The outer coil, not being yet bent in, cannot be held in the stud. It is therefore gripped in the clamps of the spring-holder while timing. When one is found of suitable strength, it is pinned to the collet and again more closely timed, as directed for the flat spiral. The point held in the clamps, when it gives correct time, will when the overcoil is bent towards the center reach a quarter of a turn further around the center than before, *i.e.*, 13¾ turns when held in the tweezers will make 14 turns when bent in, and will then make even turns, which is considered the proper method of pinning for Breguet springs. As the Breguet spring is liable to prove more slow than expected, it should gain slightly when held at the point which makes 13¾ turns before bending. But if it should nevertheless lose, it can be broken out at the center a little if necessary. Next should come the position trials, if the watch is to be adjusted for positions, the spring being held in the clamps of the spring-holder at the correct time point, as directed for the plain flat spiral. Being assured by the position trials that our spring will not require to be changed, we now form the overcoil.

(639.) *Length of the overcoil.*—The overcoil is generally made one turn in length. Before deciding whether the spring will be suitable, hold the outer coil rigidly in the tweezers at a point one turn from the point where it was held when it gave correct time, and *spring* (*not bend*) that coil around the center in such a way as to bring the correct time point to the stud hole. This will show, very closely, how much further the correct-time point will reach around the center after the terminal is formed.

(640.) *Position of the elbow.*—We have now to consider the position of the elbow. It is generally supposed that the placing of the elbow correctly is a point requiring great experience and judgment, and renders the making of a Breguet spring a very difficult and complicated job. The exact position of the elbow is not an essential matter, its object being merely to raise the final or supplementary coil so that we can curve it towards the center as we find needful, without interfering with the other coils. The terminal curve need not begin at the elbow, unless we find it necessary, upon trial, to make it so long as to reach to that point. The curve may begin at any distance from the end of the spring which will secure isochronal vibrations. The position of the elbow has nothing to do with that adjustment, provided it is far enough from the end of the spring to be out of our way. It simply, on the flat spiral, enables us to enjoy the same freedom in forming the terminal curve that we have in the helical spring.

(641.) *Action of the elbow.*—My meaning will be more evident by supposing that, with the exception of the outer coil being *raised up* by the elbow, no change has been made in its shape, the outer coil having the same size and distance from the center as before. The spring would therefore perform nearly the same as before, except so far as this elbow has made it shorter and stiffer. Accordingly, whether the elbow is a half, three-quarters, or whole turn from the end makes very little difference practically, although it is considered well to make it as near the end of the spring as will give room for the terminal curve. *That* is the real means of securing isochronism, not the elbow. The stiffness of the elbow is, of course, a disturbing influence or cause of irregular action in the spring, to a certain extent, but it is unavoidable, and we must correct or neutralize its effect in our adjustment of the terminal curve, along with all other unavoidable irregularities, such as resistance of the air to the balance, unequal springing out of the sections of the rim by centrifugal force, effects of friction in the balance jewel holes and the escapement, the oil, mechanical imperfections of all kinds, in the spring itself, as well as elsewhere—so that in spite of all of them the vibrations shall be isochronal, or as nearly so as we can make them. Many workmen insist that the supplemental coil must be just one turn in length, from the elbow to the stud. It will be noticed that following my directions will generally make it so. But that length is not imperative, for it may be either more or less, without harm. Instead of a single supplemental coil, some workmen have used two, three, or even more coils.

(642.) *Making the elbow.*—The usual way of forming the elbow is to make two bends in the outer coil of the spring, one causing it to rise above the level of the other coils, the other bending it down again and making it parallel with them, but on a higher plane. The spring must not be twisted sideways to throw the overcoil up or down, but the coil must be kept truly vertical, as it was made, and actually bent, edgewise, *i.e.*, one edge will be stretched and the other compressed a little. This strains the metal, and is to some extent injurious; hence the bend should not be too abrupt. The American watch companies employ a gradual incline extending some distance along the spring, in place of the usual more abrupt elbow. That is less injurious to the metal, but if the incline is too long it causes more or less side twisting during the vibration.

(643.) *Tool for making the elbow.*—This is done very easily and quickly with a pair of tweezers such as described in section (250.) As the tweezers hold the coil firmly and flat while bending it, any side twist or doubling up at the bend is prevented. The first bend is made a little more than one turn from the correct time point, giving the coil an upward inclination considered suitable, and, at a point which will secure the proper clearance for the overcoil, it is bent down. The tweezers are preferably heated, and the part to be treated must get thoroughly warmed up before bending, then held till cool. With care, even the hardest spring can be safely bent in this way. The novice should first practice a little on an old spring till he knows what is safe, and how to do it properly.

(644.) *Explanation of angles.*—For the benefit of those who do not understand "angles," Fig. 43 is inserted. At the point b, a line bd is drawn perpendicular to abc 5, and the arc of a circle from c to d is 90° or one-quarter of a circle. If d 1 is drawn parallel with bc 5, the line abd 1 will have two angles of 90°,—at b and at d.

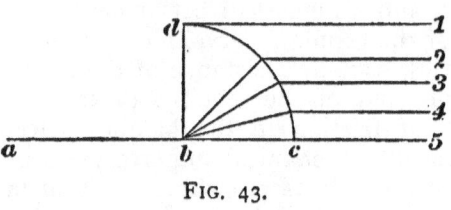

FIG. 43.

Next measure half the distance from c to d, and from that point draw lines to b and 2; in the line ab 2, there will be two angles of 45° each, *i.e.*, half of 90°. In the same way, if we measure any other fraction of cd, we will get that fraction of the angle of 90°. Thus, one-third the distance from c to d will give us the line ab 3 having two angles of 30°; one-sixth that distance gives the line ab 4, with angles of 15°. These angles are about as abrupt as the spring should be bent, although the elbow frequently has more inclination than that. It will of course be understood that the part ab corresponds to the body of the spring, the incline to the elbow, and the horizontal part to 4 represents the overcoil.

(645.) *Height and position of the overcoil.*—The overcoil is to be raised so that there will be, between it and the other coils, a space about twice the breadth of the spring. Some give even more, but that necessitates a longer elbow and increases the amount of torsion or side twist which it produces upon the spring when vibrating. The space named gives ample clearance, which is all that is necessary. Some good makers give only one and a half times the width of the spring, but that is bringing the two parts rather close. The less the spring will bear to be bent without producing the slightest injury, or the greater the clearance to be given, the longer the straight portion of the elbow, between the bends, must be, and *vice versa*. After the elbow is formed, if the clearance is found too great, the bends can be made a little less abrupt by simply squeezing them between the heated tweezers, (249, 250,) or even the jaws of a pair of very narrow flat pliers, smooth inside, which by the help of the heat flatten the bends and so partly straighten them. The clearance must be sufficient to prevent the under coils touching either the supplemental coil or the stud, even when subjected to violent shakes or thumps. The Breguet spring being long, the middle coils are liable to a greater amount of trembling and displacement by shocks than others, and require a greater space for clearance.

(646.) The supplemental coil must be parallel to the other coils. If not, it can be made so by flattening one of the two bends. If the supplemental points upwards from the body of the spring, flattening the first bend will bring it down. Or, if it lies too low, flattening the last bend, or the one nearest the end, will cause it to point higher and be parallel. This flattening is done by squeezing the spring flatwise, not by applying force to its edges. The supplemental may also be leveled by twisting the elbow sideways to throw the end upwards or downwards. But this should only be done for very slight errors, as the edges of the elbow as well as other parts should be truly vertical, *i.e.*, the breadth of the spring-wire should invariably be at right angles to the horizontal plane of the spring, and parallel to the balance axis.

(647.) *The terminal curve.*—The overcoil, or so much of it as may be needed, is now to be formed into a terminal curve, to make the long and short arcs equal, *i.e.*, isochronal. The length of the terminal will depend on the amount of position error to be corrected—the greater that error, the longer the terminal must be. If the position adjustment has been made, as before directed, (638,) you will know the amount of the error to be corrected. If the error is a *gain* in the short arcs, make the terminal as long as you can—$\frac{3}{4}$ turn to 1 turn, for you will probably need all the length you can get. If the error is a *loss* of, say, 6 seconds per day, in the short arcs, make the terminal $\frac{1}{2}$ turn; if over that, make it $\frac{3}{4}$ turn; if over 12 seconds per day, make it 1 turn in length. These lengths are only first approximations, and may require to be modified on trial. You will of course remember that a minus curve is required to correct a gain, and a plus curve for correcting a loss, in the short arcs.

(648.) *Ascertaining the position errors.*—If the position adjustment has not been made, time the watch specially to ascertain the position errors—12 hours in the horizontal position, and 12 hours in vertical positions, pendant up; or the lengths of the trials may be double those stated. The watch should be fully wound up at the beginning of each trial, to get the motive force the same, and eliminate the isochronal error of the spring from the results, so far as possible. From the results thus obtained, you can estimate the proper length and form of your terminal curve, for a first trial. See section (655.) But, of course, if you are working on a timepiece of a certain uniform or standard character, which is known to require a certain form of terminal, you can make your terminal that way. Or if you have the old one for a model, which was correct, copy it as closely as you can. If not, make a gauge for testing the form (616.) The difference per day between the horizontal and one vertical position is taken as the position error.

(649.) *Forming the terminal curve* is governed by the rules already given under the head of the cylindrical spring. (See Chapter XXXIII.) The form generally called "the Phillips' curve" is shown in Figs. 27 and 36. A better form is given in Fig. 39, showing a terminal about ¾ turn in length. This can easily be lengthened or shortened as needed, as directed for the cylindrical spring.

(650.) *Breguet spring vise.*—Fig. 44 shows a very convenient little tool for holding the spring while working on the terminal.

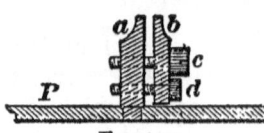

FIG. 44.

It consists of a pair of brass jaws, one upright *a* being fixed in a brass base *p*, such as an old watch plate, while the other jaw *b* is free on the screw *d*, and is drawn towards *a* by the central screw *c*. To keep the jaws parallel, a short piece of the same spring is put between them at the bottom, while the elbow is clamped between them at the top. This tool leaves both hands free to work with. The insides of the jaws are properly curved to fit the shape of the spring. Two or three such vises, having different curvatures, can be arranged in a circle of ½ inch diameter, with the heads of the screws towards the center of the base, and the spring will then be outside, over *a*. The curves of the jaws should be parallel, polished, and without sharp edges to scratch the spring, as directed for the tweezers.

(651.) *Breguet overcoil with a regulator.*—I have said that the terminal curve of the Breguet spring should be made precisely the same as that of the helical spring. This is the rule when a regulator is dispensed with. The theory of the terminal curve requires its ends to be rigidly fixed, so that the angle at which it meet the stud may be as invariable as possible. But when a regulator is used in conjunction with a Breguet spring, a new element is added to the problem. Whether the regulator pins are open or close, they are injurious to the proper action of the spring. If they are open, they interfere with the normal effect of the curve, by preventing it from flexing and vibrating naturally and properly. On the other hand, even if the pins are so close as to constitute the ideal regulator and virtually become the stud, they would derange the action of the curve by changing its operative length and its place and angle of attachment to the (supposed) new stud. For if the pins were made to conform to the position of the curve as they were moved along it, the further they were from the stud the further they would be from the center of the spring, and therefore the curve would not be attached to the supposed new stud at half the radius, as required. But if the pins retained their proper distance from the center, as they moved along the curve they would draw it to their own circle, and obviously force both it and the entire spring out of place and entirely destroy the isochronism. This is the usual result, when the ordinary Breguet spring is "regulated" by an inexperienced workman.

(652.) *The concentric arc of the Breguet spring.*—It is common, therefore, to form a portion of the last coil, next to the stud, concentric, *i.e.*, bend it so that it will form a part of a true circle, having the center of the spring for its center and half the radius of the spring for its radius; as if, for instance, the terminal curve, dc^1cb, Fig. 31, joined on to a concentric, semicircular arc reaching from e to d, and the spring was pinned in the stud at e, instead of at d, where the terminal curve ends. This concentric portion is sometimes made as much as half a coil in length, as just described, and is acted upon by the pins of the regulator the same as the outer coil of the ordinary flat spring.

It is an undoubted advantage to have the use of a regulator for rating a watch, and another advantage of having a concentric portion at the end of the spring is that, if necessary, it may be moved through the stud without thereby changing the distance of the end of the terminal curve from the center and so necessitating a remodeling of the shape of the remainder of the curve.

(653.) *Disadvantages of the concentric arc.*—But this arrangement has also its disadvantages. At the junction of the concentric portion and the true terminal curve, the spring is not rigidly fastened, as the theory of the curve requires, unless the regulator pins clasp it firmly, precisely at that point, and act as a stud. But if the pins are in the least open, the yielding of the spring at and behind the pins would allow the entire terminal curve to move more or less without changing its form at all, and during the remainder of the vibration the amount and direction of its flexion would be modified by the amount of yielding in the concentric portion of the spring behind the pins. This yielding, in turn, would depend on the position of the regulator between the junction and the stud. The nearer it was to the stud, the greater this yielding would be, and it would also involve the further difficulty that the junction, or real end of the terminal curve, would not even be fixed at half the radius, but would be at all sorts of distances from the center, sometimes further than it should be, sometimes less—and every movement of the regulator, nearer to or further from the stud, giving it greater or less liberty and scope of motion, would change the entire position, condition, and action of the terminal curve.

(654.) *The Breguet terminal curve.*—All these difficulties are easily removed by abandoning the use of a concentric arc in combination with a terminal curve, and use only a terminal curve, the end of which, next to the stud, may be concentric with the balance axis, as $e\,d\,b^1$ in Fig. 31, or concentric with the regulator center at a^1, as $e\,d\,c\,b$ in Fig. 32. There is no more objection to the portion $e\,d$ having a circular form than any other, provided that shape can properly be a part of the terminal curve we require. And if a regulator *must* be used, it can be planted concentrically with that portion. But the spring should be timed in such a way that the regulator may be kept as near the stud as possible, because shifting it from the stud cuts off that length of the terminal curve, and alters its action as a terminal.

(655.) *Testing the curve.*—Having decided upon the proper form for the curve, (647, 648,) and made it so, you will now test the spring to find whether that curve will correct the position-errors, and if not, how it should be altered. To do this, you make two trials, one in the horizontal position, the other in the vertical position, (648,) and we will suppose that the error in the vertical position was 16 seconds per day loss. You use the motive-force controller (673,) if necessary, to get an arc of $1\frac{1}{4}$ to $1\frac{1}{2}$ turns in the first trial, and one of, say, $\frac{3}{4}$ turn in the vertical position—each trial being for 12 hours. Note how much the short arcs are faster or slower than the long ones (or horizontal position arcs), and follow the indications given in the table (667) for the proper change to make in the curve, by the rules given in section (624.) The isochronizing of the spring is then completed according to the general rules for adjusting, in Chapter XXXVI.

(656.) *Special points about the Breguet spring.*—In altering the curve, move the spring through the clamps to lengthen or shorten the terminal (putting the watch in beat again by merely turning the arbor f around in the head e, Fig. 11, (238,) sufficiently to restore the beat,) until the long and short arcs have the same amount of error per day, when the spring will of course be isochronous, although the watch may still gain, or may lose, in both long and short arcs. You now pin the spring in the stud, and finish the job. If you have no spring-fitting tool, the terminal must be shifted through the stud as described, instead of in the clamps. When the isochronal point is found, as above, the timing must be made correct. If the watch loses, a part of it will be corrected by the regulator, (the point which was held in the clamps being pinned just outside of the stud,) and the rest by altering the mean-time screws in the balance. The latter alteration will also correct a gain in the rate. It should also be remembered, when fitting with any tool except mine, that the spring will be considerably slower when finally bent into shape and pinned in the stud than it was when held in the tweezers, and proper allowance (from half a minute to two minutes,) must be made before bending. The amount can only be found by experience in similar cases.

CHAPTER XXXVI.

THE ISOCHRONAL ADJUSTMENT.

(657.) *What is the isochronal adjustment?*—What does it consist in? From what has already been said, and repeated over and over again, it must be clear to all that the true object of the isochronal adjustment is to produce in the spring an error which is equal to and the reverse of the errors caused by frictions, the action of the escapement, the imperfections of the movement, etc. If these disturbing influences cause a certain loss of rate in the short arcs, the spring must be so manipulated that it will gain that amount, and *vice versa.* The rate will then be correct, the vibrations will be isochronal, and the watch will be "adjusted for isochronism."

(658.) *Proper order for the adjustments.*—It must also be clear, from the foregoing considerations, that before we can adjust for isochronism, or know what errors we are required to adjust for, those errors should be reduced to as small an amount as possible, the mechanical treatment of the movement finished, and its condition be such that the errors which are found to be unavoidable shall not afterwards be increased, for it would be a waste of time to adjust for certain errors and then have them doubled or greatly increased. It follows from this, that the adjustment for positions should *precede* that for isochronism. The position adjustment, when rationally conducted, is a process of mechanically perfecting and adjusting the mechanism, to reduce *the difference* of the frictions, and other disturbing influences, in the different positions to the smallest possible amount, and also to reduce the error *in any position* as low as possible. That is a purely mechanical proceeding, governed by the amplitudes of the vibrations, and properly has nothing whatever to do with timing. The common practice of deferring the positional adjustment till after the isochronal, and even the compensation, adjustments have been finished, is therefore as ill-judged and foolish as it would be for the jobber to wait till he has cleaned his watch nicely, before he attended to the repairing and mechanical alterations.

(659.) *When this adjustment may come first.*—There is only one case in which such a course would be excusable. If the workman is fitting a new Breguet or cylindrical spring, and has no spring-holding tools (such as are described in Chapter XVII, or something similar,) and cannot make the position tests until after he has brought the spring approximately to time, *i.e.*, after he has ascertained the proper length and made the terminal curve, so that he can pin it in the stud and screw the balance cock in place,—he will of course be compelled to first do that. In doing so, however, he should make no attempt to secure a fine isochronal adjustment, because that would consist in getting the spring to make the short and long arcs in the same times,—the watch being kept in the horizontal position, and the arcs changed by mechanical means. Such correction of isochronal errors is a waste of time, because he will afterwards have to *produce* such errors to correct the position errors, and that adjustment will thus be destroyed again. But if he has such a tool, he can grip the spring wherever he finds it most convenient, instead of pinning it in the stud. By screwing the balance cock in position, with the stud removed to get it out of the way of the spring, he can run the watch in any position, and make any tests required, before isochronizing the spring.

(660.) *What the isochronal adjustment can accomplish.*—It is well known that this adjustment can only correct a limited error arising from frictions, etc. But this is partly due to the workman himself. According to the common practice, he first gets the spring as free from "isochronal error" as possible, (*i.e.*, theoretically isochronous,) and then complains because it cannot correct a position error greater than its own—just as if he should tie up his hands and then complain that he could not do much work. The rational method of adjustment would be to first find the nature and amount of the unavoidable position errors, paying no attention whatever to getting the spring (theoretically) isochronous and correcting its errors, but then *increase* its errors (in the proper direction) till they balanced the position errors. Then he has at the same time corrected the position errors and perfected the isochronal adjustment. This will possibly explain why such eminent chronometer makers as Mr. Kullberg and others should advocate so improper a course as setting the spring excentrically, (575 to 578.) They probably felt the necessity of producing an error in some way, which would balance the opposite position error; but they did not perceive that, instead of removing the isochronal errors of the spring, they ought to *increase* them, and make *them* correct the position errors, instead of the frictions; then, they would seldom need to set the spring excentrically. It will probably explain why many other practices, known to be wrong, are sometimes advised by good workmen. It is evident that when the adjustment is conducted on such principles as I have urged, it will correct greater errors, and correct them more perfectly.

(661.) *What it cannot accomplish.*—Many suppose that if a spring corrects position errors, etc., in the "long and short arcs," it will be isochronous for all arcs. The explanations given of the action of terminal curves will show that a spring has *a different rate for every change of arc*, from the smallest to the largest. We can make its rate correct in two arcs, say, the arcs given when hanging and when lying down, by correcting the rate in one position by the timing screws in the balance, and that in the other by causing the error of the spring to balance the position errors, *i.e.*, adjusting the isochronism for that position. That is what is usually done. The rate in the hanging position is made perfect by regulating, and taken for the standard; then the short arcs are corrected by the spring.

(662.) *Example.*—Let us suppose that the foregoing adjustment is done for arcs of $\frac{3}{4}$ turn and $1\frac{1}{4}$ turns, for the short and long vibrations, respectively. When the watch is carried the vibrations will be made sometimes larger and sometimes smaller, by shaking, etc. If it is a going-barrel watch, the arcs will become smaller as the spring runs down, till it becomes necessary to wind it again. Under various conditions, the arcs might be anything from $\frac{1}{2}$ turn to nearly 2 turns. In the two arcs of $\frac{3}{4}$ turn and $1\frac{1}{4}$ turns the error of the spring balances the position errors, etc., but it will not balance them *in any other arc*, unless the position errors increase and decrease with the amplitudes of the arcs, in the same ratio that the errors of the spring vary with the arc of vibration, and in the contrary direction. If the spring *loses* less and less as the arcs become larger, the position errors must cause *a gain*, and one just equal to that loss, in each different extent of vibration. Such a coincidence may never occur, and while the rate may be correct when the vibrations are just $\frac{3}{4}$ turn and $1\frac{1}{4}$ turns, it will not be correct for any other arc. The greater the errors of the spring, the greater will be the error of rate in the unusual arcs, for the error of the spring varies with the arc, but the position errors would remain nearly the same during quite a change in the arcs. This error we may call the "middle-arc error," corresponding to the middle-temperature error of the compensation.

(663.) *What this teaches.*—We see, therefore, that the isochronal errors of the spring should be small, *i.e.*, differ but little in the different arcs; and in order that they may be small, the position errors which they are required to correct must also be small. The position adjustment should be made as close as possible, and the position errors small, then the isochronal errors of the spring may also be small, and the smaller their difference at the extreme arcs, the less error there will be at other or unusual arcs. This again corroborates my claim that the position adjustment should be made perfect before the isochronal adjustment is begun. In the cases where that cannot be done, (659,) the isochronal adjustment should only be carried far enough to render it practicable to adjust for positions, (if it is to be adjusted for positions,) and that should then be done; after which the isochronal adjustment can be finished, as described in the following sections.

(664.) *Adjusting for theoretical isochronism.*—In case it should be desired to have the spring theoretically isochronous, or as nearly so as possible, for testing purposes, as in section (706), first find what the arcs are in the hanging and lying positions, then get those two arcs with the watch in *the same horizontal position, in each arc*, and accurately note the rate for each one. By this method of testing, position errors and errors of poise are avoided, and the frictions are made as nearly equal as can be done. It is impracticable to get the errors of the spring alone, free from frictions, etc., for if the balance was not connected with the movement its vibrations could not be kept up nor could they be timed. By testing in the same horizontal position and the same temperature for each arc, we reduce the extraneous influences to the smallest amount and avoid irregular disturbing elements. The rates thus obtained show the behavior of the spring in the different arcs, very slightly modified by the frictions and the action of the escapement. The isochronal adjustment can then be made, in any of the ways already described, to correct the errors, till the rates are the same in the two arcs.

(665.) *Finding the variations from theoretical isochronism.*—The fact that they are the same will not show that the spring has the exact progression of force required for theoretical isochronism, *i.e.*, that its force increases in proportion to the angle of flexion, but it will approximately be theoretically isochronous. If we wish to know what the effect of the escapement and frictions is upon the rate, we can test the spring in a spring gauge or dynamometer, alter its terminal till the progression of force *is* correct, then again time it in the watch, getting a second set of rates, and being careful to have exactly the same length of spring in action as before. The best way to insure that is not to remove it from either stud or collet during those alterations. Comparison of the two sets of rates in the different arcs would show where the variation from the isochronous progression was greatest. The spring being now theoretically isochronous, if the rates obtained in the different arcs and positions are not the same, the deviations from equal rates must necessarily be due to the position faults, frictions, etc.

(666.) *Adjusting for practical isochronism.*—This adjustment is for making the spring isochronous when running, no matter what the peculiarities of the movement are, which is a very different thing from the foregoing. Here it is of no consequence whether the spring is theoretically isochronous naturally, or not, so long as there is no imperfection in the material or making of it. Our sole object is to get the same rate in different arcs and positions.

(667.) *Analyzing the observed rates.*—In adjusting, we really ought to know which is the predominant error in the rates we obtain. For instance, if the watch loses 8 seconds in the short arcs, there are many possible causes for it. The isochronal error of the spring and the other errors (of the movement) may vary relatively in many ways, and would require different treatment in different cases, as shown by the following table:

ANALYSIS OF SHORT ARC ERRORS.

Observed Rate.	Error of Spring.	Other Errors.	Required Error of Spring.	Change made in Spring.	Resulting Rate.
−8″	− 4″	− 4″	+ 4″	+8″	±0″
−8″	−10″	+ 2″	− 2″	+8″	±0″
−8″	+ 2″	−10″	+10″	+8″	±0″
−8″	+ 8″	−16″	+16″	+8″	±0″
−8″	− 2″	− 6″	+ 6″	+8″	±0″
−8″	0″	− 8″	+ 8″	+8″	±0″
−8″	−16″	+ 8″	− 8″	+8″	±0″

(668.) As will be seen from the third and fourth columns, the error of the spring must in every case be made to *balance all other errors*, in order to secure the perfect rate of the last column. In every case the spring is made to go 8 seconds faster than it did in the short arcs, (as shown by the fifth column,) but after that is done, the spring must still lose in some cases, while in others it must gain, as shown by the fourth column. In the former cases, we must not change a minus curve into a plus, but merely lessen the effect of the former; in the latter cases we must make that change, or make a plus curve longer or more pronounced.

(669.) *Separating the different errors.*—If the spring has terminal curves, we can generally tell by inspection whether its error is gaining or losing, (see second column,) from the nature of its curve, and act accordingly. In other cases, the course I have recommended in the position adjustment (708) will solve the problem. One series of timing trials is to be made in different positions, with the same motive force each time, and with nearly the same arc, $1\frac{1}{4}$ turns, in each position, thus largely eliminating isochronal errors of the spring from the observed rates, *i.e.*, the difference between the positions is free from errors of isochronism. A second series is made in the same positions, also with an equal motive force in each trial, but with an arc of, say, about $\frac{3}{4}$ turn in each position. This series contain the errors of poise, etc., in addition to the errors previously found, but still nearly free from isochronal differences, when the positions are compared, owing to all being in the same arc. The second series shows the total error which the spring must correct.

(670.) By comparing the same positions in the two series, we find the isochronal errors of the spring. For instance, by comparing pendant up with long arcs, (first series,) with pendant up in short arcs, (second series,) we have the action of the spring in different arcs, shown by difference in the rates. So with the rates for dial up (or down) in the long and the short arcs. Having thus found the position and other errors to be corrected, and knowing the characteristics of the spring, it should be easy to correct them. These trials were designed to assist the workman in discovering the causes of the errors in different positions, but they would also be useful in a close job of isochronizing. They need not occupy much time, if made in only two positions, say, hanging up and dial up (or down,) and it is generally done so.

(671.) *Varying the extents of the vibrations.*—As it is usual to adjust by causing the arcs of vibration to vary considerably, in the manner that is most convenient, and accurately observing the rate of the watch for an equal period with the long and with the short vibrations—in order to test the isochronal action of the spring, an easy and effective way of getting arcs of any required amplitude is desirable.

In Marine Chronometers it is generally done by keying up or letting down the main spring by the ratchet—making the motive force stronger or weaker and thereby changing the arcs. The same thing can be done with fusee watches, but not to so great an extent, as their mainsprings are generally so short that there is little extra length for keying up or letting down. In such cases we may change the arcs as follows: Wind the chain entirely up on the fusee, hook it to the barrel and key up the spring one turn. This gives the weakest force of the mainspring, with the chain upon the smallest part of the fusee, where the power of the spring is transmitted to the train at the greatest disadvantage, so that the vibrations will be very small. We then take the time for four hours; or, if that is not enough, wind it up and repeat till the desired length of time for the trial is passed. Next try it with the chain wound only one turn on the fusee, while the mainspring is keyed entirely up. This gives the other extreme, or the greatest strength of the spring acting on the fusee at the greatest advantage, and giving the largest vibrations the movement is capable of. Take the time as before, either for four hours, or any desired period, winding it up at intervals as needed to prevent running down. All this is easily done if the barrel arbor has a good square on its projecting end.

(672.) *Usual methods.*—The above is an extremely severe test, and any hair spring that will bear it may be considered practically perfect. The more common method is to wind the chain entirely up on the fusee, then hook it to the barrel, and key up the spring enough to run the watch say six hours; then, without disturbing the fusee, key up the spring enough for another six hours, and so on, till the chain has all left the fusee, when the mainspring will generally be properly keyed up for the ordinary running of the watch. The times must be carefully taken for each period of six hours, and if the different times are alike the spring is isochronous. In watches with going barrels, the time may be taken first with the spring wound entirely up, rewinding at regular intervals to keep up the motive power; then with the mainspring wound up only one turn, rewinding as before to prevent running down.

When no other convenient way is available, the watch may be tried first in the horizontal, then in the vertical position, and the motion of the balance will generally vary enough for our purposes in the different positions, unless it has been adjusted to positions. When the arcs are changed in this way, *the same* vertical position should be adopted in each trial, unless there is a difference of rate in the four vertical positions, arising from defective pivot fittings, want of poise in the balance, etc. If so, it will be necessary to divide the time of the trial between two opposite vertical positions and take the mean of the two in order to neutralize the errors in the opposite positions.

(673.) *Motive-force controller.*—A far more workmanlike and effective way than any of these is to make a pulley or collet like that shown in Fig. 45, which can be placed on the winding square or on the center or hand-setting square, and a cord with a weight can be arranged to increase or decrease the motive force to any desired extent. The two outer circles represent the periphery and the bottom of the groove for the cord. This pulley has a changeable center, which is let through the pulley; the fourth circle from the outside shows the diameter of the center-piece, the third shows the flange on the center, which is let into the pulley, and held by two screws, as shown—both flange and screw heads being let in level with the surface of the pulley. The inner circle and the two fine lines crossing exactly at right angles, are to be carefully marked on the metal, as guides for getting the central opening perfectly square and *at the centre of the piece.* The corners come at the junctions of the lines with the circle. This hole should be exactly in the center, or the force of the weight will not be uniform as the winding

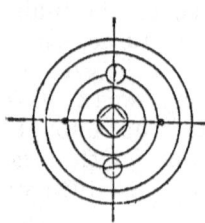

FIG. 45.

square revolves. By having half a dozen sizes of holes, any square can be fitted—the same pulley, cord and weight answering for all of the center-pieces. A pulley half an inch in diameter will be most suitable. A hole is drilled from the bottom of the groove diagonally outward, and the outer end cupped to receive a knot in the end of the cord, to prevent it pulling through.

(674.) *Use of the controller.*—If one of the spring-holding tools, such as Fig. 11, is used to hold the movement, a screw-post carrying another pulley can be secured in one of the holes, 5, in Fig. 12, (239.) The cord runs from the controller over that pulley, and can carry one or more small lead weights, in the same way as the weights of a grocer's scales are changed. When placed on a fuzee arbor, if the cord runs in the same direction as the chain, it increases the effective motive force and makes the arcs larger. By turning it the other way around the pulley, it lessens the motive force and makes the vibrations smaller. Any desired arc can be obtained and maintained in this way. In a going-barrel watch, the pulley must be put on the center square, or hand-setting post.

(675.) *Separating friction errors.*—The use of the controller enables us to separate the errors due to increased friction from the others. For example, if a watch is timed in the horizontal position with long arcs, and then timed in the same position with short arcs, it will gain in the short arcs; if then tried in the vertical (hanging) position with the same short arcs as before, it will run just right, (supposing the spring to be practically isochronous,) because the additional frictions will cause a retardation equal to the gain of the spring. This shows that there is a difference of rate with the same arc of vibration, and the gaining error of the spring, which would just balance the excessive friction of the vertical position, would show itself as an error of rate when that friction was absent. By thus lessening the arcs (in the horizontal position), without increasing the frictions, as above described, we obtain an indication of the action of the spring in different arcs. If the rate does not change under such circumstances, the spring is (almost) theoretically isochronous (664); if it does change, and in such a way as to balance the friction errors in the different positions, it is practically isochronous.

(676.) *Testing the isochronism.*—Let us now take an example. The tests are always to be made in a room at the same temperature (say, about 65° Fahr.,) because the balance is supposed to be not yet compensated, and if the temperature varied, the observed rates would contain errors not due to the isochronism but to the variation of the balance by heat and cold. First the watch is run dial up for 24 hours, and is found to have gained 6 seconds; it is then tried pendant up for 12 hours and loses 8 seconds, and then when tried pendant down 12 hours it loses 10 seconds. For comparison, we write them thus:

```
24 h.,        dial up,        + 6″
    12 h.,    pendant up,            −  8″
    12 h.,       "    down,          − 10″
─────────────────────────────────────────────
24 h.,  24 h.,                + 6″   − 18″ = − 24″
```

Put the length of trials and the errors in different columns, for the long arcs and the short ones. Add the items in the different columns, and compare the totals for the long arcs with those for the short arcs. The times are equal, being 24 hours for each; but the long arcs gained 6 seconds, while the two short arcs lost 18 seconds by the regulator. The short arcs were therefore 24 seconds slower than the long ones, and are said to have lost 24 seconds. We then alter the isochronal action of the spring to make the short arcs gain, and try again, with the following result. Dial up (or down) gives the long arcs, and the vertical positions give the short arcs.

(677.) *Testing in the quarters.*—This time the errors are:—

```
24 h.,        dial up         + 10″
    12 h.,    pendant up             + 6″
    12 h.,       "    down           + 4″
─────────────────────────────────────────────
24 h.,  24 h.,                + 10″  + 10″ = 0″
```

The watch is now said to be isochronous, because the rates are the same in both the long and short arcs, but there is a position error of 2 seconds between pendant up and down. We then try in the other two quarters, and the errors are:—

```
            12 h.,  pendant right   + 10″
            12 h.,     "    left    −  2″
```

showing a position error of 12″ between pendant right and left.

(678.) *Correcting the rate.*—We first see how we can get the rate as nearly alike as possible for the two *most important positions* in actual use, pendant up and dial up. For ease of comparison we arrange all the rates together, as they would be for 24 hours in each position, as follows:—

```
24 h., dial up            + 10″ (−  1″)
  "    pendant up               + 12″ (+  1″)
  "    pendant down             +  8″ (−  3″)
  "    pendant right            + 20″ (+  9″)
  "    pendant left             −  4″ (− 15″)
─────────────────────────────────────────────
       Make the rate slower, − 11″    − 11″
```

Subtract 11″ from each, as that will be half-way between dial up and pendant up; then dial up will be 1 second slow and pendant up 1 second fast, as shown in parentheses after each. The other positions will also be improved, with the exception of pendant left, which is made worse, as shown by the error in the parentheses. To cure that, we can alter the poise of the balance to make pendant left 12 seconds faster, (718 to 721,) which will also make pendant right 12 seconds slower; pendant right will then lose 3 seconds per day and pendant left will also lose the same. Every case is different, but by arranging the errors as above, a little study will show the best arrangement. In the above case we altered the mean-time screws to cause a loss of 11 seconds in the rate. But we might have made pendant up just right, by a loss of 12 seconds; then dial up would have lost 2 seconds, instead of 1, as shown.

(679.) *Correcting the isochronism—its limitations.*—The foregoing example proves the necessity of close position adjustment before isochronizing the spring. It is impossible for the spring to correct all errors. All that it can do is to give a certain rate (gain or loss) in the long arcs, and another rate in the short ones. If that rate balances the errors in a certain position, the error in that position will be "corrected," but the errors in other positions will not be. Let us consider another example:—

24 h., dial up		$+3''$
" pendant up		$-5''$
" " down		$+2''$
" " right		$-7''$
" " left		$+11''$

(680.) If we regulate the watch to keep correct time pendant up, the errors will be as shown in the first column below:

Dial up	$+8''$	$0''$	$0''$	$0''$	$0''$
Pendant up	$0''$	$-8''$	$0''$	$+4''$	$-4''$
" down	$+7''$	$-1''$	$+7''$	$+11''$	$+3''$
" right	$-2''$	$-10''$	$-2''$	$+2''$	$-6''$
" left	$+16''$	$+8''$	$+16''$	$+20''$	$+12''$

Instead of that, if we had made the rate correct with dial up, the errors would have been as shown in the second column. Then suppose we caused the spring to gain 8 seconds in the short arcs, the result would be shown in the third column. That is as far as we can go with the isochronal adjustment, for if we make the short arcs gain any more, say, 4 seconds more, the rates would be poorer as seen by the fourth column; and if we make them 4 seconds slower the rate would be as in the fifth

(681.) *True purpose of the isochronal adjustment.*—Consideration of the foregoing details will prove that the common practice of adjusting for only two positions is right. That is all that the isochronal adjustment can possibly correct. Anything more than that belongs to the positional adjustment and should be corrected by that. It cannot be done in any other way. It is also plain that the practice of adjusting for certain *arcs of vibration*, (long and short,) has no proper place in the adjustment for practical isochronism, (except for investigations as to the causes of observed errors,) but that the latter adjustment is simply for correcting the errors in the two chosen *positions*. Any positions preferred may be taken, but, of course, the two positions in which accuracy is most desirable should be chosen, and they are generally pendant up (hanging) and dial up or lying down. Such an adjustment relates to actual conditions, and is therefore practical. Anything beyond that is not so.

(682.) *In adjusting marine chronometers*, which are always kept in the same position, the common practice is to let down the mainspring to reduce the arcs from $1\frac{1}{4}$ turns down to from $\frac{3}{4}$ to $\frac{5}{8}$ turn, and time the instrument for the same length of time as with the long arcs; if the rate is absolutely the same in the long and the short arcs it is called isochronous, on the supposition that the short arcs so obtained will be equivalent to the short arcs caused by the thickening of the oil after two or three years' service. Any intelligent adjuster must see that this is entirely wrong. The conditions of actual use are, a slight decrease of motive force, due to thickening of the oil on the pivots of the train, and a great increase of friction from the thickening of the oil on the balance pivots. The artificial conditions produced to imitate the actual ones are, a large decrease in the motive force, and no increase in the frictions, a very different state of things. If a spring was practically isochronous, it would *gain* from 3 to 10 seconds in 24 hours when tested in the short arcs in that way; on the other hand, if it is adjusted so that it will give the same rate on the long and short arcs so produced, when exposed to actual conditions it will *lose* 3 to 10 seconds *more than if it had not been adjusted*, on account of the thickening of the oil. Turning it up into the vertical position will not duplicate the actual conditions, because there is no certainty that the side friction would be *equal to* that of the oil, but especially because the rate would then also contain the errors due to lack of poise, roundness of pivots or holes, improper sizes, and close or loose fitting, etc., etc.

(683.) *The realistic and practical methods of adjusting.*—The "realistic" method of imitating the natural conditions, would be to slightly weaken the motive force, and put thick oil on the balance pivots, then adjust the short arcs. But there would be no certainty that the effect so produced might not be too great or too small. We can therefore only follow what we may call the practical method. If we know by experience how much such instruments lose, on an average, we can adjust our spring to *gain* that amount in the short arcs, when tested in the horizontal position, with the short arcs produced by letting down the mainspring or by the controller. Even that is merely *guessing* what the loss would be at the end of two or three years, but it is the best we can do, and is far better than the usual method. The short arcs should then be the same that they usually are after the chronometer has been in use two or three years, and they should gain on the long arcs to the amount before stated.

(684.) In adjusting a going-barrel watch, the long arcs should be timed in the horizontal position, with the mainspring wound entirely up, and re-wound every 4 hours, to keep it up; the short arcs should be in the vertical (pendant up) position, with the mainspring wound only 1 turn, and re-wound every 4 hours to the same extent as before, *i.e.*, to keep it wound 1 turn during the trial. During the short arcs it should give the same rate as in the long ones, as keeping the arcs small all the time, in the manner described, will practically equal the future thickening of the oil. In adjusting a fuzee watch, take the horizontal position for the long arcs, and the vertical (pendant up) position for the short ones, either letting down the mainspring or using the controller to make them $\frac{1}{2}$ turn smaller than the long ones, and make them *gain* on the long ones from 3 to 5 seconds per day. As pocket watches are cleaned more often than chronometers, this will be ample to cover the thickening of the oil, etc. In ordinary watches, no such allowance is made, but the long and the short arcs (so produced) are made to give the same rate.

(685.) *The adjustment difficult.*—The workman may think that it is a good deal of trouble to isochronize a spring. Well, it *is* some trouble to do a good job. But nothing really good is to be had without trouble. But it is not so hard as it might seem at first, from the number of details given. I have endeavored to touch every point important to know, have even occasionally repeated directions in different ways, have used ungrammatical and unscientific expressions, have been diffuse and redundant in style, from a desire to make sure that my meanings should be *noticed* and clearly understood by all. But when once comprehended and become familiar, when the principles or models which are to be copied are fixed in the mind, the numerous details I have found it necessary to explain and dwell upon will become matter-of-course, and the practical work simple and easy, so that we may hope for an improvement in the manner of treating springs which seems to prevail at present with many makers. Judging from their work, a good share of workmen now merely try the spring by some "quick test," (524 to 526,) and let it go at that. But from what has been said, it will be seen that it is little better than a barefaced swindle to pass off such a spring as isochronal, for a spring may stand that test or even a severer one, and yet not be adjusted for isochronism at all. One has no more moral right to call such a spring isochronal than he has to represent a chain as gold because it has a few grains of that metal in it or on it.

(686.) *Practice required.*—I have now given all directions necessary for selecting and fitting hair springs in the very best manner, and making all adjustments required even in the finest watches or chronometers. It is not to be expected that the workman will observe all the niceties explained, in common watches or on low-priced jobs. But if he understands fully what has been said in these articles, and uses a reasonable amount of thought and judgment in applying it in practice, he can, with little or no loss of time, do even his common jobs in a manner approximating correctness, and which will not only please his customers, but satisfy other workmen, into whose hands they may come, that he understood his business. Above all will be the satisfaction to himself of working from knowledge, instead of blind groping and guess-work—and the ability to judge whether work is properly done or not. In order to get the most benefit from his knowledge—to both learn and *improve*—he should put it into practice at every opportunity, even if it involves extra trouble or doing a little more than he gets paid for. He will be amply rewarded by his improvement in information and dexterity. But without practice his knowledge will be both useless and fleeting.

(687.) *Rating sheets for isochronizing.*—The workman should keep a regular record of all his trials, rates, alterations made, and, in general, everything which is done in connection with the job, and which would be necessary for another man to know if he should have to take up the job and finish it. He must not imagine that keeping such a record is a mere matter of form, or even convenience. It is a legal necessity. The law requires every man to keep proper books showing the details of his business, and to produce them as proof of the truth and justice of any claims he may seek to enforce in the courts. If an adjuster should have occasion to sue for the collection of pay for his work, he would probably be unable to give legal proof of what he had done, unless he could produce some systematic record, such as is given on the next page.

(688.) *The law of evidence.*—In such suits, the first and original entries of what was done, made at the time, are always called for, and in some cases no other entries or books will be accepted as conclusive proof. The workman must be able to swear that he made those precise entries, just as they stand, at the time they purport to have been made, and that they were and are correct. Otherwise, he could only swear that he *believes* them to be true, but could not swear positively, and he believes that he did work about as stated in the entries—while the other party could bring other adjusters to say that they had examined the watch and that they did not believe any such work, or work to that value, had been done, etc., etc.,—which would imply that his claim for services was not an honest one. It is therefore not only a question of doing business in a proper and business-like way, but may also involve his reputation as an honest business man, as well as affect the collection of money due him for work performed. These remarks, of course, apply with equal force to the other adjustments, and I have given specimens of suitable records for each case.

(689.) *Isochronism record.*—[See page 286.]

(690.) *Explanation of the rating sheet.*—This can be easily ruled off as shown, and gives opportunity to make an entry for every detail useful for reference in perfecting the work, aside from its legal value. The entries are not in connected form, as they would be in a real case, but merely to show the different details which might occur in different cases. The usual course is merely to note the rates in the long and the short arcs. But it is obvious that that leaves all the most important points to the memory. In other words, such a record is legally no record at all. And it is of little or no assistance to the workman himself in trying to recall details of what he had done, the effect, etc. The record should show, for each trial, the position, the motive force, the arc of vibration, the length of trial, and the actual error observed. For the short arc trials, the way the short arcs were obtained should be stated—for different ways will produce very different results. The last column states any other point of interest or useful to remember. The entries for the short arcs are not inserted, but are made like those for the long arcs.

(689.) Isochronism Record.

(Name of owner, description and number of the watch, etc.)

Date of Trial 1894.	Long Arc.				Short Arc.				Circumstances, Alteration made at end of trials, Remarks, etc.
	Position.	Wound.	Arc of Vib.	Hours.	Gain or Loss by Clock.	Position.	Winding.	Arc of Vib.	Hours.	Gain or Loss by Clock.	How Short Arc was obtained.	
Feb. 1	p. up	up	1¼	24	+ 1′ 12″						By controller	Changed screws — 11″.
	d. up	½	1¾	12	+ 4″						By winding	Took up spring $\frac{1}{16}$ inch.
	3 up	1 t	1	12	− 11″						By winding	Set spring exc. to 3.
	9 up	2 t	1½	12	− 2′ 40″						Let down m.-spg.	Changed poise, top of bal. heavier 12 up.
	12 up	3 t	385°	12	18″						Vert. position	
	6 up	4 t	540°	12	+ 1″							
	p. d.	3½ t	680°	6	0″							

(691.) *Making the entries.*—The abbreviations are simple: *p* means pendant; *d* is dial; a figure shows what hour on the dial was up; any position in that column means up, except one: *pd* means pendant down. In the winding column *up* means wound entirely up; ½, is wound half-way up; 1 *t* means wound up one turn from the bottom of the fuzee; or, in a going-barrel watch, 1 turn from the point where the stop works prevent the spring from running further down. If the stop works are gone, it means 1 turn of the barrel arbor from the position reached after running 24 hours. The arc of vibration may be expressed in turns, as 1¼, 1, ¾, etc., or more closely in degrees, which means the vibration from one extreme to the other. In expressing the rate, *1h 10′ 11″*, would mean 1 hour, 10 minutes, and 11 seconds; + signifies a gain, and − means a loss. The entries in the last column mean that we changed the mean-time screws in the balance to make the rate 11 seconds slower; that we set the hair spring towards the III on the dial; that we made the top of the balance heavier than the bottom for the position XII up, etc. If you are particular to keep such records in the manner described, they will not only be useful for the purposes already stated, but will be a mine of valuable information to you, in case you wish to investigate any point, and a pleasure for you to look them over.

PART SEVENTH.

THE ADJUSTMENT FOR POSITIONS.

CHAPTER XXXVII.

Position Faults.

(692.) *Adjustment for different positions* should, theoretically, be unnecessary, because a watch made on correct principles, and well executed, would already be as perfect as it could be, and would therefore give as close a rate in the different positions as it could be made to do. But in practice there are many shortcomings, both in designing and executing the mechanism, and in consequence both the amplitude of the vibrations and the rate are more or less irregular when the position is changed from hanging to lying, or to the different vertical positions. The object of the position adjustment is to discover the causes of these errors, and correct them, wholly or partially, according to the quality of the watch, or of the job.

(693.) *Position variations of rate* are due to the total amount of frictions and other resistances being different in the different positions, affecting the movement of the balance and the time kept by the watch. It is generally supposed that the causes of these resistances and frictions are merely errors in the shapes or sizes of the balance pivots or in the poise, and that correcting the poise and changing the pivots will remove the errors. But, in reality, the causes are very numerous and diverse. They may be divided into several classes, as: position errors; rotating or varying errors; escapement errors; errors of proportion or design.

(694.) *Class first.—Position errors*, properly so called, are those due to a change in the position of the watch, and they do not change while that position remains the same. Among others, the following faults of that class may be mentioned:

1. *The weight of the balance* and its fixed attachments, such as

the rollers, hair-spring collet, etc., even when perfectly poised, causes a difference in the friction, between the horizontal and vertical positions. But as this weight cannot be changed to equalize the frictions, we can only accomplish that by modifying the size of the pivots, or by altering the jewels, etc., as hereafter explained. In case the weight of the balance is not correct, we can then change it to a correct proportion, as stated in the section devoted to the fourth class of errors.

2. *The weight of the central coils of the hair spring* rests on the balance axis, the same as that of the balance itself. How much of its weight is supported by the stud and how much rests on the balance staff, it is impossible to say. In the horizontal position, probably all but the last coil or half coil is supported by the balance pivot, if the spring is so pinned in the stud that it stands perfectly free, as was directed in Chapter XVIII, on Fitting Hair Springs. But by pinning it a little low in the stud, the whole weight of the spring comes on the end of the pivot, and exerts an additional mechanical pressure downward, besides,—which increases the friction on the pivot. The same effect is produced by raising the collet up on the staff. If the watch is then reversed so that the balance rests on the other end of the staff, there will obviously be *less* friction on that end, because, not only is the weight of the spring supported by the stud, but it exerts an upward pressure, tending to lift the balance off the pivot. In ordinary watches, the weight of the spring is so small that it would not count much as affecting the amount of friction on the pivot ends, but the mechanical pressure described might be a very effective means of increasing the horizontal friction, and so equalizing the horizontal and vertical frictions. But it must not be carried so far as to affect its isochronal action—and the latter should be tested when this procedure is followed.

3. *The weight of the spring in the vertical position.*—A similar method of varying the weight and the attendant frictions is often adopted in the vertical positions, by so shaping the outer coil that the stud will support nearly the whole weight of the spring in any desired vertical position. For example, if the spring shown in Fig. 25, (296,) is pinned perfectly free in the stud, and then held in the different vertical positions, a little more of the spring will rest on the balance staff when held stud up than with stud down—probably enough more to compensate for the greater weight of the outer halves of the coils, (295); and the same is true when held stud right, or stud left. So that, practically speaking, the weight of the spring resting on the staff will be equal in the different vertical positions, if

pinned in the stud so as to stand perfectly free. But if it is desired to take the weight off the pivots in one position, say, stud up, and increase the weight with the stud down, the outer coil is bent inward a little at *c*, throwing it towards the stud. The whole weight, and a pressure besides, will then rest on the pivots when the stud is down. To lessen the weight when the stud is at the right, the spring is bent inward between *c* and *d*.

4. *Side pressure of the hair spring.*—With a tolerably stiff spring, this method can produce many times more effect by the pressure than the weight alone could do. Whenever there is too much friction in any vertical position, see if the spring is out of center and is exerting a side pressure in that direction. If so, correct the excentricity, or make it excentric in the opposite direction. The rule is, to shift the center towards the dial figure which is uppermost when the friction is greatest. If the greatest error is with XII up, the outer coil is bent to throw the center towards the XII, and it will tend to lift the balance whenever the XII is up. The bending is done outside of the regulator pins, but if the effect should be to change its position between the pins, the stud should be slightly turned to restore it to the correct position between the pins. If the stud cannot be turned, bend the spring at the stud. But as observed in the second paragraph, this procedure should not be allowed to go so far as to injure the isochronal action of the spring, for that is more important than the position adjustment, and the latter can be changed in other ways, which are less objectionable.

5. *Escapement frictions* may vary in the different positions. The most common cause is the balance pivots being too loosely fitted in the jewel holes, so that the balance and its attachments work more deeply when it falls towards the rest of the escapement than when it falls from them. If this fault is serious, it should be corrected, as there is no other way of neutralizing the effects. If not too serious, setting the hair spring excentric, as directed in paragraph 4, may hide the error.

6. *Lever not poised.*—In lever watches, if the lever is not poised, it will require a greater expenditure of the energy of the balance to lift its weight in one position, than to merely unlock it in the opposite position and let it drop by its own weight. The remedy for this is obvious.

7. *Difference of friction on sides and ends of pivots.*—The difference of friction on the sides or on the ends of the pivots is a very difficult fault to overcome. We know that in nearly all watches the balance has a larger motion, or longer vibration, in a horizontal position than when it is in a vertical position, or

with its edge up. This is caused by a greater friction on the balance pivots in the latter case. The adjustment to positions is effected by equalizing the frictions, so that the hair spring will be able to move the balance through the same arc in any position in which it may be held. Even when the pivots and jewel holes are correctly formed and finished, the friction on the sides may be much greater than on the ends and produce a serious difference in the rate between the horizontal and vertical positions. If the size and condition of the pivots are correct, we can flatten the ends, not so much to increase the surface in contact with the end-stones as to increase the distance of the contact from the center of the pivot. If the end friction could all take place at the outer edge, the radius of friction would be practically the same on the ends as on the sides of the pivots. To secure that, many workmen not only make the ends perfectly flat to the edge, but it has even then been proposed to hollow out the center, so that it could only touch the end-stone at the outer edge. But that is rather difficult to do.

8. *Increasing the end friction.*—The end friction can be increased in different ways. But the only one which is worthy of consideration is to slightly incline the end-stone, so that the end of the pivot only rests on it at its extreme edge. This unquestionably does increase the friction, but it is liable to wear off the end of the pivot around its edge, unless it is burnished very hard and the end-stone very highly polished. But it produces a still greater effect by the side friction which results from the pivot sliding down the inclined surface and being forced against the side of the jewel hole. This is only allowable when the hole is perfectly polished and the side of the pivot is hard burnished. The inclination of the end-stone should not be too great, or it may cause a much greater error than the end friction did. Besides, it is a cardinal rule that in all cases the equalizing of the frictions is to be done by *lessening the greater* ones—never increasing frictions unless that is unavoidable. On the other hand, when there is an error in the rate, or a lack of proper vibration, in the horizontal position, see if the fault is not an end-stone that is inclined, instead of being vertical to the pivot and giving it a level and easy support.

9. *Lessening the end friction.*—When the side friction is very much greater than the end friction, the ends of the balance pivots may be round, or, at least, not flat. The remedy, of course, is to flatten the ends, either perfectly flat, or as nearly so as may be found necessary on trial, till the balance will keep

up about the same motion in both the horizontal and vertical positions.

10. *Excessive end friction* may be due to jewel holes being too thick, or pivot too short, or end-stone too far from the hole jewel, whereby the shoulder of the balance pivot rubs the jewel.

11. *Another cause* is the cup in the jewel being too small and deep, containing too much oil, and clogs or retards the shoulder of the pivot. Or the oil may be too thick or viscid, or dirty.

12. *Excessive side friction* is also caused by jewel holes too thick, so that the rubbing surfaces are too great, and the adhesion of the oil between the hole and the pivot causes a retarding effect. As a general rule, the length of the hole should equal the diameter. If the jewel holes are not perfectly polished the error produced is still greater. Holes which are too long can be chamfered or rounded out at the ends, to shorten the rubbing surfaces.

13. *The side friction of large pivots* will cause slowness in the vertical positions. The friction increases with the size of the pivot, and very rapidly when the pivot is too closely fitted in the hole. In such a case reducing the size of the pivots, and at the same time giving it more freedom in the hole, will greatly lessen the side friction, increase the arcs and make the short arcs faster.

14. *If the pivot holes are not round* the pivot may fall into the narrow side, and pinch, when in one of the vertical positions, causing excessive side friction, and retarding the balance or almost stopping it. The same effect may be produced if the jewel hole is chipped on one side, and the edges dig into the side of the pivot as it revolves, or cause excessive friction and error. When in the opposite vertical position the pivot may be perfectly free, thus causing a difference of friction and rate in the different vertical positions, and also a difference between the vertical and horizontal positions.

15. *Poor alignment of jewel holes.*—If the jewel holes are not in line with each other, or even if one hole is in line with the balance axis while the other is not, the holes (or the one of them which was out of line) would be equivalent to oval jewel holes, as will be seen by Fig. 46, where the right and left circles represent the two ends of the hole, as seen with the eye in line with the balance axis, and their intersection shows the oval opening left free for the pivot, which is drawn with shaded lines. If the watch is held in such a position that the oval opening is vertical, as shown, the pivot will pinch in the hole, all the time; when the oval opening is horizontal, the pivot will wabble about loosely

in the hole. This action may assist in detecting the error, for if the pivot is very loose in one direction and tight in the transverse direction, while the hole is seen to be round when examined with a powerful glass, we may infer that the jewel holes are out of alignment. There would seem to be no remedy but to fit in other jewels and set them properly. If the error is caused by one of the holes not being vertically over the other, it will be shown by the balance not being level with the plate. If level, hold the movement inclining downward from you, so that the balance pivots fall into the further sides of the holes, and gently press on the top of the rim (part nearest to you) with a stiff bristle. If loose, then press on the sides and it will be tight — or both will be the reverse of the above. Whenever you take a watch apart, test the alignment of the balance holes (with the end stones off) by putting a round broach in them. If the broach is not vertical to the plate, or cock, the hole is out of level. Do not put the broach in too tightly, or you will crack the jewel in getting it out.

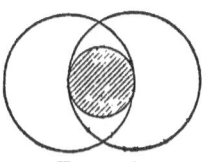

FIG. 46.

16. *If the jewel holes are too thin*, so that the pivots have too little surface to rest upon in the vertical positions, the oil will be forced out from between them, and leave the pivot to run on a dry surface, causing greater side friction and variations of rate between the vertical and horizontal positions. This is more noticeable when the balance is heavy.

17. *A magnet* near the watch will attract the balance and the lever, the attraction being greatest at the ends of the center-bar and the lever. When the position of the watch is changed, the direction of the magnetic attraction will be changed relatively to the lever and balance, thus producing different effects in different positions, and causing very serious errors of rate, almost stopping the watch if the attraction is strong.

18. *Inequalities.*—When the balance pivots are not of the same size, or the jewel holes not of the same thickness or shape, the pivots differently formed on the ends, or differently fitted in their holes, the total frictions will be different in the different positions, causing a difference of rate when the positions are changed.

19. *Horizontal frictions of pivots unequal.*—This may be due to one pivot being shorter, (or end stone further away,) or one jewel hole too thick, causing the shoulder of the pivot to graze the jewel, or clog in the oil. If so, the remedy is obvious. Sometimes one end-stone is poorly polished; or too soft, and

the end of the pivot wears it. Occasionally, a pivot has been dressed down with diamond dust, emery or diamantine, and particles of it are imbedded in the steel, making it a veritable drill. In such cases, the end should be scraped with a sharp graver, held so that the edge cuts and will lift the particles out of the metal, not rub over them and press them further in; then finish hard with a pivot burnisher. If the pivot is long enough to bear it, turning off the surface of the end in the lathe is still better.

20. *End frictions unequal.*—When unequal horizontal frictions are due to a difference in the ends of the pivots, they are equalized by making the ends of the balance pivots equally flat and well polished. The extent of the vibrations can be readily observed when the dial is upwards, by setting the movement holder upon a piece of looking-glass on the bench. The balance and works can even be examined with the eye-glass while in that position, by looking from one side at such an angle that its image will be reflected into the glass. This is much better than holding the movement above one's head in order to see its under side, insures a true and equal horizontal position each time, and obviates the trembling of the hand while holding it, which interferes with the motion of the balance—and is, besides, easier and safer.

21. *Side frictions less than end frictions.*—If the vibrations are greater in the vertical than in the horizontal position, and the fault is known to be in the pivots, the end friction being too great, we slightly round off the end of the pivots to increase the arc in the horizontal position to an equal extent. These changes of the shape of the pivots should be done in a lathe, and very slowly and cautiously, lest we do too much. The best tool is a pivot burnisher, as that both polishes and hardens the surface. If a stone or lap is used, the burnisher should finish the job. In rounding off the end, the departure from a perfect flatness on the end of the pivot should be only sufficient to prevent actual contact with the end-stone, so that the rounding off shall be barely perceptible to the eye. First remove a narrow ring around the outer edge and try. If not enough, take off a little nearer to the center of the pivot. If too much is taken off, we shall have to flatten the end again, which will shorten the pivot. Therefore we take off but little at a time, and as equally as possible off each pivot. Always remove any "feather-edge" that may appear at the corners of the pivots, with an oil-stone slip.

(695.) *Class second.*—*Rotating or varying faults* are those which vary while the watch is stationary, such as lack of poise, pivots not round, and the like. In a fine watch, and a good job, all such errors should of course be corrected; but very often they are either intentionally caused or intentionally left so, for the purpose of balancing or neutralizing some worse error. If we take a common-sense view of the situation, it is better to have every part in the watch out of poise and get a fair rate, than to have everything perfectly poised and have a poor rate. What we are after is a good running rate, not perfection in the poise, or in any other condition. If perfect poise (or anything else) will give us the best rate, we make it perfect; if imperfect poise will do that, we make it imperfect. We look at the results, not methods. Right or wrong, that is business, and we are doing what we are paid to do. But when everything is ordered to be made perfect, we of course do that. The following are the principal faults of this class:—

1. *Defective poise of the balance and its fixed attachments*, the rollers, the hair-spring collet, and the inner end of the hair spring reaching to the regular spiral or cylindrical portion. The subject of poise is fully treated in Chapter XIX.

2. *Excentricity of the balance.*—If the balance is not riveted concentrically on the staff, or the staff pivots are bent, or one or both of the balance segments are bent out of the true circular form, (at mean temperature,) or any similar error exists, it will cause the same effect as lack of poise or as pivots not round (No. 4.) This can generally be detected by testing the balance in the calipers to see if the rim is perfectly concentric with the axis.

3. *Hair spring out of poise.*—This fault can be detected in the same way as the last one, if the spring is cylindrical. Test it with the balance staff *vertical*. With a flat spiral spring, see if the coils rise regularly from the center as the balance is gently whirled around in the calipers (277). The spring should always be concentric at the center, although it is sometimes made excentric at the outside. (See (694), No. 3.)

4. *Pivots not round.*—The effect of the pivots being oval, three-sided, flattened on one side, or otherwise varying from a true cylindrical form is shown by Figs. 47, 48, 49, in which the circles represent the jewel holes, and the interior ovals are the pivots. In Fig. 47, the pivot is so well fitted in the hole that it does not fall so far below the center as in Fig. 48, but the effect is just as bad, for the nearer vertical the side contacts are, the more the pivot will wedge and pinch in the hole, clogging or almost stopping the motion. In Fig. 48, the pivot does not pinch so much, but it lets the balance down further, the distance of

the fall being shown by the two dots. In vibrating a quarter of a turn, to the position of Fig. 49, the entire weight of the balance has to be lifted, by the pivot, as shown by the dots, the lower one being the axis of the balance as in Fig. 48, and the upper one is the distance it has been lifted when in the position shown in Fig. 49. This of course implies heavy friction, and a great expenditure of the momentum of the balance in overcoming it. In every vibration of 1¼ or 1½ turns, this lifting occurs three times, and the pinching occurs three times, so that it really is a worse fault than a lack of poise, and is much more frequent. The heavy pressure also forces away the oil, and the pivots virtually run dry.

Of course, pivots are never *so much* out of shape as has been shown in the cuts for the sake of clearness, but the principle is the same, and even when the pivot is but little out of round, barely enough to *remove the supporting part underneath*, the effect is as great as if the whole under third of the pivot was gone. Although but little is thought about this fault, there can hardly be a doubt that it (including No. 5, below, and No. 15 in class

   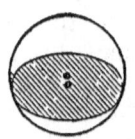   

Fig. 47.   Fig. 48.   Fig. 49.

1,) is the cause of a large share of the excessive frictions in vertical positions and of position errors of rate. Detecting the error, when slight, is difficult, (715.) The best way is probably to whirl the balance in the calipers, watching the pivots with a strong glass. There is only one remedy for the jobber, and that is to center the staff *perfectly* in the lathe and turn the pivot off true, (removing as little metal as possible,) almost finishing it with the graver, then burnish it hard while running at high speed. In the factories, the pivot could be ground true, both wheel and pivot revolving in opposite directions at high speeds.

5. *Bent pivots; poor alignment of pivots.*—When a pivot is bent in a certain direction, it is mechanically oval, or spread out in that direction, as shown in Figs. 47, 48 and 49, and its action in the hole is the same as above described for an oval pivot. If one pivot is not in line with the other, one or both of them will act in the hole as before described, being virtually oval. This will be evident from Fig. 50. If the eye is directly in line with

the axis of the staff, and the right-hand circle shows the outline of the pivot at the shoulder, and the left circle is its outline at the end, it will be mechanically equivalent to the pivot shown in Fig. 47, and the friction and error of rate will be as there described.

The remedy is the same as for that, except when the pivot is bent, in which case it should be straightened. A pivot out of line can be bent to bring it into line with the other, but then it will probably also require a smaller jewel hole. This shows the necessity of care in turning pivots. In turning the first pivot, the other end of the staff should have a well formed and conical point, and be *perfectly centered* till the outer end is finished truly. When reversed, this pivot should be *perfectly* centered while the other pivot is being turned. Both pivots should be either turned or ground so that nothing is required to finish them except a hard burnishing, which should be done while the pivot revolves at high speed.

FIG. 50.

6. *Magnetized balance.*—A magnetized balance has its North and South poles, and is attracted by every piece of iron or steel near it, whether in or out of the watch. This alternately attracts and repels it, producing such irregular vibrations that rating the watch is out of the question until the fault is removed. For the method of detecting and removing magnetism see Chapter IV.

(696.) *Class third.*—*Escapement errors* are fully considered in special articles. See Chapter XXV for the cylinder escapement, Chapter XXVI for the duplex, Chapter XXVII for the lever, and Chapter XXVIII for chronometers.

(697.) *Class fourth.*—*Errors of proportion or design* include faults in the design or proportions of the different parts, generally the fault of the maker. Among those which affect the timing in positions are:—

1. *Balance too heavy.*—It is well known that a heavy balance causes great errors between the horizontal and vertical positions, and if much too heavy correct timing in positions is impossible. The method of testing the proper weight of the balance is given in Chapter X, sections (141) and (142.)

2. *Motive force considerably too great for the balance.*—It is well known that if this is the case, the watch will be difficult or impossible to time in positions. The only method of testing this point open to the jobber is first to ascertain as above if the balance is too heavy (in proportion to the balance spring) to admit

of getting the same rate in the two positions, (horizontal and hanging,) and if not, then weaken the motive force in any convenient way, as widely as possible, to find a strength which gives but little difference of rate in the two positions, even when the strength is varied within the limits which are unavoidable with the going-barrel.

3. *Train too quick.*—In watches with very quick trains, (19,000 to 21,000 beats per hour, and upward,) there will be a loss in the hanging or vertical positions, as compared with the horizontal position, which is very difficult to overcome. See No. 4.

4. *Balance too light.*—In this case, also, the above error is found, and is thought to be due to the frictions in the vertical positions being too great in proportion to the weight of the balance. If the watch is free from the faults before stated, especially pivots or holes out of round or out of alignment, there would seem to be no remedy except to make the balance pivots smaller, and fit new jewel holes, or else shorten up the hair spring to quicken the vibrations in the vertical position. This fault is especially noticeable in very small watches, and the spring sometimes has to be shortened up as much as two turns, to produce the desired effect.

5. *Hair spring too long*, causing a loss in the vertical positions. This is practically the same as the previous one.

6. *Balance pivots too closely fitted* is sometimes the cause of the watch losing in the vertical positions. In such cases, making them very slightly smaller by burnishing will enlarge and quicken the short arcs and remedy the error.

7. *Fourth and escape wheels too heavy*, adding to the frictions, making the escapement sluggish, diminishing and retarding the impulse, and causing a loss in the vertical positions.

CHAPTER XXXVIII.

Adjusting for Positions.

(698.) *Order of the adjustments.*—The usual order is to test the isochronism first, then regulate closely to time at mean temperature, adjust for heat and cold, then for positions, first at mean temperature, and afterwards in heat and cold, again poise the balance, if needed, then rate as closely as possible. That will do very well, when the adjustment for positions is only attended to as far as may be required to detect some glaring fault of poise or fitting. The position adjustment is generally treated as a very small and unimportant matter. In ordinary watches, it is not done at all, and even in good watches most workmen adjust only very slightly, for hanging and dial up. But the foregoing list of position errors shows that it is a matter of the very highest importance, and, if properly attended to, will improve the condition and performance of the watch as much as any other adjustment. Whenever it is to be thoroughly done, as it always should be in fine watches, the preferable order of adjusting would be: positions, isochronism, compensation. But the usual order is isochronism, positions, compensation. Also, see section (663.)

(699.) *Requisites for adjusting.*—Supposing that the fitting of the hair spring has been done in accordance with the directions given, there will be no probability of our having to change the spring or the balance after adjusting for isochronism, and even if we did have to change the spring, it could be isochronized without disturbing the position adjustment. The watch should (after the isochronal adjustment is finished,) be closely regulated at mean temperature, which must be the same throughout the trials. We require a movement holder, by which the movement can be held either vertically or horizontally, such as shown in Fig. 51, in which S is a heavy stand or base, carrying a table having two clamps, $i\ i$, for receiving the edge of the watch or movement, the other edge being held by another clamp l, which slides on the rod r, and is secured by a thumbscrew n. The table, with the rod and watch, turns on a joint N underneath, and is secured in any position by thumbscrew.

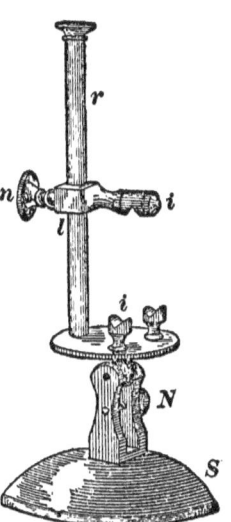

FIG. 51.

The spring-holding tool, Fig. 11, (238,) can also be used for position timing, by securing in the holes $5\ 5$, Fig. 12, four screw posts, whose upper ends are bent (L-shaped) outwards as far as the edge of the base A to hold it upright when resting on the edge and the points of the screw posts. This holds it in any of the vertical positions. Holes 5 can be put at all the corners, for this purpose. If these posts reach up higher than the end of the runner f, the whole tool can be inverted and rest on the ends of the posts, thus holding the movement in the other horizontal position. We also need sheets of paper, with columns ruled for the arcs and the times, *i.e.*, the gain or loss, in each position, (734). Much of the adjustment, however, will be mechanical tests and observations of the arcs, irrespective of timing, if the foregoing directions are carefully followed.

(700.) *The different positions of the movement.*—Much confusion is caused by different ways of naming the positions, some workmen meaning the position of the watch or movement, others that of the balance, or that of its staff. The vertical position of the staff would be the horizontal position of the balance and of the movement. In order to have a definite and invariable meaning for every term, let it be understood, once for all, that the positions always mean the positions of the watch. When "the vertical position" is spoken of, it means the hanging position of the watch. But as that does not indicate the position of the movement, the figure on the dial which is uppermost should also be specified when more than one vertical position is considered, *i.e.*, call it XII up, or III up, as the case may be. The horizontal or lying position is lying down, with the dial uppermost, and is often called dial up. The reverse horizontal position would be dial down.

(701.) When the different vertical positions are concerned, specify them by the dial figure which is uppermost, as: XII up, III up, VI up, IX up. Many workmen express it pendant up, pendant down, pendant right, pendant left, but those terms do not indicate any particular positions of the movement, for pendant up may mean XII up or III up, and pendant right may mean either XII up, III up, IX up or VI up, according to whether the dial or the plate is facing us, or whether it is a hunting case or open face watch. If the term pendant is used at all, always accompany the first use of the term "pendant up" with the dial figure which is then up, thus, "pendant (XII) up," which makes the meaning of pendant up definite; and always specify the other positions of the pendant *with the dial facing you*. But it is better to go exclusively by the dial figures, or at least to use only the term pendant up, as indicating the hanging position.

(702.) *The top of the balance.*—In expressing the position of the balance, it is supposed to be still, and free from any pressure tending to rotate it. The watch is in the hanging position. A vertical line drawn through the axis of the balance, will touch the rim at the top and bottom points. The upper point touched by that line is the top of the balance, and the upper half of the rim is the upper side of the balance. In the same way, the lower point is the bottom, and the adjacent portion of the rim is the under side of the balance.

(703.) *Measuring the vibrations.*—The mechanical position errors are discovered best by observing the exact *arc of vibration* in each trial. To know what the arc is, mark on the plate, (with whiting and oil,) just outside of the balance rim, the position of some conspicuous point or part of the rim when the balance stands freely at rest, (702.) This point may be the cut in the rim, some screw, or anything else which can be easily and clearly seen at the end of each vibration. Then make another mark exactly opposite the first one, *i.e.*, half a circle from it, and two marks just midway between them. These latter will be one-quarter of a circle, or 90°, from the former. Now make smaller marks midway between the others, and you have marks which will be one-eighth of a turn apart. When the balance vibration ends at one of these marks, its distance from the first or central mark measures one-half of the vibration. Thus, if the balance cut or screw stops opposite the third mark, that is $\frac{3}{8}$ turn from the center, and the balance is vibrating $\frac{3}{4}$ of a turn; if it stops at half the circle from the start, it is 1 turn; if it stops half-way from that mark to the next one, it is $1\frac{1}{8}$ turns, and so on.

(704.) *Detecting mechanical position faults by the arcs.*—Most of them can be detected in the ways already described, and corrected before the trials by running the watch are commenced. Those not so disposed of are detected or tested by running the watch in the different positions with the mainspring wound up an equal distance for each trial, and noting down the exact *arc of vibration* in each position. It is only necessary to continue each trial long enough for the balance to attain its normal vibration for those conditions,—two or three minutes being generally enough. The mainspring should not be wound entirely up, as there is often an extra pull on the spring just after winding, and it is better to let it back a quarter or half turn after winding, being careful to let it down the same amount each time. This precaution is not necessary with a fuzee watch. First find the extent of the arcs in the horizontal positions, dial down and dial up. If not equal, they should be made so. See 19 and 20, in section (694). The horizontal arc is the standard of comparison for the vertical arcs. The latter are then tested in the alternate positions, XII up and VI up, then III up and IX up. Each pair of opposite arcs are carefully compared, the cause of the difference studied out, and then corrected.

(705.) *Cause of the error.*—The balance may be out of poise; the balance jewel holes may not be round, not evenly polished inside, or too large for the pivot—allowing the balance to fall towards the lever, escape wheel, etc., or away from them, and interfere or change the action of the parts—or any one out of a score of other faults may cause the trouble. It must be remembered that *the arcs should be equal* in the different positions. If they are not, the change of the arcs when held in the different positions will guide us to the cause. Inasmuch as the greater the friction is, the smaller the arc will be, we know in which position to remedy the inequality of the friction, and we may also ascertain the effect of our alterations, by simply noting the change in the arcs while the motive force is the same as before. It is desirable to equalize the frictions in the different positions as nearly as possible, as it leaves less to be accomplished by isochronizing the spring, and there is a limit to the amount of irregularity which this adjustment can compensate for. Besides, the more perfect all the parts of the watch are the finer the performance which we may hope to obtain from the spring. Whenever the error seems to be a lack of poise in the balance or hair spring, let it pass for the present, as it may have been intentionally put out of poise. But if you are under orders to do a *perfect* job, correct it. After you have made all the corrections you can from the mechanical indications, and got the arcs of vibrations as nearly alike as possible in all positions, as above, the timing trials may now begin.

(706.) *Manner of testing.*—If it is not known that the isochronal adjustment is correct, we must make our trials in such a way as to eliminate isochronal errors from the result, as far as practicable. Otherwise it would be difficult or impossible to tell whether the observed variations in the rate were due to position faults or to isochronal faults in the spring. If it was known that the hair spring alone would give the same rate with different arcs—all being in one position, (665,) then any error in the different positions would evidently be due to some faults in the escapement, pivots, or other points referred to in sections (694) to (697). But inasmuch as we expect the isochronal adjustment to correct the error which remains after we have adjusted for positions as closely as we can, it is clear that we must conduct the position adjustment in such a way as to first discover the true nature and *the full extent* of all position faults, unhidden, unmodified and uncorrected by the spring, so that we can deal with them on their own merits.

(707.) *Distinction between the isochronal and positional adjustments.*—It should be remembered that the object of the positions adjustment is (1) to get the arcs equal in the different positions, and (2) to get the frictions, position faults, and disturbing influences of all kinds, as small and as nearly equal as possible in the different positions. It properly has nothing to do with correcting the rates isochronally in order to make them equal in the long and short arcs. It deals only with the rates in different *positions*, as *means* of detecting position faults, and ascertaining what effect mechanical alterations have in correcting those faults. We are not adjusting or correcting the rates, but the mechanical condition of the escapement—and are doing it exclusively by mechanical alterations. The arcs and the rates are merely our *guides* in the work.

(708.) The isochronal adjustment, on the contrary, has for its objects (1) to get the same rate in long and short arcs, and (2) to "correct" position errors, *i.e.*, to hide them by the action of the spring, which is done by producing an isochronal error just equal to, and the reverse of, the position error, which is thus balanced, and the rates made "equal or correct." Many of the methods of adjustment I have named are found in *both* adjustments, because they produce analogous or equivalent effects in both. But if those mentioned in the positional adjustment are properly carried out there, they will not be needed in the isochronal adjustment, for they will have already produced all the effect and done all the good they can, in the positions adjustment, and the isochronal adjustment will be narrowed down to mere alterations of *the spring*, for correcting the small errors which remain. That is as it should be. But I have felt compelled to specify the remedies applicable in each adjustment, from knowing that neither of them may be thoroughly done, and the remedies may be needed in either, or in both.

(709.) *The trials by timing in positions.*—Having first tested the position faults by observation of the *arcs* in different positions, and corrected them, so far as we could, *as mechanical faults*, we must now test the condition of the escapement by *timing* it in different positions, and be guided by the errors in the *rates*. If the previous mechanical trials have been thoroughly made, (704, 705,) there will probably be little left for the timing trials to accomplish. But in order to cover all contingencies, I will describe the latter as fully as if they were the only ones. We first make position trials as directed in section (711), and then poise trials as in section (713,) and compare the rates so obtained as described in section (714). This comparison of results will clearly indicate what the trouble is, and enable us to correct it with certainty. It is only necessary to point out here that when the pivots are not round, the arc and the rate will be the *same* in the *opposite* positions, but when the errors are faults of poise or escapement defects, the arcs and rates will both be *different* in the *opposite* positions. I have described the adjustment by extent of arcs and that by the rates separately, in order to make the principles clear, but in practice both the arcs and the rates can often be observed at the same time and in the same trials.

(710.) *The best arc of vibration.*—It is known that when the arc is $1\frac{1}{4}$ turns, the watch is least affected by errors in the poise of the balance, etc., (also, least affected by magnetism,) and the trials designed to discover the position errors, separate from the poise errors, should therefore be made with arcs of $1\frac{1}{4}$ turns. The poise trials, on the contrary, should be made with arcs as far from $1\frac{1}{4}$ turns as convenient to obtain, in order that the errors of poise may produce their full effect in the rate. It is evident that the best arc for running pocket watches would be $1\frac{1}{4}$ turns, or in the case of going-barrel watches, in which the arcs differ when the mainspring is wound up or run down, they might vary from $1\frac{1}{2}$ turns down to 1 turn, the average being $1\frac{1}{4}$ turns. They will thus be most free from position errors. In *testing* such watches, however, the arcs must be caused to *differ* considerably from $1\frac{1}{4}$ turns, because the rate might be very fair with that arc, even when the poise was greatly at fault, and would yet cause serious errors when running with arcs which were smaller.

(711.) *The timing trials for position errors.*—Having the rate with pendant up as a standard, you time the watch in the 4 vertical positions, for 6 hours each, with the motive force the same in each trial, and such that the arcs will be as near $1\frac{1}{4}$ turns as possible. You thus get the position errors, nearly free from errors of poise or isochronism. A loss in any position, as compared with the opposite vertical position, indicates greater resistances or frictions in the former. The cause is to be sought by the indications known to be given by different faults, as fully described in the preceding Chapter.

(712.) *Meaning of loss and gain.*—The term loss or gain is a relative one. There may be a gain in both positions, as compared with the regulator, but the one which gains the most is said to gain on the other. Or there may be a loss in both, but the one which loses the most is said to lose on the other, or we may reverse it, and say that the latter gains on the former. If one loses and the other gains, as compared with the regulator, the difference is the *sum* of both errors, and that is the amount by which one gains or loses on the other.

(713.) *Timing trials for errors of poise.*—Make another set of

4 trials, similarly to the above, but with a very different arc—preferably about ¾ turn, but with the *same motive force in each trial*. This fully develops the effects of lack of poise in the different positions, but is still nearly independent of isochronal errors, owing to all the trials being made with nearly the same arc. In comparing results, say, with XII up and VI up, (or with the two other opposite positions,) if there is a gain with XII up, as compared with VI up, it indicates that the top of the balance is heavier than the bottom in the latter position, *i.e.*, supposing the balance to be brought to rest, with VI up, the heavy side of the balance is at the top. The rule is that when there is a loss in a certain vertical position, (as compared with the opposite vertical position,) the top of the balance is heavier than the bottom, *i.e.*, provided the error is caused by lack of poise. This rule is only for arcs of less than $1\frac{1}{4}$ turns; over that, the error is the reverse of that stated.

(714.) *Comparing position and poise errors of rate.*—It is now in order to study out the causes of the errors of rate and correct them. If the position errors observed in the first set of trials, in any two opposite positions, are found to be increased in one position and also reduced in the other, in the second set, it may be inferred that in the latter trials poise errors were added to the position errors, and it will be well to test the poise, according to the rule in the preceding section, *i.e.*, in the position where the loss was increased the top of the balance would be heavier than the bottom, if the trouble is in the poise. But if the second trials do not show any such opposite effects in opposite positions, as described, when compared with the first set, the change may be due to other causes than the poise, which act differently with different arcs, and they should be sought out, by the indications in Chapter XXXVII, and corrected as far as may be. It should be remembered that while the effects produced by imperfect poise are reversed in the two opposite positions and neutralized or absent in the two transverse positions, the errors caused by escapement frictions are very similarly disposed, but those due to pivots or holes not round are *alike* in the two opposite positions and reversed in the transverse positions. As it is easy to test the poise mechanically, as well as the roundness of the holes and their alignment, it should not be difficult to locate the fault, which should be at once corrected.

(715.) *Cause of errors.*—To detect the cause of the variations between the different vertical positions, we also have the following indications, supposing the balance to be properly poised.

As a general rule any increase of friction in the *escapement* tends to retard the short arcs more than the long ones. If the trouble is in the escapement it will be detected by moving the roller or rollers of the lever or chronometer around on the balance staff, putting in beat and trying, when the errors will take place in the same positions with reference to the roller as before, irrespective of the position of the balance. But if they occur in the same positions with reference to *the balance* as before, then, if the balance is in poise, the pivots are not round, and their revolution causes them to alternately raise the balance and let it down, according as the greatest width of the pivot is horizontally or vertically across the jewel hole. Sometimes moving the rollers half-way around on the staff will neutralize the errors, if they are not too great. But pivots being sensibly out of round is a very serious fault and ought to be corrected. The amount of position error that the isochronism can cover is very limited, and it should be called upon to hide only those position errors which it is found impossible to remove by mechanical corrections and adjustments. I will therefore give the mechanical methods of correcting them.

(716.) *Equalizing the horizontal and vertical positions.*—We can equalize the arcs and the rates in the horizontal and the vertical positions by increasing the frictions in the horizontal positions, as described in Chapter XXXVII. Also, see the section (722) on setting the hair spring out of center, or changing the length of the hair spring or replacing it with a spring of the same strength but shorter. See section (697,) No. 5. That will only leave the different vertical positions to be equalized. But such changes are not advisable unless the error is large.

(717.) *Equalizing the vertical positions.*—For doing this, we have the following possible courses: changing the poise of the balance, setting the hair spring excentrically. Neither of these methods should be adopted unless the error is too large to be otherwise corrected, as it is very important to have the rate *the same* in the different vertical positions. The other courses open to us should have already been carried out before this, if such changes were necessary.

(718.) *Rules for changing the poise.*—The balance may be in perfect poise, but it can be put out of poise to cause a gain or loss in a certain position of the watch. If the watch gains in one vertical position as compared with the opposite—supposing them to be XII up and VI up,—a small amount of metal is removed from the bottom of the balance, (*i.e.*, the bottom when at rest with XII up,) thus making the top heavier, and causing a falling back or loss in the former position. On the other hand, if the gain occurs with VI up, the metal is removed from that part of the rim which is at the bottom when at rest with the VI up, and causes a slight loss of rate in that position. Care must be taken not to remove too much. In screw balances, turning the screws in corresponds to removing metal, as it makes that side virtually lighter. The same effect is produced by turning the screws out on the opposite side, as making one side heavier is equivalent to making the other side lighter. But the screws should be turned in on one side the same distance as they are turned out on the other, else the rate will be affected.

(719.) *Changing the poise of a compensation balance.*—The screws of a compensation balance must not be changed, except the timing screws, and they must be moved equally, as just observed. In the case supposed above, when the watch gained with XII up, the balance is brought to a free rest, and the timing screw which is then nearest to the XII, *i.e.*, at the top, is drawn out and the opposite screw turned in, thus virtually making the balance heavier on the former side and lighter on the latter, at the same time, without affecting the rate. If there was a gain in two vertical positions, as with XII up and III up, the timing screws nearest to the XII and III are drawn out and those nearest to VI and IX turned in equally. The rule is, when the balance is at rest, turn out the screw nearest the fast position and turn in that nearest the slow position. By fast position is meant the position in which the watch gained the most; the slow position is that in which it either lost, or did not gain so much, compared with the opposite vertical position.

(720.) *When useless.*—This change of poise is not adapted for watches which at one time vibrate over $1\frac{1}{4}$ turns and afterwards fall off and become less than that, but only for those whose arcs are always more, or always less, than $1\frac{1}{4}$ turns. At and near $1\frac{1}{4}$ turns, this change produces little or no effect.

(721.) *Timing in reverse.*—Above $1\frac{1}{4}$ turns the effect is the *reverse* of that above described, consequently, if the poise was changed to correct a certain error, the change would be inoperative at $1\frac{1}{4}$ turns, and would make the error worse when the arc was over $1\frac{1}{4}$ turns. When the timepiece always vibrates over $1\frac{1}{4}$ turns, the poise is sometimes altered to secure a loss or gain in certain positions, and in such cases the directions already given *are reversed*. Such procedure is known as "timing in reverse."

(722.) *Rules for setting the spring excentric.*—When there is a loss in one vertical position, say, XII up, as compared with the opposite position, the spring is so bent in the outer coil as to carry the center towards the XII. It of course cannot actually move in that direction, but it exerts a pressure and forces the pivots against the sides of the jewel holes, thus lessening the pivot frictions when XII is up, and of course increasing them when VI is up. It tends to lift the balance in the former position, and presses it down in the latter, adding to the friction as if the balance was heavier. It is evident that this could be caused to change the frictions similarly in two adjacent positions. If the watch loses both with XII up and III up, the spring can be set towards the point midway between XII and III on the dial, and it will quicken the vibrations in both the positions stated, but not so much as if it was bent directly towards one of them, because the effect is indirect and divided between them. This procedure not only changes the relative amounts of the frictions in the vertical positions, but it also increases the frictions in the two horizontal positions, and causes a falling off in the arcs and a loss in the rates in those positions—an effect which should be borne in mind when making such changes.

(723.) *Disadvantages of this method of adjusting for positions.*—It must also be remembered that setting the spring out of center, if carried too far, will injure the isochronism, and damage the watch in all positions, for the sake of a little apparent improvement in one or two. Besides, the effect is not great, and can correct only slight errors. In some cases it does not appear to correct the error at all, but it probably is just able to neutralize some error, which would otherwise show itself in the rate. Whenever the effect of this procedure is to injure the isochronism, it must be abandoned, and the spring either restored to concentric position or sufficiently so to avoid disturbing the isochronism. In pocket watches which are carried so loosely that they take all positions in the pocket, neither this method nor the change of poise is of any advantage, and may even be a disadvantage. Watches which are treated by either method should be worn in a closely fitting pocket, with the chain drawing upon the pendant, to maintain it in that position.

(724.) *Equalizing the vertical and horizontal positions by the length of the hair-spring,* as mentioned in section (716, 697, Nos. 4 and 5,) comes properly under the head of isochronal adjustment, and will be found fully treated there. If that adjustment has been accurately made, there will be no need of doing it as a part of the adjustment for positions. But if the vertical positions are excessively slow, and no other method seems open for trial, the spring can be shortened up, or a shorter spring of the same strength substituted.

(725.) *Choice of methods.*—In making the mechanical adjustments, the only course is obviously to correct the faults, whatever they may be; but in subsequently equalizing the arcs or correcting by the errors of rate, we have a choice of methods. As a general rule, the more usual methods are preferable in the following order:—

(726.) For equalizing the horizontal and vertical positions, making the ends of the pivots flat or sloping, to increase the horizontal frictions, or round to lessen them; or making the pivots smaller or the jewels thinner, or better polished, to lessen the vertical frictions. If the jewel holes are too long, instead of making the cup deeper or chamfering out the ends of the holes, make an extra cup on the back side, next to the endstone. To equalize the horizontal and the pendant-up positions, bend the spring towards the pendant.

(727.) *For equalizing the different vertical positions.*—If the watch is in good condition, there should be little or no difference between them. Look for pivots or holes out of round or out of alignment; loose pivots causing difference in the action of the escapement; change of poise, when it is applicable, (720); setting the hair spring excentric; turning the roller and other parts on the balance staff (715); etc.

(728.) *Necessity of equalizing the frictions in different positions.*— It must be repeated that the isochronal adjustment, which is usually depended on to counterbalance the errors arising from position faults, is able to do so only to a very limited extent; consequently, if the position errors are so great that the isochronal spring is barely able to correct them, or perhaps cannot correct them fully, it will not be able to provide for excessively large arcs of vibration, such as are constantly caused by carrying, shaking, etc., nor even for the additional differences due to variations in the motive force when the spring is more or less wound up. The watch will then run as if the spring was not isochronous, when it is really doing all that such a spring can do. The trouble is not with the spring, but with the excessive position faults. This will show the necessity of following the suggestion before made, that the position faults should be treated as mechanical defects, and corrected as such, as thoroughly as possible, by equalizing the arcs and the rates in the different positions, before calling on the isochronal adjustments to finish the work.

(729.) *Finishing the adjustment.*—When we have done that, (728,) the adjustment for positions is finished, for that adjustment properly includes nothing more, as I have already explained, (707, 708,) and any further alterations belong to the isochronal adjustment. I am perfectly well aware that it is customary to alter the isochronal action of the hair spring to correct for the remaining errors of rate, and to call that "adjusting for positions," but it is not so. It is adjusting for isochronism to hide position errors which the positional adjustment has failed to remove. Although it is no part of the positional adjustment, I will describe the method usually followed, so that the reader may have both the old and new ways before him.

(730.) *Correcting the remaining errors.*—The trials are conducted in the same way as trials of the isochronism, *i.e.*, by comparison of rates in long and short arcs, the mainspring (in a going-barrel watch) being wound up the same distance, to get the motive force the same in each trial. And in order that they may apply to position errors, the rates in the horizontal positions are supposed to represent the long arcs, and those in the vertical positions correspond to the short arcs. The trials are made in two opposite vertical positions for the short arcs, for 12 hours each, and their variations added together. This rate for the short arcs is compared with the rate in the long arcs for 24 hours, making the times equal. If the two rates are the same, for long and short arcs, the spring is said to be isochronous; if the rates were also the same in the two vertical positions, the watch is also adjusted for those positions; but if those rates differ, there is still a position error. The other two opposite positions are tested in the same way. If the position errors are small, the watch is already practically adjusted for positions. But supposing that they are still large, what shall we do? The isochronal adjustment is absolutely useless in such a case. As stated in section (661,) it can only be adjusted for two positions. at the most. Whether we like it or not, we shall be compelled to return to the positional adjustment for their correction, or else leave them uncorrected. Those who confound the two adjustments by such methods as the above are therefore taking a short cut to perform both of them at once—and slighting both. The better way would be to adjust for positions as perfectly as possible, then turn back to sections (669, 675, 679,) and adjust the isochronism properly to correct for the remaining position errors.

Before leaving this subject, I would say that the custom

among experts, and even those who consider themselves first-class, is first to get a large vibration in the two horizontal positions, equalizing the two rates by rounding the ends of the balance pivots; secondly, make the rate in the hanging positions equal to that in the horizontal by altering the poise of the balance (718); thirdly, make the rates in the two transverse quarters like the others by setting the hair spring excentrically (722) as required. In this way they get the watch adjusted "for all positions." This may do for practical jobbing, when the pay is small, but I think the reader will agree with me that putting balances out of poise and hair springs out of center does not deserve to be called first-class work unless the mechanical faults have previously been removed as completely as they can be. In that case, such alterations are excusable, because nothing else can be done. With strictly first-class watches for example, that method of adjusting would give the best practicable results.

(731.) *Testing stock watches.*—The foregoing directions are for *adjusting* watches and chronometers. For merely *testing* stock watches, a much simpler procedure will suffice. The watch should have a good free motion when half wound up, and, to the eye, the motion should be the same in all positions. To test it by timing, set it exactly with the regulator, and run it for 6 hours in each position, with the mainspring wound the same in each trial. The first trial is with pendant up, and the time in that position is the rate of the watch, and the standard of comparison for the other positions. Then test with pendant down, dial up, and dial down. In any of these positions it should not differ more than 3 seconds from the rate, (pendant up,) or it must be considered not closely adjusted. If it is a really fine movement, it can also be tested in the other two vertical positions, and should not vary from the rate more than 5 seconds per day in any one of the positions tested. Ordinary watches are adjusted for only two positions, pendant up and dial up. Better ones are also adjusted for the two transverse quarters, that is, if pendant up is XII up, the transverse positions or "quarters" would be III up and IX up; if the hanging position is III up, the quarters would be XII up and VI up.

(732.) *Example of position-timing adjustment.*—A watch which gains 12 seconds in 24 hours, hanging, *i.e.*, pendant (XII) up, is tried in the horizontal positions, and gains 4 seconds in 12 hours, dial up, and 2 seconds in 12 hours, dial down. It is then tried for 12 hours, fully wound, in the other three vertical positions, or "quarters." With VI up, it gains 6 seconds; with

III up, it gains 8 seconds; with IX up, it gains 2 seconds. As the watch gained the same amount in the hanging position and the two horizontal positions, $(4'' + 2'' = 6'',)$ it is said to be isochronous.

(733.) But dial up gains on dial down, and the end of the balance pivot is flattened a trifle in the former position to nearly equalize them. The rate with XII up and VI up is the same (for the same length of time, 12 hours,) but there is a position error in the other two quarters, and we draw out the timing screws nearest to III, to make the gain less with III up and greater with IX up, and the gain is then 5 seconds in each position. This is both easier and better than bending the spring. The mean-time screws are then drawn out, reducing the rate to $+ 3$ seconds in 24 hours, and the position errors vary from $- 1$ second to $+ 2$ seconds daily, in the different positions. All of the trials are made at 60° Fahrenheit, with the watch fully wound at the beginning of each trial. It will be noticed that the timing adjustment is short and easy, which is owing to the fact that the watch had previously been through a rigorous *mechanical adjustment*, as already recommended, and was in first-rate mechanical condition, with the arcs equalized, and therefore required only a few finishing touches.

(734.) *Explanations of positions record.*—By reference to the explanations of the isochronism record, (689,) this one will be readily understood. The "hours" refers to the length of the trial. No separation is made between the hours and the error of rate, as the $+$ or $-$ mark between them is sufficient. A space is left at the head of the column before the word "up," for the insertion of the dial figure which is up, at the place where the dots are. The amount of winding and the extent of the vibration are important items, and should be noted. If *all* the position trials are made with *the same* amount of winding and the same arc, they can all be entered on the same line, as shown. But if different, only the trial or position in which that winding or arc was used should be entered on the line with it. If the arc or motive force was varied by the controller, state the fact in the last column—also, any other point of importance.

THE WATCH ADJUSTER'S MANUAL.

(735.) POSITIONS RECORD.

(Name of owner, description and number of the watch, etc.)

Date of Alteration 1894.	Hours.	Pendant up.	Hours.	Pendant down.	Hours.	Dial up.	Hours.	Dial down.	Hours.	up.	Hours.	up.	Wound.	Arc of Vibration.	Circumstances, Alterations made, Remarks, etc.
Feb'y 2	24+1'15" 12+1'11"		12+1'19" 6+1'2"		24+1'40"		12+1'12"		12—44"		12—1'21"		Up. 1t.	680°	

PART EIGHTH.

THE ADJUSTMENT FOR HEAT AND COLD.

CHAPTER XXXIX.

COMPENSATION.

(736.) *Adjustment to temperatures.*—The compensation for heat and cold completes the list of adjustments which are found in the modern fine portable timepiece. It may be accurately adjusted to positions and isochronism, and yet be utterly untrustworthy for time. Every change in the weather, or other circumstance, however trivial or unavoidable, which warms or cools the movement, will produce an error in the rate, which may vary from a few seconds to as many minutes in a single day.

(737.) *Methods of compensating.*—The first attempts to remedy these errors were by contrivances acting upon the hair spring—an example of which is the "parachute regulator," often seen in old escapement or anker watches, which opens or closes the pins of the regulator by means of a compensating quadrant, as the temperature changes. It would be very interesting to examine the various methods of compensating for the effects of heat and cold which have been proposed at different times, and trace the progress of invention from the first crude ideas through successive discoveries and improvements, but the practical character of this book forbids. At the present day the means almost universally employed for that purpose are embodied in what is generally known as the expansion or chronometer balance, more correctly termed the compensation balance of ordinary construction.

(738.) *The compensation balance of ordinary construction* consists of a center-bar, upon the ends of which the rim is supported. The rim is made of two different metals or alloys, one of which expands and contracts more than the other when exposed to changes of temperature. The two metals which are generally employed are steel and brass. (Balances of other materials are described in Chapter IX.) The brass expands and contracts much more than the steel, and it is by means of this difference that the rim "compensates." When the balance is exposed to heat it expands and the watch would consequently run slower. But this is counteracted by the action of the rim, which, from the brass being outside and expanding more than the steel, curves the free end of the rim inward, and carries the weight or screws upon it towards the center of the balance. In cold the whole balance contracts, and, from being smaller, would vibrate more rapidly, but the brass exterior contracting more than the steel, tends to straighten the rim and carry its screws outward, thus neutralizing the effects of the cold. As has been explained in Chapter X, the virtual size of the balance is governed by the distance of the center of its weight from the axis, and the object of the compensation is to keep that distance at the proper point in all temperatures.

(739.) *What is compensated for.*—Change of temperature affects the time kept by a watch or chronometer in different ways:— 1st. Heat expands the balance, making it, for the time being, of larger diameter, and causing it to vibrate more slowly. 2d. It expands the hair-spring, making it stronger but at the same time diminishes its elastic force to a still greater degree, and thus causes a loss of time. 3d. It acts upon the mainspring in a similar way, greatly weakening the motive force. 4th. It affects the fluidity of the oil, affecting the balance vibrations and the quickness of action of the escapement. 5th. It affects the action of pivots in their holes, and all similar parts, when they are closely fitted. The opposite of the effects above noted takes place in cold. We will consider each of the actions separately.

(740.) *Action of heat on the balance.*—It is popularly supposed that the object of compensation is to neutralize the effect produced by the expansion of the balance. But that effect is only about one-sixth of the total effect produced by the heat upon the watch. A plain balance, when exposed to a rise of 60° Fahr., will cause a loss, by its expansion, of about 60 seconds in 24 hours, while the total loss by the action of heat upon the watch will be from 385 to 393 seconds per day, so that from 325 to 333 seconds per day must be attributed to other causes than the expansion of the balance. If the latter was all we had to compensate for, the compensation would be comparatively easy.

(741.) *Action of heat on the hair spring.*—The expansion of a spring by heat of course increases all of its dimensions, *i.e.*, its length, breadth and thickness, by an equal percentage. The increase in length makes the spring weaker, but the increase in width and thickness makes it stronger. If we represent its length by l, its breadth by b, and its thickness by t, the formula for calculating the strength of a spring (S) from its dimensions is $S=\dfrac{bt^3}{l}$. If we could suppose that the heat doubled its length, and the other dimensions in the same proportion, the increase in width would double its strength, but the increase in length would reduce it one-half, so that the effects of the two would be just equal, and leave the strength as it was at first. The increase in thickness would make it $2 \times 2 \times 2 = 8$ times as strong as at first, and the watch should go so much faster. The fact that it actually loses, however, shows that there is some very potent weakening influence at work, to cause a loss of over six minutes per day, instead of the gain we should naturally expect.

(742.) *Action of heat on the elastic force of the spring.*—That influence is generally supposed to be the loss of elastic force caused by heat; and to it is attributed the loss of six minutes per day, in place of a gain. Such a belief is clearly a mistaken one. No doubt, heat does lessen the elastic force, and cause a large portion of that loss, but it does not cause the whole of it, for the other effects of heat mentioned in section (739) are included in the total loss. But this effect upon the spring is much greater than that upon the balance, and the compensation is therefore needed for the correction of the errors of the spring, much more than for those of the balance. It is found that the variation in the force of the spring almost exactly follows the changes of temperature, *i.e.*, the elastic force of the spring varies inversely with the temperature, becoming greater as the temperature becomes lower, and less as the temperature rises.

(743.) *Better material than steel needed.*—As most of the errors in different temperatures are caused by the action of steel in heat, the remedy should be sought in some other material, whose elastic force is not affected so much by heat. Glass springs have been found to be much less affected. DENT experimented with springs of different materials, his chronometers having balances made of glass, and which were therefore not compensated. One of them, with a steel spring, lost 6 minutes and 25 seconds in a day for a rise of 68° Fahr., while another with a glass spring lost only 40 seconds. As steel only expands about 25 per cent more than glass, the different effect must be due to the fact that the elastic force of the glass spring is less affected by heat than that of steel. Glass is not suitable for hair springs, but some other metal or alloy may perhaps be found which would be nearly as insensitive to heat as glass, or, at least, much less so than steel. The compensation could then be easily made almost perfect. Palladium springs are less affected than steel, but they do not compare with glass in that respect. Gold springs are affected more than steel.

(744.) *Action of heat on the mainspring.*—As heat causes a loss of elastic force in steel springs, (and perhaps in those of all other materials,) it must necessarily weaken the mainspring, also. This effect I have not seen mentioned before, but as the loss is so enormous in the hair spring, it must be correspondingly important in the mainspring, causing a serious diminution in the motive force, smaller arcs of vibration, with the attendant errors of rate unless the hair spring is isochronal, and also less ability to overcome imperfections in the train, dirt, etc. Whatever the loss may be, it forms a part of the error which the compensation is expected to provide for.

(745.) *Action of heat upon the oil.*—The action of heat can hardly be said to be detrimental, unless it is sufficient to damage the oil, or make it so fluid that it runs from the pivots, etc., or permanently change its consistency by evaporating or drying it up. But the effect of lowering the temperature is well known. By thickening the oil, it causes a clogging or retarding action upon the vibrations; makes the escapement more sluggish, slower in starting and throughout the action; the oil is more sticky and adhesive, catches the dirt more easily, and retards all rubbing surfaces; and whenever the fitting is very close, in either side-shake or end-shake, very seriously affects the motion of the moving parts. When the balance pivots are closely fitted, the effect of low temperature upon the running must be considerable, and that has to be covered by the compensation.

(746.) *Action of heat upon closely fitted pivots, etc.*—As steel expands much more than the jewels employed for holes, a closely fitted pivot could easily expand so much as to become almost bound in the jewel hole. Other closely fitted parts can become too close in the same way, especially if oiled with a rather thick lubricator. On the other hand, if the pivot or bearing runs in a brass hole, cold could contract the brass around it sufficiently to cause binding. The same thing can occur when the endshake of an arbor or staff is very close. The holes being held by cocks or other parts of brass, which contracts in cold more than the steel, they are drawn together upon the shoulders or pivots, or too close for freedom. There is no doubt that the running is seriously affected by this fault in many watches, and that, also, must be covered by the compensation.

(747.) *What is compensation?*—Having our balance in the watch and running, let us consider what it should do. We have already seen that in heat the greater expansion of the brass exterior of the rim will curl the segments inwards, and carry the screws or weights towards the center. In cold the greater contraction of the brass carries the weight outwards, and thus compensates for the contraction of the entire balance, which would otherwise cause a gain in time. Obviously, the weight should be carried inward in heat, and outward in cold, just enough to make up for the expansion or contraction of the balance, the effects of heat or cold on the hair-spring, and all other changes resulting from the change of temperature. When this is accomplished, the compensation is correct, and the watch is said to be compensated or adjusted for heat and cold. Whether it does so or not can only be told by actually trying it in heat and cold. Even when marked "adjusted," balances seldom can be safely guaranteed to be closely compensated, till they have been tested and their actual performance ascertained. The custom with most manufacturers is to test them, and those which perform with tolerable accuracy are marked "adjusted," while the rest are sold as unadjusted. Watchmakers who have many customers for fine watches can frequently make it profitable to buy these unadjusted movements, and adjust them themselves, thereby raising them to the value of the adjusted movements of the same class. The process is somewhat tedious and troublesome, but this is largely compensated for by the number which may be under way at the same time, with but little more trouble and expense than one would be, and the experience gained is of great value to any watchmaker who aspires to do fine work.

(748.) *Over-compensation.*—Instead of the weights or screws on the rim being moved inward and outward just enough to compensate for heat and cold, they may be moved too far, or not far enough. In the former case, the watch is said to be "over-compensated." It will gain in heat, because the weights are carried too near the center, thus making the balance virtually smaller; in cold, the weights will be carried too far outwards, and cause a loss of time. The segments act too strongly, but as we cannot change their action, we must find some means to lessen its effects. It would not do to lessen the weights, as that would cause a gain in time by making the balance lighter. But we can move the weight or screws back from the cut ends of the segments towards the center-bar. The motion of the segments inward and outward being greatest at their free ends, the further back we place the screws, the less they will be moved. So that we can regulate the effect produced to almost any degree. For it is evident that if the weights were placed just at the ends of the center-bar, there would be no compensation at all, except that produced by the weight of the segments themselves. And we have the entire length of the segments as a range for the weights, according to the effect we desire. Sometimes the action of the segments is so strong that they compensate too much, even when the screws are all moved back as far as they can be. In such case, we must substitute lighter screws in place of those nearest to the ends of the segments, and correspondingly increase the weight of those next to the center-bar.

(749.) *Under-compensation.*—On the other hand, if the watch loses in heat and gains in cold, the weights are not carried far enough to produce the required effect, and it is said to be "under-compensated." The remedy for this is the opposite of that for over-compensation, viz: to move the weights or screws nearer to the ends of the segments, and increase the effect produced by their motion. In making these changes, the screws must, of course, be moved in pairs, to prevent destroying the poise of the balance. Take out one of the screws, and change to another hole, nearer the end, if we wish to strengthen the compensation, or further from the end, if we desire to weaken it. Then move the screw which is exactly opposite to it, in the same way. We frequently need to move several pairs, and not merely one hole, but perhaps change their position by several holes, according to the indications of the trials. If the compensating action is so weak that even massing the screws at the ends of the segments does not produce sufficient effect, we can substitute heavier screws for those nearest the ends, and lighter ones for those further back,—as, for instance, screws of gold or platinum for those of brass or aluminum; and the reverse may be done for over-compensation. But in making these changes, the total weight of the balance must be kept the same, otherwise the rate will be altered.

(750.) When a balance is properly compensated, the adjustment is not altered by changing the hair spring, or changing its length in bringing it to time, although it may be considerably longer or shorter than before, or than the old one was. The explanation of this lies in the fact that the heat or cold affects the spring in the same proportion, or percentage, whatever its length may be. For instance, if we suppose that the heat is sufficient to expand a spring one-fiftieth in length, it does not matter what the real length may be. One spring may be twice as long as another; then the increase of length in the former will be twice the amount of that in the latter,—but both will be *increased by one-fiftieth.* So if the cold increases the effective strength of a spring ten per cent., the precise strength of the spring is immaterial. We are now only concerned with the proportion or ratio by which its strength is changed, and having compensated our balance to cover that progressive increase or decrease of strength found at the temperatures for which it is adjusted, the compensation will be correct for any other hair spring having that progression, *i.e.*, having about the same form, nature and temper. But if a soft spring be substituted for one hardened and tempered, or the reverse, or its temper considerably changed, then the progression will be altered, and the compensation would require a readjustment to suit the changed conditions. For it must be remembered that the rate depends upon the absolute quantity of effective force in the spring, but the compensation is affected only by the ratio of its increase or decrease under the influence of different temperatures. Such a spring can easily be fire-hardened and tempered, as described in section (263), and so avoid such trouble.

CHAPTER XL.

Apparatus for Adjusting the Compensation.

(751.) In adjusting the compensation for heat and cold, we need an apparatus for obtaining an elevated temperature which may be of any degree required and may be maintained nearly constant for a considerable time; and another for producing cold in the same way. The former is called the adjusting-oven, the latter the cold-box. Many different constructions are in use, and some of them are described herein. When only an occasional watch is to be tested or adjusted, any simple and inexpensive means available may be adopted for producing heat or cold; care only being taken that the heat never exceeds 120°, which is as high as can be employed without danger of injuring the oil, or perhaps the movement. The movement must also be so inclosed as to be protected from dust or moisture, as, by a closely fitted movement box, with the glasses set in wax. And when great accuracy is required and the tests are short, it should be remembered that the duration of the trials must be computed as beginning *after* the movement has become thoroughly heated or cooled to the proper temperature in every part, which may take from half an hour to an hour. By this means, the times of exposure to the proper degrees of heat and cold will be alike. But if it is set and then put into the oven or cold-box, unless they were so constructed as to occupy the same length of time in attaining the required temperature in each case, the times during which it would actually be affected by the proper degree of heat or cold would be different, and cause an apparent error even when the compensation was correct.

(752.) *For testing in heat*, some watchmakers put the movement in a tight tin box, which they bury in a vessel of sand which has been heated on a stove, in the oven, or in any other convenient way, and its temperature is kept as uniform as possible by frequent examination of a thermometer also immersed in the sand. Others use a cubical box of tin, zinc, or copper, which is divided into four or five air-tight compartments by means of horizontal metal partitions inside. The upper compartment should be large enough to take in a thermometer with the watches to be tested, and then tightly closed. It is well to have a double glass window in the door in the top, so that the thermometer can be watched without opening the chamber. Heat slowly by means of a small alcohol lamp underneath, till the thermometer shows the proper temperature, where it should be kept, either by reducing the size of the flame or moving it further from the bottom of the box, or else by alternately removing and replacing the lamp as needed. It is well to have a wood or pasteboard casing to set over the box, leaving the bottom exposed, to prevent loss of heat by radiation, and preserve a more uniform temperature.

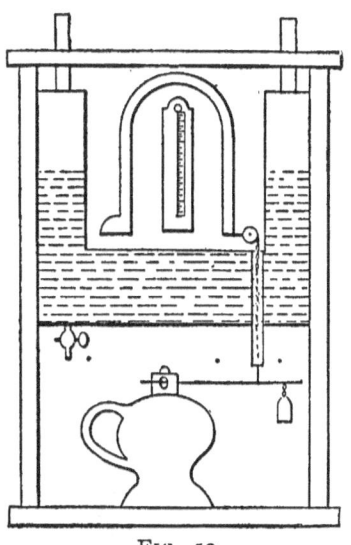

FIG. 52.

(753.) *Adjusting-oven.*—A very complete apparatus, and one not expensive, can be made as shown in Fig. 52. This consists of a reservoir containing water, made of zinc or copper, the bottom portion about eight inches front, by six back, and two deep, with two side branches four or five inches high and about one inch deep. The bottom and branches extend from front to back inside the casing. These branches are closed over at the top, and have each a short pipe extending to the outside of the casing, for use both in putting in water, and allowing the safe escape of the vapor arising from the heated liquid. These tubes should ordinarily be stopped with a loose plug of paper or cotton, to prevent evaporation. Every joint of this reservoir must be securely soldered up, so that no moisture or vapor can enter the chamber containing the movements. The water should not fill it quite to the bottom of the pipes. One or two glass shelves, for receiving the watches, are supported by wires or cleats soldered on the sides of the branches, and at such a height as to bring them about midway up the sides of the branches, and leave unobscured the scale of the thermometer fastened at the back of the chamber, or on the inside of the door. It will be observed that the front, back and top of this chamber are formed by the wood casing, leaving the reservoir containing heated water only below and at the sides of the movements. Experience has shown that the temperature is more even when arranged in this way than when the source of heat *surrounds* the watches.

(754.) The casing should be either of thick wood, or made double, with an air chamber between the walls, which is preferable but not indispensable. Pine, whitewood, or any soft wood will answer. Not only should the door fit the front of the case tightly, (or be packed with tailors' listing,) but the bottom of the reservoir should fit snugly both to the box and the door, to prevent the fumes from the lamp beneath entering the chamber. Two doors can be used, one reaching up to the bottom of the watch chamber, the other opening into the chamber and reaching to the top of the box. In the upper door and the top of the casing, double glass windows are inserted to allow of observing the movements and the thermometer without opening the door. One glass should be fastened to the outside of the wall, the other to the inside, making a tight, non-conducting air-chamber between them.

(755.) *Automatic heat regulator.*—A compound bar of steel and brass, fastened by one end to the back of the chamber, regulates the heat by the motion of its free end, which curves and straightens similarly to the compensating segments of the balance. The brass is double the thickness of the steel, which may be a piece of clock spring, while the former is any hard or springy brass, the two being soft-soldered together in the form of a common magnet, with the brass outside. To one end is riveted or soldered a flat piece for screwing it in position. When finished, this bar should be well washed and cleaned from the soldering fluid, (212.) To the free end is attached a cord which passes over a grooved pulley and through a small hole to the outside of the casing, thence to the valve which regulates the supply of gas to the burner. When oil or alcohol is used, the cord passes down inside the casing, through a tube which passes through the bottom portion of the reservoir, to the wheel which turns the wick of the burner. This tube is soldered in both the upper and lower sheet of the reservoir perfectly water-tight, and should extend down a little lower than the row of holes provided for the exit of the heated air from the lamp chamber, so that the fumes will not rise through it into the movement chamber. For this reason the tube should be of small diameter.

(756.) The gas valve, or wick turner of the lamp, is turned by means of a lever attached to it, having a weight near the end heavy enough to pull it down. This lever is supported by the cord, which is tied to it, and it is only when the motion of the compound bar allows the cord to yield that the lever can drop and shut off the gas, or reduce the flame of the lamp, more or less, according to the motion of the bar. When the temperature falls, the bar contracts, draws up the cord and lever, turns on the gas, or enlarges the flame, and an increased temperature in the reservoir results. The cord is attached to the lever at such a distance from its pivot or center of motion that the movement of the bar will give sufficient motion to the lever. For instance, if the free end of the bar moves half an inch for the increase of temperature from the mean to 95°, or any other degree chosen for the heat-extreme, then the cord should be attached to the lever at a point where that half-inch of motion will turn the valve or wick down enough to just maintain the desired temperature, and no more. This can be told by a little trial, moving the lamp to suit the changes of the cord. If preferred, the temperature can first be raised to the right degree in the chamber, then turn down the wick or valve to about the proper amount, as above mentioned, attach the lever to the valve in a horizontal position and connect the cord. Then any increase or decrease of temperature from that degree will cause the lever to be moved in the proper direction to correct it. The gas valve, or wick turner, should be made to operate very easily, and the lever made with a sort of spring clamp to slip on the thumb-piece of the valve, or the wheel of the burner, and hold itself tightly in place. In the case of a gas cock, the lever might be permanently fitted to it, if desired; but with a lamp it could not, because there is no certainty in the position of the thumb-wheel. Every trimming or alteration of the wick will change the position of the wheel, and the lever must be capable of being slipped on after the right position is found.

(757.) Air holes are made in the lamp chamber, through the casing, in two rows. The upper row should be an inch or so below the bottom of the reservoir, in order to retain the most highly heated portion of the air in the chamber, in contact with the reservoir,—only allowing it to escape after it has yielded up some portion of its heat and fallen to the level of the holes. Another row of holes for entrance of air is made near the bottom of the casing. Three or four half-inch holes are generally enough for each row, and all should be made on the same side, or on adjacent sides, to prevent wind blowing through the chamber, and disturbing the flame or putting it out. The height of this lamp chamber should be made to conform to the requirements of the lamp or flame which it is proposed to use for heating. A still cheaper oven is made by omitting the side door, and having only the opening at the top. Any similar construction can be adopted. But the use of iron or tin is objectionable, because very liable to become magnetized.

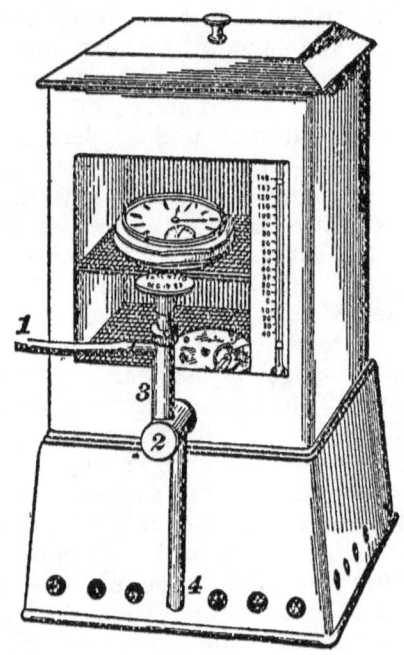

FIG. 53.

(758.) *Logan's adjusting oven* is a well known construction, which can be bought already made. It is shown in the cut, Fig. 53, which will be readily understood after reading the foregoing explanation of the requirements of such apparatus. The dimensions are: height, $9\frac{3}{4}$ inches; width, 5 inches. Base, $5\frac{7}{8}$ inches; height, $3\frac{1}{2}$ inches. It is heated by a gas burner,—the gas pipe, *1*, coming from the left side, and entering the box at the bottom, *4*. The flow is automatically regulated by steel and brass compensating laminæ in the horizontal tube *2*, seen in the center, which they control by approaching towards or receding from openings in the vertical pipe *3*, which contains a perforated plug, adjusted by the milled head at the top. A small side opening in the plug allows sufficient gas to pass to avoid extinguishing the flame, even when the main gas supply is closed.

(759.) *The cold-box.*—For testing watches in cold, they may simply be kept in a cold room, if the season is suitable, or placed in a tight metal box and kept in an ordinary refrigerator. It is much better, however, to have an apparatus constructed with special reference to that use, an example of which is shown in Fig. 54. It consists of a tight wooden box, preferably with double walls, packed between with sawdust, and lined with zinc so as to be watertight. The zinc has the same shape as the

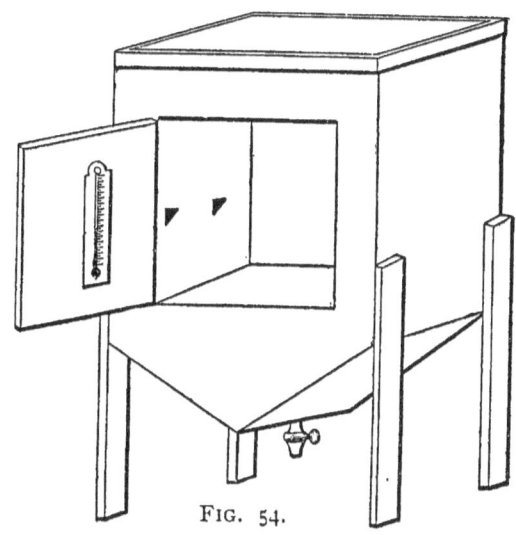

FIG. 54.

box, and will set down into it when the cover is off. The chamber is soldered water-tight to the zinc casing, in the position shown, open only in front. The door is attached to the wooden box. The ice is contained in the water-tight zinc casing, which is supported by the wooden casing around it. It comes to an edge at the bottom, both for convenience of drawing off the water by a cock inserted at the lowest point, and to insure contact of the ice with the metal chamber which holds the movements during the trials. This chamber may be about six inches square, and there should be at least $1\frac{1}{2}$ inches space between it and the sides of the casing, to prevent the ice packing and clogging, instead of passing on to the bottom. This whole space— above, at the sides of, and below, the metal chamber, is to be filled with broken ice, well packed down with a flat-ending stick. One or two glass shelves are used in the chamber, as in the oven. The thermometer is here attached to the door, and windows for observation are omitted, as the condensation of moisture upon them by the cold air within would prevent seeing inside. Besides, the box must not be opened till the trial is ended, (762,) and the thermometer is only used as an assurance that the temperature was correct up to the moment of opening the box. Legs are attached to support the box; and when the cover is removed, the whole top should be open for convenience of filling and packing the ice.

(760.) *Degrees of cold.*—If ice alone is used, a pretty constant temperature of about 35° will be maintained. When a greater cold is desired, common coarse packing salt should be mixed with the powdered ice, throwing in two or three handfuls of ice, then a handful or two of salt, mixing and packing down with a stick; then another layer, and so on. This will give a temperature of about zero. As the ice melts by contact with the salt, and the water passes off, it should be poked down occasionally with a stick and a fresh supply added at the top. When the cold-extreme chosen is only 50° or 55°, less ice must be used, and no salt. Sometimes it will be sufficient to keep a supply of ice on the top of the chamber, not being necessary to pack the whole space around it. For so moderate a degree of cold as that, the ordinary household refrigerator will answer every purpose, by enclosing the watches in an air-tight box. For regulating the temperature of the chamber in the cold-box, a compensating bar would be useless, but is sometimes used to *indicate* the temperature within the chamber. In that case it is attached to the door, and the cord passes over a pulley, with its axis penetrating the door, and on the outside carrying a pointer, which is set to point to an index corresponding to the degrees of the thermometer inside. But it is much better, as well as less troublesome, to choose for the cold-extreme a temperature which can be easily produced, and kept at the same point without watching and regulating it,—as, that of 35°.

(761.) For breaking up the ice, the best way is to make a stout wooden box, about a foot square and six inches deep inside. Put in ice enough at a time to fill it about an inch deep when broken up. Pound it with a hard-wood pestle, with perfectly flat bottom, say three or four inches square. A stick of stove-wood, with one end cut down small enough for a handle, makes a good pounder,—its weight helping along the powdering process. Break the ice pretty fine, leaving no pieces over an inch square, and empty each boxful into a tub, till enough has been broken up to fill the cold-box, before you begin to pack it. When packed, protect it from the sun, and throw an old rug or piece of carpet over it to keep it as cool as possible and save ice.

(762.) *Precautions in using the cold-box.*—When the watch is removed from the cold box and opened, the moisture in the air condenses on the cold metal, and is sure to rust all steel parts. Many plans are employed to prevent this, as it is well known that the slightest rust on the balance spring will destroy and prevent its perfect action. Some chronometer makers go so far as to take the balance and hair spring out and wash them in alcohol or benzine to absorb any film of moisture and prevent rust. But probably as good a way as any is, to notice the difference between the watch and the regulator, as quickly as possible, and then place it in the oven with chloride of calcium (763), and let it slowly warm up to the temperature of the room, (which may take 10 or 15 minutes,) when it can be safely opened and handled. Always remember not to open a refrigerated watch in a warm room till it has been brought to or nearly to the temperature of the surrounding air. If possible, open it only in a cold room.

(763.) Also remember to always place in the chamber, just before closing it, a watch crystal containing a teaspoonful of chloride of calcium in powder or fine lumps. This substance is a powerful absorbent of moisture, and prevents the moisture of the air in the chamber being deposited on the watch as it becomes cold. It must be kept in a tightly closed bottle until the moment of using, to prevent it from absorbing moisture and becoming useless. The portions used can be kept in another bottle until a quantity is collected, then heat it on a metal plate over an alcohol lamp to dry it out, when it can be used again. It can be obtained from any chemist's shop. Place the crystal where the currents of air pass over it in the chamber.

CHAPTER XLI.

Adjusting the Compensation.

(764.) *The adjustment of the compensation* consists in changing the positions and weights of the screws, until the balance compensates correctly for the effects of heat and cold and the watch will keep the same rate in all temperatures. As already explained in sections (748) and (749), if it gains in heat and loses in cold, (when running correctly at the mean temperature,) the screws or weights must be moved back from the ends of the segments towards the center bar. If it loses in heat and gains in cold, they must be moved towards the ends of the segments; if the error is not corrected when the screws are all massed at the ends of the segments, metallic washers are put under the screw heads, or heavier screws are used. Whenever the weight of the adjusting screws is thus increased or diminished, the weight of the timing screws must be correspondingly changed to keep the total weight of the balance exactly as it was at the beginning, else the rate will be disturbed. In all cases, move two opposite screws at the same time, and equally. If, however, it should become necessary to alter the hair spring, in length or otherwise, the timing must be again gone over, as carefully as at first.

(765.) *Requisites of the adjustment.*—It is always desirable, and is supposed to be the case, that before the trials for compensation commence, the movement shall be in perfect order,—the escapement particularly being as closely adapted as possible, adjusted to positions, the hair spring closely isochronized, regulated closely to mean time, and observations made by a regulator whose rate may implicitly be depended upon as correct and uniform. If there is any doubt on any of these points, the adjustment trials should be repeated, before changing the screws, to ascertain if the results coincide. If not, it is evident that the errors arise from some other source than the compensation,—perhaps the balance is defective. If the adjustment to positions has not been made, the movement must be placed in exactly the same position during each trial.

(766.) *Range of the adjustment.*—The range of temperature for which the balance is adjusted varies with the ideas of the manufacturers, or the climate in which the chronometer is expected to be used. For temperate climates, a range from 50° to 90° is thought to be sufficient. Many makers adjust only for 50° to 70°. For hot climates, 60° to 90° is considered ample to include all ordinary vicissitudes of temperature. 50° to 85° will generally cover the temperatures to which ship chronometers are exposed on board. And instruments have been carried with expeditions to the polar regions without experiencing any greater range than that, owing to the care taken of them. But pocket watches should be adjusted for a range from 35° to 95°, in order to cover the temperatures to which they will be frequently exposed. During the day they are kept warm by contact with the person, while at night they are often exposed to the temperature of freezing, zero, or even lower. Some American watch companies have adjusted from about zero to about 130°. This, however, is rather more than is necessary or beneficial, as the residuary error spoken of in a subsequent section becomes very considerable in so extended a range. And besides, the errors at such extreme temperatures do not always indicate or correspond to those found at the more ordinary temperatures in which it is commonly used. For a balance may perform quite satisfactorily in the latter, and then afterwards show a considerable error when exposed to the former, so that such tests are not necessarily trustworthy guides as to the real value of a balance. We should adjust for a range that will include the reasonable exposures to be expected, and then divide up the error between the mean and the two extremes, so that it shall nowhere be very large.

(767.) *Length of trials.*—The length of time the trial should last also varies according to the circumstances of the case. In the first trials, six hours will generally be sufficient to show the error clearly. But as each correction diminishes the error, the length of the trial must be increased to twelve, and finally to twenty-four hours. When great accuracy is required, chronometers are often kept for a week in heat and cold alternately. In all cases, the same period must be taken for heat, cold and mean temperature, so that the results can be safely compared. If the trial in one temperature is for six hours, the others must also be for six hours. The longer trials not only give time for the errors of compensation to accumulate to an appreciable quantity, but they have the further advantage of averaging errors due to other causes, as lack of isochronism, mechanical defects, etc. In the final trials, in order that the adjustment may be relied upon as perfect, the chronometer is kept a week in cold, then a week in heat, and lastly a week in cold again. This gives time to develop the actual performance of the instrument. Now test the poise of the balance, both at the mean temperature and in extremes, as in sections (154, 779), and the variations between the times in the hanging and horizontal (dial up) positions. Then finally test for a week at the mean temperature, and get the rate as correct as possible if it has been disturbed by any of the changes made during the adjustment, or by the tests, for when a chronometer has been going for some time at a very high or low temperature, the rims frequently "set" a little, causing a change of rate at mean temperature.

(768.) *Proper order of trials.*—Everything being ready, as in section (765), the watch being closely regulated to mean time, and set exactly, or its variation from the regulator noted down, we subject it first to cold for six hours, (767,) and put down the precise error of time in the adjustment-book (780); then expose to heat, and again note down the error. Many workmen expose first to heat, then to cold, but I prefer the order recommended, for the reason that when the movement is taken from the cold-box it condenses upon itself the moisture always present in the atmosphere, owing to its being colder, causing a liability to rust. But by then exposing the movement to heat, it is dried off and all danger obviated. A good custom followed by many workmen, is to expose first to heat, then to cold, then to heat again, to verify the correctness of the first heat trial. This is for the final tests.

(769.) *Disturbing the rate.*—After altering the screws to change the compensation, the trials should include not only cold and heat, but also mean temperature, to see if the alterations have disturbed the rate. If so, the two (or four) mean-time screws should be changed to correct that, at the same time that the other screws are moved to change the compensation. If the error of rate is very small, as a second or so per day, it will generally be sufficient to turn *one* of the timing screws as little as it can be seen to move. But the screw thus changed should be noted, so that any similar change afterwards required may be made upon its opposite, otherwise the balance might be thrown out of poise. It must also be remembered that the timing or "quarter-screws" should not be moved from their holes for the purpose of correcting the compensation, but the screws on either side of them may be moved *past* them, to the other side, if necessary. The timing screws are not designed for acting upon the compensation, but only for correcting the rate or the poise.

(770.) *Rating and compensating at the same time.*—After both the timing and compensating screws have been changed as above, the next series of trials should commence with a test at the mean, to ascertain the rate, then in cold and heat, comparing the three results to find the error of compensation. For instance, if the rate was discovered to be two seconds slow in six hours; the loss in cold, four seconds; the gain in heat, six seconds, then, if the rate had been correct, the real loss in cold would have been only two seconds, and the real gain in heat, eight seconds. (This is on the supposition that the watch is set exactly, at the beginning of each trial.) This was the actual effect of the compensation, but the error of rate increased the apparent loss and decreased the apparent gain. It is in the highest degree important, however, that the rate be as nearly correct as it can be got before testing the compensation, for it is often hard enough to make out the real cause of the error even then, and any further complication would make "confusion worse confounded," with the beginner. Some workmen follow a different system. Having first determined the rate at mean temperature, they test in cold, alter the screws for the error, test again in cold, and so on till the error in cold is removed;

then test in heat, and proceed in the same way; then test in cold again, removing the error in each extreme before they leave it. This is quicker than the method above mentioned, but is not so good, unless a saving of time is the paramount object.

(771.) *Irregular compensation.*—As already stated, if the watch loses in cold and gains in heat, the compensation is too strong, termed over-compensated, and the remedy is to move the weights back on the segments. If it gains in cold and loses in heat, it is under-compensated, and the screws should be moved towards the free ends of the segments. But we find in practice that there is a greater difference between the rates in cold and mean than there is between heat and mean, so that the rate cannot be adjusted so that it will be the same at the mean and both extremes. If the watch gains in both heat and cold, the compensation is too strong in heat and too weak in cold. If the screws were moved back to lessen the error in heat, we should thereby increase the error in cold to a nearly equal extent; or, if we lessen the error in cold by moving the screws forward, we shall increase the error for heat. For this there is no remedy. All we can do is to get the error equal in both heat and cold, which will of course reduce the error in each extreme to the smallest amount possible. In exceptional cases, where a chronometer or watch will seldom be exposed to one of the extremes, we can locate nearly all the error in that extreme, and thus free the other extreme, in which it will be generally used, almost entirely from variation. For instance, if the balance is adjusted for 35° and 95°, as the two extremes, the middle temperature will be 65°. Now if the instrument will only be exposed to temperatures between 65° and 95°, we can correct the error for heat by moving the screws in the proper manner to make the mean temperature rate and heat rate alike, and so place all the error in the extreme of cold, where it will rarely or never trouble us. Nearly as good results may be obtained with such balances by adjusting them from 65° to 95°, with the mean at 80°, but it is more trouble to adjust for a limited range, both from the difficulty of keeping the temperature just at the exact point,—which is more necessary in this case because the entire range of temperature is so small that any variation would reduce it to little or nothing,—and from the greater difficulty of noting the error of rate produced by so slight a change of temperature, requiring a longer time for it to accumulate into an observable amount.

(772.) If the watch loses in both heat and cold, (as compared with the mean temperature rate,) which is usually the case, the compensation is too weak in heat and too strong in cold, *i.e.*, the weights or screws are not carried fast enough, or far enough, towards the center of the balance, in heat, to compensate for the effects of heat on the balance and the hair spring; and they are carried outwards in cold too rapidly, or too far, causing a loss of time in both cases. For this error, like the one just mentioned, there is no remedy. We can only hide it, or get it out of the way, as above noted, (771.) All the foregoing errors are due to the construction of the balance being such that it cannot secure the weights being moved in accordance with the law which governs the number of vibrations, and in such a way as to compensate not only for the effects of heat and cold upon the balance itself, but also upon the hair spring, the oil, and the mechanism generally.

(773.) *Middle temperature error.*—Even when the balance is as nearly correct in construction and performance as it is possible to make it, it is very seldom practicable to adjust it so that there is no error at all when the temperature is changed. The smallest error is found when the difficulty in the balance is over or under-compensation. In these cases, by moving the screws judiciously on the segments, the variation between the rate at the two extremes and that at the mean can be reduced to a very slight error. This residuary error, which remains in spite of all we can do, is technically termed the middle temperature error. Even the best made and most carefully adjusted chronometer balances, when adjusted to give *the same* rate at 35° and 95°, or the two temperatures chosen for the heat and cold extremes, will have a different rate at the mean. Of course, the more limited the range of temperature between the extremes, the less this error will be; but it is never entirely eliminated in balances of the ordinary construction, varying from a part of a second to several seconds per day, according to the range, the skill and patience of the adjuster, and the peculiarities of the balance, its hair spring, etc. Sometimes the rate at the extremes will be a trifle faster than the mean temperature rate, but, almost invariably, when the rate has been made alike at the two extremes, it will be slower than the mean temperature rate; that is to say, the chronometer being regulated at the mean temperature, it will lose time as the temperature becomes higher or lower. Or, if the rate be made the same at the mean and either extreme, the loss will be all located in the other extreme, as already stated.

(774.) *Locating the error.*—Chronometer makers generally get the rate as correct as possible at the two extremes to which the instrument will probably be exposed, and it will then (almost invariably) gain as the temperature changes from either extreme towards the mean, and will of course gain most at the mean temperature—generally from 2 to 4 seconds per day. For temperatures outside of the extremes it will lose. Watches, however, are more often adjusted for mean temperature, and when the rate is correct at the mean, there will be a loss of 2 to 4 seconds at either extreme, and still more outside of the extremes. In many cases, they are adjusted to get the rate correct at the mean and one of the extremes, and the total error will then be located at the other extreme, *i.e.*, a loss of from 4 to 8 seconds per day.

(775.) *Secondary or auxiliary compensation.*—As the ordinary compensation balance is not capable of being manipulated so as to remove this residuary error, various devices have been added to it for producing a separate and additional adjustment to accomplish that purpose—some acting in cold, some in heat, and some at all temperatures. This additional compensation is called secondary or auxiliary compensation, and balances provided with them are termed balances with auxiliaries. These, however, are generally added only for some special requirements, (766, 789,) and have not come into any general use in pocket watches and instruments sold for purely commercial purposes, being mostly unstable, and therefore unreliable for a permanent action, besides their cost being greatly increased. As the number of these devices is probably several hundred, acting on all sorts of principles, and by all sorts of means, it is impossible to give directions for constructing or adjusting even the more prominent makes. (I describe the two kinds most used, below.) Frequently the conditions of success are known only to the makers, or could only be ascertained by many experiments and failures. It will generally be found more profitable and satisfactory not to meddle with auxiliary compensations or unusual constructions at all, unless the workman has skill and experience enough to make them himself. In that case, he would probably be able to study out the principles of the particular device before him, without any further instruction than his knowledge of the theory of compensation. His experience will then have taught him both wisdom and *caution* in making alterations. The average workman would do well to confine his practical operations to the primary compensation, or adjustment of the ordinary compensation balance, and, before going any further than that, he should again read and remember the advice in the last paragraph of the introduction.

(776.) *Molyneux's auxiliary for heat.*—This acts in the heat extreme. It consists of a short segment or arc, either of steel, or of steel and brass laminæ similar to a section of a balance rim, arranged inside of the real rim near its cut end, and carried by a light spring *1*, Fig. 55, screwed to the end of the center bar by a foot piece *6*. Ordinarily, this stands free, with the heel *2* resting against the rim at *a*, and is carried around by the balance the same as the rim. But if it is desired to increase the compensation at the heat extreme, a banking screw, *5*, in the end of the balance segment hits the arc *2*, *3*, at the proper time, and forces it to move inward with itself. The weight of the auxiliary is thus added to that of the rim and the effect increased. The banking or adjusting screw, *5*, in the end of the long segment of the rim can be adjusted to touch the auxiliary sooner or later, as required, and one or more screws, *4*, in the latter vary its weight. The spring *1*, which sustains the auxiliary arc, yields easily when the balance rim (by screw *5*) presses against the auxiliary. *7* is the usual mean-time screw or nut.

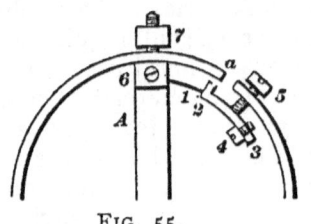 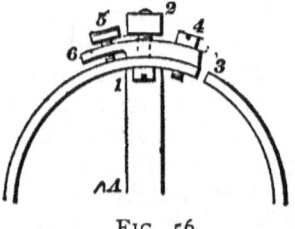

FIG. 55.   FIG. 56.

This device can be made of compensating laminæ, with the steel inside, like the balance, in place of *1*, *2*, *3*, in which case it compensates by itself, besides aiding the balance to compensate. In Mercer's chronometer balance this construction is employed. The auxiliary arc is screwed to the rim at the end of the center-bar, and carries screws at its free end, which can be moved to vary the effect, as is done with the balance. It is sometimes used to lessen the error in cold, and then the steel lamina is outside of the brass, and the banking or adjusting screw is in the short segment of the balance rim. The foregoing description will sufficiently explain how to adjust them.

(777.) *Poole's auxiliary for cold*, Fig. 56, is merely a slip of brass *3*, *6*, rigidly screwed to the outside of the balance rim at the center bar by a screw *4*, and extends a short distance along the long segment. A banking screw *5* in the end of the slip strikes against the segment when it moves too far outward and stops further outward movement there, but leaves the free end of the segment still at liberty to respond to cold. This banking screw is turned in or out to vary the time (or temperature) at which the rim banks against it, as required for removing the error in cold. It can be placed further to the left when a greater effect is desired. *1* is the usual mean-time screw with its nut, *2*.

(778.) *Finishing the adjustment.*—Whenever any changes are made which affect or may affect the rate, *i.e.*, the time at mean temperature, a careful test of the rate should first be made as a standard of comparison for subsequent tests. Also, whenever any change might affect the isochronism of the hair spring, that should be tested, by varying the arcs of vibration, in the same position, and at mean temperature. And testing at mean temperature does not mean testing at any temperature which happens to prevail in the testing room at the time, but at a certain fixed temperature, which has been chosen as the mean between the two extremes for which the watch is being adjusted. The testing room must be kept at that temperature.

(779.) After the compensation has been perfected, the poise is then tested, both at mean and extreme temperatures (154, 291), and tests are also made for any position errors at mean temperature. If it is a fine watch or chronometer, the position tests are repeated at extreme temperatures, *i.e.*, test in the hanging and the horizontal positions in cold and in heat. If any errors are found and corrected, the compensation is again tested, to see if the corrections have affected it. If no corrections were made, the horizontal positions tests in heat and cold would suffice to show if the compensation is correct. Lastly get the rate at mean temperature as perfect as is possible to do, and the watch or chronometer can honestly be called "fully adjusted." When only the compensation is to be adjusted, (not for positions or isochronism,) the hair spring should be fitted as directed in Chapter XVIII, the balance poised, get the compensation correct, test the poise, if any change is made in it then test the compensation, and finally rate the watch.

(780.) *Rating book, or rating sheets, for compensating.*—For use in adjusting the compensation, the workman will find that paper ruled as shown on the following page, (338,) will be very convenient, and will greatly simplify the work and assist in avoiding mistakes. Many workmen set the watch exactly with the clock at the beginning of each trial, but that involves considerable trouble, and is not at all necessary. It is only requisite to note the exact difference between the watch and clock at the beginning and end of each trial. A comparison of the two will show the exact gain or loss during the trial, while any other system will cause confusion and frequent mistakes. The form shown, (782,) gives all the data needed, is easy to fill out, and will be found preferable to the usual forms for practical use.

(781.) *Example of record of adjustment.*—A careful study of the record given on the following form (782) will afford the workman a better idea of the method of adjusting and of making a record of it, than any amount of explanation alone could do. At the head is sufficient description to identify the watch. The first column gives the date of the trial, and the second column states its duration. The third and fourth columns contain the data of all trials in cold, the fifth and sixth those of trials at mean temperature, and the seventh and eighth columns those in heat. The temperatures chosen for the adjustment in this case are 60° for the mean, and 35° and 85° for the extremes. The last column is for miscellaneous memoranda, which may explain the circumstances connected with the trial and need to be remembered or recorded. In such matters it is *never* safe to trust to the memory, and all such points should be at once recorded in detail.

(782.) *Form for rating sheet.*—[See page 338.]

(783.) *Recording the difference from the regulator.*—It will be noticed that in the record of the first trial, there are two differences from the regulator. The first one, in parentheses, is the difference from the clock at the beginning of the trial, while the principal difference, below the former, is found by comparing the watch at the end of the trial. The first difference is given as + 1′ 12″, which shows that the watch was not set, but its error merely noted at the beginning of the trial. The safest way is to *always* state the difference at the beginning. If the watch was set with the clock state that fact, as is done in several trials on the sheet. If the watch is compared with the clock at the end of one trial, and without alteration is immediately subjected to another trial, it is not absolutely necessary to state the difference at the beginning of the new trial, because it would be merely repeating the record already made of the difference at the *end* of the previous trial. In the trials on April 4, the difference at the beginning is thus omitted in each case, and it is understood that the difference at the beginning of the trial is the same as that stated at the end of the last preceding trial. But, as before stated, it is much safer to state it in plain figures each time, as is done in all the other trials.

(784.) *Recording the error.*—It will also be noticed that there are two entries of the error, in each case, in the trials for heat and cold. The reason of this is, that we have to make allowance for the error of rate. In the record, the watch had a mean-time error of 10 seconds per day, and even if the compensation had been so perfect that there was no compensation error at all, in either heat or cold, the watch would still show an error of 10 seconds per day. Consequently, that error would not be an error of the compensation, and in order to ascertain what the real compensation error is, we first record in parentheses the variation which has occurred during the trial, and below we enter *the real error* after allowing for the daily rate. Thus, in the first trial of April 4, the difference from the regulator at the beginning was + 1′ 22″, and at the end was + 1′ 52″, showing that the watch gained 30″ during the trial—which we enter in parentheses. But 5″ of that gain was due to the error of rate, (12 hours, at 10″ per day,) which leaves + 25″ as the real error of the compensation in cold. In the second trial of April 4, the watch fell back from + 1′ 52″ to + 1′ 24″ during the trial, the actual loss of time was therefore — 28″, which we enter in the parentheses. But the real error in heat was 5″ more, (on account of losing — 28″, in spite of the daily-rate gain of + 5″,) or — 33″.

(785.) *Computing the real error.*—The easiest way to find the real error is to write down the difference from the clock at the beginning of the trial, + 1′ 52″, add to this the error of rate, + 5″, to find what the difference from the clock would be if there was no error in the compensation,—and compare this sum, + 1′ 57″, with the actual difference from the clock at the end of the trial, + 1′ 24″, and we find that the latter falls short to the amount of — 33″. In the trial of April 7, in heat for 1 day, the difference at the beginning was + 6″, to this add + 10″ for the rate-error for 1 day, making + 16″; but the actual difference from the clock at the end of the trial was only + 12″, showing that the compensation error in heat caused it to fall back — 4″. While there was a gain of + 6″ during the trial, as shown by comparison with the clock, there was a real loss of — 4″ due to the compensation, for if there had been no compensation error, the difference would have been + 16″. In making the allowance for rate, always compute the rate error *for the length of the trial.*

(786.) *The daily rate.*—In the case recorded, the error at the mean temperature was called the daily rate. But, as before stated, the watch can be adjusted for either extreme, if preferred, and then the error in that extreme would be the daily rate, and the error at mean temperature would be called the " real error " at that temperature. The computation of the daily rate is very simple, being the actual loss or gain of the

(782.) FORM FOR COMPENSATION TRIALS.

R. Brown, Pocket Chronometer, Frodsham, No. 2,118.

Date of Trial 1894.	Length of Trial.	TEMPERATURES OF TRIALS.							Circumstances of Trial, Positions, Alterations made, etc.
		35°		60°			85°		
		Difference from Regulator.	Real Error.	Difference from Regulator.	Daily Rate.		Difference from Regulator.	Real Error.	
April 3	1 day	....	....	(+ 1′ 12″) +1′ 22″	+ 10″		....	....	Dial up.
" 4	12 h.	+ 1′ 52″	(+ 30″) + 25″	....	"		....	....	Dial up.
" 4	12 h.	....	....	....	"		+ 1′ 24″	(− 28″) − 33″	Moved comp. screws forward, and set.
" 5	12 h.	Set − 25″	(− 25″) − 30″	....	"		....	....	Moved screws back a little and set.
" 5	12 h.	Set − 12″	(− 12″) − 17″	....	"		....	....	Moved screws back. Dial up.
" 6	1 day	Set + 6″	(+ 6″) − 4″	....	"		....	....	Dial up.
" 7	1 day	....	....	....	"		(+ 6″) + 12″	(+ 6″) − 4″	Poised balance, changed mean-time screws, and set. Dial up.

Date					Tested in cold again. Dial up.	Dial up. Tested in heat.	Changed mean-time screw. Tested at mean. Dial up.	Tested hanging up.	Set, and delivered to owner to carry.	Tested 4 days more, carried.	Tested 1 week, carried.	O.K.
April 9	2 days	…	…		…	…	$(-2'')$ $-4''$	…	…	…	…	…
" 10	1 day	$(+4'')$ $+2''$	$(-2'')$ $-4''$		"	…	$(+2'')$ $0''$	…	…	…	…	…
" 11	" 1			$+2''$	Set $+4''$	…	…	Set $-1''$	$(-1'')$ $0''$	Set $+4''$	$(+4'')$ $+1''$	$(+1'')$ $-2½''$
" 13	" 2			"				$-½''$	$+1''$	$+2''$	$-¾''$	$-½''$
" 14	" 1											
" 16	" 2											
" 20	" 4											
" 27	" 7											

THE WATCH ADJUSTER'S MANUAL.

watch during the trial, as compared with the clock. There is no allowance to be made for anything, except the length of the trial. In the two-days trial ending April 16, the watch gained $+4''$, and the daily rate was $+2''$, that is, it gains $+2''$ in each 24 hours. In the four-days trial it lost $-3''$, which would be $-\frac{3}{4}''$ per day; in the seven-days trial it lost $-3\frac{1}{2}''$, which makes the daily rate $-\frac{1}{2}''$, or $-.5''$. The daily rate varied a little while being carried in the different trials, but that is to be expected in the pocket. But taking the last 13 days together, the mean daily rate for that period was only $-\frac{1}{5}''$, which might fairly entitle the watch to be marked "O. K."

(787.) *Performance when adjusted.*—If a watch keeps the same time in heat, cold, and mean temperature, it is accurately compensated. But this is very seldom the case with the ordinary compensation balance, except by accident, when the limits within which it is tried are very circumscribed. And it may be valuable to the novice to know what performance may be considered good, average, or poor. Marine chronometers come nearest to perfection, and the very best made and most accurately adjusted instruments will gain daily, on an average, from five to six-tenths of a second more at the mean temperature than at the extremes,—supposing the former to be, say 70°, and the latter 55° and 85°. What may be called superior instruments, but not *the best*, will lose from one-tenth to one-fifth of a second for each degree of change of temperature either way from the mean, in twenty-four hours. When exposed to temperatures 10° to 20° beyond these extremes, they will lose from one-quarter to three-quarters of a second daily, more than at the extremes. So regular are these variations, that when the connection between certain temperatures and the daily rate of a chronometer has been ascertained, the error of rate may be computed from observations of the thermometer. It will be sufficient for all practical purposes to determine the rate in the three temperatures for which it is adjusted, or the mean and the two extremes, and also say 15° outside of each extreme. In good instruments this connection will remain constant for a long time. The rate at the middle temperature is generally the standard or starting point, from which variations are noted. But cases sometimes occur when it is desirable to regulate to mean time at one of the extremes. As, if a chronometer is exposed habitually to a temperature of 95°, it can be regulated to mean time at that temperature, and the rate at the mean, or say 60°, will then be said to be so much slower or faster than the mean rate. Sometimes instruments are even adjusted with three rates,—as if, for instance, the rate was made correct with mean time at 95°, but there was an error at the other extreme, or 35°, and still another rate at the mean, or 60°. The owner being furnished with a schedule of the rates corresponding to certain temperatures, could very easily compute the approximate error of his instrument by noticing the degrees on the thermometer, as already stated.

(788.) *Ordinary rates.*—But the above-named results are shown only by the finest instruments. Ordinary chronometers will vary from one or two, up to five or six seconds daily when the temperature changes from the extremes for which they are adjusted, to the extent of 10° to 20° beyond. Pocket-watches may be made to come nearly as close as marine chronometers, but they seldom do so. Watches marked "adjusted" will frequently vary from three to ten seconds in twenty-four hours, at the temperatures of 55° or 95°. A closely adjusted movement of the first quality ought not, however, to vary more than one to three seconds in twenty-four hours, when the temperature is changed from the mean of 75°, to 55° or 95°. At the first trials, an unadjusted balance may vary from thirty seconds to two minutes in twenty-four hours heat or cold. And a variation of only fifteen or twenty seconds per day may be considered good for the first trials. All the foregoing rates apply only to the true compensation balance. Uncut balances, and the ordinary ones of one metal, will vary from three to six minutes when the temperature is changed from 35° to 95°.

(789.) *Marine chronometers.*—It must not be supposed that all ship-chronometers are good timepieces, and reliably compensated for heat and cold, for they are not. The majority of those in use are hired by the month, and in order to save a few shillings per month in the rent, shipmasters will deliberately choose instruments which are inferior in performance to a decent watch. So well is this understood by chronometer-makers, they are in a great measure deterred from experimenting for the sake of improving the compensation or from availing themselves of the discoveries of others, well knowing that they can scarcely hope to make good their outlay. A large share of their customers will pass by a really good instrument at a fair price, and take a "thing" offered by some competitor at a dollar less per month. It is only for some special uses that the most accurate performance is insisted upon, such as instruments for observatories, expeditions, watchmakers' time, and a few first-class vessels. As a matter of ordinary business, a perfect compensation is not profitable, and consequently not sought for. Of course, instruments designed for competition are made and adjusted regardless of time, trouble, and expense, if only they may take the first or at least a leading place in the list of competitors. And for this purpose almost innumerable devices have been employed to reduce or remove the error which always remains after adjusting the ordinary compensation balance. The two auxiliaries which are most used by chronometer makers have been described in sections (776) and (777), with directions for adjusting them.

INDEX.

NOTE.—The references are to the numbers of the *sections*, not of the pages:

A.

ABSOLUTE isochronism, 547, 551, 554, 556, 660.
Accelerating forces, 532, 533, 558.
    "   short arcs, 593. (See *Isochronal adjustment*.)
    "   "   " by plus curves, 602 to 607.
Acceleration in rate, 86, 381, 382, 383.
"Adjusted" balances, distinguishing, 145, 347, 348.
    "   "   performance of, 787, 788, 789.
Adjusting, automatic heat regulator for, 755, 758.
    "   cold box for, 253, 759 to 763.
    "   "   " precautions in using, 762, 763.
    "   oven, 253, 751 to 758.
Adjusting for isochronism, 657 to 691.
    "   "   " by terminal curves, 602 to 605.
    "   " positions, 698 to 735.
    "   " practical isochronism, 666.
    "   " theoretical " 664, 665.
    "   " temperatures, 764 to 789.
    "   " the different escapements, 389 to 514.
Adjustment for heat and cold, 736 to 789.
    "   "   "   " finishing, 778, 779.
    "   " positions, 657, 692 to 735.
    "   "   " object of, 707.
    "   realistic and practical methods of, 683.
Adjustments, proper order of the, 658, 663, 698.
Adjustment, the, for isochronism, 515 to 691.
    "   "   "   " difficult, 685.
    "   "   "   " object of, 708.
    "   "   " of fuzee watches, 684.
    "   "   " " going-barrel watches, 684.
    "   "   " " marine chronometers, 682.
American watch springs, 96, 97, 103, 104.
Angles, explanation of, 644.
Annotating the book, 6.
Arcs of vibration, see under *Vibration*.
    "   "   " best for trials, 710.
    "   "   " large and small, 662.
Auxiliary compensation, 775.
    "   Molyneux's, 776.
    "   Poole's, 777.

INDEX.

B.

BALANCE, proper size and weight, for cylinder escapement, 318, 319, 423, 456; for duplex, 449; rules for, 139.
" spring, see under *Hair Spring*.
" timing-, 218 to 220.
" " top" of, 702.
Balance, the, 27.
" compensation, 738.
" effect of heat on, 740.
" elastic, 524.
" magnetized, 30, 31, 41, 695 (6).
" making heavier, 332, 333; lighter, 349.
" Mercer's, 776.
" out of poise, 152, 154. See under *Poising*.
" pivots bent, 29, 514.
" " side pressure of, 544, 623, 660, 694.
Balances, "adjusted," 347.
" apparatus for hardening, 120.
" calculating number of vibrations, 128 to 138.
" " proper size of, 126.
" correcting and finishing, 147 to 156.
" excentric, 148 to 150, 695.
" expansion or imitation, 348.
" faults of expansion, 155, 695.
" " " plain, 156, 695.
" irregular, 153.
" making compensation, 110 to 117, 120, 122.
" " expansion, 144.
" " gold, 108.
" " non-magnetic, 123.
" " palladium, 123.
" " plain, 108.
" " spring-steel compensation, 118 to 121.
" poising in extreme temperatures, 154.
" proper size and weight for, 12, 125, 139, 694, 697.
" " " " " testing for, 141, 142.
" selecting and testing, 124 to 146.
" " " " compensation, 143 to 145.
" tempering or setting, 151.
Banking, in auxiliary compensation, 775, 776.
" " chronometer escapement, 482, 505.
" " cylinder " 406, 407.
" " lever " 472.
Bar magnets, care of, 51.
" " making and charging, 40.
Bascule escapement, 473.
Bath, cyanide, 63, 102.
" lead, 62.
" of melted alloy, 66, 67, 70.
" oil or tallow, 66, 70, 78.
" quenching, 65, 78.
Beat, putting in, 287.
" " " chronometer, 287, 487 to 490.

INDEX.

Beat, putting in, cylinder escapement, 288, 404, 405.
  "   "   "   duplex, 287, 429.
Beginning or end of terminal curve, 596.
Bell, timing, 209.
Bent pivots, 29, 514.
  "   "   to straighten, 415.
Bending terminal curves, effect of, 631 to 636.
  "   "   "   tweezers for, 250.
Book, Prof. Phillips', 541, 549.
  "   rating, see under *Rating Sheets*.
Box chronometer, 170.
Breguet elbow, 640 to 646.
  "   "   benders, 250, 643.
  "   overcoil, 589, 606, 607.
  "   "   concentric arc on, 579 to 582.
  "   "   hardening in form, 96, 97, 102.
  "   "   regulator on, 579, 581, 651 to 654.
  "   "   shape of, 104, 638 to 656.
  "   "   terminal curve on, 647 to 649.
  "   springs, 604; making, 95.
  "   "   fitting, 237, 242, 638.
  "   "   number of coils, 103, 104, 105, 637.
  "   "   pinning, 638.
  "   "   regulating by regulator, 354 to 358, 652 to 654.
  "   "   vise for holding, 253, 650.
  "   "   with concentric arc, 356 to 358, 652 to 654.
Bulged hair springs, to correct, 262.

C.

CALCIUM, chloride of, in cold box, 762, 763.
Calculating revolutions of fourth wheel, 185.
  "   size and weight of balance, 124 to 127.
  "   vibrations of balance, 129 to 138, 182 to 192, 264.
Cannon pinion, 24.
Cap jewels, 17 to 19.
Care of magnets, 51.
  "   " watches, 323 to 325, 334, 335.
Center of gravity of Phillips' curves, 543 to 546.
  "   square, 24.
Central coil of spring, 274.
Chloride of calcium, to absorb moisture, 762, 763.
Chronographs, 176 to 179.
  "   recording times by, 161, 180, 181.
Chronometer, box or marine, 170.
  "   escapement, 473 to 514.
  "   "   description of, 482 to 486.
  "   "   drops in, 496 to 500, 572.
  "   "   faults of, 474, 475, 476.
  "   "   hair spring for, 474, 479.
  "   "   in beat, 487 to 490.
  "   "   oiling, 480.
  "   "   proper condition of, 473 to 509.
  "   setting, 341 to 343.
  "   "   to time, 510 to 512.

Chronometer, timing in positions, 698 to 735.
Clark's method of demagnetization, 42.
Cleaning blackened steel, 59.
" colored or tarnished steel, 60, 92, 103.
Clock, secondary, 171.
" standard, 157, 158.
Coils of Breguet spring, number of, 103 to 105, 637.
" " cylindrical " " " 86, 397.
" " flat spiral " " " 103, 105, 397, 427, 453, 474, 479.
" " " " distance apart, 547.
" " " " opening the, 260.
Collet, pinning spring to, 273 to 277, 282.
" poising the, 290.
" -turning tool, 289.
Color-piece, 81, 82.
Coloring cylindrical spring, 81 to 84.
" flat spiral " 94, 103.
Colors for hardening steel, 64.
" " tempering " 66 to 68, 92.
" " " palladium, 101.
Common ideas on isochronism, 521, 528.
Comparing vibrations by opposition, 221.
" " " reversal or coincidence, 222.
" " with another watch, 214 to 217.
" " " timing balance, 218 to 223.
" watch by the seconds hand, 367 to 375.
" " " vibrations of balances, 366.
" " with an assistant, 375, 376.
" " with the regulator, 365.
Compensated for, what is, 739.
Compensating, methods of, 737.
" and rating at the same time, 770.
Compensation, adjusting the, 764 to 789.
" apparatus for, 253, 751 to 763.
" auxiliary, 775.
" " Molyneux's, 776.
" " Poole's, 777.
" balance, ordinary, 291, 738.
" changing spring does not affect it, 750.
" for heat and cold, 736 to 747.
" irregular, 771, 772.
" natural, 389 to 514, 518.
" over-, 748; under-, 749.
" rating sheets for, 780 to 785.
" requisites of, 765.
" secondary, 775.
Concentric arc on Breguet spring, 579 to 582.
Contradictions, seeming, 14.
Controller, motive force, 673, 674.
Correcting the poise, 695.
Counting, 193 to 209, 271, 272, 310, 311.
" the vibrations of balance, 197, 208.
" " " till reversal or coincidence, 205.
Cracking, to prevent, 61.
Criterion, for hair springs, 254.

INDEX. 347

Cross-references, 7.
Current, alternating, for demagnetization, 47.
Curves, adjusting by the, 602 to 607.
" effect of bending the, 631 to 636.
" " " the form of, 634 to 636.
" " " " " "Excelsior's" theory of, 634 to 636.
" forming the, 649.
" minus, 596, 598.
" mixed, 596, 599.
" of flat spiral spring, 629 to 636, 654.
" Phillips', 548, 549.
" plus, 596.
Cyanide bath for heating, 63, 102.
" " " tempering, 72, 102.
Cylinder escapement, 396 to 425.
" " escape wheel in, 400, 414.
" " faults of, 408 to 415.
" " hair spring in, 397.
" " in beat, 404, 405.
" " methods of isochronizing, 419 to 421.
" " "natural compensation" of, 416 to 418.
" " oiling, 424, 425.
" " proper condition of, 396 to 407.
" " setting, 345.
" " testing the balance in, 421, 423.
" " vibrations, 397.
Cylindrical hair springs, 73 to 87.
" " " coloring, 81 to 84.
" " " hardening, 77.
" " " length of, 620.
" " " making, 75.
" " " number of coils, 86, 397.
" " " pinning, 618, 621, 622.
" " " poising, 299, 546.
" " " polishing, 80.
" " " ready made, 611.
" " " tempering, 80.
" " " terminal curves for, 87, 612.
" " " " " changing, 624, 625.
" " " " " proper forms for, 617, 619.

D.

DAILY rate, 362, 590, 600, 786; correcting, 678. See under *Rate*.
Demagnetization, 38, 53.
" apparatus for, 50.
" Clark's method of, 42.
" Maxim's " " 45.
" Mayer's " " 44.
" Waldo's " " 43.
" of tools, etc., 52.
" with alternating current, 47.
" " electro-magnet, 48, 49.
" " horse-shoe magnet, 46.
Detecting position faults by extent of arcs, 704, 705.

Detecting position faults by timing, 709; in positions, 711.
Dial, excentric, 334, 339.
" fastening the, 21, 338.
" imperfect, 334, 369, 373.
" testing the, 340.
Diameter gauges for springs, 210, 252.
Difference between isochronal and positional adjustments, 707.
" " the different escapements, 393.
Different escapements, merits of the, 391, 392.
" " require different treatment, 389.
" " the four, 389 to 395.
" opinions on isochronism, 536 to 541.
Distance of coils apart, 106, 547.
Drawing hair-spring wire, 56.
Drops, in chronometer, 496 to 500, 572.
" " duplex, 431 to 433, 571.

E.

EFFECT of bending the curve, 631 to 636.
" " changing balance pivots, 569.
" " " the coils of spring, 574.
" " " " drops, 572.
" " " " escapement frictions, 571.
" " " " other frictions, 568. See under *Frictions*.
" " " " length of spring, 560, 563.
" " " " mode of attachment, 622, 624, 634 to 636.
" " " " motive force, 573, 697.
" " " " poise of balance, 718 to 721.
" " form of curve, 629, 634, 636.
" " frictions greatest in short arcs, 556, 567, 568.
" " heat on elastic force of spring, 742, 743.
" " moving the regulator, 350 to 358, 584.
" " " " " on Breguet overcoil, 579 to 581.
" " pinning in even or fractional coils, 563 to 567.
" " running down, 385.
" " setting the spring excentric, 575 to 578, 633, 660, 694.
" " the regulator pins, 585 to 588.
Elastic balance, 524.
Elastic force of the spring, 742, 743.
Elasticity, imparting to steel, 55; to gold, 98, 99; to palladium, 100, 101.
Elbow-forming tweezers, 260, 643.
Electro-magnet, demagnetizing by, 48, 49.
End-stones, 17 to 19.
End or beginning of terminal curve, 596.
" virtual, of spring, 591, 592.
Enlarging a spring, 260.
Error, personal, of observer, 180, 181.
Errors, escapement, 696 (5), 714.
" frictional, separating, 675, 714.
" middle-arc, 662.
" " -temperature, 384, 773.
" must balance each other, 657, 669.
" of compensation, 784, 785.
" " isochronism, 558, 657, 668.

INDEX. 349

Errors of poise, 695; trials for, 713.
" " proportion or design, 697.
" positional, 662, 694, 695.
" rotating or varying, 695.
Escapement frictions, 571, 694.
" the chronometer, 473 to 514.
" " " description of, 482 to 486.
" " " drops in, 496 to 500, 572.
" " " faults of, 474, 475, 476.
" " " hair spring in, 474, 479.
" " " in beat, 487 to 490.
" " " oiling, 480.
" " " proper condition of, 473 to 509.
" " " setting to time, 341 to 343, 510 to 512.
" " " timing in positions, 698 to 735.
" " " vibrations, 477, 478.
" the cylinder, 396 to 425.
" " " faults of, 408 to 415.
" " " " " cylinder, 401 to 403.
" " " " " escape wheel, 400.
" " " " " " " pinion, 414.
" " " hair spring in, 397.
" " " in beat, 404, 405.
" " " methods of isochronizing, 419 to 421.
" " " "natural compensation" of, 416 to 418.
" " " proper condition of, 396 to 407.
" " " testing size and weight of balance, 421, 423.
" " " vibrations, 397.
" the duplex, 426 to 450.
" " " drops in, 431 to 433, 571.
" " " faults of, 444, 445.
" " " hair spring in, 427.
" " " in beat, 429.
" " " "natural compensation" of, 446, 447.
" " " proper condition, 426 to 443.
" " " setting in, 344.
" " " vibrations, 428.
Escapement, the lever, 451 to 472.
" " " faults of, 472.
" " " hair spring in, 453.
" " " in beat, 455.
" " " oiling, 457.
" " " proper condition of, 451 to 471.
" " " setting, 345.
Escapements, the, separately considered in Part Fifth.
" " adjusting, 393, 395.
" " four principal, 389 to 395.
" " mechanical conditions required, 394.
" " merits of, 391, 392.
" " " Frodsham's opinion on, 391, 392.
" " the "natural compensations" of, 393, 416 to 423.
Even turns, 564 to 566; or fractional coils, 567.
"Excelsior's" hair-spring tools, 224 to 244.
" " " " mode of using, 229 to 237, 611, 659.
" magnetism tester, 37.

"Excelsior's" method of detecting magnetism, 37.
" " " making hair springs, 106, 107.
" " " " spring-steel compensation balances, 118 to 121.
" motive-force controller, 673.
" "Practical Treatise on the Balance Spring," see Introduction.
" theory of flat spiral springs, 629 to 636.
" " " terminal curves, 589 to 607, 629 to 636, 654.
Excentric balance, 148 to 150.
" dial, 334, 339; testing do, 340.
" spring, 575 to 578, 633, 660, 694.
" " rules for setting, 722.
Expansion balance, the, 144, 348.
Experts, different opinions from, 608, 609.
" information from, see Introduction.
Extent of vibrations, measuring, 703.
" " " varying, etc., 671 to 673.
" " " detecting position faults by, 710.

F.

FAULTS of compensation balances, 155, 695.
" " plain balances, 156, 695.
" " hair springs, see under *Hair Springs*.
" " poise, 713.
" " proportion or design, 697.
" " the chronometer escapement, 474, 475, 476.
" " " cylinder " 408 to 415.
" " " duplex " 444, 445.
" " " lever " 472.
" escapement, 696, 714.
" positional, 665, 694, 704, 705, 711.
" rotating or varying, 695.
Finding proper number of vibrations, see under *Balance* and *Vibrations*.
Finishing balances, 147 to 156.
Fitting balances, 124 to 146, 147 to 156.
" Breguet hair springs, see under *Breguet*.
" cylindrical " " " *Hair Springs*.
" flat spiral " " " " "
Flat spiral hair springs, adjusting for isochronism, 629 to 636.
" central coil, 274.
" cleaning, 92; coloring, 94.
" distance of coils apart, 106, 547.
" excentric, 575 to 578, 633, 660, 694.
" " bending, 631.
" fitting, 237, 242, 255 to 303, 627.
" hardening, 92, 103, 263.
" improvement suggested, 106, 107.
" isochronizing, by excentric setting, 575 to 578, 694.
" " " fractional coils, 567.
" " " openness of coils, 574.
" " " regulator, 584.
" " " " pins, 585 to 588.

INDEX. 351

Flat spiral springs, making, common method, 88.
" " modern American method, 102, 103.
" " number of coils, 103, 105, 397, 453, 474 to 479.
" " pinning to collet, 273 to 277, 282.
" " polishing, 93.
" " selecting, 258, 259, 268, 626.
" " " by hair-spring gauge, 265.
" " " " " " rule for, 266.
" " " " vibrating balance, 269, 272.
" " taking up and letting out, 630.
" " tempering, 92, 103.
" " winding, 91, 103.
" " " tool for, 89, 90.
Flattening hair springs, 261.
Force, motive, varying the, 518, 573, 697.
" " controller, 673.
Form, changing the, 624, 625. See under *Curves*.
" effect of, 634 to 636.
" for Breguet overcoil, see under *Breguet*.
" " flat spiral, 547, 575 to 578, 629 to 636, 660, 694.
" " terminal curves, 87, 548, 589, 595, 612, 617, 619.
" reverts after bending, 625.
Flexion, influences affecting, 533.
" irregular, 533.
" isochronal, 536, 544.
Fractional coils in hair springs, 567.
" " " " " effect of changing, 567.
Friction, effect of, 530 to 533, 556, 568, 569, 571, 601, 664.
" " greatest in short arcs, 556, 557, 568.
" " in different positions, 518, 693, 694.
" errors, separating, 675, 714.
" escapement, 571, 694, 696 (5), 714.
Frodsham's opinion of the different escapements, 391, 392.
Functions of terminal curves, 590, 594.
Fuzee watch, adjusting for isochronism, 684.

G.

GAIN or loss, 527, 557, 600, 601, 712.
Gauges, hair-spring, 211, 212, 248.
" " " using do, 265; rule for, 266.
" " " for diameter of, 210, 252.
" terminal curve, 616.
Going-barrel watch, adjusting for isochronism, 684.
Gold balances, making, 108, 109.
" hair springs, 98; properties of, 99.
Gravity, center of, of Phillips' curves, 543 to 546.
Grinding hair springs, 328, 329.

H.

HAIR springs, altering, 327; in stud, 336.
" " better material needed for, 743.
" " bulged, 262; central coil of, 274.
" " collet turner, 253, 289.

Hair springs, criterion for, 289.
" " curves of, see under *Curves* and *Terminal Curves*.
" " diameter gauges for, 210, 252.
" " enlarging, 260.
" " excentric, 575 to 578, 694.
" " " rule for setting, 722.
" " fitting, see under *Breguet*, *Cylindrical*, and *Flat Spiral*.
" " flattening, 261.
" " gauges, 211, 212, 248.
" " " using, 265; rule for, 266.
" " grinding, 328, 329.
" " hardening, 72.
" " " drawn, 263.
" " heating, in lead, 62; in cyanide, 63.
" " holding, 269, 270.
" " " tools, 224 to 247.
" " " vise, 253, 650.
" " isochronizing, see under *Isochronal*, *Isochronism*, and *Isochronous*.
" " number of coils, see under each escapement.
" " pinning excentric, 575 to 578, 694.
" " " in even coils, 279.
" " " level, 276, 694.
" " " " and concentric, 277, 694.
" " " to collet, 273 to 277, 282, 618, 621, 622.
" " " " stud, 278, 281, 282, 284.
" " poising, 293 to 297, 546, 694.
" " " difficulty of, 295, 296, 297.
" " putting in beat, see under *Beat*.
" " quick test for, 223.
" " ruined, 257.
" " selecting, usual way, 268.
" " " by vibrating the balance, 269, 272.
" " shaping tweezers and pliers, 249, 250.
" " testing, 210 to 220.
" " " by comparing with timing balance, 218 to 223.
" " " " " " watch, 214 to 217.
" " " " hair-spring gauges, 211, 212.
" " " " opposition of vibrations, 221.
" " " " vibrating the balance, 213.
" " " " "weighing," 210.
" " " freedom of, 285.
" " timing by comparing balances, 305 to 309.
" " " " counting vibrations, 310, 311.
" " " " opposition of vibrations, 306.
" " " " reversal or coincidence, 307.
" " " for errors of poise, 713.
" " " " position errors, 711.
" " " "in reverse," 721.
" " " quick ways of, 305 to 311.
" " " see under *Timing*, *Rating*, and *Regulating*.
" " vibrators, 247.
" " weakening with acid, 330.
" " weight of, 694.
Hands, fitting the, 20 to 25.

INDEX.

Hands, fitting the, of the regulator, 166.
" " seconds, 22, 337.
" putting on and taking off, 511.
" " " tool for, 512.
" setting the, 319.
" " " to seconds, 320, 341 to 345, 510 to 512.
" should be in center of dial, 334, 338.
Hardening and quenching bath, 65.
" Breguet overcoil in form, 96, 97.
" drawn and soft hair springs, 263.
" expansion balances, 120.
" steel, 62; cylindrical springs, 77 to 79.
" " colors for, 64.
" " temperatures for, 64, 78.
Heat and cold, the adjustment for, 736 to 789.
" effect on closely fitted pivots and parts, 746.
" " " the balance, 740.
" " " " elastic force of the spring, 742, 743.
" " " " hair spring, 741.
" " " " mainspring, 744.
" " " " oil, 745.
Heating, in cyanide, 63; in lead, 62.
" the new way, 63, 103.
Heavier, making the balance, 332, 333.
Holder for Breguet springs, 253, 650.
" " hair springs 224 to 246.
" " holding watch in different positions, 699.
Holding springs by putty powder, 627.
Horseshoe magnet, for demagnetization, 46.

I.

IDEAS, common, about isochronism, 521, 528.
Imitation expansion balances, 348.
Imperfect dial, 334, 369, 373; testing do., 340.
Improper weight of balance, 125, 694, 697.
Improvement in making hair springs, 106, 107.
Impulse vibration of chronometer, 485.
Influences, accelerating, 532, 533, 558.
" affecting flexion, 533.
" " friction in different positions, 693, 694.
" " isochronism, 530 to 534.
" disturbing, 534, 658.
" retarding, 530, 531, 533, 558.
Irregular balances, 153.
" compensation, 771.
" rate, 321, 322, 334.
Isochronal adjustment, 515, 657, 660 to 685.
" " true purpose of, 681.
" " what it can do, 660.
" " " " cannot do, 661, 662.
" errors must balance other errors, 657, 669, 675.
" springs, action of, 280, 517, 522.
" vibrations, 553.
" also see under *Adjusting*.

23

354 INDEX.

Isochronism, 515 to 534.
" common ideas of, 521, 528.
" correcting the, 679.
" depends on special adjustment, 609.
" different methods of securing, 550; also, see under *Isochronism, securing.*
" " opinions about, 536 to 541.
" effect upon the, of moving the regulator, 350 to 358.
" influences modifying it, 530 to 534.
" law of, 551.
" middle-arc error of, 662.
" no one method always successful, 609.
" only true test for, 525.
" on what it depends, 535, 551.
" practical, 547, 551, 554, 556, 660.
" "quick test" for, 524.
" requirements of, 520, 528.
" testing the, 522, 523, 676.
" theoretical, 536, 547, 554, 555, 660.
" true explanation of, 556 to 558, 601.
Isochronism said to depend—
 on balancing isochronal and other errors, 558.
 " the length of the spring, 537, 539.
 " mode of pinning, 538, 539.
 " relation of the ends, 539.
 " terminal curves, 541.
Isochronism can be secured—
 by a certain length of spring, 560.
 " " " allowance for adjustment, 560, 561.
 " " " rules for the length, 560.
 " altering the balance, 570.
 " " " " pivots, 569.
 " " " drops, 572.
 " " " escapement frictions, 571.
 " " " frictions, 568.
 " " " motive force, 573, 697.
 " even turns, see *Pinning in even turns*, below.
 " excentric spring, 575 to 578, 694.
 " fractional coils, 567.
 " " " effect of changing the coils, 567.
 " isochronous stud, 550, 559.
 " pinning in even turns, 564.
 " " " " principle of this method, 565, 566.
 " regulator, on Breguet overcoil, 579 to 581.
 " " " flat spiral spring, 584.
 " " " terminal curves, 582, 583.
 " " " pins, 585 to 588.
 " taking up or letting out the spring, 563.
 " terminal curves, 589 to 610.
Isochronized, soft springs cannot be, 533.
 " to ascertain if a spring is, 516.
Isochronous springs, 535, 556, 558.
 " " practically, 660, 668, 671, 672.
 " stud, 550, 559.
 " theoretically, 660, 664, 668.

J.

JEWEL cupped on the back side, 726.
" holes not in line, 695.
" " not vertical, 694.
" " side pressure in, 544, 623, 660, 694.
Junction of terminal curve with the spring, 590, 594, 596.

K.

KULLBERG, setting springs excentrically, 575 to 578, 660.

L.

LARGE and small vibrations, 662.
Law of evidence, 688.
" " isochronism, 551.
Lead bath for heating, 62.
Length, isochronism said to depend on, 537 to 539, 560.
" of trials for compensation, 767.
" virtual, 591, 592, 593.
" " lengthening, 599.
Letting out and taking up the spring, 563.
Lever escapement, 451 to 472.
" setting the hands of, 345.
Line, pivots not in, 674 (15), 695 (5).
Linseed oil for tempering steel, 66, 70, 78.
Location of the standard or regulator, 169.
Long and short arcs, testing in, 386.
Loss and gain, 527, 557, 600, 601, 712.
" of rate in soft springs, 383.

M.

MAGNETIC metals, 35, 36.
Magnetism, 30, 34; detector, 37; testing for, 37.
Magnetized watches, 30, 31, 41, 695 (6).
Magnets, 33, 694 (17).
" bar, making, 40; care of, 51.
" electro-magnet, 48, 49.
" horse-shoe, 46.
Making balance heavier, 332, 333, 348; lighter, 349.
" hair springs, see under name of each form.
" " " weaker with acid, 330.
" steel elastic, 55.
Mainspring, effect of heat on, 744.
" see under *Motive Force*.
Manner of attaching spring, 621, 622.
" " " effect of changing, 622, 624, 634 to 636.
Marine chronometers, adjusting for isochronism, 682.
" " performance when adjusted, 787 to 789.
Maxim's method of demagnetization, 45.
Mayer's " " " 44.
Materials for making hair springs, 54, 98, 100.
" better needed, 743

Manner of testing in positions, 706.
" " " stock watches, 731.
Marker, vibration-, 175.
Mean daily rate, 363.
Measuring extent of vibration, 703.
Mercer's compensation balance, 776.
Metallic baths for heating, 67, 68.
Methods of adjusting for positions, choice of, 725.
" " compensation, 737.
" " demagnetizing watches, 38 to 53.
" " forming terminal curves, 612 to 615.
" " isochronizing, see under head of *Adjusting*.
" " " none successful in all cases, 609.
" " " various, 550 to 610.
" " regulating, see under *Rating, Regulating*, and *Timing*.
" " testing in positions, 706.
Middle-arc error, 662.
" temperature error, 384, 773.
Minus curves, 596, 598; see also under *Curves*.
Mirrors, getting time by, 172; positions for, 173, 174.
Mixed curves, 596, 599.
Modern American method of making hair springs, 102, 103.
Molyneux's auxiliary or secondary compensation, 776.
Motive force, adjusting isochronism by, 573, 697.
" " controller, 673, 674.
" " equal, 518; varying, 573.
Movement holder, for different positions, 699.
Moving regulator, effect on isochronism, 350 to 358, 579, 584.

N.

"NATURAL compensation," 393, 416 to 423, 446, 447, 518.
New way of heating, 63, 103.
Non-isochronous springs, action of, 517.
Non-magnetic balances, 123.
No one method of isochronizing applies in all cases, 609.
Number of coils, for Breguet spring, 103, 104, 105, 637.
" " " " cylindrical spring, 86, 474, 479.
" " " " flat spiral, in cylinder, 397.
" " " " " " " duplex, 427.
" " " " " " " lever, 453.

O.

OBSERVATORY certificates for watches, 388.
" trials, 387, 388.
Observing the vibrations, 694 (20).
Oil, effect of heat on, 745.
" for tempering, 66, 70, 71, 78.
Olive oil, 66.
Only true test for isochronism, 525.
Openness of coils, effect of, 574.
Opinions on isochronism, conflicting, 536 to 541.
Order of adjustments, 768.
Over-banking, 408 to 410.

INDEX.

Over-compensation, 748.
Overrunning, in chronometer, 476, 498, 499.
" " duplex, 444.

P.

PALLADIUM balances, 123; springs, 100, 101, 611.
Pendulum of regulator, 167.
Personal error of observer, 180, 181.
Phillips' book, 541, 549.
" curves, 542, 548, 549, 594, 597.
" " center of gravity of, 543 to 546.
" theory of terminal curves, 541 to 549.
Pinning springs level, 276, 694.
" " " and concentric, 277, 694.
" " excentric, 575 to 578, 694.
" " " rule for, 722.
" " in even coils, 279, 564.
" " " " " principle of, 565, 566.
" " " fractional coils, 567.
" " " " effect of changes, 567.
" Breguet springs, 103, 104, 105, 637, 638; see under *Flat Spiral Springs.*
" helical or cylindrical springs, 86, 397, 618, 621, 622.
" the flat spiral spring, 103, 105, 397, 427, 453, 474, 479.
" to the collet, 273 to 277, 282.
" " stud, 278, 281, 282, 284.
" " " testing freedom of, 285.
Pivots bent, to straighten, 415.
" not in line, 694 (15), 695 (5).
" " round, 694 (14), 695 (4).
" other faults, 694, 695.
" side pressure of, 544, 623, 660, 694.
Plus curves, 596.
Poise, correcting the, 695.
" errors of, 695.
" " " trials for, 713.
" rules for changing the, 718 to 721.
" testing the, 302.
Poising, 290 to 302.
" difficulty of poising hair springs, 295, 296, 297.
" the balance, 152; in extremes, 154.
" " Breguet spring, 298.
" " collet, 290.
" " compensation balance, 291.
" " cylindrical spring, 299, 546.
" " flat spiral spring, 294.
" the hair spring, 293 to 297, 546, 694.
" tools, 251, 300; using, 300, 301.
Polarity of magnetized pieces, testing, 40.
Polishing cylindrical springs, 80; flat spiral springs, 93.
Position errors, 662, 694, 695; balancing do., 662; cause of, 705.
" " detecting by extent of vibrations, 704, 705.
" " " " " timing, 709; by timing in positions, 711.
" " " " " example of, 732, 733.

INDEX.

Position errors, trials for, 711.
" faults, 665.
" holder for watches, 699.
" record or sheets, 734, 735; form for, 734.
" of regulator, 282, 284, 315, 352.
" " " clock, 169.
" " " pins, 284, 315, 316, 352, 585 to 588.
" " " " effect of moving, 350 to 358, 579, 584.
" " timing mirrors, 173, 174.
Positional adjustment, choice of methods for, 725.
" " difference from isochronal, 707.
" " finishing, 729, 730.
Positions, adjusting for, 698 to 735.
" adjustment for, 681, 692.
" " defined, 700 to 702.
" " nature of, 699.
" " requisites and apparatus for, 699.
" friction in different, 518.
" manner of testing in, 706.
" " " " stock watches, 731.
" the four "quarters," 677.
" timing in, chronometers, 698 to 735.
" " " cylinders, 422.
" " " duplex, 448.
" " " levers, 698 to 735.
Poole's auxiliary compensation, 777.
Practical isochronism, 547, 551, 554, 556, 660.
Practically isochronous spring, 660, 668, 671, 672.
Practice needed, 5, 686.
Precautions, with cold box, 762, 763.
Prerequisites of regulating, 15, 314, 315.
Pressure, side, of balance pivots, 544, 623, 660, 694.
Prevent steel from cracking, 61.
Progression of force, of spring, 352, 526, 532.
" isochronal, 544, 547, 552, 555.
Proper condition, chronometers, 473 to 509.
" " cylinders, 396 to 407.
" " duplex, 426 to 450.
" " levers, 451 to 471.
" extent of vibrations for trials, 710.
" forms for terminal curves, 548, 589, 595, 609, 617, 619.
" length " " " 619.
" number of revolutions, 185.
" " " vibrations, calculating, 182 to 192, 264.
" " " " counting, 193 to 209, 271, 272.
" " " " finding, 264.
" " " " " by hair-spring gauge, 266.
" " " " for chronometers, 477.
" " " " " cylinders, 397.
" " " " " duplex, 428.
" " " " " levers, 454.
" order for adjustments, 658, 663, 698.
" " in regulating, 318.
" time for regulating, 317.
" weight and size of balance, for cylinder, 318, 319, 423, 456.

INDEX.

Proper weight and size of balance, for duplex, 447.
Proportion or design, position faults of, 697.
Putting in beat, 287.
" " " chronometers, 287, 487 to 490.
" " " cylinders, 288, 404, 405.
" " " duplex, 287, 429.
" " " levers, 287, 455.
Putty powder for holding springs, 269, 270.

Q.

"QUARTERS," the, 677.
Quenching bath, 65.
Quick test for isochronism, 524.
" " " springs, 223.
" ways of bringing springs to time, 305 to 311.
Quickening the short vibrations, 593.

R.

RANGE of compensation, 766.
Rapping, 411.
Rate, acceleration of, 381, 382.
" book, 377, see under *Rate sheets*.
" causing it to correct middle-arc error, 384.
" " " " " temperature error, 384.
" change of, 381 to 383.
" correcting the, 678.
" daily, 362, 590, 600, 786.
" errors in, 387.
" loss of, 383.
" mean daily, 363.
" ordinary, of compensated watches, 788.
" sheets, 377 to 380; law bearing on, 688.
" " for compensation, 780 to 785.
" " " isochronism, 687 to 691.
" " " positions, 734, 735.
" " form for compensation, 782; for isochronism, 689; for positions, 734; for rate, 379.
" testing in long and short arcs, 386.
Rates, analyzing, 667 to 670.
" observatory certificates for, 388.
" required in observatory trials, 387.
Rating, 361 to 388.
" and compensating at the same time, 770.
" duration of trials, 385.
Ready made cylindrical springs, 611.
Realistic and practical methods of isochronizing, 683.
Recoil, 412.
Recording times, apparatus for, 176 to 179.
" " by chronographs, 161, 180, 181.
Records, law of, 688; see under *Rate Sheets*.
References, cross-, 7.
Registering and comparing times, 176 to 181.
" vibrations, 196; apparatus for, 194, 195.

Regulating, 304, 312, 350 to 353.
"   by altering spring, 327; in stud, 336.
"   " grinding spring, 328, 329.
"   " making balance heavier, 332, 333, 348; lighter, 349.
"   " regulator, 163, see under *Regulator*.
"   " timing or quarter screws, 346 to 348, 764.
"   " weakening spring with acid, 330.
"   choice of methods for, 326.
"   how done, 334, 335.
"   in one temperature, 347.
"   prerequisites of, 315.
"   proper order in, 318.
"   " time for, 317.
"   to a fraction of second per day, 309.
"   varying watches, 321, 322, 334.
Regulator, heat-, for adjusting ovens, 755, 758.
Regulator, the, cap, 284.
"   " effect of moving, on isochronism, 350 to 358, 579, 584.
"   " isochronizing by, on Breguet spring, 579 to 581, 594.
"   " " " " flat spiral, 584.
"   " " " " the regulator pins, 585 to 588.
"   " " " " on terminal curves, 582, 583.
"   regulating by, on Breguet spring, 354 to 358, 651 to 656.
"   " " " with concentric arc, 356 to 358, 652 to 654.
"   on concentric arc, 582, 583.
"   pins, 16, 284, 315, 316, 352, 585 to 588.
"   the, 283.
"   " position of, 282, 284, 315, 352.
Regulator clock, 157 to 169.
"   " altering and setting, 163, 164.
"   " dial and hands, 165, 166.
"   " winding, 168.
Relation of ends of springs, 539.
Requirements and apparatus for positional adjustment, 699.
"   of isochronism, 520, 528.
"   " the different escapements, 389.
Retarding influences, 530, 531, 533, 558.
Reversal of vibrations, 307.
Reverting of form after bending, 625.
Revolutions, calculating number of, 185.
Rigidity of curve of spring, 591.
Rotating position faults, 695.
Ruined springs, 257.
Rule for changing the poise, 718 to 721.
" " finding desired number of vibrations, 266.
" " isochronizing by length of spring, 560.
" " selecting springs by gauge, 266.
" " setting the spring excentric, 722.
Running down, effect of, 335.

S.

SECONDARY clock, 171.
" compensation, 775 to 777.
Seconds-hand, comparing watch by, 367 to 375.

INDEX. 361

Seconds-hand, fitting the, 21, 165, 337.
" of regulator clock, 166.
" setting to seconds, 320, 510 to 512.
" should be central, 334 to 339.
" taking off and putting on, 511.
" timing to fraction of second, 309.
" tool for putting on, 512.
Securing isochronism, different methods of, 550.
Selecting and testing compensation balances, 143 to 145.
" " " plain " 124 to 146.
Selecting hair springs, by gauge, 211, 212, 265, 266.
" " " " vibrating balance, 269, 272.
" " " usual way, 268.
" steel, 57.
Separating friction errors, 675, 714.
"Setting," 413, 445, 472, 476, 499.
Setting hair springs excentric, 575, 578, 660.
" the regulator, 164.
" to seconds, 319, 320, 510 to 512.
" " time, chronometers, 341 to 343, 500 to 512.
" " " duplex, 344.
" " " levers or cylinders, 345.
Shape of Breguet overcoil, 104, 638.
Shaping tweezers and pliers, 249.
Short arcs, 662.
" " to make faster or slower, 593.
Shortening of spring, virtual, 598.
Size of balance, 126 to 142, 318, 319, 423, 449, 456, 697.
Soft springs cannot be isochronized, 533.
Special adjustment, isochronism depends on, 609.
Spring steel compensation balance, 118 to 121.
" winding, 91, 103; tool, 89, 90.
Springs, effect of heat upon, 741 to 743.
" gold, 98, 99; palladium, 100, 101, 611.
" holding, by putty powder, 627.
" isochronous, 535, 556, 558.
" " practically, 660, 668, 671, 672.
" " theoretically, 660, 664, 668.
" non-isochronous, action of, 517.
" tools for fitting, 224 to 253.
" " using, 229, 230, 234, 265 to 267, 611, 659.
" vise for holding Breguet, 253, 650.
Standard time, getting by observations, 162; by telegraph, 159.
" " by box chronometer, 170.
Steel, annealing, 58.
" cleaning blackened, 59; tarnished or colored, 60, 92, 103.
" coloring, 81 to 84, 94, 103.
" drawing, etc., 56.
" hardening, 62, 92, 96, 97, 103.
" " colors for, 64; temperatures for, 64.
" heating, the new way, 63, 102, 103; colors for, 64.
" imparting elasticity to, 55.
" tempering, 66, 80, 103; colors for, 69, 70, 71, 81 to 84.
" " in air, 69; in cyanide, 72, 102; in melted alloys, 66, 68, 71.

Steel, tempering in metallic baths, 67, 68; in oil, 66, 70, 71, 78.
" " " tallow, 66; with thermometer, 72.
" to prevent cracking, 61.
Straightening balance pivots, 415.
Stud, pinning to the, see under head of *Pinning*.
" the isochronous, 550, 559.
" removing the, 286.

T.

TAKING off and putting on seconds-hand, 511, 512.
" time off telegraph wire, 160, 161.
" up and letting out spring, 563, 630.
Tallow for tempering, 66, 70, 78.
Telegraph, getting time by, 159 to 161.
Temperatures, adjustment for, 736 to 789.
" for annealing, 58, 61.
" " coloring, 81 to 84, 94.
" " hardening, 64, 78.
" " tempering, 66, 68, 69, 70, 71, 72.
Tempering cylindrical springs, 80; spiral, 92, 103.
" gold springs, 99; palladium, 101.
" or setting, 151.
Tempering, springs or steel, see under head of *Steel*.
Tendency of modern manufacturing, 2.
Terminal curves, 589; plus, 596; minus, 596, 598; mixed, 596, 599.
" " adjusting isochronism by, 602 to 607.
" " beginning or end of, 596; junction, 596.
" " bending, effect of, 631 to 636.
" " effect of form, 634 to 636.
" " form reverts after bending, 625.
" " forming, 649.
" " " gauge for, 616; tools for, 249, 250.
" " functions of, 590, 594.
" " manner of attachment, 621, 622.
" " " effect of changing, 622, 624, 634 to 636.
" " Phillips', 542, 548, 549, 594, 597.
" " " center of gravity of, 543 to 546.
" " proper form of, 548, 589, 595, 609, 617, 619.
" " " length of, 619.
" " regulator on, 582, 583.
" " rigidity of, 591.
" " tweezers and pliers for forming, 249, 250.
" " with concentric arcs, 579 to 582.
Terminal curve, the, mathematical theory of, by Phillips, 541 to 549.
" " " mechanical " " " "Excelsior," 589 to 607.
" " " spiral, "Excelsior's" theory of, 629 to 636, 654.
" " " " " "Excelsior's" theory of form of, 634 to 636.
Testing balance, size and weight of, 141, 142.
" " of cylinder watch, 421, 423.
" dial, 340.
" for magnetism, 37; tester for, 37.
" in long and short arcs, 386.
" " positions, manner of, 706, 709, 711.
" " " stock watches, 731.

INDEX. 363

Testing the isochronism, 522, 523, 676.
" " " only true test, 525.
" " " "quick test," 524.
" " poise, 302.
" " polarity of magnetized objects, 40.
Testing hair springs, 210 to 220.
" " " by hair-spring gauge, 211, 212.
" " " " " " quick test, 223.
" " " " opposition of vibrations, 221.
" " " " reversal or coincidence, 222.
" " " " vibrating the balance, 213.
" " " " "weighing," 210.
" " " for freedom of pinning and position, 285.
" " " for poise, 295, 296, 297, 302.
Theoretical isochronism, 536, 547, 554, 555, 560.
Theoretically isochronous springs, 660, 664, 665, 668.
Thermometer for tempering, 72.
Theory of flat spiral springs, "Excelsior's," 629 to 636, 654.
" " form of springs, "Excelsior's," 634 to 636, 654.
" " terminal curves, see under head of *Terminal Curves*.
Tight, dial should be, 21, 338.
Time, setting to, 307; also, see under head of *Setting*.
" standard, getting by observation, 162; by telegraph, 159.
" " with box chronometer, 170.
" " " mirrors, 172 to 174.
" " " regulator, 157 to 169.
" " " secondary clock, 171.
" " " vibration marker, 175.
" taking off telegraph wire, 160, 161.
Times, comparing, 334.
" recording, by chronographs, 161, 176 to 181.
" registering and comparing, 176 to 181.
Timing-balance, 218 to 220; bells, 209.
Timing in reverse, 721.
" or quarter-screws, 346 to 348, 764.
" prerequisites of, 15, 314, 315.
" watch in "Excelsior's" tool, 243.
" " " positions, 422, 448, 698 to 735, 709, 711, 732, 733; also, see under head of *Positions*.
Tools, demagnetizing, 52.
" for fitting hair springs, 224 to 247.
" " putting on seconds-hand, 512.
" " winding hair springs, 89 to 91, 103.
Top of balance, 702.
Treatment of steel, 54 to 72.
Trials for faults of poise, 713.
" " position faults, 711.
" observatory, 387, 388.
" of isochronism, best arcs for, 710.
True explanation of isochronism, 556 to 558, 601.
True purpose of isochronal adjustment, 681.
Turns of spring, complete, 564 to 566; fractional, 567.
Tweezers, automatic, for holding spring, 246.
" curve forming, 249, 612; uses of, 612 to 615.
" elbow bending, 250; heating, 613 to 615.

INDEX.

U.

UNDER-COMPENSATION, 749.

V.

VARIOUS temperatures for tempering, 69 to 71.
Varying watches, 321, 322, 324.
Vibrating tool for springs, 247.
Vibration, dumb-, of chronometer, 485; impulse-, 485.
Vibration-marker, 175; registers, 194, 195.
Vibrations, calculating proper number of, 128 to 138, 182 to 192, 264.
" comparing, by opposition, 221, 366.
" " " reversal or coincidence, 222.
" " with timing-balance, 218 to 223.
" " " watch, 214 to 217.
" counting, 193 to 209, 271, 272, 310, 311.
" " till reversal or coincidence of, 205.
" extent of, best for trials, 710.
" " " detecting position faults by, 704, 705.
" " " measuring, 703; varying, 518, 519, 662, 671 to 673.
" finding desired number of, 264; by gauge, 266.
" large and small, 662.
" observing the, 694 (20).
" proper number, for chronometers, 477; for cylinders, 397.
" " " " duplex, 428; for levers, 454.
" registering the, 196.
" short, to quicken, 593; to retard, 593.
" testing springs by the, 213.
Vise for holding Breguet springs, 253, 650.

W.

WALDO's method of demagnetization, 43.
Watch, taking time off telegraph wire by a, 160, 161.
" timing in "Excelsior's" tool, 243.
Watches, comparing with regulator, 365 to 375.
" " " " with assistant, 375, 376.
" compensated, ordinary rates of, 788.
" fine, regulating, 336 to 360.
" magnetized, 30, 31, 41, 695 (6).
" regulating, 312 to 335.
" setting to time, see under head of *Setting*.
" varying, 321, 322, 334.
" winding and regulating, 317.
Ways, quick, of bringing a spring to time, 305 to 311.
Weakening spring by acid, 330.
Weight and size of balance, 12, 125, 126, 139, 449, 694, 697.
" " " " " for cylinders, 318, 319, 423, 456.
" " " " " testing, 141, 142.
What is compensated for, 739.
What isochronism depends on, 535 to 551.
What rating is, 361.
" the isochronal adjustment can do, 660.
" " " " cannot do, 661, 662.
Winding springs, 91, 103; tool for, 89, 90.
" the regulator, 168.
Workman, to become a good, 3, 9.

www.ingramcontent.com/pod-product-compliance
Lightning Source LLC
Chambersburg PA
CBHW031751220426
43662CB00007B/368